FINANCIAL MANA

Made Simple

The Made Simple series has been created especially for self-education but can equally well be used as an aid to group study. However complex the subject, the reader is taken step by step, clearly and methodically, through the course. Each volume has been prepared by experts, taking account of modern educational requirements, to ensure the most effective way of acquiring knowledge.

In the same series

Accounting
Administration in Business
Advertising
Basic
Biology
Book-keeping
British Constitution
Business Calculations
Business Communication
Business Law
Calculus
Chemistry
Child Development
Commerce
Computer Electronics
Computer Programming
Computer Programming Languages in Practice
Computer Typing
Cost and Management Accounting
Data Processing
Economic and Social Geography
Economics
Education
Electricity
Electronics
Elements of Banking
English
Financial Management
First Aid
French
German
Graphic Communication
Italian
Journalism
Latin
Law
Management
Marketing
Marketing Analysis and Forecasting
Mathematics
Modelling and Beauty Care
Modern European History
Money and Banking
MSX
Music
Office Practice
Personnel Management
Philosophy
Photography
Physical Geography
Physics
Politics
Practical Typewriting
Psychology
Russian
Salesmanship
Secretarial Practice
Social Services
Sociology
Spanish
Statistics
Systems Analysis
Teeline Shorthand
Typing

FINANCIAL MANAGEMENT
Made Simple

Wilfred Hingley, BSc (Econ), FCMA
Frank Osborn, FCMA, MBIM

Second edition

MADE SIMPLE
BOOKS

Made Simple Books
An imprint of Heinemann Professional Publishing Ltd
Halley Court, Jordan Hill, Oxford OX2 8EJ

OXFORD LONDON MELBOURNE AUCKLAND SINGAPORE
IBADAN NAIROBI GABORONE KINGSTON

First published 1978
Reprinted 1983
Second edition 1989

British Library Cataloguing in Publication Data
Hingley, Wilfred
Financial management made simple.—2nd ed.
1. Business firms. Financial management
I. Title. II. Osborn, Frank III. Series
658.1′5

ISBN 0-7506-0865-X

Contents

Relation of Chapters to Syllabuses

Chapter		CACA	CIMA	ICAEW	
		Financial Management	*Management Accounting*	*Management Accounting and Financial Management*	
		3.2	*4*	*PE 1*	*PE 2*
		Section	*Section*	*Section*	*Section*
1	Objectives, Forecasting, Planning	A	DM1/FM1	104	154
2	Interpreting the Financial Requirements	C	DM2/FM2	115/8	
3	The Investment Decision	D, E	DM3/4	112	153/7/9
4	Corporate Finance	B, C	FM2		160/1/2/6
5	Analysis of Performance	E	FM3		156
6	Controlling Capital Expenditure	D	DM1/4	113	154
7	Valuation of a Business	D	FM3		163/4/5/6
8	Growth and Failure	D	FM2		163
9	Accounting under Inflation	C	FM2		150
10	Investment Management	C, E	FM2		165/6

DM, Management Accounting—Decision Making
FM, Management Accounting—Financial Management

Preface

This book has resulted from considerable years' experience in preparing students for all levels of the subject of Financial Management and for a variety of courses. It seeks to supplement knowledge of the techniques with a greater degree of understanding of related business operations and management. The aim is to show the general way in which a business operates as it sets about its task, dependent upon finance for its resources for survival and development. The text develops this theme emphasising basic theory but nevertheless developing each aspect to the level of the final professional stages of the professional bodies listed in the Acknowledgements.

Experience in teaching Financial Management suggests the major requirements are as follows:

(*a*) The need to give depth to subjects in which students have attained a satisfactory performance at previous levels either in terms of examination success or experience.

(*b*) The need to bring an integrated and analytical approach to problems which embrace several academic areas and require application of skills possibly acquired previously as separate disciplines.

(*c*) To achieve a balance between the student's objective of examination success and the lecturer's objective of ensuring a level of competence suitable for meeting the challenge of practical work in the business environment.

One text cannot cover the whole area of this subject at one time, much less a moderate size publication such as this. Effort has therefore been made to emphasise areas repeatedly stressed in all examinations on the subject and those most required in practice, and practically all the examples have been drawn from final papers of the bodies mentioned. It is suggested that students of all the accounting bodies will find this book appropriate for the subject, whether termed Financial Management, Management Accounting, or Business Finance, so long as the paper is concerned with the topics listed in the contents. Sufficient theory is included for it to be a suitable introductory text for CNAA and other degrees, BTEC courses, etc., concerned with sources and control of finance. At the same time each section has been developed from first principles and mathematical treatment kept to a minimum so that it may also appeal to others concerned, be they practising managers or others having a general interest in the area.

Unlike certain other disciplines whose content changes slowly over a long time, the area of financial management is one that is continually changing and whose boundaries are almost infinite. Changing economic conditions, taxation systems, political influences and controls render the detailed description of particular topics dated almost before printed. This is one further reason why greater attention has been given to fundamental aspects which remain more general to the requirements of student, practitioner and general reader alike.

Descriptions of developments in the more contentious areas of the subject are therefore those applicable at the time of writing.

WILFRED HINGLEY
FRANK OSBORN

Preface to Second Edition

On original publication this book was awarded the prize presented annually by the SCCA for the best-buy textbook. The following extracts are from reviews made at that time:

> 'A wide ranging book which undoubtedly succeeds in simplifying financial management. Excellent for the non-specialist and will justifiably find a following with students preparing for professional examinations; in undergraduate work and in post-experience courses.'
>
> *Accountancy*

> 'Students should be well rewarded with a study of this work—a great aid to students in attaining their goal.'
>
> *Accountants Record*

> 'The book should provide valuable material for students whose study time does not permit more leisurely perusal of theoretically based texts.'
>
> *Association of University Teachers in Accounting Review*

The opportunity has been taken in this edition to update various sections, particularly those dealing with Investment and Inflation. The extent to which the original text still applies justifies the attention given to fundamental aspects of the subject as stated in the original preface. For the benefit of students of the major accounting bodies a summary is given on page x showing the chapters referenced to the appropriate syllabus sections. The book is suitable for students working for Business Studies and Accounting degrees, BTEC awards, the Diploma in Management Studies and courses run by the following:

- Professional Accounting Bodies
- Institute of Bankers
- London Chamber of Commerce and Industry
- Chartered Institute of Transport

It is also suitable for the non-specialist and general reader, requiring an appreciation of the management of business finance. Opportunity has been taken to include specimen questions from the most recent examination papers including some from the Institute of Chartered Accountants new syllabus proposals. Space and cost preclude inclusion of answers to all.

WILFRED HINGLEY
FRANK OSBORN

Acknowledgements

We wish to extend our acknowledgements to Unilever Ltd for permission to quote from their booklet *Profits in Time of Inflation* and thank the following bodies for permission to include questions from their final examinations as demonstration examples in the text and as questions at the ends of chapters:

Institute of Chartered Accountants in England and Wales (ICAEW)
Chartered Association of Certified Accountants (CACA)
Chartered Institute of Management Accountants (CIMA)
Society of Company and Commercial Accountants (SCCA)

We also wish to record our appreciation of assistance from friends and colleagues at City of Birmingham Polytechnic for suggestions and advice on selected areas. Responsibility for the final text does, however, rest with the authors.

WILFRED HINGLEY
FRANK OSBORN

1

OBJECTIVES, FORECASTING AND PLANNING

Business Objectives

At first sight it might appear that the primary objective of a business is to make a profit. Certainly growth and even survival will depend upon it. However, closer reflection suggests that profit is the outcome of successfully performing what the business set out to do; the challenge for business is to decide what it should do to accomplish a profit.

Defining business objectives is the process of defining what the business should do in a given time period that will not only produce a profit but the amount of profit the business needs for survival, security and advancement. Formulating the objective begins with the recognition of a need by the community and then finding the means to satisfy this identified need in such a manner as to attract buyers in sufficient volume at a price to leave a surplus of income over total expenditure, i.e. profit.

Admittedly many businesses begin with ideas of a product or service but they then have to test the market to establish and quantify the need for it. Peter Drucker, a well-known author on the subject of management, made the point that there are few things as useless as the engineering department that, with great despatch, industry and elegance, turns out the drawings for an unsaleable product.

The Need for Forecasting

Forecasting is founded in the challenge to management to demonstrate how it proposes to achieve the corporate objectives it has defined. Management thus needs to make plans to formulate how and in what manner this can be brought about, going on to define who does what, when, and what resources will be required, in the course of which there will be highlighted certain limiting factors operating upon the business.

Although physical resources and the cash to provide them comprise the more obvious limitations, the skills and abilities of the management itself can prove to be important. In the main a management sets its objectives, certainly of a mid-term nature, within the realms of what it is good at.

The forecast is a financial interpretation of the plan, and the plan begins with a review of the physical things that need to be done. Each of the main functions of the business make their contribution and the range of possibilities is jointly examined and compromises are arrived at to ensure that all can subscribe with some degree of commitment. This involves examining and defining the resources each responsibility will require, including the numbers and the skills of the people. Courses of action are rehearsed for the variable conditions likely to be met and performance expectations tested for practical feasibility. The financial interpretation of the plan will demonstrate among others, two main judgment areas:

(*a*) The resulting amount of profit and rate of profitability upon investments.
(*b*) The financial investment required.

The former is tested against the profit needs and expectations of the particular business and the latter against the ability of the business to find the necessary capital, either from the profit it expects to generate or from external sources. Much of this judgment is exercised while the plan is being formulated. Each idea, investment or project will be evaluated financially as it is tabled and considered, and it will be included in the plan only if financial appraisal justifies it.

Thus the plan for the business demonstrates how it is proposed that the objectives will be achieved and the forecast provides the financial interpretation of the plan.

Ideal solutions to embrace all of the alternatives and the variety of constraints that may occur in the future may be rare. Management does its best with the information available at the time and uses its best judgment about what conditions are most likely to occur. Much depends upon the period of the forecast, of course: the longer this is the more uncertain will be the information. Management therefore will tend to keep a high degree of versatility in its plans so that it can change course or make amendments to accommodate changes of circumstance and still achieve its objectives. Anticipation is one of the skills of management and the forecast is a manifestation of this skill in operation.

The Time Period

The time period to be covered by the forecast will vary considerably between different types of business and the outlook of particular managements. A term generally adopted is five years ahead of the current year, itself operating against its own budget. The general format as each year passes is for the first year of the forecast to be firmed into the budget for the next immediate year and the forecast to embrace the next year ahead. The new forecast incorporates all the revisions and amendments necessary upon a reassessment of the factors influencing the business so that a regular process of updating takes place.

Extensions to a period of five years will largely depend upon the time-span between the decision to proceed and output commencing. In cases of large-scale chemical processing plants and oil refineries, to incorporate the very latest techniques as they develop may require a forecasting time-span as long as 15 or 20 years.

A key matter in the forward planning is to demonstrate when the commitment decisions need to be made in relation to the implementation dates. The introduction of a new product either as a replacement or an addition to the range will require a series of intermediate decisions before and after the key commitment. Research and development, with marketing, must outline the main features and performance of the product and evaluate its potential market. Research will proceed to translate the ideas into practical form and ensure by cooperation with the production function that problems of manufacture are minimised in the design. A small quantity of the product needs to be made, often at high unit cost, to ensure by tests that the product performs to the set requirements. Funds for these purposes must be provided. Viability of the project will be evaluated against the criteria laid down by the firm's objectives and a formal commitment decision made. The proposed volume and/or complexity of the product may call for new buildings requiring time to find a site, design the building and construct.

Meanwhile, specialised equipment and tooling may be required involving design, manufacture and proving. The production function will need a pre-production period to test the manufacturing equipment and methods and ideally a base stock of the finished product is desirable for delivery once it is launched on the market.

The greatest psychological impact upon consumers and competitors is sought in the launching of the product and a great deal of preparation is required with potential consumers, agents and other outlets to ensure the acceptability of the product and the ideal launching conditions.

Throughout this sequence of events there will arise a variety of intermediate decisions, invariably affecting other areas of the plan, and the completion time of each feature of the plan must dovetail together. These respective completion times will provide the time-span for the relevant decisions to be made beforehand. In the course of these planning stages it often becomes necessary to make adverse decisions about a project as new facts come to light and appraisal reveals inadequacy when contrasted with the judgment criteria. Abortive effort and expense is thus a consequence of progress.

As the years of a forecast period pass and the progressive decisions are taken or amended, it is not unusual that firm commitments about capital expenditure are made considerably in advance of a budget year, as are also expectations about revenue and the revenue expenditure arising from it. In this way a well formulated forecast which is progressively updated will merge into a firm budget for the next immediate year of the business.

Reliability of Data

It is a general truism that notwithstanding the sophistications of subsequently applied evaluation techniques the decision data are only as good as the initial input data. In forecasting, therefore, it becomes necessary to check the basic data by as many means as practical for accuracy. This can be done by identifying variables relative to the components of the forecast—e.g. sales units, price, labour rates—and using alternative sources to check predictions. Sales projections could be checked against published indicators for items having correlated movement such as statistics produced by government and trade association sources. Similarly, price movements may have to be determined because different factors may have differing rates of inflation.

Many a 'good sense' test can prove invaluable as to what is practicable for the business to achieve. Most enterprises are complex organisations and their ability to accept change, especially of a fundamental nature, can be limited and a fair timetable should be allowed for the full integration of all that is necessary to be done. For example, the introduction of a single major design change to an established product can be as much as one organisation can absorb at one time. Multiplicity of changes can strain a business to breaking point. Often, therefore, a valuable check can be upon the limiting factors of the business and assessing what is within the practical attainments of the organisation.

Statistical Techniques and Sources

The art of effective forecasting is a discipline in its own right and preferably should be done with expert assistance from trained statisticians. The financial manager or accountant should at least, however, have a working knowledge of the tools available and the following list is merely indicative of the basic techniques or terms used.

Trend Analysis

The past is not necessarily a good indicator of the future, and some statistical books dismiss the usefulness of techniques which take the past as a guide to the future as of limited or no practical significance. In the absence of a crystal ball or firm information about the future, however, one might be forced to utilise the statistics of past performance. Sufficient, therefore, to say that any predictions made by using techniques such as those described here should obviously be adjusted if evidence is there to suggest changing conditions. Similarly, it needs to be borne in mind that the accuracy of the basic data and therefore that of the results produced is not enhanced by increasing indefinitely the number of decimal places to which a statistical coefficient is computed.

Past data can be screened to ascertain whether evidence of seasonal or cyclical variations exists. The seasonal movement is probably known and allowance can therefore be made in short-term planning but evidence does exist of five- to seven-year cycles in some industries.

Extrapolation

This is the term used when predictions for the future are 'extrapolated' (i.e. projected) from figures already known—usually past results. The initial data is usually plotted on a graph over a time-scale to indicate whether any consistent or repetitive 'trend' exists, or whether data appears to be purely 'random', i.e. has no pattern.

Smoothing

Various techniques are used to smooth the data if evidence of some basic form of relationship exists. These include:

(i) Moving averages
(ii) Exponential smoothing
(iii) Logarithmic charts
(iv) Lorenz curves
(v) Regression analysis

All these are used in an endeavour to see if there is some basic or fundamental relationship which can be used and expressed in a formal mathematical rule or model to simplify the problem of forecasting.

Measures of Dispersion

Sometimes termed averages of the second order, these statistical tools are used to quantify the degree of deviation or difference which observed results show when compared with a forecast or prediction. Alternatively, they can be used to show the effect of errors or differences if the actual performance should deviate by a specified amount or proportion. The more common measures are:

(*a*) The range
(*b*) The quartile deviation
(*c*) The standard deviation

Correlation

This is a technique used to ascertain if there is any relationship between two or more variables. If it can be established that there is such a relationship then variation in one variable can be examined to predict or confirm forecasts or variations in others. It is not necessary that movement of the one variable be 'caused' by another, merely that two or more groups of data move in sympathy with each other. Such movement may be direct, indirect or lagging. Elementary tests of relationship are scatter diagrams, tests for evidence of linear regression and calculation of coefficients of correlation.

Sensitivity Analysis

This is a term to describe the technique used when the various **parameters** or variables involved in a problem—in our case a business situation requiring a decision—are subjected to separate examination in order to determine to which particular variable the ultimate objective is most sensitive. If a small change in one particular variable results in failure to achieve the objective, or changes the choice of alternative the desired result is sensitive to that particular variable. This is dealt with in more detail in Chapter 3.

The greater the number of variables the more complex the exercise. Most variables are interrelated, e.g. a reduction in price could stimulate an increase in sales. It is the intermatching of the variables to provide optimum solutions under differing specified conditions which provides opportunity for a more sophisticated use of this technique. Nevertheless even in its simplified form it is a method which can appeal to a practical manager desirous of seeing at least some indication of the effects of error in predicted results.

Simulation

This technique is usually used in combination with sensitivity analysis and/or model building. The word is self-explanatory in that it literally means that actual happenings are 'simulated'. Management may be considering increasing the selling price of a particular product or group of products. Before such a decision is implemented they would probably attempt to assess the effect on other factors such as demand, costs, etc. The effect of a variety of alternative outcomes using a range of prices can thus be 'simulated'. The variables can sometimes be expressed in terms of comparative simplicity; for example, in the basic profit equation

$$\text{Profit} = \text{Sales} - \text{Total Costs}$$

or

$$P = S - TC$$

Total costs, however, comprise a multiplicity of variables such as rents, rates, labour rates, production times, material costs and so on. Further, they can be classified as fixed, variable or semi-variable. Nevertheless, they are a subdivision of Total Costs. The alternative computations under a variety of simulated conditions may be complex but calculations can be made fairly quickly and results produced by standard or special programmed computer packages.

Model Building

Most people are familiar with the general interpretation of the term model as being a miniature representation of an actual physical unit. In business or financial planning the term is used when the elements of a situation are expressed in formal relationships and the results of alternative choices of action are examined by substituting differing values in the framework of relationships established. The simple model used for computing total cost in elementary break-even analysis can be used as an example.

	If unit variable cost	$= m$
	Volume of output	$= x$
	Fixed costs	$= c$
then	Total cost	$= y = mx + c$

It is obviously much more practical to examine past and predicted results by using such tools than to attempt to assess the result by undisciplined estimating.

The above paragraphs represent a mere listing of the more basic techniques with which the financial manager or student should be acquainted. There are other more complex applications of the techniques that he should make himself aware of, particularly in the fields of systems analysis and data processing. It is not necessary that he be an expert himself but that he knows the services available to him from the skilled analyst or statistician, of the aid in forecasting they can provide and also of the limitations of the systems in relation to the accuracy of the basic input and deductions made from them.

Sources of Data

External

(*a*) Government departments produce information from which general 'indicators' of economic significance may be acquired. Most well known and useful categories are:

National Income and Expenditure
Finance and Banking
Population and Vital Statistics
Manpower and Labour Statistics
Production and Wholesale prices
Consumption and Retail prices
Trade, Transport and Communications
Social Statistics

(*b*) The above can be supplemented by reference to regular and *ad hoc* surveys produced by:

Bank of England
Commercial banks
Trade associations
Trade and financial press

(*c*) Specialist services are available from market research consultants, who may tend to specialise in product areas or specific markets.

Internal

Sales and order records
Production statistics
Salesmen's and agents' field reports
Special market surveys

Conclusion

All forms of enterprise should have major and subsidiary objectives. Whenever possible they should be quantified. In this respect subsidiary objectives are frequently seen as **targets** of functional executives, e.g. budgeted sales, output per manhour. A suitable unit should be selected and a target level of performance set. Profit as such is an absolute measure and gives no indication of efficiency of performance. £10 million profit achieved in one year by a large public limited company (plc) may represent much less effective utilisation of scarce resources than £10,000 attained by a sole trader. **Profitability** implies a ratio or group of ratios such as return on capital employed (ROCE); profit per employee or per £ of added value. Other measures of performance may use elements which contribute to profit and these subsidiary objectives may be measured, for example, as rate of growth of sales; proportion of market share; and the familiar earnings per share. Non-profit oriented, or non-economic objectives may be broadly stated. These include such desired goals as better labour relations, better product reliability and satisfying environmental conditions. Even so, to be effective they should be quantified, e.g. reduction in noise intensity or lower volumes of smoke and fumes. Most service industries and public services have problems since their achievements are not necessarily profit oriented. To help in this respect the techniques of **Cost Benefit Analysis** have been developed.

Individual managers and executives may set, or have set, different and conflicting objectives. It is essential that top management achieves consensus of subsidiary objectives to achieve the primary one. This is termed **goal congruence** and must be related to all levels in the corporate plan, e.g. each company level must mastermind subsidiary functions and departments and similarly the group must weld together the conflicts of operating or marketing divisions. More detailed analyses of the measures of performance are given in Chapters 5 to 7.

Questions

1. You are required to discuss the extent to which the concept of maximisation of wealth is relevant to the formulation of company financial objectives. In doing this, you should make reference to a valuation formula based on dividend growth and to the importance of statistics of earnings per share. (CIMA)

2. A recent board meeting of Acre plc discussed what financial objectives the company should have. Four different views were expressed:

(i) The company should maximise profits.
(ii) The company should maximise turnover.
(iii) The company should maximise shareholder wealth.
(iv) The company should maximise benefits to employees and to the local community.

Comment on the implications of the four views.

(CACA)

3. Discuss how managers' objectives might differ from those of shareholders, especially if managers are not closely monitored by shareholders, and are not subject to constraints and/or incentives imposed by shareholders. For these differing objectives illustrate the policies that managers might adopt that are likely to be considered sub-optimal from the shareholders' point of view. (CACA)

4. (*a*) Outline the factors that a company should consider when developing a long-term financial plan of 3 years or more in duration. Briefly describe the major types of financial model that might be used to assist in the preparation of such plans, and discuss the problem that companies face in long term planning.

(*b*) Oxold Ltd uses linear programming to assist in its financial planning. The company wishes to estimate its investment and borrowing levels for the next year.

Divisible investment opportunities exist that would require funds of up to £2 million. These investment opportunities are all expected to produce perpetual annual cash flows (after tax) with an internal rate of return of 15% per year. The stock market is expected to capitalise these project cash flows at a rate of 17% per year.

Oxold has £1,500,000 cash available. Any surplus cash, after investments have been undertaken, will be paid out as dividends. The company does not wish to issue new equity capital, but is prepared to finance up to 40% of any investment with new long term debt which may be assumed to result in a permanent increase in the company's capital. The company pays tax at 35%.

Oxold Ltd wishes to maximise the total value of the company.

You are required to:

(i) Formulate a linear programming model which could be used to estimate the optimum levels of investment and borrowing for the next year. (Modigliani and Miller's formula for the valuation of a company in a world with taxation might be helpful in this process.) Do not calculate the optimal solution.

(ii) Discuss briefly whether Oxold Ltd is likely to undertake any investment during the next year:

1. If no new funds are borrowed.
2. If the company borrows funds through new long term loans. (CACA)

5. The 1986 annual report of T plc, a company engaged in the leisure industry, states its objectives as:

'to adjust to new circumstances so as to preserve our service to our customers and to provide shareholders with steady capital and dividend growth prospects.'

The five-year financial summary contained in the report includes the following information:

	1986	*1985*	*1984*	*1983*	*1982*
	£000	£000	£000	£000	£000
Net revenue	12,203	10,433	9,346	7,727	7,055
Profit on ordinary activities	1,515	1,124	1,007	551	482
Less: Taxation	(621)	(511)	(424)	(181)	(225)
Extraordinary items			(385)	36	
	894	613	198	406	257
Dividends	210	176	160	134	114
Retained profits	684	437	38	272	143
Ordinary shareholders' funds					
Issued share capital	840	840	840	420	420
Revaluation reserve	961	897	790	694	634
Profit and loss account	2,384	1,700	1,264	1,645	1,373
	4,185	3,437	2,894	2,759	2,427

The financial press dated 31st March 1987 provides the following share service information relating to T plc and seven other companies (A–G) in the same type of industry:

		Share price						
	Nominal	*1986/87*		*Today*	*Div.*		*Yield*	
Company	*value*	*High*	*Low*		*Net*	*Cover*	*Gross*	*P/E*
T plc	25p	151	74	124	3·13	3·6	3·5	11·1
A plc	25p	318	176	318	8·5	2·7	3·8	13·9
B plc	25p	704	263	689	18·15	2·2	3·7	17·4
C plc	25p	462	219	459	9·5	1·9	2·9	25·8
D plc	25p	282	136	279	6·25	2·9	3·2	15·3
E plc	10p	99	27	97	2·0	3·5	2·9	14·0
F plc	10p	491½	175	490	10·5	3·3	3·0	14·1
G plc	5p	82½	31	82	2·05	2·6	3·5	15·6

You are required to:

(*a*) Appraise the company's objectives as stated.

(*b*) Relate those objectives to the information provided in the question.

(*c*) Compare the performance of T plc with that of its competitors.

(CIMA)

6. It is said to be important to retain a high degree of flexibility of operation in the forward planning of a business. Discuss this and give examples to illustrate your understanding of flexibility in achieving corporate objectives. (SCCA)

7. 'Effective corporate planning depends on the prior formulation of a business policy with clearly defined objectives for the company which will lead to a co-ordination of all the various activities and their orientation towards the corporate objective.' Discuss the factors which need to be considered in defining this corporate objective and especially the financial factors which will influence it.

(SCCA)

2

INTERPRETING THE FINANCIAL REQUIREMENTS

Determining the Needs for Finance

Once a forecast has been prepared a process of conversion takes place. A forecast of sales will be converted into expected revenue and associated costs at the appropriate production level. The translation of expected performance can be against a background of change experienced by the enterprise, aspects of which may not occur at the same time in the one business, namely:

(i) Where a particular enterprise is just being started or being purchased (taken over) as a complete operating medium.

(ii) In an 'on-going' situation for an existing business where a review of the resources needs regular decisions in respect of

(*a*) Replacement investment
(*b*) Unavoidable investment such as that required by law for environmental or employee protection.
(*c*) Expansion investment involving marginal additions to the existing capital structure of the firm.

A company may produce forecasts on a rolling basis—say five years. Some features of such a forecast may not have the same time-span as others but the approach and techniques used to assist judgments are similar regardless of the time-scale involved in various projects. Specific areas of study are:

(i) Cash flow forecasting
(ii) Plant investment appraisal
(iii) Project investment appraisal
(iv) Group corporate plans and strategies
(v) Operating budgets

The next section is mainly concerned with the overall position and techniques of cash flow forecasting. Techniques (ii) to (v) above are dealt with in the appropriate sections. These latter techniques may already have been utilised before the funds forecasting is done. If the objective is to determine the maximum funds or cash requirements then investment appraisal will already have been performed and the funds required in respect of approved projects will be included under the forecasts of revenue income and requirements for funds. On the other hand, the level of operations with existing plant may have been agreed and the forecast need is to determine how much surplus cash will be generated by the profit made. Opportunities for extra investment may be explored after this has been done and in this event investment appraisal will be undertaken on projects competing for these internally generated funds. The process may be repeated until final figures are produced around which management objectives and strategies are constructed for the forecast period ahead.

Fixed Capital

Reference was made in Chapter 1 to the technique of model building and a simple example of this technique would be the formulation of the basic equation for the balance sheet of a business, i.e.

$$\text{Liabilities} = \text{Assets}$$

This can be expanded and symbols can be substituted

Let E = Owner's equity
M = Long-term loans
C = Current liabilities
F = Fixed assets
I = Investments held by the firm
D = Current assets

Then if $\text{Liabilities} = L = E + M + C$
$\text{Assets} = A = F + I + D$

substituting $E + M + C = F + I + D$

If five of these variables are known or forecast we can determine the sixth

$$E = (F + I + D) - (M + C)$$

or $C = (F + I + D) - (E + M)$, and so on

The original format for a balance sheet showed the two groups of items on differing sides, whereas the modern format is for a single vertical formation. Reverting to the former, the major variables above would be laid out as in Fig. 1.

Liabilities		*Assets*
Ordinary and preference share paid up capital Revenue plus Capital Reserves Long Term loans Deferred Liabilities	equivalent to	Intangible Assets, e.g. goodwill Fixed Assets less depreciation Net Current Assets

Fig. 1

Alternatively the major variables may be laid out in a vertical format.

	£	£
Fixed Assets		xxx
plus: Current Assets	xxx	
less		
Current Liabilities	xxx	
Net Current Assets/Liabilities		xxx
		xxx
less Long term loans		xxx
		xxx
Equivalent to		
Ordinary and Preference Share Capital		xxx
plus Reserves		xxx
		xxx

It is always desirable that in normal circumstances long term capital sources should exceed long term capital uses, i.e. part of working capital should be financed by long term sources. Reasons for this will be examined in depth later but the basic one is that if the situation is reversed—i.e. long-term capital uses are financed by short-term sources—then the firm is very vulnerable to short-term influences and this results in an instability which is not conducive to the best long-term performance. The margin by which the short-term commitments should be financed by long-term sources will, however, vary, among other factors, with the industry, with particular firms, with size and with the general economic situation. These factors can be given different weightings and thus different data can be used in the basic model in order to see how the other factors and the end result are affected.

Whether we are dealing with a completely new business or a new project, i.e. a marginal addition to an existing business, the model remains the same. If we know or have estimated the cost of plant, buildings, stocks and debtors—namely, the total resources required—and are prepared to estimate the level of credit we in turn will take from suppliers, then

$$\text{Long-term capital required} = \text{Total assets} - \text{Current liabilities}$$

or

$$E + M = (F + I + D) - C$$

If it is decided that it is unlikely that any long-term loans will be available, then

$$M = \text{zero}$$

$$E = (F + I + D) - C$$

If the current cost of financing by means of equity is 20 per cent and profits are forecast at £10,000 p.a., then the model can be taken a stage further. If £10,000 p.a. is the maximum sum available to reward suppliers of funds who are at present demanding a 20 per cent return then the maximum amount of capital this profit level will support will be

$$\frac{£10{,}000}{20\%} = \frac{£10{,}000 \times 100}{20} = £50{,}000$$

So long as the return required remains at 20 per cent and profits are not expected to exceed £10,000, then under these constraints the maximum capital sum is restricted to £50,000.

$$\therefore \quad F + I + D - C \leqslant £50{,}000$$

which is a shorter way of saying Fixed assets plus Investments plus Current assets less Creditors must be equal to or less than £50,000. Present data may indicate a forecast requirement of £60,000. In this event all the variables would be scrutinised and if no compromise could be found the project would not be recommended. Details of the techniques used for each element of the analysis are given in the appropriate chapters but the objective here is to show how even the basic business problem can be formalised quite simply. It is the number and complexity of the variables within each major group which make the forecasting complex. One could, however, argue that it is because of this very complexity and the severe penalties of an incorrect decision in the early stages that maximum advantage should be taken of the assistance obtainable from other disciplines.

Working Capital

This is the term used when referring to assets and liabilities which are subject to short-term fluctuation and commitment. The most usual current assets are:

Stocks: Finished goods
Work in progress
Raw materials
Debtors
Bank and cash balances

The most usual current liabilities are:

Current taxation
Creditors

Current taxation is normally shown separately as it is usually a major item and to distinguish current commitment on past year's profits from future provisions for taxation on the current year's profits. Similarly, if the bank balance is an overdraft then it is shown as a separate item. In forecasting these elements regard is taken to company policy and planned growth (or decline) together with other relevant parameters such as sales activity, credit policy and changing economic conditions. These items are dealt with in detail in subsequent chapters. It should be noted in passing that the term 'working capital' is not standardised. Sometimes it is used to refer collectively to the above items and sometimes to the difference between them. It is suggested that the term should be used to describe all the items concerned and when the difference only is being considered this must be referred to as 'net working capital' or 'net current assets'. Ideally, in most instances this difference should be in favour of the current assets and is referred to as 'surplus' working capital. Conversely, if the current liabilities exceed current assets this is referred to as a deficit. The term 'net' is therefore an inclusive term which could summarise a movement either way and the nature of the balance would indicate a surplus or otherwise.

Again, forecasting a specific element of working capital would entail subjecting that particular item to scrutiny and building a model. This can best be illustrated by considering the simplest version of a stock control model—that in respect of items bought for resale by a wholesaler. In this case the stock is all finished goods. The objective of the wholesaler is to minimise the costs of carrying stocks commensurate with satisfying his customers' demand. The variables involved are:

Q = Quantity ordered at any one time.
A = Annual demand for the product.
C = Cost of placing an order or costs which vary with the number of orders placed, e.g. delivery costs if paid by the purchaser.
P = Price of one item.
R = Rate of interest applicable to stockholding (as a decimal) or other costs of holding stock provided they are expressed per unit.

The simplest case would be where sales of the item were at a constant rate—i.e. each period's sales were the same—and the supplier would guarantee immediate delivery upon receipt of order, or a firm delivery date which was always observed. In these circumstances the quantity Q would be exhausted over a constant time period and a graph of the position would always show the characteristic sawtooth formation of Fig. 2.

(*a*) Under the conditions stipulated stock cannot exceed the quantity ordered since the wholesaler will receive the quantity required. With a constant demand rate the stock will decline at a steady rate indicated by the sloping line. When stocks are zero a new consignment is delivered and therefore stock goes up again temporarily to the maximum Q and the cycle is repeated. Further, it can be seen that in one half of the period half of the batch purchased will have been consumed, so the average stock held in any period—and therefore the average stock overall—will be $Q/2$.

(*b*) The number of deliveries per annum $= A/Q$; therefore if $C =$ cost per order placed the annual ordering and delivery costs will be AC/Q.

(*c*) The average quantity in stock is $Q/2$. The stockholding cost per unit is equal to RP, where R is the stockholding costs per unit (expressed as a decimal) and P the price paid per unit. If, for example, we can borrow money at 15 per cent and the unit price is £10 per unit then the stockholding cost per unit will be $0{\cdot}15 \times £10 = £1{\cdot}5$ p.a. This would be multiplied by the average stock of $Q/2$ to give the total annual cost of stockholding as $RPQ/2$.

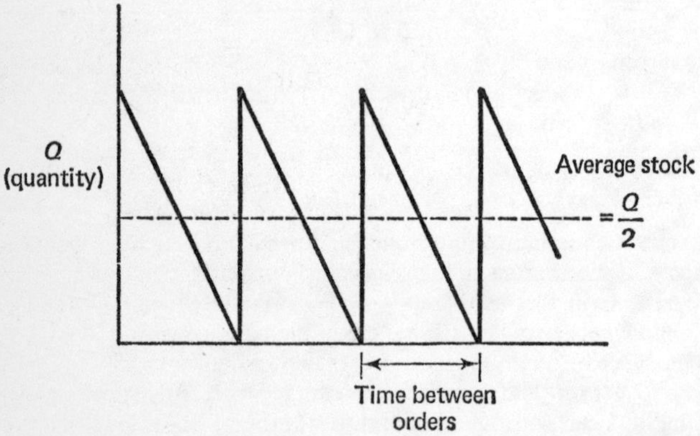

Fig. 2

The total variable costs involved are the sum of stockholding cost and delivery/ordering costs, i.e.

$$\frac{RPQ}{2} + \frac{AC}{Q}$$

These two elements are interdependent since if we attempt to minimise the stockholding costs by stocking small quantities we must order more frequently. Conversely, if we order large quantities we must have a greater investment in stocks and larger storage capacity. It is the combined cost of these elements which we wish to make as small as possible.

The answer as to which batch quantity (Q) will make total costs a minimum can be found by

(*a*) Simulation or trial and error, i.e. computing costs at a variety of levels until the minimum figure can be obtained by inspection.

(*b*) Drawing a graph of the variables at a variety of values for Q.

(*c*) Using a basic formula derived from application of algebra and calculus thus:

$$\text{Total variable cost} = \frac{RPQ}{2} + \frac{AC}{Q}$$

Differentiating with respect to Q

$$\frac{d}{dQ}(\text{Total variable cost}) = \frac{RP}{2} - \frac{AC}{Q^2}$$

This step represents an elementary application of differential calculus and the proof is not included here. For application only knowledge of the formula and ability to identify the variables concerned is needed. For total cost to be a minimum this expression must be equated to zero, i.e.

$$\frac{RP}{2} - \frac{AC}{Q^2} = 0$$

$$\therefore \frac{RP}{2} = \frac{AC}{Q^2}$$

$$\text{and } Q = \sqrt{\frac{2AC}{RP}}$$

This is the most fundamental formula. It can be modified to take account, among other things, of:

(i) Internal manufacturing conditions involving batch set-up costs as opposed to costs of ordering.

(ii) Variations in the 'lead time', or what happens when suppliers cannot deliver immediately or when partially completed work is involved.

(iii) The effect of quantity discounts offered by suppliers.

(iv) The effect of 'stock-outs', i.e. using probability analysis to assess the possible loss due, on the one hand, to not being able to satisfy customers' immediate delivery requirements and, on the other hand, carrying excessive safety stocks.

It should be noted that only the variable costs of stockholding are reflected in the formula. If the *fixed* costs are to be taken into account then it must be remembered that storage facilities must cater for the maximum stock, so the number and size of warehouses needed will depend upon Q itself not $Q/2$. The divisor RP above represents costs of holding stocks and in alternative versions of the formula may be indicated by a single letter. The symbols used vary from text to text but it is a matter of identifying into separate groups those costs which (*a*) vary with the number of orders placed or batches of production commenced, and (*b*) are related to the costs per item purchased and associated storage facilities.

Example

A manufacturer requires 1,000,000 components for use during the next year which it is assumed will consist of 250 working days. The cost of storing one component for one year is £4·00 and the cost of placing an order is £32·00.

There must always be a safety stock equal to two working days' usage and the lead time from the supplier, which has been guaranteed, will be five working days throughout the year.

Assuming usage takes place steadily throughout the working day, delivery takes place at the end of the day of delivery, and orders are placed at the end of a working day, you are required to:

(*a*) calculate the economic reorder quantity;

(*b*) calculate the reorder point;

(*c*) show graphically the physical stock and order position during seven consecutive working days.

(CIMA)

This question can be used to illustrate and expand the use of the model.

(*a*) *Calculate the reorder quantity*

$$Q = \sqrt{\frac{2AC}{RP}}$$

A = 1,000,000 components p.a.
C = £32 per order
RP = £4, i.e. the cost of the component and the charges associated have already been combined.

$$Q = \sqrt{\frac{2 \times 1{,}000{,}000 \times 32}{4}}$$

$$= 4{,}000 \text{ units}$$

Note. The fact that there is a required safety stock means that there will be a permanent addition to the stockholding costs which will be independent of the Economic Order (Batch) Quantity (*EOQ*). There must always be in stock a supply equivalent to two days' usage $= \frac{1{,}000{,}000}{250} \times 2 = 4{,}000 \times 2 = 8{,}000$ units. The storage costs per annum will therefore be:

		£
8,000 × £4 in respect of safety stock	=	32,000
$\frac{4{,}000}{2}$ × £4 in respect of average stock during and between reorder periods	=	8,000
		£40,000

The costs of ordering per year will be

Number of orders placed × cost of ordering each order –

$\frac{1{,}000{,}000}{4{,}000} \times £32$ = £8,000

Combined costs will be £40,000 + £8,000 = £48,000 p.a.

(*b*) *The reorder point*

This must be equal to the safety stock plus usage during the lead time.

The lead time is 5 days.
The present rate of demand is 4,000 per day.
Therefore, the Reorder level = (5 × 4,000) + 8,000 = 28,000 units.

Note that in this case the ordering schedule on the supplier is made out from orders on hand. The quantity of 28,000 is never physically stocked. If the supplier delays more than two days beyond his normal lead time in his delivery, there will be a **stock-out**, i.e. zero stock. If it was felt desirable to keep a safety stock equivalent to requirements during the lead time, then the safety stock would be equal to 5 days at 4,000 units (20,000) and total costs involved would increase to $(20{,}000 \times £4) + \left(\frac{4{,}000 \times £4}{2}\right) = £88{,}000$ p.a.

Computation of the *EOQ* has not been affected. The graph shown in Fig. 3 would appear the same in format but would start at 28,000 units and decline to 20,000. Storage facilities would then be required for 28,000 units as opposed to 12,000 units. The question would then arise of the costs of building the stores— i.e. as an investment proposition. This is a separate element of the problem to the stockholding element of the working capital—although the cost of financing such building or amortising their original cost can be incorporated into an adapted version of the model.

(*c*) The graph in Fig. 3 is similar to the basic version of Fig. 2 except that the line corresponding to the safety stock (8,000) provides the lowest point as

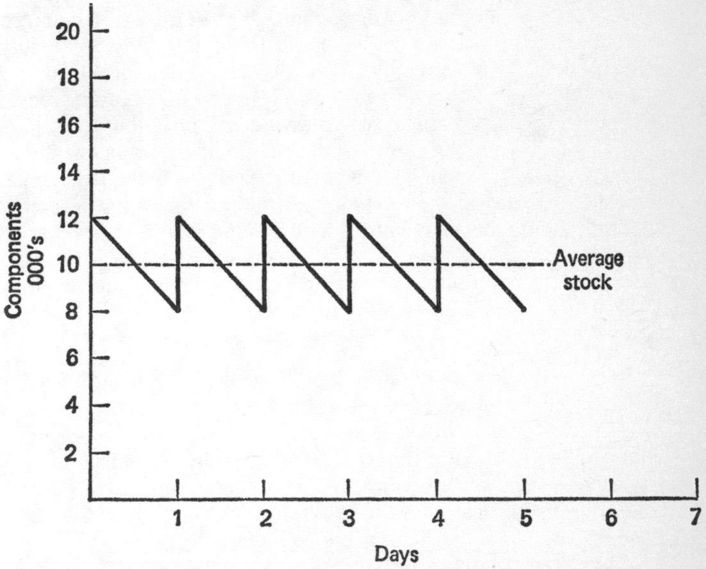

Fig. 3. Physical stock and order position during seven consecutive working days.

compared with zero earlier. It is a coincidence here that the *EOQ* of 4,000 is equivalent to the daily usage rate. The important thing from the point of view of capital utilisation is that a safety stock will increase the requirement for working capital to finance the stockholding and also the requirement for capital to provide storage facilities, i.e. fixed capital.

This example on stocks has been dealt with in detail as it is a fairly common exercise in model building. Also it can be adapted to develop models of the other elements of working capital such as debtor levels, credit management and control of cash.

Planned Funds Flow and Liquidity

The methods which are used for funds forecasting may be used for estimating overall capital requirements. The major differences in applying them are that a greater degree of approximation is acceptable as figures become more tentative and total capital required may on occasion be satisfied by methods other than cash. The main purpose of the capital requirements projection are:

(*a*) To ascertain the maximum or peak cash commitment over the forecast period.

(*b*) To determine the extent to which this can be met by short-term borrowing at the relevant time.

(*c*) If the balance is to be determined from long-term sources, how this best might be raised. This entails checking the capital required against the earnings accruing from its use and ensuring that the costs and other items can be met.

The basic methods of funds forecasting are now dealt with.

Receipts and Payments Basis

This is in effect a summarised cash account. A pro forma of the end result of this type of analysis is shown in Fig. 4, but this is normally preceded by a detailed worksheet if done manually and a worked example of this method is given on page 20 onwards as a demonstration. This format can be used when the new capital intake is unknown. All known items, including the minimum acceptable cash balance either as an absolute figure or that which is the result of a desired ratio, are inserted. The figures necessary to make the tabulation balance are then inserted in the receipts from other sources in whatever form of capital injection it is considered possible. When the receipts other than those of a capital nature are sufficient to increase or maintain the cash balance required no more external funds are required, and the minimum requirement can be obtained by accumulating all periods prior to this.

Forecast Funds Flow Statements

These can be produced in a variety of forms depending upon whether it is desired to emphasise changes in net liquid funds, total financing, working capital movements or some other particular aspect. They can commence with profits before or after taxation, and subsequently items which do not involve movement of funds—but which affect profits—such as depreciation are separated from those which do involve such movement, such as the purchase of fixed assets. An example is given in Table 1 (page 20).

On page 321 reference is made to Statements of Standard Accounting Practice (SSAPs). The standard dealing with funds flow is SSAP 10. A simple version of the particular layout recommended is given as an example only and would be similar to that shown in Table 2 (page 21).

The major objective of the standard is to try to ensure some uniformity of layout and treatment in published accounts where the flow of funds is being

Cash forecast	Periods No. 1-4			
	Period 1 £	Period 2 £	Period 3 £	Period 4 £
Balance b/f				
Receipts from trading				
Debtors				
Cash				
Total				
Payments				
Direct materials				
Indirect materials				
Expenses				
Wages and salaries				
Other trading items				
Total				
Surplus/deficit on trading				
Add				
Receipts from other sources				
Interest/dividends received				
Loans				
Sales of assets				
Capital issues				
Deduct				
Non-trading payments				
Interest				
Dividends				
Taxation				
Purchase of assets				
Balance c/fwd				

Fig. 4

explained on a past or historical basis. When the objective of a forecast can be improved by varying the presentation then this is a matter for the management accountant concerned. If, for example, the objective was to emphasise the additional long-term capital required then the layout could be modified into a form similar to that shown in Table 1.

Requirements for additional fixed assets and investments would come from the capital appraisal procedures and resulting approvals. The profit and loss figure would come from the forecast accounts and changes in working capital and would largely depend on established ratios between the elements in this section and the volume of activity concerned. It would be necessary also to set a minimum working cash balance either in absolute terms or as a ratio. In the example in Table 1 the increase in cash has been set at £100,000 in each period. A more extensive example is shown on pages 24–6 and also on page 147.

Table 1. Forecast of Long-Term Capital Requirement (£000)

	19x6	*19x7*	*19x8*	*19x9*
Application of funds				
Purchase of fixed assets	2,500	1,500	1,000	—
Investments proposed	800	1,000	—	—
Debentures redeemable	—	—	—	—
Taxation payable	250	215	300	400
Dividends payable	650	650	650	650
	4,200	3,365	1,950	1,050
Increase/(Decrease) in working capital				
Increase in stocks	200	100	300	100
Increase in debtors	200	100	200	100
Increase in creditors	(200)	(150)	(150)	(100)
Increase in cash	100	100	100	100
	300	150	450	200
Total applications	4,500	3,515	2,400	1,250
Sources of funds				
Profit before tax	750	800	900	1,200
Depreciation	500	550	600	800
Sale of assets	—	50	—	—
Others	—	—	—	—
Subtotal internal sources	1,250	1,400	1,500	2,000
Required from other sources	3,250	2,115	900	(750)

Notes

(i) No allowance has been made for increasing cost of servicing capital, i.e. increased dividends or interest charges, since this depends on the form in which the capital is raised.

(ii) The cumulative capital requirement over the three years is (3,250 + 2,115 + 900) thousands = £6,265,000. This is reduced at the end of year 19x9 by the surplus of £750,000 created by the build-up of profit-earning assets and investment.

(iii) The final stage would be to decide whether and in what form these capital requirements could be satisfied in a manner profitable to the firm.

Table 2. Source and Application of Funds

for the year ended 31st December 19—

	£	£
Source:		
Profit before taxation		70,000
Items not involving movement of funds:		
Depreciation		12,000
		82,000
Application:		
Purchase of fixed assets	40,000	
Loans repair	10,000	
Taxation paid	21,000	71,000
Increase in working capital		11,000

Represented by:	
Increase in stocks	5,000
Increase in debtors	17,000
Increase in creditors	(10,000)
	12,000
Decrease in net liquid funds:	
Increase in bank overdraft	(1,000)
	11,000

Worked Examples

1. Calculation of a Cash Budget

You are required, given the following information, to prepare a cash budget for each of the three months, October, November and December:

	June	*July*	*Aug.*	*Sept.*	*Oct.*	*Nov.*	*Dec.*	*Jan./ Mar.*
Weeks in month	4	5	4	4	5	4	4	
Profit forecast	£000	£000	£000	£000	£000	£000	£000	£000
Contracts invoiced	688	560	1,600	2,000	320	600	720	800 per month
Material consumed ex stock		190	190	180	180	160	210	
Direct purchases to contract		550	626	511	400	330	400	
Direct wages		50	60	60	75	60	72	
Direct input to work-in-progress		790	876	751	655	550	682	
Decrease/(Increase) in work-in-progress		(400)	300	610	(395)	(75)	(102)	
Direct cost of sales		390	1,176	1,361	260	475	580	
Factory overhead		60	70	80	75	60	80	
Selling and administration costs		72	72	92	102	82	72	
Royalties		27	80	100	15	30	35	
Premises charges—rent and rates		8	8	8	8	8	8	
Depreciation		5	5	5	5	5	5	
		562	1,411	1,646	465	660	780	
Net profit before tax, subject to commissions		(2)	189	354	(145)	(60)	(60)	
Materials in stock at month end	196	176	200	229	250	240	250	

You are informed that:

1. Of the total sales invoicing, about one quarter will be on the basis of 'net cash one month'. The remaining three quarters will be subject to the following payment conditions:

   20 per cent with order, on average three months before invoicing;
   50 per cent on delivery, on average one month before final invoice;
   20 per cent on one month's credit after invoicing;
   10 per cent on acceptance, on average three months after invoicing.

2. Commissions are to be calculated to the nearest £1,000 at the rate of 2 per cent on cash collections, and will be paid one month in arrear.
3. Of the total purchases for stock and contract, about one third will attract $2\frac{1}{2}$ per cent cash discount, and will be paid for in the month following delivery. The remaining two thirds will be paid for on average $2\frac{1}{2}$ months after delivery.
4. Direct wages are paid one week in arrear.
5. Factory and selling and administration overhead are in general paid in the month when they arise.
6. Royalties are paid quarterly in February, May, August and November, one month in arrear.
7. Rent is paid on the usual Quarter Days, and rates are generally paid about the same time.
8. Outlays on capital purchases in the months given above are expected to be:

	£000
August	80
October	40
December	100

9. The cash balance at 30th September is £120,000. The normal minimum requirement for working purposes is considered to be £250,000.
10. At 30th June there is a bank loan of £900,000. It is proposed reducing this by £450,000 as soon as the cash flow permits. (CIMA)

For workings see page 23.

Cash Budget

For Period October–December

	October (£000)	*November* (£000)	*December* (£000)
Receipts			
Debtors	1,187	638	810
Payments			
Purchase creditors—1 month	234	195	156
$2\frac{1}{2}$ months	520	520	440
Commission	18	24	13
Direct wages	75	60	69
Factory overheads	75	60	80
Selling and admin. overheads	102	82	72
Royalties	—	195	—
Rent and rates	—	—	24
Capital expenditure	40	—	100
	1,064	1,136	954
Monthly balance	123	(498)	(144)
Opening balance b/fwd	120	243	(255)
Monthly closing balance	243	(255)	(399)

Workings

Payment for credit purchases — 2½ months:

	Oct. (£000)		*Nov.* (£000)		*Dec.* (£000)
½ July	240	½ Aug.	280	½ Sept.	240
½ Aug.	280	½ Sept.	240	½ Oct.	200
	520		520		440

Commissions

	Oct.	*Nov.*	*Dec.*
One month in arrears	18	24	13

Wages	*Sept.*		*Oct.*		*Nov.*		*Dec.*	
As charged	60		75		60		72	
Number of weeks	4		5		4		4	
£000 per week	15		15		15		18	
Carry forward	15	→	15	→	15	→	18	→
Payment	—		75		60		69	

Royalties—Paid in November:

Sept.	100
Aug.	80
Oct.	15
	195

Rent and rates—Paid in December:

Oct.	8
Nov.	8
Dec.	8
	24

Debtors

Payment proportions:

	25% Net sales—one month	= 25%
Of 75%	20% With order—3 months before invoice	= 15%
	50% On delivery—1 month before invoice	= 37·5%
	20% One month's credit after invoice	= 15%
	10% On acceptance 3 months after invoice	= 7·5%
		100%

	Sept.		*Oct.*		*Nov.*		*Dec.*	
%	£000	£000	£000	£000	£000	£000	£000	£000
25	of 1,600 =	400	of 2,000 =	500	of 320 =	80	of 600 =	150
15	of 720 =	108	of 800 =	120	of 800 =	120	of 800 =	120
37·5	of 320 =	120	of 600 =	225	of 720 =	270	of 800 =	300
15	of 1,600 =	240	of 2,000 =	300	of 320 =	48	of 600 =	90
7·5	of 688 =	52	of 560 =	42	of 1,600 =	120	of 2,000 =	150
		920		1,187		638		810

Purchases

	July £000	*Aug.* £000	*Sept.* £000	*Oct.* £000	*Nov.* £000	*Dec.* £000
Closing stocks	176	200	229	250	240	250
Issues	190	190	180	180	160	210
	366	390	409	430	400	460
Opening stocks	196	176	200	229	250	240
Purchases for stock	170	214	209	201	150	220
Purchases direct	550	626	511	400	330	400
Total purchases	720	840	720	601	480	620
$\frac{1}{3}$ thereof	240	280	240	200	160	207
$2\frac{1}{2}$% discount	6	7	6	5	4	5
Net cash	234	273	234	195	156	202
Balancing $\frac{2}{3}$	480	560	480	400	320	414

2. Preparation of a Profit and Loss Budget, Cash Budget and Budgeted Balance Sheet

Trendy Ltd produces two products for the tourist market. The management are now planning production for the three months from 1st July. Estimates and other information relating to the three months in question are as follows:

Sales	*Units*	*Price*
Product A	10,000	£1·00
Product B	15,000	£1·20
Stocks of finished goods	*30th June*	*30th Sept.*
Product A (units)	2,000	4,000
Product B (units)	3,000	6,000
Standard direct costs per unit	*Product A*	*Product B*
Material X	20p	25p
Material Y	10p	10p
Labour	40p	50p

Production and purchases are to be at a constant monthly rate throughout the period. Materials stocks are not to be increased or decreased. All sales on 2 months' credit. All material purchases are on 3 months' credit. Work-in-progress remains at a constant level. Overdraft facilities are available up to £10,000.

Overhead expenses for three months are estimated at:

Manufacturing	£3,000
Administrative and selling	£2,000

These overhead expenses can be assumed all to be paid in cash except for £400 depreciation on fixed assets included in manufacturing overhead.

Summarised balance sheet at 30th June

	£	£
Fixed assets		
Cost		4,000
Depreciation		1,600
		2,400
Stock at standard direct cost:		
Finished goods		
Product A (2,000 units)	1,400	
Product B (3,000 units)	2,550	
		3,950
Work-in-progress		
Product A	280	
Product B	510	
		790
Materials		
X	500	
Y	300	
		800
Debtors for sales of products		3,000
Balance at bank		1,000
		11,940
Creditors for materials		2,500
		9,440
Share capital		5,000
Reserves (retained profit)		4,440
		9,440

You are required to prepare the management profit and loss budget and the cash budget for the three months, and the budgeted balance sheet at 30th September. Stocks are to be valued at standard direct cost.

Preliminary Workings

	Product A £	*Product B* £
Standard product costs		
Material X	0·20	0·25
Y	0·10	0·10
Labour	0·40	0·50
Total direct (marginal) cost	0·70	0·85

Since stocks are valued on a direct cost basis the profit and loss account can be constructed using marginal costing for the volume of sales forecast.

Profit and loss budget for three months to 30th September

	Product A		Product B		Total
	Unit	Total	Unit	Total	
	£	£	£	£	£
Sales	1·00	10,000	1·20	18,000	28,000
Less Direct costs	0·70	7,000	0·85	12,750	19,750
Standard contribution	0·30	3,000	0·35	5,250	8,250
Less Fixed costs					
Manufacturing (excluding depreciation)					2,600
Depreciation					400
Administrative and selling					2,000
Net profit for period					3,250

Cash budget

		£
Sources of funds		
Profit as above		3,250
Adjustment for items not involving the movement of funds: Depreciation		400
Total generated from operations		3,650
Funds from other sources		—
		3,650
Application of funds		
Divdends paid	—	
Tax paid	—	
Purchase of fixed assets	—	Nil
		3,650
Increase/Decrease in working capital		
Increase in stocks	3,950	
Increase in debtors	15,667	
(Increase)/Decrease in creditors	(7,400)	
		12,217
Movement in net liquid funds		
Increase/(Decrease) in cash balance		(8,567)
Balance at bank 1st July		1,000
Projected balance 30th Sept.—Debit/(Overdraft)		(7,567)

Note. The only differences between this format and that recommended by Statement of Standard Accounting Practice Number 10 is in the rearrangement of the last two lines. Items not requiring entries have been included to indicate the position of major items likely to occur in other problems. If, for example, the above overdraft position was not acceptable the limit required would be inserted and the forecast examined to see if profits could be increased or other items changed to produce the necessary figure.

Budgeted Balance Sheet as at 30th September

	£	£	£
Fixed assets			
Cost		4,000	
Depreciation		2,000	
			2,000
Net current assets			
Stocks (at standard direct cost)			
Finished goods			
Product A (4,000 units)	2,800		
Product B (6,000 units)	5,100		
		7,900	
Work-in-progress			
Product A	280		
Product B	510	790	
Materials			
X	500		
Y	300		
		800	
		9,490	
Debtors		18,667	
		28,157	
Less Creditors	9,900		
Bank overdraft	7,567	17,467	
			10,690
			12,690
Represented by:			
Share capital			5,000
Reserves			7,690
			12,690

Notes

(i) Finished goods stocks are the forecast figures at standard direct cost per unit.

(ii) Work in progress and material stocks are unchanged.

(iii) Debtors will be equal to $\frac{2}{3} \times$ £28,000 = £18,667.

(iv) Creditors: Material requirements will be for 12,000 units of A and 18,000 units of B respectively. This is because we need to purchase sufficient materials to produce the sales quantities and the *increased* stock requirements in the quarters.

Materials X 12,000 × £0·20 + 18,000 × £0·25 = £6,900
Y 12,000 × £0·10 + 18,000 × £0·10 = £3,000

£9,900

(v) Reserves will be increased by the profit made in the period (£4,440 + £3,250) = £7,690.

Questions

1. Runswick Ltd is a company that purchases toys from abroad for resale to retail stores. The company is concerned about its stock (inventory) management operations. It is considering adopting a stock management system based upon the economic order quantity (EOQ) model.

The company's estimates of its stock management costs are shown below:

	Percentage of purchase price of toys per year
Storage costs	3
Insurance	1
Handling	1
Obsolescence	3
Opportunity costs of funds invested in stock	10

'Fixed' costs associated with placing each order for stock are £311.54

The purchase price of the toys to Runswick Ltd is £4·50 per unit. There is a two week delay between the time that new stock is ordered from suppliers and the time that it arrives.

The toys are sold by Runswick at a unit price of £6·30. The variable cost to Runswick of selling the toys is £0·30 per unit. Demand from Runswick's customers for the toys averages 10,000 units per week, but recently this has varied from 6,000 to 14,000 units per week. On the basis of recent evidence the probability of unit sales in any two week period has been estimated as follows:

Sales (units)	*Probability*
12,000	0.05
16,000	0·20
20,000	0·50
24,000	0·20
28,000	0·05

If adequate stock is not available when demanded by Runswick's customers in any two week period approximately 25 per cent of orders that cannot be satisfied in that period will be lost, and approximately 75 per cent of customers will be willing to wait until new stock arrives.

Required:

(*a*) Ignoring taxation, calculate the optimum order level of stock over a one year planning period using the economic order quantity model:

$$\text{EOQ} = \sqrt{\frac{2\text{FS}}{\text{CP}}}$$

Where: F is the fixed cost per order.
S is the annual sales.
C is the cost of carrying a unit of stock per period expressed as a percentage of its purchase cost.
P is the purchase price per unit of stock.

(*b*) Estimate the level of safety stock that should be carried by Runswick Ltd.

(*c*) If Runswick Ltd were to be offered a quantity discount by its suppliers of 1 per cent for orders of 30,000 units or more, evaluate whether it would be beneficial for the company to take advantage of the quantity discount. Assume for this calculation that no safety stock is carried.

(*d*) Estimate the expected total annual costs of stock management if the economic order quantity had been (i) 50 per cent higher (ii) 50 per cent lower than its actual level. Comment upon the sensitivity of total annual costs to changes in the economic order quantity. Assume for this calculation that no safety stock is carried.

(*e*) Discuss briefly how the effect of seasonal sales variations might be incorporated within the model.

(*f*) Assess the practical value of this model in the management of stock. (CACA)

2. A company needs to hold a stock of item X for sale to customers. Although the item is of relatively small value per unit, the customers' quality control requirements and the need to obtain competitive supply tenders at frequent intervals result in high procurement costs.

Basic data about item X are as follows:

Annual sales demand (d) over 52 weeks	= 4,095 units
Cost of placing and processing a purchase order (procurement costs – C_s)	= £48·46
Cost of holding one unit for one year (C_h)	= £4·00
Normal delay between placing purchase order and receiving goods	= 3 weeks

You are required to

(*a*) *Calculate*

(i) the Economic Order Quantity for item X, using the formula:

$$EOQ = \sqrt{\frac{2C_s d}{C_h}}$$

(ii) The frequency at which purchase orders would be placed, using that formula.

(iii) The total annual procurement costs and the total annual holding costs when the EOQ is used.

(*b*) Explain why it might be unsatisfactory to procure a fixed quantity of item X at regular intervals if it were company policy to satisfy all sales demands from stock and if:

(i) The rate of sales demand could vary between 250 and 350 units per four-week period or

(ii) The delivery delay on purchases might vary between 3 and 5 weeks

suggesting in each case what corrective actions might be taken.

(*c*) Describe in detail a fully-developed stock control system for item X (or other fast-moving items), designed to ensure that stock holdings at all times are adequate but not excessive. Illustrate your answer with a freehand graph, not to scale. (CIMA)

3. Trade credit is one of the most common sources and uses of short-term finance. Discuss the factors which should be taken into consideration in determining the level of trade credit that should be extended to customers.

A supplier who had previously been supplying your firm on the basis that all accounts had to be paid within 30 days of receipt of goods with a 3 per cent cash discount for goods paid within 10 days has notified you that as from the beginning of the next trading period it is extending the period of payment to 90 days with a reduced cash discount of 1 per cent if paid within 20 days. What are the implications for this as far as your organisation is concerned? (CACA)

4. A new company to be known as Stratoscope Ltd is to be formed on 1st January for the purpose of taking over an existing wholesale business dealing in fancy goods as from the same date, when the present proprietor retires. The purchase consideration of £100,000 is payable in two equal instalments on 1st January and 31st March.

The purchase price includes freehold buildings valued at £60,000, furniture and equipment valued at £15,000, two delivery vans valued at £5,000 and stock-in-trade valued at £20,000. A preliminary budget for the first year includes the following information:

(i) Sales in the first quarter will be £20,000 per month, in the second £18,000 per month, in the third £24,000 per month and in the fourth £30,000 per month. Gross profit averages 50 per cent on cost.

(ii) Fixed cost is budgeted at £5,000 per month. Variable overhead expense is budgeted at 10 per cent of sales value. All expenses are payable on the last day of the month in which they relate.

(iii) Debtors are allowed two months' credit—that is, they can be expected to pay for goods on the last day of the second month following that in which the sales are made. Trade creditors allow one month's credit and stocks are to be maintained at £20,000 throughout the year.

(*a*) Prepare a cash flow statement to calculate the minimum capital required by the new company for the first year. (Assume that the company will not be able to borrow further funds during the year.)

(*b*) Prepare an Income Statement for the year taking into account depreciation at 10 per cent on furniture and equipment and 20 per cent on the delivery vans. (Ignore any possibility of paying loan interest during the year.)

Note: Price level changes should be ignored. (SCCA)

5. DEF Ltd is the United Kingdom agent for the installation and servicing of a new type of infra-red coffee-roasting machine. The company is currently selling the machine to a variety of grocers and other retail outlets and believes it could have an appeal to householders on a mail order basis. Over the first two years of operation about 3,000 machines have been installed and, although many of these have given technical trouble, it is believed that the major causes of malfunctioning have now been overcome.

The gross margin on these machines is low. The company has kept its overhead to a minimum but has still failed to show a net profit. It has experienced fairly heavy bad debts. The normal credit terms require payment in the month following installation of the equipment, but slow payment by a significant number of retail customers has added to the shortage of liquid funds.

In reviewing the position the board has asked for the chief accountant's comments on four possible lines of action:

(*a*) To give longer credit in the hope of attracting more sales which would improve the overhead/sales ratio.

(*b*) To offer, say, 5 per cent discount for payment within the existing allowed credit period.

(*c*) To pass the whole sales ledger and debt collection procedures to a factor in order to obtain quicker access to funds.

(*d*) To insure the book debts so as to minimise the impact of bad debts.

You are asked to give your views on the practicability and possible benefits of these various courses of action and include any further comments or suggestions which appear to be relevant to the company's liquidity problem. (CIMA)

6. You are given the following information concerning Z Ltd and are required to:

(*a*) Forecast the operating capital required at sales values per annum of: (i) £4,250,000, and (ii) £1,800,000.

(*b*) Comment on the internal availability of capital as sales rise or fall.

(*c*) Review the profit effectiveness of capital employed in the business and suggest methods of improving it.

The amounts of capital in use at various annual sales values are as follows:

Annual sales value (in £000)	2,150	2,500	2,850	3,200
Average capital employed:				
Current assets:	£	£	£	£
Cash	122,455	134,250	146,045	157,840
Accounts receivable	223,075	251,250	279,425	307,600
Stocks and work-in-progress	420,900	465,000	509,100	553,200
	766,430	850,500	934,570	1,018,640
Current liabilities	226,360	251,000	275,640	300,280

	£	£	£	£
Net working capital	540,070	599,500	658,930	718,360
Fixed assets at cost	676,170	684,500	692,830	701,160
Total operating capital	1,216,240	1,284,000	1,351,760	1,419,520

The following information is taken from the profit and loss account:

Variable costs per £100 of sales

	£
Direct labour	10·80
Direct material	46·88
Indirect salaries	5·00
Other indirect costs	14·67
	£77·35

Fixed costs, per annum £478,500 (CIMA)

7. The ABC Company Ltd will require to find during the next three months £60,000 for the financing of some new equipment. It had been anticipated that the company would have been able to find the funds for this from internal sources but by the end of June the bank overdraft will have reached the overdraft limit of £25,000. The company does not operate a detailed budgetary planning system but you have been able to obtain the following sales estimate.

	Cash sales	*Credit sales*	*Total sales*
	£	£	£
July	40,000	200,000	240,000
August	45,000	220,000	265,000
September	50,000	220,000	270,000

The sales mark-up is estimated to give a gross profit margin of $33\frac{1}{3}$ per cent on gross cost and £240,000 of goods at sales value will be needed as stock to enable the above sales forecasts to be met.

All company purchases are paid for on receipt in order to get the benefit of a 5 per cent discount, and likewise a cash discount of 3 per cent is offered to customers who pay within 15 days. Only 50 per cent of customers pay in time to take the benefit of the cash discount—unlike in the previous year when about 90 per cent did so—20 per cent pay at the end of 30 days and the remainder at the end of 60 days. On average 25 per cent of the credit sales in any one month to customers who take the benefit of the cash discount will be in debtors at the end of the month.

The estimated other expenses payable monthly are:

Fixed	£50,000
Variable	$12\frac{1}{2}$ per cent of gross sales

Cash sales for June—a high sales month—were £20,000 and credit sales £285,000 of which £185,000 were still outstanding. The opening balances for the beginning of July are:

Stock	£220,000
Debtors	£275,000

You are required to prepare a cash budget for the months of July, August and September along with a report commenting on any other matters you would wish the directors of the company to consider. (CACA)

3

THE INVESTMENT DECISION—BASIC TECHNIQUES

Introduction

The previous chapter concentrated on the capital structure *as a whole* but this situation is in practice the cumulative result of large numbers of prior decisions. Most investment decisions are marginal—that is, we have to consider the effect on an existing situation. This does not necessarily mean that the amount of capital involved is small. We may be, at one end of the scale, contemplating buying another factory or at the other merely replacing one of the firm's cars. Ideally each decision to invest—or not to invest—should be based on accurate factual information and prior knowledge of what the economic and political situation will be over the life of the investment. These factors are inevitably unknown and the decision must therefore be made as much on a subjective basis as an objective one. The manager relies largely on information provided by the accountant. This information is formalised in the Capital Asset Pricing Model, which is simply another way of saying that the accountant makes use of statistical and mathematical techniques to assist him. The sophistication of some of the techniques should not be allowed to obscure the fact that they in no way improve the accuracy of the original information.

The simplest case for decision is where the funds are available and only one project for investment has been put forward. In this situation it is a question of deciding whether the return from this investment will increase or reduce that being made at present. The case for investments which do not yield a financial return will be considered later.

Example 1

Alpha Ltd is at present making a return of 15 per cent on its capital employed. A proposal is under consideration to invest £10,000 in a machine which engineers claim will reduce costs by £3,000 p.a. and last at least five years before being scrapped with no residual value. There are various ways in which even this simple exercise can be approached.

	£
(i) Cash generated by investment—5 × £3,000	15,000
Original Cost	10,000
Profit after five years	£5,000

A surplus has been generated and therefore the project should be accepted.

	£
(ii) Original Investment	10,000
Annual return	3,000
Annual return as percentage of investment	30%

This is in excess of the present return of 15 per cent; therefore the project should be accepted.

(iii) We may claim that it is unreasonable in (ii) to consider a return which does not allow for repayment of the original cost; therefore we get

		£
Original Investment		10,000
Annual return	3,000	
Less annual depreciation	2,000	1,000
Annual return as a percentage of investment		10%

This is less than the existing return of 15 per cent and therefore the project should be rejected.

However, this example includes many factors which are open to question:
(*a*) The cost of the project
(*b*) The source of funds for the project
(*c*) The certainty of future cash flows
(*d*) The timing of the cash flow
(*e*) The existence of alternative opportunities for investment.
(*f*) Taxation
(*g*) Government policy

(a) The Cost of the Project

This may vary from obtaining the cost of a standard machine from a supplier to questionable estimates ranging over a considerable period of time in uncertain conditions, such as the construction of entirely new types of plant for offshore oil drilling.

There is also the matter of defining 'cost' in relation to the nature of the problem. A comparative cost study prepared on a conventional accounting basis would not necessarily be in the best form on which management could base a decision. The statement may well be based on sound accounting conventions, but it would not emphasise those variables which are relevant to the decision-making. Sometimes it is stated simply that only marginal costs and revenues should be considered, i.e. the net income arising from a project should be compared with the increment of capital required to produce that income. This is sometimes termed marginal analysis, or the economic approach, to distinguish it from the historical cost method. The difference can best be illustrated by considering the following problem.

Example 2

Ajax Manufacturing Company Ltd has been considering the launching of a new product. It has to date spent £10,000 on market research and £20,000 on development. If it is decided to go ahead with the manufacture and sale of the product new plant costing £80,000 will be required. The production costs of the model in the first five years of operation have been assessed as follows:

Variable costs (per unit)	
Materials	£3·00
Labour	£2·00
Expenses	£1·00

The accountant has stated that fixed overheads in respect of items such as rent, rates, insurances and administration would, on the allocation basis used, amount to £40,000 p.a. The marketing manager anticipates that sales in the first three years will be at a rate of 10,000 units p.a. and for the next two years 20,000 units p.a., all at a price of £8 each.

The plant will be scrapped at the end of the project and has no residual value. Prepare a statement showing the result of the project, (i) on a historic cost accounting basis, and (ii) on an economic cost basis.

(i) Historic Cost Basis

Five-year period

Units produced and sold		70,000	
	Unit		*Total*
	£	£	£
Sales	8·00		560,000
Less Variable cost of sales			
Materials	3·00		210,000
Labour	2·00		140,000
Expenses	1·00		70,000
	6·00		420,000
Contribution	2·00		140,000
Less Fixed costs			
Plant		80,000	
Market research		10,000	
Development		20,000	
General fixed costs alloated		40,000	150,000
Deficit			10,000

This statement suggests that as total revenue does not exceed total costs the project should not be proceeded with.

(ii) Economic Cost Basis

Five-year period

Units produced and sold			70,000	
	Unit		*Total*	
	£	£	£	£
Sales	8·00		560,000	
Less Variable cost of sales				
Materials	3·00	210,000		
Labour	2·00	140,000		
Expenses	1·00	70,000		
	6·00		420,000	
Contribution	2·00		140,000	
Less 'Relevant' fixed costs				
Plant			80,000	
Surplus			60,000	

The £30,000 for marketing and development has already been spent and is therefore not pertinent to the decision as to whether to proceed or not. The alternative presentation apparently transforms a loss of £10,000 into a profit of £60,000. Both statements cannot be correct, but they do endorse one cardinal principle, and that is that as far as possible **each accounting document should be designed specifically for the purpose intended.** If it is not, then confusion arises when figures which were produced for an entirely different purpose are made the basis on which decisions are made.

The primary difference in this simple example is entirely in the fixed costs section. In the conventional statement three types of costs are included:

(i) Expenses specific to the project which have not yet been spent.
(ii) Expenses specific to the project which have already been incurred.
(iii) Expenses of a continuing nature for the enterprise as a whole but not specific to the project.

If the costs on the two latter categories are ignored, then the result of the second exercise is the same as the first, i.e. costs are reduced by £70,000; therefore, the difference will be £70,000 – £10,000 = £60,000 gain. This implies that *in the absence of any alternative investment* the effect on the enterprise as a whole if we do not proceed is a lost opportunity of improving cash flow by £60,000. The term 'deficit' and 'surplus' have been used specifically to endorse this emphasis on cash flow. The terms profit and loss, in common with the use of the word cost, without amplification, can be confusing, since among other things it may include non-monetary items in its computation.

This does not imply that statements produced in the conventional fashion have no purpose or importance. In the long run all costs incurred by a business must be recovered if it is to prosper. Nevertheless the expenditure of £10,000 on marketing and £20,000 on development *has been spent* and no decision taken now can affect this. Similarly, by definition the general fixed costs are allocated—i.e. they will have to be borne by the *enterprise* whether or not this particular project is proceeded with and therefore do not have the same classification as the plant, since this is the only fixed cost in this example in relation to which we still have freedom of choice.

Accurate data in respect of capital costs and anticipated cost savings or increased revenues is the most important stage in the task. It is repeatedly stressed in management literature that no systems, quantitative or otherwise, can produce results more accurate than the reliability of this basic information. This applies particularly in the case of investment projects and requires the effective cooperation of all personnel in the function concerned, i.e. technical, accounting, marketing and managerial.

(b) The Source of Funds for the Project

In most instances the necessary finance will have to be provided by either (i) borrowing from some external source or (ii) utilising money which has been retained in the enterprise from profit made out of previous transactions.

In the first instance it will be necessary to ensure that the return is in excess of the cost of funds from the external source; in the second case it will be necessary to ensure that the return is at least equivalent to that being earned on the existing capital, otherwise the *average* rate of return will simply be reduced for the enterprise as a whole.

(c) The Certainty of the Future Cash Flows

The income arising from the investment may be the result of a high degree of subjective assessment. In the simplest case, if the investment consists of a purchase of fixed-interest stocks, the amount of the monetary income is fairly certain. For example, if we purchase £1,000 worth of 10 per cent local government stocks the income would be £100 p.a. At the other extreme, if the proposal is to market a new product then all figures relating to quantities, costs and revenues are estimates which will vary in reliability in relation to an extensive list of factors, such as skill of estimators, accuracy of market forecasts, changing economic environment and consumer tastes.

(d) The Timing of the Cash Flows

The timing of the cash flow is extremely important. Some simpler methods of investment appraisal ignore this. Other schools of thought maintain that its importance in recent years has been overemphasised and while it may be academically sound for projects with a reasonable life, other factors are so difficult to predict that the techniques used to take it into account can give an impression of precision where such accuracy does not exist.

The importance of the timing lies in the simple fact that money received in the future is worth less than money already in our possession. This argument is not based on the assumption of erosion through inflation (although the techniques used can be adapted to allow for this factor) but on the concept of opportunity cost.

Suppose that in selling an article the buyer offers payment of £100 now or £110 in a year's time. Which would be more acceptable? The two price elements of the problem are known. If it is further known that £100 could now be invested in bonds yielding 12 per cent p.a., then the choice is obvious. The income received from the bond—assuming it is payable once a year at the end of the year—is £12, a gain of £2 should the £100 be accepted and invested immediately. Furthermore, in a large number of projects increased income is anticipated in the latter years of its life. The extent to which the increase in absolute figures is offset by the time involved in waiting for its generation is assessable by using the techniques of **discounted cash flow** (see page 45).

(e) The Existence of Alternative Opportunities for Investment

The factors listed above apply to any single investment choice, but in most practical situations there are various projects likely to be under consideration at any one time. Since few, if any, organisations either have or would obtain an unlimited amount of resources priorities have to be established between the competing claims for investment. In most instances this will be a matter of deciding which is the most profitable alternative, although there are occasions when some alternatives will be non-profit-generating—for example, money spent on welfare facilities for employees.

(f) Taxation

The taxation policies in respect to investment and claims on income arising could be the most important factor in making the final decision to invest. There are two major factors to consider. First, the amount and timing of any allowances in respect of the project under review against profit arising in the first instance from other sources. Second, the effect on total taxation liability and timing of cash income when profits from the new investment begin to flow in.

(g) Government Policy

In addition to direct intervention by means of taxation the Government of the day may for a variety of reasons influence the particular investment situation. Cash grants may be made available as an inducement to move to a development area or special facilities in the form of cheaper buildings or lower rates on industrial sites may be offered. Alternatively, firms may be forbidden to expand in a particular area, and thus forced to consider additional costs which would not otherwise have arisen. See page 127.

Methods of Investment Appraisal

The methods which can be used to assess the relative profitability of projects can be grouped into three major sections:

(i) Techniques which evaluate the returns but ignore the timing of the proceeds and the risk.
(ii) Techniques which evaluate the timing of the proceeds but ignore the risk.
(iii) Techniques which are used to compel some quantitative assessment to be given to the risk factor.

Techniques which Evaluate the Returns but Ignore the Timing of the Proceeds and the Risk

Implicit in any method in this section are several basic assumptions, stated or implied: (i) money received at some future date is worth as much as money received now; (ii) the costs and net revenues from the projects are known with certainty.

Generally the data are prepared and the method chosen to emphasise one of two aspects of the problem: either the time taken to repay the original cost from the cash flow receipts, or the relationship between profit and the capital required, i.e. the return on the investment.

Payback Period Method

This is defined as the number of years required for the stream of cash proceeds generated by an investment to equal the original cost of that investment.

Example 3

The Alpha Manufacturing Co. Ltd is considering its capital investment programme. Table 3 indicates the net cash flow per annum associated with five mutually exclusive projects each having the same initial capital cost £20,000. Evaluate the ranking of each alternative using the payback method as the criterion for choice. ('Mutually exclusive' implies that only one project is possible and the choice eliminates the remainder.)

Examination of Table 3 will show that the results are as follows:

Project A: This investment produces a return of £20,000 after one year and the whole of the capital cost is recovered in this time. The payback period is therefore one year.

Project B: This is producing equal annual cash flows of £10,000 p.a. Two years is sufficient to recover the capital cost incurred and the payback period is therefore two years.

Table 3. Investments and Income

Project	Capital cost (£)	*Net cash flow (before depreciation) Year 1 (£)	Year 2 (£)	Year 3 (£)
A	20,000	20,000	—	—
B	20,000	10,000	10,000	10,000
C	20,000	3,000	9,000	12,000
D	20,000	12,000	16,000	10,000
E	20,000	16,000	16,000	—

*i.e. profit with any provision for depreciation added back.

Project C: By the end of the second year the gross proceeds are £3,000 plus £9,000, i.e. £12,000. This leaves a balance of £8,000. Assuming the cash inflow during Year 3 is at an even rate throughout the year, two thirds of this year would have elapsed before the remaining £8,000 was recovered. The payback period is therefore 2·66 years.

Project D: In Year 1 £12,000 is recovered. The annual inflow for Year 2 is £16,000 of which £8,000 is required. Again assuming an even rate of cash inflow it would take six months of Year 2 for the total sum recovered to amount to the original cost of £20,000. The payback period is therefore 1·50 years.

Project E: In Year 1 £16,000 is recovered and a further £4,000 is required for the sum recovered to equate with £20,000. At an annual rate of cash inflow for Year 2 of £16,000 p.a. it would take one quarter of the year for the remaining £4,000 to be recovered. The payback period is therefore 1·25 years.

These results are best summarised in a 'priority ranking' table. This is a tabulation which formally summarises the results and expresses the ranking or order of preference which the particular method of investment appraisal being used produces—see Table 4.

Project A is the most favourable choice and is therefore ranked 1, whereas the least favourable investment is C, having the longest payback period of 2·66 years, and therefore ranked last.

Table 4. Payback Period

Project	Payback period (years)	Rank
A	1	1
B	2	4
C	2·66	5
D	1·50	3
E	1·25	2

The major **disadvantages** of this method are as follows:

(i) It ignores income arising after the payback period. The total income over the three years from project D is £38,000 but it is ranked third by this method as the income for the last 1½ years is not taken into account.

(ii) The method is biased in favour of projects having higher cash flows in the early years. There are arguments in favour of this—particularly in economic conditions creating stringent cash-flow problems—but from the long-term standpoint, this may not be so good. In the case of a large number of projects the cash inflow is slow to start for a variety of reasons, such as increasing market impact, phasing out of development expenditure, gradual production build-up and so on. These products may produce a steady cash inflow for a considerable period and add to the overall stability of the firm's position.

(iii) The method ignores the timings of the cash flow from the point of view of the cost of funds. Consider investment A in Table 5. The cost of the project has been fully recovered by the end of Year 1. The cash would probably, in practice, be coming in during the year at an irregular rate—that is, there would be delay between the incurring of the capital expenditure and receipt of the benefits. It would be necessary to forecast these delays. In most academic examples, however, simplified assumptions are normally made. First, we assume that capital expenditure was incurred immediately at the beginning of the period and secondly that the cash inflow occurred in one sum at the end of the period—in this case one year. Second, if we know that money could be invested at the rate of at least 10 per cent p.a., we could test the validity of A being the first choice. Given an interest rate of 10 per cent, £1·00 invested at the beginning of the year would amount to £1·10 at the end of it. If the £20,000 is invested at this current rate it would be worth £22,000 at the end of year one, which is £2,000 more than the project will produce. It would therefore be a better proposition to invest the money outside the enterprise. This point can be further emphasised by considering the position assuming that the cash inflow from project A does not commence until the beginning of Year 2: the first two entries in Table 3 would then appear thus:

			Net cash flow	
	Capital cost	*Year 1*	*Year 2*	*Year 3*
Project	(£)	(£)	(£)	(£)
A	20,000	—	20,000	—
B	20,000	10,000	10,000	10,000

Both these projects have a payback period of two years, and would therefore be ranked equally under this method. However, the £10,000 received in Year 1 from investment B would be free for reinvestment at the current rate, or in a new project, and B would therefore be a better choice. The arguments relative to this concept are treated in detail from page 97 onwards.

(iv) Net cash flow when used in this method is normally defined as profit after tax, but before charging depreciation. It is essential that all comparisons are made on a common definition of cash flow, acceptable and known to all concerned in a particular organisation.

(v) No formal assessment is given to the risk factor. Estimates of cash flows are likely to be less reliable the further into the future they are made. The payback method assumes all cash flows are equally certain.

In spite of the formidable list of disadvantages given above the payback method is used by a majority of firms in this country and abroad as a primary basis on which the investment choice is made. Attention should therefore be given to its **merits**, which are as follows:

(i) It is easy to understand, simple to compute and uses data in a form familiar to most levels of management.
(ii) It emphasises the importance of cash flow as a dominant factor in the problem.
(iii) It will bias a firm's investment programme away from longer-term projects where the risk that projected returns will not be realised is greater. From the manager's point of view it is important that he be able to show a record of success and he will therefore tend to favour medium-term, minimum risk projects—hence the attraction of this method to him.
(iv) Most firms have some idea of the life of their projects by relation to other items marketed; therefore, while it would be a hazardous method for firms having lengthy cycles complicated by development problems—for example, aero engines—it would be useful with fashion projects where it could be anticipated that demand would cease after, say, three years.

Finally, the continued and preferred use of this technique demonstrates that sometimes managers collectively act in an apparently illogical fashion in their decision-making. The results of research done in 1964/5 by Merrett and Sykes, subsequently published in their book *Capital Budgeting and Company Finance* two years later, indicated that 78 per cent of companies were using the payback method. A decade later an English Institute Research Committee paper still found payback the most popular single criterion of investment choice. In fact, the high interest rates and later high inflation rates seemed to add to its preference. A summary of the position at the time of writing (1988) has confirmed its pre-eminence as the single most popular approach. See reference to article by Dr Roger W. Mills contrasting the various methods on page 60.

Average Annual Rate of Return on Investment Methods

The methods used in this section relate the return earned by the investment to its original cost and rank the desirability of the investment accordingly. In the payback method emphasis was placed on the speed with which the original cost of the asset was recovered—in these methods emphasis is placed on the volume of profits generated by the investment. Two methods are in common use and are normally referred to as the **gross** and **net** methods.

Average Gross Annual Rate of Return

This is defined as the average proceeds per year over the whole of the life of the asset expressed as a percentage of the original capital cost. The higher the return the more desirable the investment is claimed to be.

Using data from Table 3 we can produce the ranking in Table 5. It will be noted that the table produces a ranking identical with that for the payback period, but this is coincidental. To emphasise this, suppose that the earnings for project B in Table 3 were £20,000 for the third year of the project. This

Table 5

Project	Capital cost (£)	Cash flow (before depreciation) Total (£)	Average p.a.* (£)	Gross annual average income (% of capital cost)	Rank
A	20,000	20,000	20,000	100	1
B	20,000	30,000	10,000	50	4
C	20,000	24,000	8,000	40	5
D	20,000	38,000	12,666	63·3	3
E	20,000	32,000	16,000	80	2
a	b	c	d	e (= $d/b \times 100$)	*f*

**Note about average p.a.:*

Project A has a life of one year only; therefore, the average annual proceeds are $\frac{£20{,}000}{1} = £20{,}000$

Project E has a life of two years and, therefore, average annual proceeds are $\frac{£32{,}000}{2} = £16{,}000$

The remaining projects B, C and D have a life of three years and, therefore, the divisor in each case for the figures in column *c* is 3.

would not affect the payback computation of two years and would not disturb the ranking by this method. It would, however, mean that total earnings over the three years were now £40,000 and the average annual earnings would be £13,333. This produces an average gross annual rate of return of $\frac{£13{,}333}{£20{,}000} \times 100 = 66{\cdot}66$ per cent, which would make B preferable to D. In computing this return the following terms should be clarified:

Capital cost. This is generally the total cost incurred or anticipated in putting the asset into a revenue-earning position. In the case of a new machine it would include its purchase price and money spent on installing it, and any additional working capital required. Should the firm use its own labour, then this should be costed and capitalised.

Cash flow. This is defined as the difference between total revenue and total operating costs (excluding depreciation). Taxation in most cases is ignored, but as will be later demonstrated the rates can be computed net of tax if required. The essential thing in practice is to define the terms on the documents concerned and to use a consistent basis. This ensures that all parties interpret the figures in the same way and make their conclusions on the same data.

Total cash flow is sometimes related to initial capital expenditure. This would produce the results in Table 6 for the data from Table 3.

This shows a different ranking from the *average* result. For example, the preference for investment A indicated in Table 5 has been reversed to last choice in Table 6. The reason for this is that only total return and total cost have been related and no account has been taken of the time involved. A major element in the cost of capital or attraction of an investment is the time for which the money is borrowed or earned. Because using total figures fails to

Table 6

Project	Capital cost (£)	Cash flow (before depreciation) (£)	Total cash flow (% of capital cost)	Rank
A	20,000	20,000	100	5
B	20,000	30,000	150	3
C	20,000	24,000	120	4
D	20,000	38,000	190	1
E	20,000	32,000	160	2
	a	*b*	*c* $\left(=\frac{b}{a}\times 100\right)$	

recognise this factor the proceeds are usually averaged over the life of the asset and the percentage thus represents an *average annual* rate of return.

If we could repeat investment A every year our average gross annual rate of return would remain at 100 per cent and this is the reason why the percentage computed for project A in both Tables 5 and 6 are identical.

The major **disadvantages** of the gross (and other) average methods are:

(*a*) They smooth the effects of irregularities in the cash inflow and suggest that an investment which produces a cash flow which is built up gradually is just as preferable as one with large cash inflows in the early years. Compare the figures in the following example:

		Cash flow (before depreciation)			
Project	*Capital cost* (£)	*Year 1* (£)	*Year 2* (£)	*Year 3* (£)	*Total* (£)
X	10,000	3,000	5,000	7,000	15,000
Y	10,000	7,000	5,000	3,000	15,000

In both cases the average cash flow is equal to £15,000 divided by 3, i.e. £5,000 p.a., and the return will be equal to $\frac{£5{,}000}{£10{,}000} \times 100 = 50$ per cent. Inspection of the figures shows that project Y has an income of £7,000 in Year 1, which could be reinvested by comparison with the alternative project X, which has an income of only £3,000. This ignoring of the *timing* of the cash flow can lead to errors of judgment in the decision to invest because of the factor already mentioned, i.e. the greater (by comparison) the cash flow in the early years the quicker the investment will pay for itself, thus releasing money for further investment and lessening the risk that a project will prove unsuccessful.

(*b*) Once averaged no indication is given of the time-span of the return; thus a return of, say, 20 per cent p.a. for one year would be equated with the same return per annum for, say, ten years.

The major **advantages** claimed for the average methods are:

(i) They are easy to compute and for management to understand.

(ii) They emphasise profitability since—unlike the payback method—proceeds over the entire life of the asset are taken into account.

(iii) The concept of 'return on capital employed' which the method employs is a familiar one to most accountants and provides a yardstick for comparison which uses familiar notions of profit and capital costs as a basis.

Once again, in general, they are methods which, while subject to criticism primarily in relation to the concept used, are often employed in practice either in isolation, or more likely as a check on the result produced by more sophisticated methods.

Average Net Annual Rate of Return

This is defined as the average annual proceeds per year—*after allowing for depreciation*—over the whole of the life of the asset expressed as a percentage of the original capital cost. The higher the return the more desirable the investment is said to be. Using the data from Table 3 we can produce the ranking in Table 7.

Table 7

			Average cash flow p.a.			
Project	*Capital cost* (£)	*Depreciation p.a.* (£)	*before depreciation* (£)	*after depreciation* (£)	*Net annual av. income (% of (capital)*	*Rank*
A	20,000	20,000	20,000	Nil	—	5
B	20,000	6,666	10,000	3,334	16·6	3
C	20,000	6,666	8,000	1,334	6·6	4
D	20,000	6,666	12,666	6,000	30	1
E	20,000	10,000	16,000	6,000	30	1
a	*b*	*c*	*d*	*e* $(=d-c)$	*f* $\left(=\frac{e}{b}\times 100\right)$	*g*

In using this method depreciation is normally charged on a straight line basis. Project A has a life of one year only; therefore the depreciation figure is equal to $\frac{£20,000}{1}=£20,000$. Project E has a life of two years only and the depreciation figure is, therefore, equal to $\frac{£20,000}{2}=£10,000$. The remaining three alternative projects have a life of three years and annual depreciation—to the nearest pound—is therefore £6,666. The figures in column *d* are identical to those in column *d* of Table 5.

The gross average annual proceeds are reduced by the depreciation figures computed and the result in this example is as expressed in column *e*. This figure is then expressed as a percentage of the original capital cost to produce the average net annual rate of return. With the exception therefore that depreciation is considered part of the cost to be charged against income arising from the project, this method is identical with the previous one. There is no consistent view from all accountants as to which is correct. Many would, in fact, agree that both methods could be used dependent upon the particular purpose to which the figures computed were going to be put. The argument for reducing income by depreciation is a parallel one to that used by economists in relation to profit. Economists generally consider a profit has only arisen when an allowance for interest on funds utilised has been incorporated into costs. Similarly, in respect of depreciation the argument is that income arises from a project only when the historical cost of the project has been or, more correctly, is being recovered. The justification of the viewpoint is illustrated by the reversal of ranking of investment A in Tables 5 and 6. In the first case we have a return of 100 per cent as the cash inflow at the end of one year is equal to the total cost of the project. However, on a straight-line depreciation basis it would mean that the full cost of the project must be charged as depreciation by the end of the year, and project A becomes the least preferable of the five.

The **disadvantages** of the net average rate of return methods are:

(*a*) They smooth any irregularities in the cash flow and thus ignore the effect of timing of the proceeds.

(*b*) In the case of the net method the effect of the previous disadvantage is heightened by the fact that the adjustment in respect of depreciation—when the straight-line method is used—results in a fixed amount being charged each year against, probably, varying annual incomes and this exaggerates the distortion.

(*c*) It particularly affects the shorter-life project, as the longer the project is expected to last the less will be the relative effect of the depreciation provision on the ultimate result.

(*d*) Objection is sometimes made to these methods on the basis that if depreciation is charged against the cash flow, then it is incorrect to relate the return to the initial capital. The argument here is that reinvestment of the depreciation provision should make the asset self-liquidating. The divisor in respect of capital employed should therefore represent the **average** amount of capital invested. For example, if the asset has no realisable value at the end of the period and the straight-line basis of depreciation is used then the effect of this will be to halve the value of the divisor and the computed rates will be higher. It is therefore essential in comparing returns under the average method to confirm which basis is being used as the relevant capital figure: the total cost of the asset or the average capital employed over the period of its life.

The **advantages** claimed for this method are:

(i) It is easy to compute and for management to understand.

(ii) It demonstrates the rate of net gain to the company, i.e. after maintaining the value of the assets intact in terms of original cost. In this respect it tends to agree with the general interpretation of 'profit' in well-known terms and so finds general acceptance.

Techniques which Evaluate the Timing of the Proceeds but Ignore the Risk

In the previous section it was stated that use of payback and return on investment methods presupposed that money received at some future date is worth as much as money received now, and that this was a questionable concept as a basis for decision-making. This doubt is not due to a decline in the value of money in real terms, i.e. inflation, but simply to the existence of alternative opportunity for investment.

The notion of **alternative investment** or **opportunity cost** is one which has long been considered by economists and it is from them that the ideas that came to fruition under this heading were originally borrowed. From 1950 onwards an increasing volume of literature questioned the validity of the techniques described previously, and various ideas and concepts were developed.

The basis from which the technique most popular in this section was developed was from the mathematical computations of compound interest. As noted earlier, a firm—like an individual—has, subject to any legal restriction, opportunity to invest money in projects offering fixed interest returns such as Government stocks or commercial debentures, or higher risk equity shares of other companies. The best of these investments from a security point of view are risk-free, i.e. it is assumed that the possibility of the original investment being lost or the creditor defaulting on interest payment is remote. The element of risk is to some degree reflected in the interest rate offered—the higher the risk, the higher the interest demanded by the investor or offered by the person or organisation requiring funds—but no other quantitative assessment of the risk factor is made.

If an investment is offering 10 per cent p.a., interest payable in annual instalments, then the value of £1 at the end of the first year would be £1·10. Provided that the money was left on deposit at this rate, the value at the end of the second year would be £1·10 plus 10 per cent of the reinvested sum of £1·10, equivalent to £1·10 plus £0·11, or £1·21. Similarly, at the end of the third year, the total sum accumulated would be £1·21 plus 10 per cent of £1·21, equivalent to £1·331.

This can be generalised into a formal mathematical expression such that the total accumulated sum at the end of any period can be expressed as equivalent to

$$P(1+r)^n$$

where P is original sum invested, r the appropriate rate of return (as a decimal) and n the number of periods for which original sum is invested.

Reference to the above figures indicates that when P is £1 then the expression becomes simply $(1+r)^n$. If P is £100 then the value of this sum after three years with interest added at 10 per cent is derived as follows:

$$P = £100 \quad r = 0{\cdot}10 \quad n = 3$$

$$\begin{aligned}\text{Total sum invested} &= £100(1+0{\cdot}10)^3\\ &= £100 \times 1{\cdot}331\\ &= £133{\cdot}1\end{aligned}$$

i.e. in order to work out any sum, if we have access to a predetermined value for the expression $(1+r)^n$, then we simply multiply this figure by the initial investment. Compound interest tables are, therefore, precomputed answers for given values of r and n and, as they are readily available the work involved in numerical computation is considerably shortened.

Discounted Cash Flow

For some purposes, such as forecasting the future terminal monetary values of fixed-term insurance policies or the value at the end of a period of a debenture investment fund, we need the compound interest valuation. For other purposes we need, however, to consider whether spending money on the project in the first place is worth while. The majority of returns from capital projects arise during future periods and we have to wait for the reward. This involves determining whether the value of these *future* proceeds is worth more than the present cost. This is not due simply to the erosion due to inflation—it would also be true in a stable monetary situation, because using money incurs a cost, as does using any other factor of production.

If we have £1 available to invest and have the opportunity to invest it at 10 per cent p.a., then there are two options available to us: either to retain the £1 or to invest it. Assuming that no risk was attached to the investment then at the end of one year, if invested, the £1 would have increased in value to £1·10—that is, the *present value* of £1·10 received in one year's time with interest rates at 10 per cent on the original £1. If this is so, the present value of *each* pound received in one year's time must be equal to $\frac{£1}{£1{\cdot}10} = £0{\cdot}9091$ (to four decimal places).

This procedure of finding the present worth of future cash flows is termed **discounting** and is the basis of investment appraisal techniques termed **Discounted Cash Flow (DCF).** A check can be made on the figure of £0·9091 by considering the results of investing this sum for one year with interest at 10 per cent. The sum receivable at the end of one year would be equal to £0·9091 plus 10 per cent of £0·9091, equivalent to £0·9091 plus £0·0909 = £1·00 (the small differences due to rounding up are ignored).

The present value of £1 receivable in two years' time can be similarly computed. The compound interest computation above showed the future value of £1 invested for two years at 10 per cent as £1·21. If this is so, the *present* value of each £1 invested must be equal to $\frac{1}{1{\cdot}21} = £0{\cdot}8264$.

It will be seen that in both the one- and two-year period the discounted figure is obtained by dividing into unity the figure previously computed for compound interest, and this is true for the general case, i.e. the value of £1 receivable in n years' time at an interest rate of r is the reciprocal of the compound interest figures for a similar period. This means that provided we have compound interest tables available, we can find an equivalent discounted figure by dividing into unity. Although for convenience most reference books contain both sets of tables, it is useful to be aware of the relationship between the figures. If the compound interest table represents computations of the formalised expression $(1+r)^n$ then the discounted cash flow table represents the reciprocal of all these values, i.e. the formalised expression $\frac{1}{(1+r)^n}$ sometimes expressed as $(1+r)^{-n}$.

Use of the Discounted Cash Flow Techniques

There is a variety of methods which use DCF techniques for investment ranking but they divide broadly into two groups:

(i) Methods used when the cost of supplying funds for a project is known and/or a minimum rate of return is given—usually referred to as the **Net Present Value** method.

(ii) Methods used when alternative projects are competing for limited funds available for investment and it is desired to invest in that investment which provides the highest return—usually referred to as the **Internal Rate of Return** method.

Net Present Value Method

Information required to implement this method is:

1. The initial cost of the project.
2. The cost of supplying the capital required or the minimum rate of return acceptable.
3. The value of the future cash flow in each period.
4. The total life of the project.
5. Tables of DCF factors for reference.

Method of Procedure

(i) Compute the present value of each year's cash inflow by multiplying the actual cash figure by the appropriate discount factor.

(ii) Add the figures so computed to obtain the *gross* net present value of the future cash proceeds.

(iii) Deduct the original capital cost of the project.

Should the answer produced in (iii) be positive the project would be acceptable; should the answer be negative the project should be rejected. If more than one project is involved, then all those producing negative net present values should be rejected, and of the remainder priority given to the projects producing highest positive net present values.

Consider the situation referred to in Table 3 (page 38), with the additional information that the firm will have to pay 10 per cent p.a. to borrow any money required for investment (tax ignored) we have the following position in respect of the first two investments:

	Project A			*Project B*		
Year	*Net cash flow* (£)	*Discount factor*	*Present value* (£)	*Net cash flow* (£)	*Discount factor*	*Present value* (£)
1	20,000	0·9091	18,182	10,000	0.9091	9,091
2	—	0·8264	—	10,000	0·8264	8,264
3	—	0·7513	—	10,000	0·7513	7,513
Gross present value			18,182			24,868
Less cost			20,000			20,000
Net present value			−1,818			+4,868

Project A produces a net present value of £1,818 (negative) and should therefore be rejected. The reasoning behind this is that if I borrow £20,000 now at a rate of 10 per cent in order to invest in a project which at the end of the year will result in an income of only £20,000, then I will be out of pocket by the cost of the overdraft, i.e. £2,000. In other words, if £0·9091 invested now for one year at 10 per cent is equivalent to £1·00 in one year's time I need invest only £20,000 × 0·9091 = £18,182 now to accumulate to £20,000 by the end of the year. This being so there is no merit whatsoever in investing in project A.

On the other hand, project B has a positive net present value of £4,868 and therefore is to be preferred if the choice is between these two investments only. However, if we have five mutually exclusive investment choices and only one sum of £20,000 available, we consider the remaining investments. The results of the calculations for all investments are as follows:

		Project C		*Project D*		*Project E*	
Year	*Factor* @ 10%	*Cash flow* (£)	*NPV* (£)	*Cash flow* (£)	*NPV* (£)	*Cash flow* (£)	*NPV* (£)
1	0·9091	3,000	2,727	12,000	10,909	16,000	14,546
2	0·8264	9,000	7,438	16,000	13,222	16,000	13,222
3	0·7513	12,000	9,016	10,000	7,513	—	—
Gross present value			19,181		31,644		27,768
Less cost			20,000		20,000		20,000
Net present value			−819		+11,644		+7,768

These results can be summarised in the priority ranking shown in Table 8.

It should be noted that this method may only be used as a direct ranking process if—as in this instance—the capital cost of the alternatives is the same. If it is not, the NPV must first be converted into an index by relating it to the original capital sum invested. Suppose that the cost of project B could be reduced by £5,000, the gross present value of the proceeds remaining unaltered; then comparing project B (as revised) with project D (as existing) we get:

	Project B (£)	*Project D* (£)
Index: Gross =	$\frac{24,868}{15,000}$	$\frac{31,644}{20,000}$
=	1·658	1·582
Index: Net =	$\frac{9,868}{15,000}$	$\frac{11,644}{20,000}$
=	0·658	0·582

Comparing the net present values, project D is still preferable to project B as the net present value of £11,644 is higher than £9,868. However, with Project B, to produce a surplus of £9,868 only £15,000 has been invested, i.e. *each* £1 invested has generated £1·658, and has returned the costs plus profits of £0·658 in present-value terms, whereas in project D each £1 has generated only £1·582, returning the original £1 plus a surplus of £0·582. Because of this the ranking would be reversed and project B would be ranked higher than project D.

Table 8. Discounted Cash Flow (NPV Method)

Project	Net present value (£)	Rank
A	−1,818	5
B	+4,868	3
C	−819	4
D	+11,644	1
E	+7,768	2

The net present value method can be represented by the formal mathematical expression

$$\text{NPV} = \sum_{n=1}^{n=n} P_n(1+r)^{-n} - c$$

or

$$\text{NPV} = \sum_{n=1}^{n=n} \frac{P_n}{(1+r)^n} - c$$

where P_n is the profit in any period n (e.g. year 1, 2, 3, . . . , year n), r the rate of return or cost of capital, and c the first capital cost of the project.

Since a table of DCF factors provides the value of the expression $(1+r)^{-n}$ for required values of r and n, the computations generally are as illustrated in the above examples.

Equal Annual Cash Flows

In Table 5 it will be noted that the cash flow in project B is the same amount, i.e. £10,000, for each year of its life. Similarly, for project E it is at the rate of £16,000 p.a. If such a condition exists the cash flow is said to be **regular** or in **equal annual instalments**, and this represents a special case for a simplified application of the DCF method. Consider again the computation set out previously in respect of project B:

Net cash flow (£)	Factor	Present value (£)
10,000	0·9091	9,091
10,000	0·8264	8,264
10,000	0·7513	7,513
Gross present value		24,868
Less cost		20,000
Net present value		4,868

The income in respect of each period is constant and we could get the same answer as above by multiplying the total value of £1 p.a. for three years by £10,000 once only, thus

$$£10{,}000(0{\cdot}09091 + 0.8264 + 0{\cdot}7513) = £10{,}000 \times 2{\cdot}4868 = £24{,}868$$

This figure agrees with the gross present value of £24,868 and since the cost remains the same at £20,000 the net figure will be the same at £4,868. When the income figures are the same in amount each year the computation is referred to as **equal annual instalments** or an **annuity** basis. Figures for annuity computations are fundamental to a variety of tasks in banking, insurance and other industrial and commercial activities and it is therefore hardly surprising that tables are available which render it unnecessary for us to add the figures ourselves each time this situation arises.

Internal Rate of Return (IRR) Method

This method has a variety of alternative names, the most relevant of which is probably the **Marginal Efficiency of Capital**. It is used either when the cost of providing funds is unknown or, particularly, when funds available are restricted, to indicate the most profitable choice of alternatives. Information required to implement this method is:

(*a*) The initial cost of the project.
(*b*) The value of future cash flows in each period.
(*c*) The total life of the project.
(*d*) Tables of DCF figures for reference.

Under this method we are required to determine the rate of interest which equates the present value of the future cash flows with the capital cost of the project. The preference will be for that project producing the higher rate of return. Computation under this method is more difficult than the NPV method as, with no rate being given, progress may have to be on a trial and error basis.

Method of procedure

Consider the data for investment C in Table 3 (page 38), i.e.

Project	*Capital cost* (£)	*Net cash flow* *Year 1* (£)	*Year 2* (£)	*Year 3* (£)
C	20,000	3,000	9,000	12,000

		Assuming percentage: 7%		8%		9%	
Year	*Cash inflow* (£)	*Factor*	*Present value* (£)	*Factor*	*Present value* (£)	*Factor*	*Present value* (£)
1	3,000	0·9346	2,803·8	0·9259	2,777·7	0·9174	2,752·2
2	9,000	0·8734	7,860.6	0·8573	7,715·7	0·8417	7,575·3
3	12,000	0·8163	9,795·6	0·7938	9,525·6	0·7722	9,266·4
			20,460		20,019		19,593·9

The above computations indicate that the cash flow discounted at a rate of 7 per cent is equivalent to £20,460 and 8 per cent equivalent to £20,019. Both these are in excess of £20,000, and since 7 per cent produces a larger figure than 8 per cent, it is necessary to continue moving *up* the discount table and try 9 per cent. This rate produces an aggregate of £19,755·9, which is *less* than the required £20,000. The *absolute* rate therefore lies between 8 and 9 per cent, although for all practical purposes 8 per cent would be accepted since a difference of £19 in excess of £20,000 would not be significant. Should it be considered necessary to adjust for the difference it would be computed by **linear interpolation** in the following manner:

Present value at 8%	=	20,019
Present value at 9%	=	19,594
Difference	=	425

The difference of £425 represents an increment of 1 per cent in the rate. The actual figure required of £20,000 is $\frac{19}{425} \times 1$ more than the 8 per cent rate (or alternatively $\frac{406}{425} \times 1$ less than the 9 per cent rate). It will therefore be much nearer proportionately to 8 than to 9, this proportion being computed by the appropriate proportion of the class interval.

$$\text{Distance from } 8 = \frac{19}{425} \times 1 = 0{\cdot}045$$

$$\therefore \text{ Rate required} = 8 + 0{\cdot}045 = 8{\cdot}045\%$$

Assuming that the tables available moved in increments of 5 per cent rather than 1 per cent the only figures available would be those in respect of 5 and 10 per cent and it would be necessary to interpolate between the class interval of 5 per cent (10 – 5) in a similar fashion:

		£
Present value at 5% p.a.	=	21,386
10%	=	19,181
Difference	=	2,205
Present value at 5%	=	21,386
Capital cost	=	20,000
Difference	=	1,386

The difference of £1,386 is equivalent to a proportionate increase of $\frac{1386}{2205} \times (10 - 5) = 3{\cdot}14$ per cent on the rate of 5 per cent, i.e. 8·14 per cent.

It will be noted that this is different from the answer produced when figures were available in 1 per cent increments. This is because linear interpolation is an approximation. It is not significant in the above example because the rate would probably be rounded to 8 per cent in either case, but the greater the amounts involved and/or the greater the class interval in the tables referred to, the greater will be the error.

Assistance in Determination of the Rate

Where the cash flow is **irregular**, as in the example above, two methods may be used to attempt to minimise the number of rates experimented with. First the total net return can be compared with the initial cost to ascertain if the return is high or low. In the above case the return is £(3,000 + 9,000 + 12,000) – £20,000 = £4,000 on an investment of £20,000 after three years. This represents 20 per cent after three years—not very high as it is equivalent to a simple average growth of approximately 7 per cent—a comparatively low return and suggesting an approximate starting point.

Secondly, the figures could be examined to see if the variations in the cash flow of individual years are significant. In the case of project B it is because Year 2 is three times that of Year 1 and Year 3 is four times that of Year 1. If the figures were less variable, we could initially average the income and use the more simple method described below for projects having regular cash flows in order to obtain a first approximation to the rate.

When the cash flow is **regular** the approach can be formalised. The annuity tables represent the present value of one pound per annum receivable for (n) years at a rate of interest (r). In this case r is unknown, but the present value of the capital cost, the annual anticipated cash flows and the number of years (n) are known. If the capital cost in any problem is divided by the annual income, this will give the necessary present value of *each* pound of the capital cost required to satisfy the condition that the discounted value of the proceeds must be equal to the capital cost.

Consider the data for project B from Table 3 (page 38):

		Net cash flow		
Project	*Capital cost*	*Year 1*	*Year 2*	*Year 3*
B	£20,000	£10,000	£10,000	£10,000

Therefore we have

Capital cost (c)	£20,000
Annual cash flow (a)	£10,000
Life of project (n)	3 years

$$\frac{c}{a} = \frac{20,000}{10,000} = £2$$

i.e. the present worth of £1 p.a. for three years at rate r is equal to 2. All that remains is to ascertain from the annuity table which rate produces the very nearest figure to £2 for three years. The nearest figures from the tables for $n = 3$ years are

24%	1·9813
23%	2·0114

The rate must therefore be between 23 and 24 per cent. Using interpolation as before

Present value at 24%	=	1·9813
23%	=	2·0114
Difference	=	0·0301
Present value at 24%	=	1·9813
required	=	2·0000
Difference		0·0187

The rate lies $\frac{0{\cdot}0187}{0{\cdot}0301} \times 1$ away from 24% = 24 − 0·6213 = 23·3787 (or 23·4% to one decimal place)

Constraint in the Use of Internal Rate of Return (IRR) Method

The examples given above are based on the situation where, except for the initial period, the cash flow in any individual period is positive. There are occasions in practice when this may not be so—for example, when capital costs are incurred in instalments so that a positive stream of cash flow is interrupted by one or more occasions where the inflow is negative. This affects the validity of the IRR method if applied as above. Suppose the data from Table 3 for investment C were reversed to imply that the capital cost of £20,000 was incurred not prior to the beginning of Year 1 but payable at end of Year 2. The revised data would be:

Year	*Capital cost* (£)	*Cash flow* (£)	*Net cash flow* (£)
1		3,000	+3,000
2	20,000	9,000	−11,000
3		12,000	+12,000

The cash flow sequence becomes +£3,000, −£11,000, +£12,000, whereas in all previous examples we have an initial capital cost (minus) followed by a continuing stream of cash inflows (positive).

The required internal rate is that which equates the present values of all gains with that of all losses after allowing for the timing of the cash flows. If this is to be the case then the sum of all the cash flows must be zero. More formally:

$$+\pounds 3{,}000 - \pounds 11{,}000(1+r)^{-1} + \pounds 12{,}000(1+r)^{-2} = 0$$

Because there are only two changes of sign in the cash flow, this can be rearranged and solved by quadratic equations to produce two possible solutions. Should the problem be extended such that there are more than two changes of sign in the cash flow, the solution becomes more complex. It can be solved by combinations of trial and error using either graphs or a mathematical programme to assist. The problem then is to decide which of the acceptable mathematical answers—these increase with the number of changes of sign—is of practical significance. Because of the complexity and restricted practical application of this method, it is more usual to use the following alternative method.

Multiple Rate of Return or Secondary Interest Rate

The argument for this method is that money which is received at the end of a period is available for reinvestment until such time that it is required for some purpose or distributed to the owners of the business. Effective financial management requires that funds should not be left idle but reinvested on such terms as are appropriate for the period for which they are available. Comparatively small sums can be invested for virtually risk-free returns for short periods, ranging from bank deposit accounts through a whole range of short- to medium-term financial alternatives. In assessing the relative worth of a project on this basis it is prerequisite that the rate—sometimes termed secondary or auxiliary rate—be specified. It could be the bank deposit rate, the cost of loan capital or the latest known or target average internal rate of return. Assuming a minimum rate of return equivalent to 10 per cent is specified this is applied to the positive returns detailed in the project in sequence.

Using figures from page 53 above, the positive cash flow at the end of Year 1 is assumed invested for one year at 10 per cent. Its worth at the end of Year 2 will therefore be £3,000 + 10% (300) = £3,300. The net requirement for investment at the end of Year 2 will therefore be +£3,300 − £11,000 = −£7,700.

This can now be stated in the simplified IRR form, i.e. at what rate will the present worth of £12,000 receivable in one year's time equate with £7,700 now?

$$£7{,}700 = £12{,}000(1 + r)^{-1}$$

This can be simplified and solved by multiplying through by $(1 + r)$, which gives

$$7{,}700(1 + r) = 12{,}000$$

$$\therefore \quad r = \frac{12{,}000 - 7{,}700}{7{,}700} = \frac{4{,}300}{7{,}700} = 0.56$$

or 56%

Since this is in excess of the borrowing rate of 10 per cent the investment is viable. Comparison may not necessarily be between the rate of return and the cost of borrowing. The firm may require a minimum internal rate of return of 20 per cent and if the return computed as above falls below this the proposal may be rejected. In effect, this method is a compromise between aspects of the NPV method and the pure application of the IRR method. Under the NPV method the assumption is that the rate given is both the rate of return and the rate at which funds can be obtained or reinvested. Under the IRR method, the assumption is that net cash flows could be reinvested at the internal rate of return. The introduction of the intermediary rate of 10 per cent is a practical recognition of the fact that most business projects proceed when the opinion is that money borrowed at one rate will be used to generate profit at a higher rate.

Some Practical Modifications to the Basic Problem

Amplification of Examples (Table 3, page 37)

Recapitulation of the original data in Table 3 indicates that the assumptions were very simplified. First, we had £20,000 available and all projects cost this amount; second, with the exception of project A, all the rest had a life of three years. In practice this is unrealistic since most likely:

(*a*) All projects will have different capital cost.
(*b*) All projects will have different lives.
(*c*) The life of the project may be limited to either:

(i) the life of the plant required;
or (ii) the period of time over which it is anticipated profits would be made. Such a period may be longer than (i) above, requiring consideration of plant replacements, or it may be shorter, requiring consideration of the salvage value of the equipment before it is worn out.

(*d*) The final decision is not on the basis of one project, but on the basis of how most effectively to spend the total amount of money available or which would be raised. A project therefore which on its own is the most desirable measured against some criteria may not be part of an ideal *combination* of projects producing the best overall result.

(*e*) The effect of taxation on the cash flow may have a considerable effect on the decision. The detailed application at a particular time requires knowledge of current legislation and the main systems are dealt with later. In elementary exercises, however, the effect in principle can be illustrated by making two assumptions:

(i) One tax rate is applied to profits as initially computed.
(ii) The taxation due in a particular one-year period is paid at the end of the following period.

(*f*) The outcome of some investment projects may be considered more predictable and more certain than others. In some instances quantification of the degree of risk may be attempted. The results when allowance has been made for the risk factor may well be different from those produced by methods of discounting which assume the funds flow is certain.

The following example is intended to illustrate the variety of results produced by the main alternative methods when used in relation to some of the factors listed above.

Example 4

The list given below represents a series of investment opportunities put forward as proposals by various operating divisions of XYZ Ltd.

Project	*Capital cost* (£)	*Life of project* (years)	*Anticipated cash flows*
A	50,000	10	£10,000 in Year 1 growing at increments of £1,000 p.a. for 4 years then regular at £14,000 p.a.
B	25,000	10	£5,000 p.a. for first 3 years, £6,000 p.a. for next 3 years, £8,000 for next 2 years and £2,000 p.a. for final 2 years.
C	15,000	5	£5,000 p.a. in equal annual cash flows.
D	20,000	3	£10,000 in Year 1, £10,000 in Year 2, £5,000 in Year 3; £5,000 out of the original cost of £20,000 is working capital assumed to be self-liquidating at the end of Year 4.
E	10,000	4	£4,000 p.a. in equal annual cash flows. In addition the trade mark will be sold at the end of Year 4 for a lump sum of £2,000.

Notes

1. It is anticipated that sufficient capital for all investments could be obtained by raising 10 per cent debentures.
2. Taxation is to be ignored.
3. All projects have zero residual value at end of life.

The projects are required to be ranked in order of preference using the following methods:

(*a*) Payback period.
(*b*) Discounted cash flow—NPV method:

(i) on the basis of net present value;
(ii) on the basis of profitability index.

(*c*) Discounted cash flows internal rate of return.

(*a*) *Payback Method*

Project	*Capital cost* (£)	*Payback* (years)	*Rank*
A	50,000	4·29	4
B	25,000	4·67	5
C	15,000	3	3
D	20,000	2	1
E	10,000	2·50	2

(*b*) *Net Present Value (10% Discount Rate)*

Project A

Year	Factor	Cash flow Gross (£)	Cash flow Net (£)
1	0·9091	10,000	9,091
2	0·8264	11,000	9,090
3	0·7513	12,000	9,016
4	0·6830	13,000	8,879
5–10	2·9747	14,000	41,646
			77,722
		Cost	50,000
		NPV	27,722

Index: $\frac{77{,}722}{50{,}000} = 1{\cdot}554$

Project B

Year	Factor	Cash flow Gross (£)	Cash flow Net (£)
1–3	2·4868	5,000	12,434
4–6	1·8684	6,000	11,210
7–8	0·9797	8,000	7,837
9–10	0·8096	2,000	1,619
			33,100
		Cost	25,000
		NPV	8,100

Index: $\frac{33{,}100}{25{,}000} = 1{\cdot}324$

Project C

Year	Factor	Cash flow Gross (£)	Cash flow Net (£)
1–5	3.7908	5,000	18.954
		Cost	15,000
		NPV	3,954

Index: $\frac{18{,}954}{15{,}000} = 1{\cdot}264$

Project D

Year	Factor	Cash flow Gross (£)	Cash flow Net (£)
1	0.9091	10,000	9,091
2	0·8264	10,000	8,264
3	0·7513	5,000	3,757
4	0·6830	5,000	3,415
			24,527
		Cost	20,000
		NPV	4,527

Index: $\frac{24{,}527}{20{,}000} = 1{\cdot}226$

Project E

Year	Factor	Cash flow Gross (£)	Cash flow Net (£)
1–4	3·1699	4,000	12,679
4	0·6830	2,000	1,366
			14,045
		Cost	10,000
		NPV	4,045

Index 1·40

Summary

Project	Net present value: Amount (£)	Rank	Index	Rank
A	27,722	1	1·554	1
B	8,100	2	1·324	3
C	3,954	5	1·264	4
D	4,527	3	1·226	5
E	4,045	4	1·40	2

(*c*) *Internal Rate of Return*

Project A

Year	Cash flow (£)	Discount factor (20%)	Discount factor (21%)	Present values (20%) (£)	Present values (21%) (£)	Interpolated result
1	10,000	0·8333	0·8264	8,333	8,264	
2	11,000	0·6944	0·6830	7,638	7,513	
3	12,000	0·5787	0·5645	6,944	6,774	
4	13,000	0·4822	0·4665	6,269	6,065	
5–10	14,000	1·6038	1·5135	22,453	21,189	
				51,637	49,805	20·9%

Project B

Years	Cash flow (£)	Discount factor (17%)	Discount factor (18%)	Present values (17%) (£)	Present values (18%) (£)	Interpolated result
1–3	5,000	2·2096	2·1743	11,048	10,872	
4–6	6,000	1·3796	1·3233	8,278	7,940	
7–8	8,000	0·6180	0·5800	4,944	4,640	
9–10	2,000	0·4514	0·4165	903	833	
				25,173	24,285	17·19%

Project C

Years	Cash flow	Discount factor (19%)	Discount factor (20%)	Present values (19%)	Present values (20%)	Interpolated result
1–5	£5,000	3·0576	2·9906	£15,288	£14,953	19·86%

Project D

Years	Cash flow (£)	Discount factor (21%)	Discount factor (22%)	Present values (21%) (£)	Present values (22%) (£)	Interpolated result
1–2	10,000	1·5094	1·4916	15,094	14,916	
3–4	5,000	1·0310	1·0021	5,155	5,010	
				20,249	19,926	21·77%

Project E

Years	Cash flow (£)	Discount factor (26%)	Discount factor (27%)	Present values (26%) (£)	Present values (27%) (£)	Interpolated result
1–4	4,000	2·3203	2·2800	9,281	9,120	
4	2,000	0·3967	0·3844	793	769	
				10,074	9,889	26·4%

Summary

Project	Rate (%)	Rank
A	20·9	3
B	17·19	5
C	19·86	4
D	21·77	2
E	26·4	1

Summary of Methods

Project	Payback	Net present value Amount	Net present value Factor	Internal rate of return
A	4	1	1	3
B	5	2	3	5
C	3	5	4	4
D	1	3	5	2
E	2	4	2	1

There is so much variation in the ranking table produced by the methods that one may well question the usefulness of any, or all, of the techniques. **The answer is that no single technique is the best for all purposes.** Indeed, an examination of the reasons as to why the ranking is different may provide a reason for acceptance or rejection according to what are the particular aims, objectives and priorities which are the essentials of the financial strategy at the particular time.

Since it is anticipated that sufficient capital could be raised at a cost of 10 per cent to finance all investments, then no problem of selecting is involved, as all the projects exceed this on both the NPV and IRR methods. However, if the maximum amount of capital available at this rate was limited to, say, £90,000 then other criteria would apply. Similarly, if the minimum internal rate of return acceptable (alternatively termed the 'cut off' rate) was 20 per cent then reference to the summary of the internal rates achieved would indicate that only projects A, D and E achieved this minimum—the remaining projects would therefore be rejected.

The subject of investment appraisal is one of continuous research and comment. In a recent article (January 1988) published in the magazine *Management Accounting*, Dr Roger W. Mills summarised the capital budgeting techniques most frequently used in the UK and the USA. Five separate UK studies were reviewed. One reported the IRR method as most popular in the UK followed by NPV method. Another reported 'qualitative judgement' first choice followed by IRR. Both gave payback in its basic form a relatively low rating. However, when payback categories were combined the payback period became the most popular. Of the DCF methods IRR is far more frequently used than NPV. **Most companies used more than one technique.** The reason for preferring IRR were given as (Pike) 'it gives immediate ranking of projects with different time scales and overflows' and it does not require a predetermined cut off rate. In medium-sized firms 80 per cent used payback by comparison with 44 per cent using DCF. Eleven years previously the order was Payback, Accounting rate of return, IRR and NPV. Of the very small companies the largest proportion used no technique at all. In the public sector a combination of techniques was used. In the USA there was evidence of greater use of DCF techniques than in the UK but payback was still most popular.

The decision to invest should therefore be the result of combined techniques and subjective assessment of the management. Each project will present different problems under different actual or anticipated economic consequences and each particular method has merits under specified circumstances and conditions. Discussion on these aspects is deferred until page 85, when the effects of uncertainty and risk on the problem will also have been considered.

Capital Residual Values

Capital investment in a project may be of a fixed nature, or working capital comprising stocks, debtors or advance payments of a special non-recurring nature such as development and market research. Consideration should be given to each, particularly as to the absorption of the expenditure against the proceeds over the life of the project.

Fixed Capital

It often helps first to define the factor which controls the life of the project: it may be the asset or the product. If it is the former, when justification for its expenditure is the prime consideration, then usually there can be seen enough work for it to perform throughout its life-span. Such fixed capital may be of a general nature which permits its application to a range of alternative work, or the work or product to which it will be applied can be foreseen for an indefinite period ahead, beyond the life of the asset. Under such circumstances the cost of the asset must be wholly absorbed from the proceeds over its life-span, at the end of which it may have a nil value, or perhaps a nominal scrap value. In the latter case any cash flow received should be incorporated at the end of the life-span thus:

			Factor	Present value @ 15%
		(£)		(£)
Year 0	Investment outflow	−10,000		−10,000
10	Residual value received for asset—inflow	500	0·25	125
Present value of net investment				−9,875

If a project is controlled by the life of the product to be undertaken by the fixed capital, then this may be shorter than the life of the asset itself. Treatment will then depend upon an assessment of the further usefulness of the asset. If it is a specialised piece of plant, then it may only be suitable to produce the product under review, and although it may be good for several more years' operation its whole initial cost should be recovered against income of the project over the life of the product, thus:

				Present value @ 15%
				(£)
Year 0	Investment outflow	−10,000		−10,000
1	Product inflow	2,000	0·87	1,740
2	Product inflow	3,000	0·76	2,280
3	Product inflow	3,000	0·66	1,980
4	Product inflow	4,000	0·57	2,280
5	Product inflow	1,000	0·50	500
5	Investment value inflow (but having five years more useful life)			nil
	Net present value of project—under recovery (Project ought not to proceed)			−1,220

On the other hand plant required for a project could be of a general nature and capable of further use after the expiry of the project life. In such a case a valuation of the plant is introduced as inflow at the end of the project's life, as if it is expected to realise that sum.

Buildings as permanent and adequate fixed assets are often assessed for interim values in this context.

First Project

				Present value @15%
		(£)		(£)
Year 0	Investment outflow	−10,000		−10,000
1	Product inflow	2,000	0·87	1,740
2	Product inflow	3,000	0·76	2,280
3	Product inflow	3,000	0·66	1,980
4	Product inflow	4,000	0·57	2,280
5	Product inflow	1,000	0·50	500
5	Investment value inflow (but having five years more useful life)	5,000	0·50	2,500
	Net present value of project—favourable (Project may proceed)			1,280

Subsequent project

Year 0	Investment outflow	−5,000		−5,000

All projects do not necessarily rely only upon a single initial investment: a forecast of growth may require an injection of further investment later in the time cycle, thus:

				Present value @ 15%
		(£)		(£)
Year 0	Original investment —outflow	−10,000		−10,000
3	Additional investment—outflow	−4,000	0·66	−2,640
8	Residual values —inflow			
	Original	500	0·33	264
	Additional	300		
	Net present value of investment			−12,376

A forecast for growth may envisage that the initial investment is replaced by a more comprehensive piece of equipment, thus:

				Present value @ 15%
		(£)		(£)
Year 0	Original investment—outflow	−10,000		−10,000
4	Sale of original —inflow	6,000	0·57	−5,130
4	Replacement —outflow	−15,000		
10	Residual of replacement—inflow	1,000	0·25	250
	Net present value of investment			−14,880

Another variation could be the introduction of a more advanced piece of equipment to replace plant currently operating and which in the example below is assumed to have four more years of life outstanding. The example assumes that the plant to be replaced is sold to make way for the new advanced version but the fact that the life span has another four years to run with an expected residual value of £1,000 needs to be demonstrated. If the replacement project has not arisen the business would have expected to receive £1,000 in four years time, but because it now becomes necessary to sell the old plant immediately—for £4,000—the opportunity to receive £1,000 in four years time is lost. The net gain to the business is thus £3,000 but over a time gap of four years and this is interpreted by the discounting process thus:

				Present value @ 15%
		(£)		(£)
Year 0	Replacement investment—outflow	−10,000		−10,000
0	Sale of original —inflow	4,000		4,000
4	Planned residual value of original (foregone) —outflow	−1,000	0·57	−570
10	Residual value of replacement —inflow	500	0·25	125
	Net present value of investment			−6,445

Working Capital

In essence working capital arises from the deferment of the cash inflow. Thus stock investment is the initial cash outflows for materials, the replacement for which is delayed until the product is sold and the cash inflow arrives, and investment in debtors is another stage of this process.

In the case of stock investment an additional cash outflow is incurred for, say, three months' usages, with this maintained throughout the life-span until the last year. Purchases in the last three months of this last year will cease and production will absorb the stocks without incurring actual cash outflow. So the net cash inflows for this last year will be greater by the value of the stocks absorbed and sold, thus recouping the initial stock investment.

In a similar way at the end of the project with the last of the production made and sold, the investment in debtors will be collected as inflow at the expiry of the credit period. For simplification the recoupment of the initial investments in stocks and debtors is assumed to occur at the end of the last year of the life-span of the project. To reflect absolute accuracy it may be considered desirable to interpret the facts in a particular context and assume the recoupment of the debtors occurs in the year following the last year of the life-span of the project.

Furthermore, in reflecting anticipated practical outcomes there may be stock losses revealed at the end of the project or irrecoverable bad debts.

			(£)		*Net present value @ 15%* (£)
Year 0	Initial plant investment	—outflow	−10,000		−10,000
0	Initial stocks	—outflow	−5,000		−5,000
1	Other net current assets	—outflow	−8,000	0·87	−6,960
2	Further current assets	—outflow	−2,000	0·76	−1,520
3	Further current assets	—outflow	−2,000	0·66	−1,320
10	Residual value of plant	—	500	} 0·25	4,375
10	Recoupment of working capital	—inflow	17,000	}	
	Net present value of investment				−20,425

Variations to reflect detail could be that the stocks were accumulated gradually once the project had started and therefore occur in Year 1. Stock losses and bad debts might occur and therefore reduce the eventual recovery of the £17,000 of working capital: the other net current assets may be interpreted as being recouped as inflow in Year 11. In the above demonstration the further additions of other net current assets would reflect the growing volume of the turnover as the project developed.

Advance Payments for Development and Market Research

In most cases advance expenditure on development will have occurred immediately prior to the commencement of manufacture, and therefore can be treated as Year 0. If such development began much earlier then a proportion could be treated as Year −1, and instead of being discounted will be cumulated at the appropriate rate.

Market research is often similarly incurred at the outset—namely, year 0—as part of the decision to proceed. Initial marketing expenditure by way of publicity may be heavy in the early years and adversely affect the net cash flow in those years.

Care should be taken to confine the data relevant to the decision to be made. If it is a test of the whole project to justify, say, a required rate of return, then all the above facts could be relevant. However, if having spent some initial development and research, the decision is whether to proceed or not, such expenditure should be excluded because having been spent it is irretrievable—only income and expenditure from the 'now' position will affect the future outcomes arising from the decision.

Taxation

The earlier examples 1 and 4 demonstrate the treatment in a basic fashion, dealing with the first two categories of difficulty, i.e. when

(i) all projects have different capital costs;
(ii) all projects have different lives.

The effect of taxation adds one more variable to the necessary analysis and it is a very important one. Its effect has to be viewed from both sides of the investment problem—that is, from the benefit that one obtains in respect of capital allowances as an encouragement to invest, and the tax advantages or otherwise of raising the money in alternative capital forms, should this be necessary. On the debit side earnings from the investment will suffer taxation and this is why the cash flow used earlier was stated to be before taxation, but with depreciation (a non-cash item) added back.

Systems of taxation vary from country to country, government to government and in terms of particular schemes from year to year as relative Finance Acts are passed. The present UK system was introduced in 1984 and the principles are simple although the practice is complex. Capital allowances are granted against expenditure incurred on new plant at a rate of 25 per cent per annum on the diminishing value. This is referred to as the Writing Down Allowance (WDA). These allowances are given until the original cost has been absorbed. If disposal of the asset takes place before all the cost has been utilised the remainder can be claimed immediately (Balancing Allowance). On the other hand if proceeds from the sale of the asset plus allowances already claimed exceed the initial cost tax on the difference is payable (Balancing Charge).

The primary reason therefore that cash flows in previous examples have been assumed before depreciation and taxes is because the emphasis is on cash flow not profit. In assessing 'profit', depreciation may be charged at any rate or on any conventional basis, but it reduces profit only—not the actual cash flow. On the other hand, taxation reduces cash flow as it results in an actual payment to the Revenue authorities. In theoretical examples the two items are quite frequently assumed to equate, i.e. the depreciation provision is taken to be equal to the capital allowances in respect of taxation. This is unlikely to occur in practice, but the specific amount and timing of the various provisions and allowances would be calculable and the actual dates or periods in which they were allowable, chargeable or payable would be known.

The time period in British practice will generally range for a year or more between the accounting periods to which allowances and assessments are made and the actual payment of tax is made. This is, again, the reason why the other assumption is made or implied: that payments or receipts in respect of taxation take place one year after the transaction or accounts to which they refer.

The broad effects of this tax system upon a project are illustrated below, using the basic data given for project B in example 4 and adding the relevant tax details.

Example 5

Project	*Cost*	*Life*	*Anticipated cash flows*
B	£25,000	10 years	£5,000 p.a. for first 3 years
			£6,000 p.a. for next 3 years
			£8,000 p.a. for next 2 years
			£2,000 p.a. for final 2 years

(*a*) Rate of Corporation Tax anticipated 35 per cent.
(*b*) Writing down allowances 25 per cent p.a. on reducing balance.
(*c*) Payments or receipts are assumed to take place at the end of each year with the exception of the original investment assumed to be made on the first day of Year 1.
(*d*) All tax payments and receipts are assumed to 'lag' by one year after the period to which they actually relate.
(*e*) The cost of capital is 10 per cent.
(*f*) Project has zero residual value after 10 years.

It is necessary in this case to determine the net cash flows before discounting. It is preferable to set up two separate tabulations: the first to indicate the net cash flows and the second to show the effect of discounting.

Project B: Cash Flows

Year	*Investment* (£)	*Income* (£)	*Allowance* (£)	*Net* (£)	*Taxation (delayed 1 year)* (£)	*Net cash flow* (£)
1	−25,000					−25,000
		5,000	6,250	+1,250	—	5,000
2		5,000	4,687	313	+438	5,438
3		5,000	3,516	1,484	110	4,890
4		6,000	2,637	3,363	519	5,481
5		6,000	1,978	4,022	1,177	4,823
6		6,000	1,483	4,517	1,408	4,592
7		8,000	1,112	6,888	1,581	6,419
8		8,000	834	7,166	2,411	5,589
9		2,000	626	1,374	2,508	−508
10		2,000	1,877	123	481	1,519
11					43	43
	−25,000	53,000	25,000	28,000	9,800	18,200
a	*b*	*c*	*d*	*e* $= c - d$	*f* $= 35\%$ *of e*	*g* $= b + c - f$

(*a*) This represents annual periods—the actual year may be substituted if known.
(*b*) The cost of the investment in the project. It may not necessarily all be made in Year 1.
(*c*) The *net* cash flow arising each year before taxation. It will normally represent net profit or cost savings arising from the investment, but with any provision for depreciation added back.

(*d*) The capital allowances computed as shown in the following summary:

Year			(£)	*Cumulative Allowances* (£)
1	Cost of Plant		25,000	
	Writing down allowance	25% × 25,000	6,250	6,250
	w/d value	c/f	18,750	
2	w/d allowance	25% × 18,750	4,687	4,687
	w/d value	c/f	14,063	10,937
3	w/d allowance	25% etc.	3,516	3,516
		c/f	10,547	14,453
4	w/d allowance		2,637	2,637
		c/f	7,910	17,090
5	w/d allowance		1,978	1,978
		c/f	5,932	19,068
6	w/d allowance		1,483	1,483
		c/f	4,449	20,551
7	w/d allowance		1,112	1,112
		c/f	3,337	21,663
8	w/d allowance		834	834
		c/f	2,503	22,497
9	w/d allowance		626	626
		c/f	1,877	23,123
10	Balancing allowance		1,877	1,877
			—	25,000

(*e*) The difference between columns *c* and *d* representing assessable income. A + sign indicates a loss subject to tax refund.

(*f*) The tax due to be paid (refunded) in the year. The rate is 35 per cent and this column represents 35 per cent of figures in Column *c* but posted one year later to coincide with cash outflow (inflow) in respect of taxation.

(*g*) The algebraic sum of columns *b*, *c* and *f* representing net cash flow for year concerned.

The discounting procedure is now as before; with a cost of capital of 10 per cent the net present value would be computed thus:

Year	Net cash flow (£)	Discount factor	Present value (£)
1	–25,000	1·0000	–25,000
	5,000	0·9091	4,546
2	5,438	0.8264	4,494
3	4,890	0·7513	3,674
4	5,481	0·6830	3,744
5	4,823	0·6209	2,995
6	4,592	0·5645	2,592
7	6,419	0·5132	3,294
8	5,589	0·4665	2,607
9	–508	0·4241	–215
10	1,519	0·3855	586
11	–43	0·3505	–15
	18,200	Net present value =	3,302

The taxation system operating prior to 1984 was much more generous from the point of view of discounting techniques. In order that the effect of such changes in fiscal policy may be appreciated the example is reworked under these prior conditions. Companies may be located or investing overseas and tax systems and timing could be the critical factor. Under the old system allowances were granted on a 'free depreciation' basis. This meant that, subject to certain conditions, a company might offset any proportion of the expenditure, up to 100 per cent against profit which would otherwise be taxable in the relevant assessment period. The basic conditions were that the company must have made sufficient profits to absorb the amount of capital allowances claimed otherwise the balance unabsorbed would be carried forward.

The broad effect of this system upon a project is illustrated below repeating the data given for project B in example 4 and adding the relevant tax details.

Example 6

Project	*Cost*	*Life*	*Anticipated cash flows*
B	£25,000	10 years	£5,000 p.a. for first 3 years
			£6,000 p.a. for next 3 years
			£8,000 p.a. for next 2 years
			£2,000 p.a. for final 2 years

(*a*) Rate of Corporation Tax anticipated 35 per cent.
(*b*) The company has sufficient profits from other sources to absorb and opts to take 100 per cent capital allowance in the first year.
(*c*) Payments or receipts are assumed to take place at the end of each year with the exception of the original investment assumed to be made on the first day of Year 1.
(*d*) All tax payments and receipts are assumed to 'lag' by one year after the period to which they actually relate.
(*e*) The cost of capital is 10 per cent.
(*f*) Project has zero residual value after ten years.

It is suggested that as previously two tabulations are used—the first to determine the timing and amount of the net cash flows and the second to show the effect of discounting.

Project B Cash Flows

Year	Investment (£)	Income (£)	Allowance (£)	Net (£)	Taxation (delayed 1 year) (£)	Net Cash Flow (£)
1	25,000					−25,000
		5,000	25,000	+20,000	—	5,000
2		5,000		5,000	+7,000	12,000
3		5,000		5,000	1,750	3,250
4		6,000		6,000	1,750	4,250
5		6,000		6,000	2,100	3,900
6		6,000		6,000	2,100	3,900
7		8,000		8,000	2,100	5,900
8		8,000		8,000	2,800	5,200
9		2,000		2,000	2,800	−800
10		2,000		2,000	700	1,300
11					700	−700
	25,000	53,000	25,000	28,000	9,800	18,200
a	*b*	*c*	*d*	*e* $= c - d$	*f* $= 35\% e$	*g* $= b + c - f$

The key to the columns is the same as the previous example except that Column *d* is less complicated. A summary of capital allowances is not required as the whole £25,000 expended ranks for allowance in Year 1. The tax benefit of this at a 35 per cent rate is £8,750. It can be claimed from the tax bill in Year 2 provided we assume sufficient profits from other sources to absorb it. The benefit is reduced by tax due at 35 per cent on the £5,000 income for Year 1. The tax due on this is £1,750 so the net reduction in tax for Year 2 payment is £7,000 as shown.

The discounting procedure is now as before; with a cost of capital of 10 per cent the net present value would be computed as follows:

Year	Net Cash Flow (£)	Factor	Present Value (£)
1	−25,000	1·0000	−25,000
	5,000	0·9091	4,546
2	12,000	0·8264	9,917
3	3,250	0·7513	2,442
4	4,250	0·6830	2,903
5	3,900	0·6209	2,421
6	3,900	0·5645	2,202
7	5,900	0·5132	3,028
8	5,200	0·4665	2,426
9	−800	0·4241	−339
10	1,300	0·3855	501
11	−700	0·3505	−245
			4,802

The result is much more favourable than the present alternative system (page 67) giving a NPV of £4,802 compared with £3,302, an increase of 45 per cent. Since practical projects may run into millions of pounds the importance of taxation systems, rates and timings should be considered very carefully.

One final point applies to most theoretical examples. In most of these, as stated above, payments and receipts are assumed to take place at the end of the year with the exception of the initial capital expenditure which is normally at commencement of Year 1. One could assume that the equipment was purchased on the final day of Year 0, i.e. immediately prior to the commencement of Year 1.

This would have no effect on the net present value computed before taxation since the present value of £1 at the very end of Year 0 or beginning of Year 1 is 1·0 for any rate of cost of capital chosen. It does, however, make a difference in the case of taxation because Year 0 precedes Year 1 and if the expenditure is deemed to be incurred in Year 0 this would be the assessment year and the benefit would be received earlier at the end of Year 1. Using the previous example in which all the capital allowances were claimed in Year 0 the table would appear as follows:

Example 7

Cash Flows

Year	*Investment* (£)	*Income* (£)	*Allowance* (£)	*Net* (£)	*Taxation delayed 1 year* (£)	*Net Cash Flow* (£)
0	–25,000		25,000	–25,000		–25,000
1		5,000		5,000	+8,750	13,750
2		5,000		5,000	1,750	3,250
3		5,000		5,000	1,750	3,250
4		6,000		6,000	1,750	4,250
5		6,000		6,000	2,100	3,900
6		6,000		6,000	2,100	3,900
7		8,000		8,000	2,100	5,900
8		8,000		8,000	2,800	5,200
9		2,000		2,000	2,800	–800
10		2,000		2,000	700	1,300
11					700	–700
	–25,000	53,000	25,000	28,000	9,800	18,200

Discounted Cash Flows

Year	Net Cash Flow (£)	Factor	Present Value (£)
0	−25,000	1·0000	−25,000
1	13,750	0·9091	12,500
2	3,250	0·8264	2,686
3	3,250	0·7513	2,442
4	4,250	0·6830	2,903
5	3,900	0·6209	2,421
6	3,900	0·5645	2,202
7	5,900	0·5132	3,028
8	5,200	0·4665	2,426
9	−800	0·4241	−339
10	1,300	0·3855	501
11	−700	0·3505	−245
			5,525

The difference between £5,525 and the previous NPV of £4,802 is £723. This is equivalent to the benefit of taking the capital allowance one year earlier. As can be seen by comparing the tabulations the results from Year 3 onwards are the same. The effect could have been computed by comparing simply the effects of discounting under both systems for years 0–2 inclusive as follows:

Year	Example 1 (£)	Example 2 (£)	Difference (£)
0	25,000*	25,000	—
1	4,546	12,500	+7,954
2	9,917	2,686	−7,231
			723

*This is shown as beginning of Year 1 in the tabulation.

Negative Cash Flows in Early Years

In some cases in addition to the outflow for capital investment the net revenue receipts could be negative in the early years. This would arise when a project is making losses in the early stages of exploitation or marketing. The losses in this case would normally be offset against the total tax charge for the company but if this were not practicable they would be carried forward for the maximum permissible period and absorbed against subsequent profits before an actual assessment would arise.

Example 8

A company invests in a project which produces the following stream of cash flows

Year 1	£5,000	Loss
Year 2	£4,000	Loss
Year 3	£3,000	Profit
Year 4	£8,000	Profit
Year 5	£10,000	Profit

Evaluate the present value of the project assuming all cash flows arise at the end of the year and taxation at 35 per cent is applicable. Payments in respect of taxation are assumed to lag one year.

Cash Flow after Taxation

Year	*Cash Flow* (£)	*Cumulative Loss* (£)	*Assessable* (£)	*Due* (£)	*Paid* (£)	*Net Cash Flow* (£)
1	−5,000	5,000	Nil	—	—	−5,000
2	−4,000	9,000	Nil	—	—	−4,000
3	3,000	6,000	Nil	—	—	+3,000
4	8,000		+2,000	700	—	+8,000
5	10,000		10,000	3,500	−700	+9,300
6					−3,500	−3,500
	12,000				4,200	7,800
	a	*b*	*c*	$e = 35\% \times c$	$f = e$ delayed 1 year	$g = a - f$

The effect of discounting this cash flow at 10 per cent will be:

Year	*Net cash flow* (£)	*Factor* (£)	*Present Value* (£)
1	−5,000	0·9091	−4,545
2	−4,000	0·8264	−3,306
3	+3,000	0·7513	+2,254
4	+8,000	0·6830	+5,464
5	+9,300	0·6209	+5,774
6	−3,500	0·5645	−1,976
	7,800		+3,665

However, if this project is introduced into a company already making a profit on all its other activities, then the initial losses in Years 1 and 2 will reduce the total profits of the company and thus the assessment. The reduced tax bill will result in more immediate cash flow benefits arising thereby as follows:

Year	*Cash flow* (£)	*Cumu-lative loss* (£)	*Assessable* (£)	*Due* (£)	*Paid* (£)	*Net Cash Flow* (£)
1	−5,000	—	−5,000	+1,750	—	−5,000
2	−4,000	—	−4,000	+1,400	+1,750	−2,250
3	+3,000	—	+3,000	−1,050	+1,400	4,400
4	+8,000	—	+8,000	−2,800	−1,050	6,950
5	+10,000	—	+10,000	−3,500	−2,800	7,200
6					−3,500	−3,500
	+12,000		+12,000	4,200	−4,200	7,800

The effect of discounting this cash flow at 10 per cent will be:

Year	*Net Cash Flow* (£)	*Discount Factor* (£)	*Present Value* (£)
1	−5,000	0·9091	−4,545
2	−2,250	0·8264	−1,860
3	4,400	0·7513	3,306
4	6,950	0·6830	4,747
5	7,200	0·6209	4,470
6	−3,500	0·5645	−1,976
	7,800		4,142

It will be observed that the net cash flow is £7,800 in each case over the full time cycle but the net present value of this cash flow improves from +£3,665 to +£4,142 wholly because of the timing of tax incidence under the differing circumstances of consolidated profit position of the company.

Risk and Uncertainty

Most literature on the subject of risk and uncertainty in the sphere of investment decisions tends to refer to the problems of risk and uncertainty as one item. It may be well to consider whether there is any merit in attempting to distinguish between the two definitions in order to make clearer the techniques used to assess them. *The Concise Oxford Dictionary* states the following:

risk. Hazard, chance of bad consequences, loss, etc., exposure to mischance.
uncertainty. Not certainly knowing.

If everything about a particular project in terms of initial cost, future costs and incomes over a perfectly predicted life-span was known with absolute certainty there would be little, if any, risk in undertaking the project. Risk arises by virtue of incomplete knowledge of the outcome of a specific course of action. Incomplete knowledge is the state of 'not certainly knowing' and we therefore complete a circle in terms of the definitions.

In general, the term 'uncertainty' tends to be used in referring to the factors which influence the problem, but on a general or wide scale, such as the general economic climate or the effect of political action, whereas 'risk' tends to be used in discussion on outcomes of particular projects, fortunes of a particular class of investor or determination of the market response for a particular product. It is a matter of degree since it is the inability to be certain which gives rise to the risk. We may, therefore, decide to increase or decrease the risk by choosing one specific course of action in preference to another, but the uncertain conditions would still apply.

If a manager is asked to furnish information about the outcome of a particular course of action, the response is usually along the lines of: 'I think that . . .' or 'Subject to so and so, I think that . . .' The use of the phrase 'I think' or 'Subject to' is a defensive reaction used immediately to convey that it is an opinion of what is likely to happen—not a guarantee. Different persons presented with the same data may give their reply or advice a varying degree of self-confidence or caution. This is a reflection of the degree of knowledge on the subject possessed by the person concerned, the extent of the data submitted and the reliability of it, and the personality of the individual. Thus if two people possessing exactly the same knowledge and basic ability were presented with the same data there could still be a large difference in the decision, due entirely to the basic personalities of the people making the decision. This may represent the extremes of super optimism and utter pessimism, and the decision choice would reflect these attributes of their personalities.

In the final analysis the decision to invest or not to invest in a project is made by an individual or at best the consensus of a committee, such as a board of directors, on a majority vote. None of the techniques described subsequently can replace this subjective assessment. The term subjective is used to indicate a decision which is influenced by individual or collective opinion as opposed to an objective appraisal which would be arrived at by a clearly defined and usually quantitative analysis.

Techniques used when the Probabilities of the Alternative Outcomes are Known or Estimated

This title is to some extent a misnomer. As was stated above, risk arises due to uncertainty about the outcome of a particular action, so how can references to 'known' probabilities be justified? Admittedly, some probabilities are known even though an individual outcome is uncertain. For example, when throwing a single dice—assuming it is not loaded—the probability of any particular number from one to six being thrown is intuitively assessed as one in six or as the fraction $\frac{1}{6}$. We know that on each occasion the dice is thrown there will be some result, i.e. an outcome is certain. On the other hand, assuming we desired a six as our particular result the *risk* that this would not be the outcome would be five in six or $\frac{5}{6}$ and this reflects the extent of our uncertainty about this particular outcome. Identical business situations do not repeat themselves with anything like the frequency with which dice are thrown and therefore we must ask if techniques applicable in one situation are applicable in another? Argument for the case that they are so applicable is based primarily on the fact that the characteristics of the situations repeat themselves—e.g. estimates of such variables as capital cost, project life, cash flows and salvage values—and the techniques will, therefore, assist in predicting the outcome on more occasions, in the long run, than would otherwise be the case.

Most Probable Outcome

This method suggests that the alternative which is chosen should be that whose outcome is most probable. It can be illustrated by considering again the example of the dice. With a balanced dice each outcome is equally likely, i.e. it has a probability of $\frac{1}{6}$. If, however, the dice were loaded so that the probability of a six being thrown was twice that of any other single number, then the most frequent and therefore the most probable outcome would be a six.

Expected Value

This method of assessing risk suggests that the alternative which is chosen should be that whose 'expected value' is the most favourable. The term expected value is here used in its particular statistical sense and has a precise meaning. It is defined as the sum of the values of the possible outcomes, each outcome being weighted by the probability of its occurrence. Considering the case of the dice, the probability of any number being the result of a particular throw is $\frac{1}{6}$ and the possible outcomes are any of the numbers one to six, if the dice is properly balanced. The expected value approach would normally assume a large number of repeated occurrences and in this case the result would be:

Possible value	*Probabilities*	*Expected value*
6	$\frac{1}{6}$	1·0
5	$\frac{1}{6}$	0·83
4	$\frac{1}{6}$	0·67
3	$\frac{1}{6}$	0·5
2	$\frac{1}{6}$	0·33
1	$\frac{1}{6}$	0·17
Total	1·0	3·50

The sum of the expected values is 3·50 and is the weighted average value of each outcome in the long run. In this case it is the same as the simple average, which would be $\frac{6+5+4+3+2+1}{6} = 3{\cdot}5$, but this is because each outcome was equally likely. Consider the situation where, as before, the dice were loaded such that the probability of a six being thrown was twice that of any other number. This factor must be taken into account in the weighting; therefore the probability of a six must be weighted twice that of any other single outcome. The total of the weighting factors must equal seven and the summary becomes:

Possible value	*Probabilities*	*Expected value*
6	$\frac{2}{7}$	1·71
5	$\frac{1}{7}$	0·71
4	$\frac{1}{7}$	0·57
3	$\frac{1}{7}$	0·43
2	$\frac{1}{7}$	0·29
1	$\frac{1}{7}$	0·14
	1·0	3·85

This reflects the fact that there is twice the probability of a six being the outcome than any other single alternative. Note that the most probable outcome is still a six, the unweighted average is still 3·50, but the sum of the expected values has increased to 3·85, reflecting the increased effect on the average of the bias towards the highest score of six.

Earlier it was demonstrated how a manager is inclined to qualify an opinion about the outcome of a particular course of action by a self-defensive statement. Similarly, when faced with alternatives and asked to assess the possibility of each of the choices occurring, the manager may use such phrases as 'a small chance', 'a reasonable chance', 'a good chance', or 'a low' and 'a very much lower' possibility, and other non-specific terms. An interpretation of such opinions can best be illustrated by reconsidering example 4 and using the project C (page 56).

Project C

The estimates of the cash flow centre around approximately £5,000 p.a. for five years, but 'there is a small chance that the outcome will be below this and a reasonable chance that it will be above this figure'. To use the techniques described above this means some quantification of the following questions:

(i) How small is a small chance?
(ii) How large is a reasonable chance?
(iii) What are the possible alternative outcomes?

Each one of these estimates, or more formally parameters, requires a subjective decision on the amount of adjustment, i.e. it is a matter of personal opinion. Once these opinions have been resolved into figures the techniques described can be applied. The techniques could not correct error in the judgments or in the initial data.

Suppose that eventually it was agreed by all that the probability of an income below £4,500 or above £6,500 was small enough to be considered insignificant. However, one half of the personnel consulted considered the probability to be 10 in 100 that income would fall as low as £4,500, whereas the second half consulted considered the probability could be as much as 20 per cent. Similarly, the first half of the personnel concerned considered the probability of achieving the higher income of £6,500 p.a. to be 20 per cent, whereas the second half considered the possibility as being only 10 per cent. In summary, the first group represented the compromise view of the optimists, whereas the second group were more pessimistic in outlook.

A specific value had been allotted to each element of the data in lieu of the general terms 'small', 'reasonable', 'low', 'high', etc. The information can now be expressed in a more formal fashion.

Project C

Possible values (£)	*Group A* *Probabilities*	*Group A* *Expected values* (£)	*Group B* *Probabilities*	*Group B* *Expected values* (£)
4,500	0·1	35	0·2	900
5,000	0·7	3,500	0·7	3,500
6,500	0·2	1,300	0·1	650
	1·0	5,250	1·0	5,050

The table illustrates the effect on the aggregate figure for the expected value of the differing subjective views of the two groups which, in turn, represented compromise by the individuals within them. The figure of 0·7 is deduced as the difference between total probability for all outcomes of 1·0 and the sum of the alternatives already accounted for, which totalled 0·3 in both cases. Thus the most probable outcome was deemed to be £5,000 p.a. by both groups whereas the expected value was computed as £5,250 for group A as compared with £5,050 for group B.

The computation in respect of expected value can be expressed in mathematical terms as

$$E(V) = V_1P_1 + V_2P_2 + \cdots V_nP_n$$

where E is the expected value, V the possible values, and P the probability of outcome. Note that $P_1 + P_2 + \cdots P_n = 1{\cdot}0$.

As stated previously, if this method is used, all other things being equal, the alternative with the largest expected value will be chosen. Note that it does not represent or correspond to any of the particular outcomes: it merely favours the choice whose *sum* of weighted possible outcomes is greatest. Some feel that the use of this technique is not justified since basic theory requires a repetitive number of trials. In the case of dice throwing, each trial is similar, whereas in the case of investment each 'trial' is likely to be different, i.e. each opportunity to invest is a unique one. On the other hand, the type of variables inherent in the decision choice are similar and protagonists of this method claim that this would give a series of better choices in the long run.

Application of the expected value approach is quite frequently combined with representation by means of a **decision tree**. This simply is a means whereby alternative courses of action which may require detailed descriptions are reduced to a generalised form of diagram.

Example 9

In simplified form, two alternative investment opportunities show the following prospects. Which of the two alternative projects would you recommend for acceptance and what further analysis of the figures would be desirable?

	Project A	*Project B*
Life of project	5 years	5 years
	£	£
Initial investment	2,500	2,500
Average annual cash inflow net	650	700

Possibility of average annual cash net flow differing from figures given above:

One chance in			Project A	Project B
			£	£
20	of being	at least	800	—
50		not more than	450	—
25		at least	—	1,700
$12\frac{1}{2}$		a loss of		(200)
100		a loss of	—	(600)

The chance of a loss on project A is considered to be insignificant.

(CIMA)

The above data set out as a decision tree would appear as in Fig. 5. In using expected value as a criterion each outcome must be weighted by the probability of its occurrence and the aggregate compared. The diagram is repeated in Fig. 6, and the expected value (EV) of each set of outcomes computed.

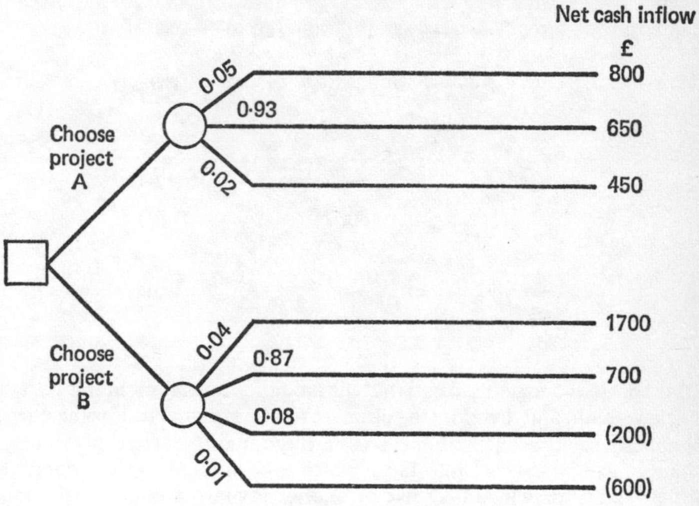

Fig. 5. A decision tree for Example 9.

Note

The symbol □ is used to indicate a point of decision.
The symbol ○ is used to indicate the possible outcomes of a particular decision.

The most favourable expected value is project B, but only marginally so. This is because of certain characteristics of the problem, which would be unlikely in a more complex practical situation. These are as follows:

(i) The costs of the projects are the same.
(ii) The lives of the projects are the same.
(iii) The most likely incomes are fairly near to each other, i.e. £650 p.a. compared with £700 p.a.
(iv) The probability of the most likely outcome relative to other possibilities is extremely high, i.e. 93 per cent for project A and 87 per cent for project B.

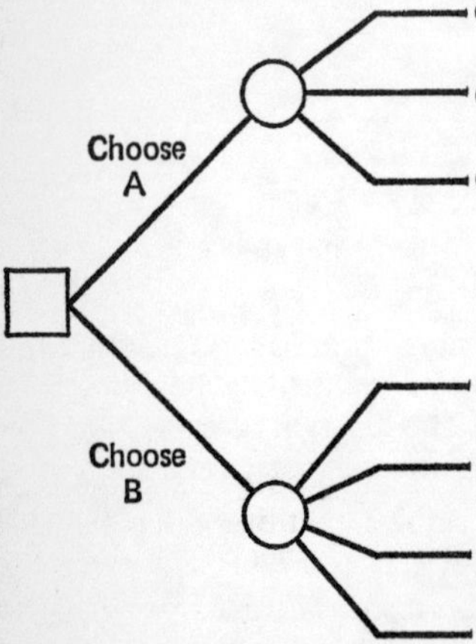

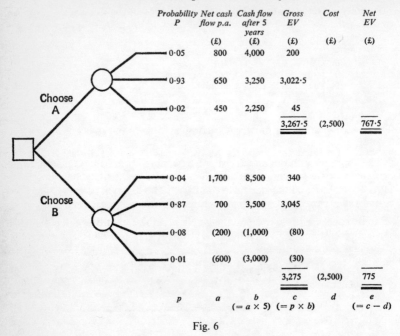

	Probability P	Net cash flow p.a. (£)	Cash flow after 5 years (£)	Gross EV (£)	Cost (£)	Net EV (£)
Choose A	0·05	800	4,000	200		
	0·93	650	3,250	3,022·5		
	0·02	450	2,250	45		
				3,267·5	(2,500)	767·5
Choose B	0·04	1,700	8,500	340		
	0·87	700	3,500	3,045		
	0·08	(200)	(1,000)	(80)		
	0·01	(600)	(3,000)	(30)		
				3,275	(2,500)	775
	p	*a*	*b* (= *a* × 5)	*c* (= *p* × *b*)	*d*	*e* (= *c* − *d*)

Fig. 6

All these factors together mean that the amount of variation in this particular problem is small, and therefore the ultimate results are similar. For the purposes of simplicity the cost of the funds has been ignored. As stated previously the techniques can be divided into those which take account of the timing of the proceeds and those which take risk or uncertainty into account. Including the cost of financing does not affect the principles of the above technique, it merely adds another factor into the computation.

Example 10

In addition to the data given in the example above, the firm normally uses a DCF rate of return of 10 per cent as a cost of capital for acceptability. Show to what extent if any, this would affect the decision.

It is not necessary to develop the decision tree yet again. The arithmetic can be simplified and data illustrated by using an alternative approach. In the answer above the annual cash flows were multiplied by 5 to give total cash flow over the life of the project before multiplying by the probability. This could just as easily have been reversed and the *annual* cash flows adjusted before being multiplied out. In some instances where cash flows vary over the life of the asset the first method may be easier to follow, but it is a matter of choice.

The Expected Annual Cash Flows

	p	*Cash Flow* (£)	*Expected value* (£)
Project A	0·05	800	40
	0·93	650	604·5
	0·02	450	9
	1·00		653·5
Project B	0·04	1,700	68
	0·87	700	609
	0·08	(200)	(16)
	0·01	(600)	(6)
	1·00		655

If the cost of capital at 10 per cent is now to be taken into account these figures need to be adjusted. From the annuity table we establish that the present value of £1 p.a. receivable for 5 years at a rate of 10 per cent is 3·7908. The present value of the expected incomes is then:

Project A £653·5 × 3·7908 = £2,477

Project B £655 × 3·7908 = £2,483

These values, however, exclude the cost of the project. The *net* present value of the expected incomes is therefore:

Project A £2,477 – £2,500 = £23 Loss

Project B £2,483 – £2,500 = £17 Loss

It should be noted that the expected value criterion used on its own indicates slight preference for project B. The net present value method criterion used on its own with an 'optimistic' view that average cash inflows of £650 per annum and £700 per annum would be maintained similarly indicates a preference for project B. When the two methods are used in combination, however, both projects produce a negative result and would therefore both be rejected. On the other hand, if the equipment used for project A had a possible salvage value of £500 at the end of year 5, compared with *nil* for project B, then this becomes the most significant fact in the study and would result in project A being recommended.

Techniques used where the Probabilities of Alternative Outcomes are Unknown

Characteristic of the situations where forecasts of probabilities will be forthcoming is the fact that there are a sufficient number of 'trials' or occasions where experience of likely outcomes can be gained and thus objective measures suggested and tested. In a continuous production situation, for example, the frequency of rejects can be observed and tested against conventional theories and hypotheses.

Many investment decisions are of a unique nature and forecasters are not prepared to put specific values to the probabilities of alternative outcomes. They may, however, be prepared to compute what they consider to be likely outcomes under alternative conditions. For example, it may be estimated that net revenue from sales of a domestic appliance it is proposed to market could be at a variety of levels depending on the rate of Value Added Tax to be applied during the period. If the computation were done at four assumed rates of taxation, this would provide four possible outcomes for this project. This is not the same as the examples in the previous section, as in that case specific probabilities of the particular alternative rates being introduced would have to be postulated.

Most of the techniques applied in this type of situation owe their origin to work done by econometricians and statisticians, in particular the *Theory of Games and Economic Behaviour*, by J. von Neumann and O. Morgenstern. Other works on decision-making processes and utility theory also apply and create a complex approach. The examples which follow are intended to illustrate application in principle of the most common methods. For deeper knowledge of any particular method reference should be made to the original work, or the more specialist books listed in the Bibliography.

Game Theory and Similar Techniques

Suppose that the outcomes of five mutually exclusive projects of the same duration had been computed in terms of net annual cash flows and the initial cost has been taken into account in computing this figure. Further suppose that these outcomes had been computed under four potential alternatives: for example, anticipated demand under four sets of economic conditions representative of possible circumstances. While not being prepared to put specific values on the probability of a particular outcome, i.e. set of conditions, occurring, the forecasters had nevertheless computed figures for each project which they thought would be likely under the four alternative sets of conditions. These four outcomes could be referred to as P1, P2, P3 and P4, the P merely signifying 'Possible'. Similarly, the projects could be designated A1, A2, A3, A4 and A5, the A signifying 'Alternative'. The estimates could be summarised in what would be termed a 'pay-off matrix'.

Example 11

		Possible outcomes (£000)			
		P1	P2	P3	P4
	A1	90	30	10	80
	A2	60	40	50	60
Alternative projects	A3	20	40	30	30
	A4	50	60	20	30
	A5	40	80	30	40

The figures therefore represent the anticipated gain to the company if a particular project is chosen for investment and varying conditions—in game theory termed 'states of nature'—occur.

Using the technique, we first examine the data to see if any one course of action is *dominated* by another. Dominance occurs when one course of action is so inferior to another that it would never be used. The particular course of action which is dominated can be removed from the matrix, thus reducing the number of variables to which attention need be given. This situation occurs in example 11 when we compare alternatives A2 and A3:

	P1	P2	P3	P4
A2	60	40	50	60
A3	20	40	30	30

Whatever the conditions prevailing the cash flow generated by project A2 is higher than or equivalent to project A3. There is therefore no case for investment in project A3. This is equivalent to an application of the exceptions rule for effective management—that is, we concentrate our attention only on those alternatives which merit it. The matrix is therefore reduced in size and would now appear thus:

		Possible outcomes (£000)			
		P1	P2	P3	P4
	A1	90	30	10	80
Alternative projects	A2	60	40	50	60
	A4	50	60	20	20
	A5	40	80	30	40

In a game situation the above matrix would represent a series of 'strategies' available to two players A and P. Each individual value in a 'cell' would represent the anticipated outcome if the two players chose individually a combination of strategies represented by that cell. Thus if player A chose strategy 4 and player P chose strategy 2 the outcome would be identified as the value intersected by row A4 and column P2, i.e. £60,000. The possible outcomes in this investment situation are probably conditioned partly by the anticipated reactions of players (e.g. sales competitors) and partly by less easily predictable factors (e.g. future economic conditions). In any event the major assumption in game theory is that each player looks at the strategies to see which is the worst possible outcome. He then chooses that course of action which corresponds to the best of the worst outcomes. Similarly, if the possible outcomes are estimates of results under various combinations of conditions he will follow the same approach. This is alternatively described as the **pessimistic** approach. Illustrations of both approaches follow.

1. The Pessimistic Approach

In the example above, if project A1 is proceeded with the worst result occurs when the conditions represented by P3 obtain as this is the point of lowest *profit* for this alternative. Similarly, all the worst outcomes can be tabulated as follows:

	Minimum cash flow (£000)
A1	10
A2	40
A4	20
A5	30

The *best* of these *worst* outcomes would be to choose A2, as whatever condition then occurred we would make a gain of £40,000. The term **maximum** is sometimes used to describe this approach when used in conjunction with a *profits* or cash flow example. (On the other hand, if the matrix represents the *costs* of alternative projects then the approach is termed **minimax** since the worst outcomes would be represented by the maximum cost figures and the chosen alternative would be that which minimised the *maximum* cost—see example 12.)

2. Optimistic Approach

This is the opposite approach to the one described above and in contrast represents the outlook of a supreme optimist. It states that the manager will select the most favourable outcome from each alternative and finally select the one which gives the most desired result. Using the figures from the example these figures would be the maximum profits from each alternative.

	Maximum cash flow (£000)
A1	90
A2	60
A4	60
A5	80

The alternative which *maximises* the *maximum* profit is A1, and this is the one which would be preferred under this method since it maximises the maximum gain. With a profit problem this approach is termed the **maximax**, but as before the optimistic approach with a matrix representing alternative costs would be to *minimise* the *minimum* cost and it is referred to in this case as the **minimin** (see example 12).

Example 12: Costs example

In order to emphasise the different terms used when the above approach is adopted, the tabulation used in example 11 is repeated below with the same figures, but treated now as *costs*.

Possible costs (£000)

	P1	P2	P3	P4
A1	90	30	10	80
A2	60	40	50	60
A3	20	40	30	30
A4	50	60	20	20
A5	40	80	30	40

Examine for dominance. If each alternative is compared with the others it can be seen that dominance occurs when alternative A2 is contrasted with A3:

	P1	P2	P3	P4
A2	60	40	50	60
A3	20	40	30	30

Whatever the outcome the costs incurred by A3 are less than, or equal to, A2. There is therefore no case for incurring the cost of project A2. (Note that this is a reversal of the choice when figures were *assumed* to represent profits.) The matrix is therefore reduced in size and possible choices reduced to four as follows:

	P1	P2	P3	P4
A1	90	30	10	80
A3	20	40	30	30
A4	50	60	20	20
A5	40	80	30	40

Pessimistic Approach. The worst outcomes are when the highest, i.e. maximum, costs are incurred. These can be listed as follows:

	£000
A1	90
A2	40
A4	60
A5	80

By choosing the alternative which minimises the worst of the possible alternatives the decision-maker restricts his loss to the better of the worst outcomes—he would therefore select A3 as this is the minimum of the maximum values, hence **minimax**.

Optimistic Approach. The best outcomes are when the lowest, i.e. minimum, costs are incurred. These can be listed as follows:

	£000
A1	10
A3	20
A4	20
A5	30

By choosing the alternative which minimises the best of the possible alternatives the decision-maker is hoping for a best set of conditions to transpire—he would therefore choose A1, since this gives the possibility of minimum of the minimum values, hence **minimin**. Note, however, that this will only produce the best outcome if the set of conditions represented by P3 prevails. Should the decision-maker choose A1 and the conditions represented by P1 occur instead of those represented by P3 then the outcome will be the worst possible.

3. Degrees of Optimism

In practice it is fairly obvious that individuals will vary between the extremely pessimistic and the extremely optimistic. Representative of work done on methods which formally take into account these shades of opinion are the efforts of Hurwicz and Savage. The econometrician Hurwicz suggested that alternative possible outcomes could be weighted by a 'coefficient of optimism' which reflected individual preference. This comes back to a variation of the expected value approach since the coefficients in total equal unity. It could therefore be stated in the form

$$EV_H = C\ (\text{maximum A}) + (1 - C)\ (\text{minimum A})$$

where EV_H is the total expected value of the two extremes. In example 11 the most optimistic forecast for project A1 was £90,000 profit and the most pessimistic forecast was £10,000 profit. If the manager was twice as favourably inclined that the outcome would be high rather than low, then the expected value of project A1 under the Hurwicz rule would be

$$\begin{aligned} EV_H &= \tfrac{2}{3}(\pounds 90{,}000) + (1 - \tfrac{2}{3})\pounds 10{,}000 \\ &= \pounds 63{,}333 \end{aligned}$$

Similarly, for project A4 if he considered there was only a quarter of the probability that this project would result in the highest figures being attained then

$$\begin{aligned} EV_H &= \tfrac{1}{4}(\pounds 60{,}000) + (1 - \tfrac{1}{4})\pounds 20{,}000 \\ &= \pounds 30{,}000 \end{aligned}$$

Values would be computed on the same basis for the remaining projects under appropriate degrees of optimism and that project would finally be selected which had the highest expected value. It should be noted that, as in the previous examples, should the figures be alternative costs rather than profits, or revenues, an 'optimistic' view would be the lowest cost and a 'pessimistic' view would be the highest cost expected. In some instances where no weighting factor is forthcoming an arbitrary fraction of $\frac{1}{2}$ is applied to both extremes. This is an implied assumption that either extreme is equally likely and does have the effect of reducing the influence of extreme values.

An alternative approach to the above is that suggested by L. J. Savage, which is generally referred to as the **Minimax Regret** rule. It is similar to the previous method except that Savage maintained that the criterion was the 'regret' the manager would experience if he did not achieve the most favourable outcome. The 'regret' value attached to a particular alternative is in effect the opportunity cost of the lost alternative. Consider the projects in the example in so far as possible outcomes P1 are concerned. These are:

		Possible outcome (£000)
		P1
	A1	90
Alternative	A2	60
choice	A4	50
	A5	40

If it was *known* that the situation represented by condition P1 would definitely occur then alternative A1 would be preferred as it shows the maximum gain. However, if it were not known that P1 would occur and A2 had been previously selected then the regret value is equal to the opportunity cost of the best alternative—in this case the difference between £90,000 and £60,000, or £30,000. Similarly, the 'regret' of choice A4 relative to A1 is £40,000 and of A5 relative to A1 is £50,000. Similar 'regret' statistics are constructed for the alternative projects under remaining conditions P2, P3 and P4. The complete regret matrix would appear as follows:

	P1	P2	P3	P4
A1	0	50	40	0
A2	30	40	0	20
A4	40	20	30	60
A5	50	0	20	40

The objective is then to select that alternative which minimises the maximum regret. The values for maximum regret can be listed as follows:

	Maximum regret (£000)
A1	50
A2	40
A4	60
A5	50

The minimum value is for A2 and under this rule this will be the project selected. To repeat: the philosophy is based on the proposition that the manager will seek to minimise the maximum effect of lost opportunities, whatever the possible conditions prevailing.

Reliability of the Basic Data

In the foregoing sections various methods have been illustrated which are used as aids to the decision-making process under the various circumstances described. In none of these was the validity of the estimate itself questioned. Consider again the figures originally given in example 12:

	Possible outcome (£000)			
	P1	P2	P3	P4
A1	90	30	10	80
A2	60	40	50	60
A4	50	60	20	20
A5	40	80	30	40

In all previous analyses these figures were taken for granted. They could, however, be questioned from two sides:

(*a*) How sure are we that all possible outcomes lie between a minimum of £10,000 and a maximum of £90,000?
(*b*) How sure are we that the outcome of P1 would be £90,000, of P2 would be £30,000 and so on?

The question can be put more formally in three stages:

(i) How wide is the *range* of values of all possible outcomes?
(ii) How great is the dispersion of the values which have been simplified into the final forecast?
(iii) Finally, and most important, what effect would an error in these figures have had on the final decision?

The tools used in assessing these factors have been briefly described in Chapter 1. Without space to develop the details of the techniques themselves—these are available in any standard work on statistics—it is salutary to reiterate that however impressive the impression of accuracy may be, errors in the original data are compounded as calculations proceed on dubious estimates and forecasts.

Capital Rationing

Finally, capital rationing exists when a firm is unable or unwilling to include in its investment programme all projects which have either a positive net present value at the given cost of capital or are similarly unable or unwilling to invest in all projects where the internal rate of return is in excess of the borrowing rate. The reason for such a decision may be made by the directors or be enforced by outside conditions. In the former case the management may genuinely feel that too many projects undertaken simultaneously will stretch too much the ability of its executives to cope with the rate of expansion. In this event the rationing may be made effective by simply increasing the cut-off rate for acceptability or use of subjective criteria such as doubts about stability of the financial data or political/economic conditions. A further factor may be protection of the locus of managerial control. If the firm raises more money by issues of ordinary shares, large blocks may be obtained by parties interested in changing the managerial pattern. Even if the capital in shares or loans is subscribed by institutional investors there is a 'watch-dog' interest exhibited by these parties which might inhibit future operations.

More fundamental is the fact that the assumption usually made in the basic approach that the firm can 'borrow or lend funds at a given rate of interest' is in practice totally unreal. A firm's borrowing rate is governed by, among other factors, its size, history, status, type of industry and gearing structure. Similarly its 'lending' rate will be governed by the amount it has to offer, the degree of risk it is prepared to take and the time-span considered. The greater the gap between the borrowing and lending rate the more serious the error in using one or the other rate exclusively as the cost of capital.

The problem is usually referred to as **'multi-period'** or **continuous capital rationing.** This is because over the period of a capital budget—say, five years—the firm's borrowing or lending position may change in successive periods due to dividend policies, increasing or decreasing liquidity arising from cash flow from other projects and the ranking of the firm by alternative forms of lenders. Complex mathematical techniques are utilised to provide solutions when the number of variables are increased in this fashion. One such is linear programming. Models illustrating this technique frequently assume that a proportionate investment in a project results in a proportionate return. In practice this is frequently not possible—investment must be in a complete machine, a complete product run or a whole new factory. Combinations of proportions of this type of investment could be completely impractical. If partial investment is possible then the standard type of simplex algorithm will provide the answer to the most profitable proportion of cash to invest. Space precludes detailed descriptions of the techniques of linear and other forms of mathematical programming suitable when linear conditions are not present. References to specialist texts are included in the reading list but a reasonable degree of mathematical knowledge is required for their appreciation.

In most practical situations the net present value methods will provide a guide to selection but a rate must be determined. If this is not available users of the internal rate of return must bear in mind the limitations described in the text. Extended study of the techniques is of little value if there is little confidence in the ability accurately to predict the required variables over the required time-span—i.e. capital costs, changing interest rates, retained profits, dividends and other items. If these are available assistance can always be obtained from operational research or computer specialist in producing the calculations by standard mathematical techniques or packages.

Concluding Comment

This chapter is concerned with describing and illustrating in simple form the more common methods of quantitative analysis used in the decision-making process. Each individual technique can be developed to a much greater degree of mathematical sophistication, but no development to date has been made which renders the art of management unnecessary. Little has been said, for example, of the effect of differing objectives, both between differing organisations and in the same organisations at differing times. For example, investment policies operating during a period of planned growth would involve different criteria and rates to those applicable during a period of consolidation or difficult environmental conditions. Some managers would question the usefulness of any or all of the techniques under practical conditions, and certainly there are indications that some of them are open to question. The fact remains, however, that the disciplinary exercise of compiling the data and presenting it in the orderly fashion which is a prerequisite of any of the methods ensures a closer and more logical examination of the alternatives that would otherwise be the case. If this aspect of the process is the sole benefit then the analysis may still have been worth while in ensuring that at least all data relative to the decision is considered. See also Chapter 6, particularly the case study on page 210.

Worked Examples

(a) A company is manufacturing a consumer product, the demand for which at current price levels is in excess of its ability to produce. The limiting factor on production is the capacity of a particular machine which is now due for replacement.

The possibilities exist either of replacing it with a similar machine (project X) or acquiring a more expensive machine with greater throughput capacity (project Y). The cash flows under each alternative have been estimated and are given below. The company's opportunity cost of capital is 10 per cent after tax.

In deciding between the two alternatives the managing director favours the payback method. The chief accountant, however, thinks that a more scientific method should be used, and he has calculated for each project:

(i) a net present value;
(ii) the discounted profitability index;
(iii) the discounted payback period.

Having made these calculations, however, he still finds himself uncertain about which project to recommend.

You are required to make these calculations and to discuss their relevance to the decision to be taken.

Project cash flow	*Project X* (£000)	*Project Y* (£000)
Immediate outlay	(27)	(40)
Inflows, year 1	—	10
2	5	14
3	22	16
4	14	17
5	14	15

(b) The variables used in calculating the cash inflows on Project X are as follows:

	Sales/production quantity (units)	*Production cost per unit (£)*	*Sales price per unit (£)*
Year 2	10,000	1·5	2·0
3	40,000	1·45	2·0
4	28,000	1·4	1·9
5	28,000	1·4	1·9

The managing director has doubts about the accuracy of these estimates, and would like to concentrate his attention on that variable for which an error in estimating would have the most significant effect on the DCF rate of return for the project as a whole.

You are required to discover by calculation which variable he should first investigate.

(CIMA)

(a)

Project X				Project Y			
Year	*Factor*	*Cash flow (£000)*		*Year*	*Factor*	*Cash flow (£000)*	
		Gross	*Net*			*Gross*	*Net*
1	0·91	—		1	0·91	10	9·1
2	0·83	5	4·15	2	0·83	14	11·62
3	0·75	22	16·50	3	0·75	16	12
4	0·68	14	9·52	4	0·68	17	11·56
5	0·62	14	8·68	5	0·62	15	9·30
			38·85				53·58
0			(27·00)				(40)
(i) Net present value			11·85				13.58

Both investments are viable at a rate of 10 per cent but project Y has the higher net present value.

(ii) Profitability index $\frac{38·85}{27} = 1·44$ $\qquad \frac{54·08}{40}$ 1·35

On this basis project X is preferred to project Y since the return per pound of original investment is superior.

(iii) Discount Payback

Year		*Year*	
1	0	1	9·1
2	4·15	2	11·62
3	16·50	3	12·00
	20·65		32·72
4	9·52	4	11·56
	30·17		44·28

27 lies between the figures of 20·65 and 30·17.

Assuming cash flow is evenly spread during Year 4 it will take

$$3 + \frac{(27 - 20·65)}{9·52}$$

$$= 3·67 \text{ years}$$

for discounted payback.

Note. The normal payback period would be exactly 3 years.

40 lies between the figures of 32·72 and 44.28.

Assuming cash flow is evenly spread during Year 4 it will take

$$3 + \frac{(40 - 32·72)}{11·56}$$

$$= 3·63 \text{ years}$$

for discounted payback.

Note. The normal payback period would be exactly 3 years.

(b) The parameters here are only three, i.e. sales quantity, production cost and sales price. The objective is to maximise cash flow and the effect of this can be considered by examining the effect of a small (say 5 per cent) change in the variables concerned.

(i) *Effect of 5% reduction in quantity*

Year	*Change in units*	*Contribution*	£	
2	−500	£0·5	250	
3	−2,000	£0·55	1,100	
4	−1,400	£0·50	700	
5	−1,400	£0·50	700	
			2,750	less cash flow

(ii) *Effect of 5% increase in costs*

Year	*Units*	*Change in contribution per unit*	£	
2	10,000	−£0·075	750	
3	40,000	−£0·0725	2,900	
4	28,000	−£0·07	1,960	
5	28,000	−£0·07	1,960	
			7,570	less cash flow

(iii) *Effect of 5% decrease in selling price*

Year	*Units*	*Change in contribution per unit*	£	
2	10,000	−£0·01	1,000	
3	40,000	−£0·01	4,000	
4	28,000	−£0·095	2,660	
5	28,000	−£0·095	2,660	
			10,320	less cash flow

The tabulations show that cash flow is most sensitive to movements in selling price, a 5 per cent reduction in these having almost four times as much effect on the cash flow as a similar percentage reduction in quantities. The managing director is therefore recommended to investigate the origins of the selling prices in an endeavour to eliminate inaccuracies and more deeply examine pricing policies.

Questions

1. The directors of Linnet Oil plc are considering whether to make an immediate payment of £20 million for a licence to drill oil in a particular geographical area. Having acquired the licence, the company would commission a seismic survey to determine whether the area is a suitable prospect, i.e. whether there are any geological structures present which could contain oil. If the area is a suitable prospect, exploration wells would be drilled to discover if oil is in fact present. If oil is present, appraisal wells would be drilled to ascertain the size and characteristics of the potential field.

The company's development expert has produced the following data about the licence area based upon the results from adjoining areas. If oil is discovered by the exploration wells, the appraisal wells will indicate one of the three following types of oil field:

Type	Probability of occurrence (%)	Millions of barrels	Expected life (years)
I	60	negligible	zero
II	32	42	4
III	8	2250	10

The annual oil production will decline over the life of the field. To approximate the decline, the expert argues that a sensible approach would be to assume that the annual production of the field during the first half of its life is twice the annual production during the second half. For example, for a type II field the first two years' annual production rate would be 14 million barrels per annum and the second two years' annual production rate would be 7 million barrels per annum.

During the entire life of the field, a barrel of oil is expected to sell for \$26·4 and the \$/£ rate is expected to be 1·2\$/£. The annual operating cash surplus is expected to be 45 per cent of sales revenue. The combined tax costs for the company are usually 77 per cent of the operating cash surplus and these tax cash flows can be assumed to arise one year after the cash flows relating to sales and other costs. Production of oil would start in one year's time and the first annual net revenues would arise at the end of the first year of production.

The cost of the appraisal well drilling will be £100 million and the exploration well drilling will cost £10 million. Both costs will be paid in one year's time. The seismic survey costs of £2 million will be paid immediately. All three of the costs, together with the cost of the licence to drill oil, will give rise to tax relief equal to 50 per cent of the cost, receivable one year after the cost is paid.

It is expected that there will be a 50 per cent chance that the seismic survey will indicate the prospect of oil and a 30 per cent chance that the exploration drilling will find oil. The company's after-tax cost of capital for this type of project is 15 per cent per annum.

You are required to calculated the expected net present value of the venture.

(ICAEW)

2. Pavgrange plc is considering expanding its operations. The company accountant has produced *pro forma* profit and loss accounts for the next three years assuming that:

(*a*) The company undertakes no new investment.
(*b*) The company invests in Project 1.
(*c*) The company invests in Project 2.

Both projects have expected lives of three years, and the projects are mutually exclusive. The *pro forma* accounts are shown below.

(*a*) *No new investment*

Years	*1*	*2*	*3*
	£000	£000	£000
Sales	6,500	6,950	7,460
Operating costs	4,300	4,650	5,070
Depreciation	960	720	540
Interest	780	800	800
Profit before tax	460	780	1,050
Taxation	161	273	367
Profit after tax	299	507	683
Dividends	200	200	230
Retained earnings	99	307	453

(*b*) *Investment in Project 1*

Years	*1*	*2*	*3*
	£000	£000	£000
Sales	7,340	8,790	9,636
Operating costs	4,869	5,620	6,385
Depreciation	1,460	1,095	821
Interest	1,000	1,030	1,030
Profit before tax	11	1,045	1,400
Taxation	4	366	490
Profit after tax	7	679	910
Dividends	200	200	230
Retained earnings	(193)	479	680

(*c*) *Investment in Project 2*

Years	*1*	*2*	*3*
	£000	£000	£000
Sales	8,430	9,826	11,314
Operating costs	5,680	6,470	7,230
Depreciation	1,835	1,376	1,032
Interest	1,165	1,205	1,205
Profit before tax	(250)	775	1,847
Taxation	0	184	646
Profit after tax	(250)	591	1,201
Dividends	200	200	230
Retained earnings	(450)	391	971

The initial outlay for Project 1 is £2 million and for project 2 £3½ million.

Tax allowable depreciation is at the rate of 25 per cent on a reducing balance basis. The company does not expect to acquire or dispose of any fixed assets during the next three years other than in connection with Projects 1 or 2. Any investment in Project 1 or 2 would commence at the start of the company's next financial year.

The expressed salvage value associated with the investments at the end of three years is £750,000 for Project 1, and £1,500,000 for Project 2.

Corporate taxes are levied at the rate of 35 per cent and are payable one year in arrears.

Pavgrange would finance either investment with a three year term loan at a gross interest payment of 11 per cent per year. The company's weighted average cost of capital is estimated to be 8 per cent per annum.

Required:

(*a*) Advise the company which project (if either) it should undertake. Give the reasons for your choice and support it with calculations.

(*b*) What further information might be helpful to the company accountant in the evaluation of these investments?

(*c*) If Project 1 had been for four years duration rather than three years, and the new net cash flow of the project (after tax and allowing for the scrap value) for years four and five were £77,000 and (£188,000) respectively, evaluate whether your advice to Pavgrange would change.

(*d*) Explain why the payback period and the internal rate of return might not lead to the correct decision when appraising mutually exclusive capital investments.

(CACA)

3. Bewcastle Ltd has received an order from a potential new customer in an overseas country for 5,000 staplers at a unit price of £1·75, payable in sterling. Bewcastle's terms of sale for export orders are a 10 per cent initial deposit, payable with order, with the balance payable in 180 days. The 10 per cent deposit has been received with the order.

Customers from the overseas country have in the past, usually taken approximately one year's credit before making payment, and several have defaulted on payment. On the basis of past experience Bewcastle's management estimates that there is a 35 per cent chance of the new customer defaulting on payment if the order is accepted and only a 50 per cent chance of payment within one year.

Incremental costs associated with the production and delivery of staplers would be £1·25 per unit and, in addition, there is an estimated cost of £500 for special attempts to collect an overdue debt, this cost being incurred one year after the sale is made. When this extra cost is incurred there is a 30 per cent chance of obtaining quick payment of the debt. If, after this action, payment is not received the debt is written off.

Bewcastle currently has some surplus funds which could be used to finance the trade credit. Prices, costs and interest rates are not expected to change significantly in the foreseeable future. Bewcastle's stapler production facilities have a large amount of spare capacity.

The company considers the granting of export credit to be a form of investment decision, with 14 per cent per year as the appropriate discount rate.

Required:

(*a*) Evaluate whether Bewcastle should accept the order from the new customer:
- (i) On the basis of the above information.
- (ii) If there is a 50 per cent chance that the order will be repeated at the same time next year. Following payment for a first order the probability of default for repeat orders is 15 per cent. No special attempts to collect an overdue debt would be made at the end of Year 2.
- (iii) If the overseas company has stated that it will definitely repeat the order in the second year.

State clearly any assumptions that you make.

(*b*) What other factors might influence the decision of whether or not to grant credit to this potential customer?

(*c*) Discuss briefly other methods which might be used to evaluate the creditworthiness of this potential customer. (CACA)

4. A South American farms 960 hectares of land on which he grows squash, kale, lettuce and beans. Of the total, 680 hectares are suitable for all four vegetables, but the remaining 280 hectares are suitable only for kale and lettuce. Labour for all kinds of farm work is plentiful.

The market requires that all four types of vegetable must be produced with a minimum of 10,000 boxes of any one line. The farmer has decided that the area devoted to any crop should be in terms of complete hectares and not in fractions of a hectare. The only other limitation is that not more than 227,500 boxes of any one crop should be produced.

Data concerning production, market prices and costs are as follows:

	Squash	*Kale*	*Lettuce*	*Beans*
Annual yield				
(boxes per hectare)	350	100	70	180
Costs	Pesos	Pesos	Pesos	Pesos
Direct:				
Materials per hectare	476	216	192	312
Labour:				
Growing, per hectare	896	608	372	528
Harvesting and packing, per box	3·60	3·28	4·40	5·20
Transport, per box	5·20	5·20	4·00	9·60
Market price, per box	15·38	15·87	18·38	22·27

Fixed overheads per annum:

	Pesos
Growing	122,000
Harvesting	74,000
Transport	74,000
General administration	100,000
Notional rent	74,000

It is possible to make the entire farm viable for all four vegetables if certain drainage work is undertaken. This would involve capital investment and it would have the following effect on direct harvesting costs of some of the vegetables:

	Capital cost	*Change from normal harvesting costs*	
		Squash	*Beans*
	(Pesos)	(Pesos per box)	
First lot of 10 hectares	19,000 total	+1·2	−1·2
Next lot of 10 hectares	17,500 total	+1·3	−1·3
Next lot of 10 hectares	15,000 total	+1·4	−1·4
Remaining land (per hectare)	1,850	+1·5	−1·5

The farmer is willing to undertake such investment only if he can obtain a return of 15 per cent DCF for a four-year period.

You are required to:

(*a*) Advise the farmer, within the given constraints:

(i) The area to be cultivated with each crop if he is to achieve the largest total profit.

(ii) The amount of this total profit.

(iii) The number of hectares it is worth draining and the use to which they would be put.

(*b*) Comment briefly on four of the financial dangers of going ahead with the drainage work.

Notes: Show all relevant calculations in arriving at your answer. Ignore tax and inflation. (CIMA)

5. A company is proposing to use a new type of machine that costs £12,000 and has expected trade-in values as follows:

Start of year	£000
2	9
3	7
4	6
5	5
6	3·5
7	2
8	Nil

The basic operating costs of the machine are £1,000 per quarter but there are special safety costs that have to be met to keep the machines up to safety standards. These are £500 at the beginning of the second year and increase by £500 at the beginning of each subsequent year. In addition, there are obsolescence costs, representing the value of lower output each year, which the company estimates at £100 per annum after the first year.

Because of seasonal variations the company's requirements are expected to be 10 machines in Quarter 1, 12 in Quarter 2 and 14 in each of Quarters 3 and 4. Its business plan, however, proposes the purchase of 10 machines and the hiring of its excess requirements in Quarters 2, 3 and 4. The cost of hiring is £2,500 per quarter per machine.

This covers all operating costs and as new machines are always provided for hire it also covers the special safety costs plus obsolescence costs.

The company is considering an amendment to its business plan whereby it would buy 12 machines instead of 10, with appropriate adjustments to its need for hiring. In any quarter when a machine that it owns lies idle, the operating costs would not be incurred but the safety and obsolescence costs would continue.

Assume that:

1. The company can claim capital allowances of 50 per cent of the original cost in each of years 1 and 2 and that it had adequate profits to absorb these allowances.
2. There is a one-year delay in the payment of tax net of allowances.
3. Corporation tax of 35 per cent is paid.
4. Any purchase or trade-in is made at the start of a year.
5. All revenue costs (including hire charges) are deemed to occur at the end of the year.
6. The company's cost of capital for this type of transaction is 14 per cent per annum.

You are required to:

(*a*) Advise, with supporting calculations:
 (i) Which one of the four-year or five-year replacement frequencies gives the lower overall cost.
 (ii) Whether it would be more economic for the company to maintain its original business plan or to undertake the purchase of 12 machines.

(*b*) Explain briefly what other considerations it should take into account in its decision on (*a*) (ii) above. (CIMA)

6. A small company in the house building industry has £201,000 cash which is surplus to current requirements. The cash will eventually be used to help finance the construction of a small housing development. The housing development depends upon obtaining permission to build the houses from the local government planning department. It is believed that this permission will be given in two years' time.

The £201,000 can be invested in the money market to yield a return of 10 per cent per year. The money market is considered to be an efficient market.

Alternatively an opportunity exists for the funds to be invested on a temporary basis in Goer, a family owned car hire business which wishes to expand its car hire fleet by thirty cars costing £6,700 each. Goer is temporarily short of funds because of recent inheritance tax payments. If the funds are invested with Goer they will produce an annual net cash inflow to the building company, but the size of this cash flow is not known with certainty, and the cash flow at the end of the second year is dependent upon the cash flow at the end of the first year. Estimates of the net cash inflows to the building company are detailed below.

End of Year 1		*End of Year 2*	
Probability	*Cash inflow* £	*Probability*	*Cash inflow* £
0·6	80,000	0·6	80,000
		0·4	90,000
0·4	100,000	0·6	100,000
		0·4	110,000

In addition Goer will make a payment to the building company at the end of the first year of £141,000 *or* at the end of the second year of £81,000. The building company has to choose at the end of the first year whether to receive payment of £141,000 then or £81,000 a year later. If the payment of £141,000 is received by the building company at the end of the first year the investment will be terminated and there will be no further cash flows to the building company from Goer.

Eighteen per cent per year is considered to be an appropriate discount rate for investments in the car hire business.

Required:

(*a*) Prepare a report recommending whether the building company should invest in the car hire business or in the money market. All relevant calculations must be included in your report. Ignore taxation. State clearly any assumptions that you make.

(*b*) Discuss the practical problems of incorporating abandonment opportunities into the capital investment decision-making process. Suggest possible reasons why a company might decide to abandon an investment project part way through its expected economic life. (CACA)

7. A company is proposing to acquire a piece of office equipment which has a life of five years, after which it would need to be replaced.

The purchase price of the equipment is £5,000. It will have no residual value at the end of its life and for tax purposes the capital allowances are assumed to be at 20 per cent per annum on a straight-line basis.

If it were to buy the equipment, the company would need to borrow the total sum from the bank. Repayment would be by a standard annual amount at the end of each year. This amount would comprise repayment of principal and interest at 16 per cent per annum before tax.

The equipment is also available on a standard five-year least at an annual payment of £1,529.

The company is not certain that it will require the equipment for the full five years because it is considering a more elaborate system that would make this equipment redundant. In these circumstances:

1. The equipment could be sold at the end of any year for 80 per cent of its book value.
2. A special lease can be taken at the same annual cost as for a standard lease but with the facility to cancel at the end of any year. There is, however, a penalty of £1,850 if the lease is cancelled at the end of the first year and a penalty of £1,000 if it is cancelled at the end of the second year. There are no penalties for cancellation at the end of the third or fourth years.

The company assesses the probability of its keeping the equipment:

for one year	0·2
for two years	0·3
for three years	0·2
for four years	0·2
for five years	0·1
	1·0

You are required to advise the company whether it should lease or buy the equipment:

(*a*) If it is certain to keep the equipment for the whole five years and is considering a standard lease.

(*b*) If it is uncertain of the time the equipment will be kept and it is considering the special lease.

Notes: Assume that interest payments are made net of tax at 50 per cent and that tax of 50 per cent on profits applies and that it is paid in the year in which profits are earned. Ignore the risk differentials other than those explicitly stated in the question. All workings should be shown to the nearest £. (CIMA)

8. A division of Bewcast plc has been allocated a fixed capital sum by the main board of directors for its capital investment during the next year. The division's management has identified three capital investment projects, each potentially successful, each of similar

size, but has only been allocated enough funds to undertake two projects. Projects are not divisible and cannot be postponed until a later date.

The division's management proposes to use portfolio theory to determine which two projects should be undertaken, based upon an analysis of the projects' risk and return. The success of the projects will depend upon the growth rate of the economy. Estimates of project returns at different levels of economic growth are shown below.

Economic growth (annual average)	*Probability of occurrence*	*Estimated return (%)* Project 1	Project 2	Project 3
Zero	0·2	2	5	6
2 per cent	0·3	8	9	10
4 per cent	0·3	16	12	11
6 per cent	0·2	25	15	11

Required:

(*a*) Using the above information evaluate and discuss which two projects the division is likely to undertake. All relevant calculations must be shown.

(*b*) What are the weaknesses of the evaluation technique used in (*a*) above, and what further information might be useful in the evaluation of these projects?

(*c*) Suggest why portfolio theory is not widely used in practice as a capital investment evaluation technique.

(*d*) Recommend, and briefly describe, an alternative investment evaluation technique that might be applied by the division.

4

CORPORATE FINANCE

Cost of Finance from Alternative Sources

In the previous chapter reference was made to the 'cut-off' rate used by a company in assessing the relative merits of investment projects and to the fact that this was sometimes termed the **cost of capital**. This rate was used as a yardstick to assess the acceptability or otherwise of particular capital projects. If new capital is required to finance the project then the cost of the *existing* capital is irrelevant to the decision: it is what the firm will have to pay to raise the *new* finance which will determine its ability to proceed with the project. The cost to the firm of the capital it is using now is determined by what happened in the past. It may have raised loan capital at a time when an acceptable rate of interest to the investors supplying it was, say, 10 per cent. If additional funds are now required in a similar form investors may be demanding at least 15 per cent due to the general economic climate and the ranking of the particular firm within this climate. Similarly, if due to adverse trading conditions a firm is paying a reduced dividend to its ordinary shareholders, in the historic accounting statements this is the cost, but the firm would be unlikely to tempt its existing—or new—shareholders to supply funds on similar terms.

If a particular investment is to be financed from a specific source—for example, if we propose to increase our material stocks by extra purchases financed by a bank loan at 15 per cent p.a.—then the cost of the extra stockholding is the interest payable. If we had surplus cash at present earning 12 per cent on short-term deposits then the cost in the sense in which we desire to use it would be the investment income lost by choosing to invest in the extra stocks, i.e. the 'opportunity' cost of increasing our stocks is the income forgone from the now reduced deposits. Potential investors—be they banks, institutions or individuals—will apply a similar approach when deciding whether to advance the necessary finance or buy our shares and it is this cost of capital we are endeavouring to assess.

One of the rates used in assessing the ranking of alternative investment projects is termed the **marginal efficiency of capital**, and this is similar to the internal rate of return used in the previous chapter. With the exception of essential but non-revenue earning projects, marginal increments of investment generate marginal additions to profit. Ranking in order of the highest internal rates of return produces an initial order of preference. Any additional project which has an internal rate of return less than that being earned as an average by the company as a whole would not be acceptable since it would merely worsen the existing performance. It is now a matter of reconciling this list of projects having acceptable internal rates of return with a (probably) restricted supply of funds. *The problem of investment appraisal is therefore largely indivisible from the problem of optimum financing strategy.*

While it is permissible in order to illustrate the alternative technique of net present value for the demonstrator to *assume* a cost of capital, or minimum cut-off rate, it is deciding what this figure should be which provides the challenge and difficulty. Major difficulties in its assessment are lack of knowledge of investors' preferences, imperfect capital markets, economic and political climate and taxation effects. Further, it is extremely unlikely in practice that the use of each small increment of investment can be identified with its particular source.

As demonstrated in Chapter 6, the calculation of capital requirements, even allowing for practical difficulties, is the easier part of the exercise. The total is arrived at by summing all the investment projects approved. Most of the projects generate income—some do not for reasons similar to those stated previously, i.e. they are required to comply with legal or safety requirements, or to provide employees with facilities in accordance with non-monetary objectives of the corporate plan. Alternatively, they may be required simply to maintain present profitability or for expansion. Given that the total amount of capital required, including working capital where applicable, has been computed and allowance for any short-term sources and retained profits made, there is the major question to be answered: in what form, debt or equity will the capital be raised?

Debt Capital

This is the general term used to describe long-term borrowing at fixed rates of interest and normally for a contracted period. It may be unsecured but more usually is secured on specific assets or (floating) on the assets of a firm in general. The subscribers or holders are legally protected in that there is a trust deed setting out the respective rights and responsibilities of the parties to the contract in regard to priority of payment of interest and capital refund.

Although the interest payment is related by a fixed percentage (contract rate) to the nominal value of the debenture, it is the relationship between this income and the current market value of the debenture which would indicate the present cost of this form of capital to a firm contemplating raising a further amount. Suppose, for example, that the debenture concerned carried a coupon or contract rate of 12 per cent, that the present price per £100 nominal value is £91, and that it was due to be redeemed at par in four years. Using our knowledge of present values we could calculate the present cost or return.

Example 1

For £91 the investor is buying an income of £12 p.a. for 4 years and a capital receipt of £100 at the end of Year 4. The rate of interest such that an annuity of £12 p.a. and a single payment of £100 will equate with £91 can be computed from the tables by trial and error as approximately 15 per cent, i.e.

	£
£12 × 2·855 =	34·26
£100 × 0·5717 =	57·17
	91·43

Assuming the company desired to issue new debentures this could provide some indication of the likely cost. The rate would need to be examined and possibly qualified by subjective decision in respect of practical considerations such as:

(i) How large a sum is the additional capital required in relation to both the existing loan capital and total capital (in market values rather than book values)?

(ii) Is the nature of the company's business such that the asset structure will provide the necessary backing in terms of security?

(iii) Are there any legal restrictions?

(iv) Allowing for the additional earnings expected to be generated by the assets purchased, will the new interest charges materially distort relative incomes of existing debenture and ordinary share holders? Each increment of debt capital increases the amount of cash income required for total interest payments. It therefore makes the position of the junior, i.e. last subscribed, debenture holders more risky and similarly increases the risk to the equity share holders of the previous profit distribution being maintained. It is this balance between the interests of debt and equity holdings which is the subject of gearing and this is so fundamentally integrated with the cost of capital concept that it is treated later in this section.

It would appear reasonable to use the cost of debt computed in this way as *minimum* cost for all capital. The figure is derived from familiar and definite data, i.e. the market price at a particular time together with the fixed coupon rate, and there is a degree of precision about the computed result which is impressive. The rate is termed the **gross redemption yield**. This is because it ignores the effect of personal taxation—income tax and capital gains tax—on the amount actually received by the investor. It can be argued that after-tax preferences of the investors are reflected in the demand price for the securities concerned, and the price being offered therefore reflects this, and the gross rate is a reasonable one on which to work.

Equity Capital

The holders of equity shares are the owners of the company and therefore carry the majority of the risk. The value of an individual's shareholding and the total market value of the firm will vary in relation to a greater number of variables than will the debt capital, although some factors are common. Among these variables are:

(i) The general economic climate.

(ii) The state of the particular industry or activity in which the company is engaged.

(iii) The recent performance and investor's assessment of the future prospects of the company concerned.

(iv) The policy of the company in respect of retained earnings relative to dividends distributed.

General theory states that the value of a firm is determined by the expectations of investors. When a share is purchased the investor is buying two rights: the right to cash dividends and the right to (it is hoped) an increase in the value of the firm over time. This implies growth, and when a share is sold the profits which have been retained by the firm are reflected in the higher selling price paid to the vendor. If it is desired to raise further equity capital, shareholders will expect the performance of the increment supplied at least to match that of the existing capital. If a growth rate is known or predicted then the return necessary to match it can be predicted. Suppose a firm is currently paying a dividend of £0·12 per share and the current market price is £2·50. If dividends are expected to grow by 3 per cent p.a. then the earnings required to meet this dividend would be

$$\frac{£0{\cdot}12}{£2{\cdot}50} \times 100 + 3 = 7{\cdot}8\% \text{ p.a.}$$

The figure of 7·8 per cent would then be expressed as the cost of equity capital, since any increment of funds subscribed in this form which failed to achieve the target would lower the return below the expectations of potential investors and be reflected in a lower market price.

The emphasis on dividends may also be questioned on the basis that it does not take into account the full earnings. If the relationship between dividends and earnings were constant—i.e. the dividend cover as a multiple was always the same—this would not affect the use of dividends as a yardstick. The implication is that the retained earnings are being effectively utilised by the company.

If the interrelationship between the cost of capital and a cut-off rate for new investment is to be emphasised then the dividend approach is not completely satisfactory. In the boom investment period of the 1960s investors were prepared to put their faith as much if not more in the increase in value of the market price of their shares as much as the amount of cash received in dividend. This was admittedly assisted by two factors. Dividend restraint imposed by the UK Government prevented autonomous decisions by the directors of companies as to what dividends would be paid. Secondly, changes in the tax structure by successive governments affected the issue. One of the intentions of the 1965 Finance Act was to favour retention of profit and encourage investment. The subsequent introduction of the 'imputation' system was to some extent an attempt to reduce the discrimination against distribution. Thus in planning overall financial strategy these factors became more important than the basic theoretical approach. On balance, the use of an earnings basis as a cost of capital would appear more practical since if a firm has no earnings then neither dividends or taxation will be paid!

An issue associated with the choice of which rate to use is a definition of the fundamental objectives of the firm. This could be stated to be the maximisation of profit—but what profit and how is it to be measured? An alternative objective stated might be **maximisation of shareholders' wealth**. Few people would argue with the tenet that this is now too narrow. With current emphasis on factors such as protection of the environment, employee participation, partial and complete takeover of industries by the State, the debate on which definition of wealth to use becomes even more academic. However, the acceptance that shareholders derive maximum satisfaction when the value of their shareholding is optimised in monetary terms can at least provide a starting point for deciding an acceptable cost of equity capital, since it is a major fact that no firm will find it practical to raise new funds unless it retains the confidence of the investors—public or institutional—and the barometer which reflects this confidence is share price. In fact, many boards of directors are reluctant to undertake the more risky investment projects simply because a steady solid appearance is preferred to the erratic performance which could be reflected if profits showed too violent a fluctuation—even if the long-term average was one of satisfactory growth.

If the company is already quoted on the Stock Exchange the current market value of a share is available. The earnings per share are also available—in fact, the company will be able to form a more up-to-date estimate of its ability to improve or maintain present performance than will the external analyst who is working from latest published information.

If the market price of one share (MV) is £2·00 and the earnings per share (E) are expected to be £0·16 then the **equity capitalisation rate** can be deduced as

$$\frac{E}{MV} \times 100 = \frac{£0{\cdot}16}{£2{\cdot}00} \times 100 = 8\%$$

If the earnings per share are expressed net of tax then the figure produced is synonymous with the earnings yield. Another way in which this relationship can be stated is the **price/earnings ratio**. This is defined as the market value of a share related to earnings per share after tax. It represents the number of years required at that rate of earnings for the original investment to be repaid. Thus using the above figures

$$\text{p/e (price/earnings) ratio} = \frac{\text{Market price of share}}{\text{Net earnings per share}}$$

$$= \frac{£2{\cdot}00}{£0{\cdot}16} = 12{\cdot}5$$

In practice, however, if we are contemplating raising additional funds we could use the existing situation as a starting point. Note that the equity capitalisation rate or earnings yield, when computed from market information, is the reciprocal of the p/e ratio. In the example above the earnings per share of £0·16 is converted into a p/e ratio by dividing it into the purchase price, arriving at a figure of 12·5. The reciprocal of 12·5 converted to a percentage is 8.

The p/e ratio can be computed from statistics for one share or for the firm as a whole.

Example 2

Issued ordinary share capital		
500,000 ordinary shares of £1 each		£500,000
Market price of one share		£2
∴ Market value of company		£1,000,000
Earnings per share		£0·16
∴ Total earnings		£80,000
p/e ratio	*Total*	*Per share*
(*a*) Earnings	£80,000	£0·16
(*b*) Market value	£1,000,000	£2·00
(*c*) p/e ratio $= \frac{(b)}{(a)}$	12·5	12·5

The nominal value of the equity and unknown figures for reserves and surplus are irrelevant to the computation since it depends solely on earnings available and market values.

If we have an investment proposal to consider, requiring an additional £150,000 of capital, we can see that unless it is anticipated that it will produce a return of at least 8 per cent net after taxation we cannot raise the capital by means of a new equity issue. If the expenses of the issue are taken into account then the return must be marginally higher to compensate for the non-producing element of capital required to meet the preliminary expenses. Suppose these were estimated at £10,000; then the total capital requirement would be increased to £160,000. Minimum earnings required to produce a return of 8 per cent would be £12,800. The project for which the money is required must produce this earnings figure, i.e.

$$\frac{£12{,}800}{£150{,}000} \times 100 = 8{\cdot}53\%$$

This means the minimum effective rate—the cut-off rate or marginal efficiency of capital rate—is 8·53 per cent. This can be proved non-algebraically by considering the position before and after the investment:

	Before	*After*
Market value of shares issued	£1,000,000	£1,160,000
After tax earnings	£80,000	£92,800
Earnings yield	8%	8%
p/e ratio	12·5	12·5

Adjustment for other forms of taxation or a change in the number of shares issued, dividend proposals and related cover add to the complexity of the computation and modify the result but do not affect the necessity to compute some rate of return to integrate with the investment appraisal procedure. In its simplest form then the minimum equity capitalisation rate for an existing quoted company can be determined by relating existing or projected maintainable earnings to market value for a start. The problem of determining whether the market value at a particular date is in the firm's view realistic still remains, but it is a question of adjusting this by some subjective evaluation or resorting to using the more theoretical growth models which could require much more sophisticated estimates.

Capital Gearing and the Combined Cost of Capital

Few firms exist with wholly equity share capital and virtually none financed entirely by debt capital. It was at one time generally accepted that firms could improve the earnings of equity shareholders by employing additional or substituting amounts of lower cost debt capital. Since the return paid to the debt subscribers had to be paid before anything was available to the equity interests, these were the 'priority' claimants on income. There are various classes of prior claims in most capital structures of companies. As was mentioned in the section on debt capital, the rights of the debenture holders are recorded in the trust deed. Among these rights is usually the position in which various classes of debentures issued rank for payment and protection of interest and repayment of capital.

The relationship between the fixed interest bearing securities such as loan capital and preference shares to the equity interest is termed the **gearing** and a firm with a relatively high proportion of fixed interest capital is said to be highly geared. The **gear ratio**, i.e. the relative proportion of fixed interest capital to other forms, can be expressed in a variety of ways (as discussed later), but when considering it from the point of view of the cost of capital it is the relative

market values which are significant. In this case the ratio is normally stated as that which exists between the total market value of fixed interest capital and the total market value of the firm as a whole.

Traditional theory maintained that there was a limit to the amount of debt capital that an individual capital structure could support. This was because as the total amount, and more particularly the proportion of debt capital to total capital, was increased higher rates of interest would be required by the later subscribers in view of the increased risk that, under adverse conditions, their interest payment would not be met. Similarly, since equity shareholders take what is left after all prior claims have been met, their position also would be open to a greater degree of risk and the rate of return demanded by them would also increase. This is shown diagrammatically in Fig. 7.

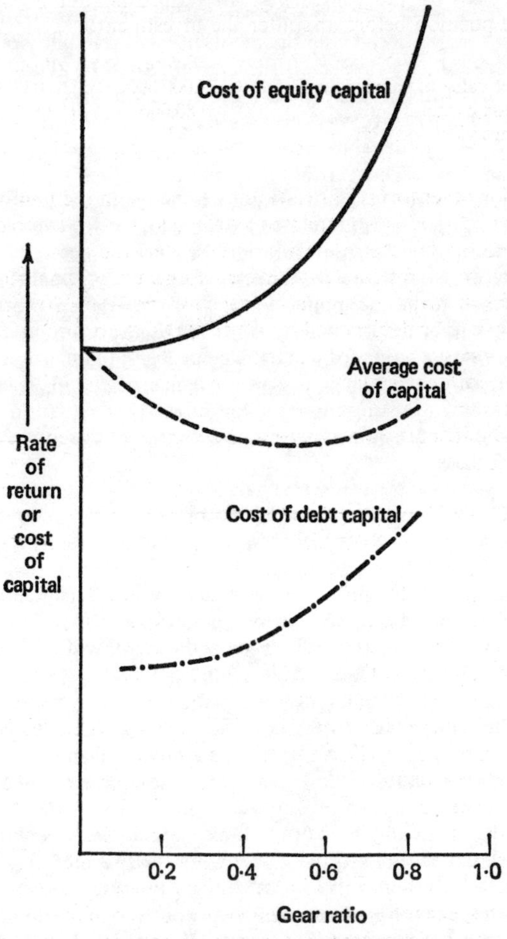

Fig. 7. The effect of gearing on the cost of capital.

With a gear ratio of only 0·1 the cost of debt capital is low because risk is low. Equity shareholders expect a higher rate of return and with no gearing at all the average cost of capital is the same as for the firm which is entirely equity financed. Injecting some low-cost debt capital increases the risk to equity shareholders and the return expected by them is slightly higher. The average or weighted cost of capital, however, falls because of the significant difference in the two rates. This fall continues until the gearing becomes substantial—about two-thirds—in Fig. 7. Beyond this both costs of capital increase at a much more accelerated rate. Both classes now face more risk; equity holders because of the large interest commitments which must be met before they share in the returns and debt subscribers because of the prior claims of the earlier debt. The average cost of capital must also rise and the optimum gearing in this instance must occur at the lowest point of the average curve. Each class of industry would tend to have its own particular relationships for many reasons, the two major ones being the regularity and reliability of income and the nature of the industry's assets. If these assets could be adaptable for other purposes, e.g. department stores, then the firms will have less difficulty in pledging them than owners of very specialised equipment, e.g. for North Sea oil.

As previously stated, the relationship of fixed interest capital and total capital is referred to as the 'gearing' of the company and a firm is said to be highly geared if its fixed interest commitments form a significant proportion of the whole. There is a variety of ratios used to express this proportion, some relating to the figures used in published accounts (but these are not relevant to the problem under review). From the point of view of the investor in a going concern, and hence from the point of view of the firm desiring to raise capital, it is the relative market values which dominate. Usually when the cost of capital is being examined the gear ratio is defined as the market value of the total fixed interest capital expressed as a proportion of the total market value of the firm; thus if

$$MV_E = \text{Market value of } \textit{equity}$$
$$MV_D = \text{Market value of } \textit{debt}$$
$$\text{Gear ratio} = \frac{MV_D}{MV_E + MV_D}$$

a figure which must obviously be between zero and unity, and it is this ratio, not one derived from the accounts, which is implicit in Fig. 7.

No mathematical model has been developed that individual firms could use to decide exactly what particular ratio would be ideal for their type of firm. Indeed, the conventional theory was challenged by two American professors, Modigliani and Miller, with a now famous thesis published in 1958 whereby they argued that using increments of fixed interest finance brought no change in the total market valuation of the firm. They maintained that as the proportion of debt capital to total capital—in market terms—increased, the equity shareholders would demand higher rates for investment in view of the increasing risk that the existing earnings rate would not be maintained. This would cause a decline in the p/e ratio and this reduction would exactly offset the increased risk. The total market values of any firm in a similar risk class would therefore tend to be determined by the one which was entirely equity financed. Instead of a flat U-shaped curve similar to that in Fig. 7 the average cost of capital would be a straight line parallel with the axis. A great deal of debate ensued with the traditional view being firmly upheld by other writers. Criticism was primarily based on the fact that by assuming perfect capital markets and ignoring taxation the M.M. conclusion was too unrealistic.

In 1963 the authors revised their original thesis and demonstrated that if the taxation system was such that interest payments on debt are an allowable expense in arriving at taxable profit then the effect of this on company financial policy is substantial. In their revision Modigliani and Miller conceded that there could be an optimal gearing structure when tax savings and other variables were taken into account. Thus they came to more modified results when more practical considerations were added into the original highly theoretical approach.

It is doubtful if any approach can provide a satisfactory model by which the actual rate required for a particular company can be predicted, as this would mean no subjective judgment at all was required. It is, however, essential that management should be familiar with all aspects of the problem when assessing rates for use in investment decisions and a clearer identification of all the variables concerned will at least ensure that none is ignored when judgments are made. We can have, on the one hand, effective utilisation of capital but pay dearly for it; alternatively, we could raise funds by effective gearing and tax planning only to see them squandered by inefficient production or marketing management.

The major benefits of gearing are:

1. The cost of borrowing is known, and even if rates are high the benefit of tax relief makes the cost to the company much lower. With a tax rate of 50 per cent a company has to earn twice as much to pay the same rate on equity as it would on borrowings.

2. The losses due to inflation fall on the subscriber of the fixed capital. When repaid in the future a debt may represent very much less in real terms than it did at the time of borrowing.

3. Once the earnings level sufficient to pay all fixed interest commitments has been reached all profits belong to the equity holders.

There are also disadvantages—for example:

1. It must be endeavoured at all times to secure sufficient profits to pay the interest commitments.

2. Dates for repayment may occur at particularly disadvantageous periods due to the firm's position or the economic situation generally. New borrowing may then be under particularly painful and costly conditions.

3. Management is continuously aware that the mortgage or loan holders are watching the security of their investment and this may inhibit certain courses of action.

Example 3

A company has the following capital structure:

	£
Ordinary shares of £1	
Authorised	800,000
Issued and fully paid	500,000
Reserves and undistributed profits	150,000
12% Debentures	200,000
	850,000
Market price per share	£2·50
Earnings per share (net after tax)	12·5p
Market price of debentures (£100 nominal)	£92
Taxation rate	52%

If the company is to maintain its existing share price the earnings level required can be computed as follows:

Earnings required to meet the interest payment on the debenture are £24,000 before tax. Earnings required to equate with 12·5p per share for 500,000 shares are £62,500 but this is after taxation at 52 per cent has been allowed for. In order to meet this net figure the gross earnings must be

$$\frac{£62{,}500}{48} \times 100 = £130{,}200$$

Total gross earnings would therefore need to be £154,200, and a simplified profit and loss statement could be arranged in conventional form to prove the figure.

	£
Profit before tax and interest	154,200
Less debenture interest	24,000
	130,200
Less tax at 52%	67,700
Earnings available to equity shareholders	62,500

Performances and gearing figures can be computed without reference to the market figures. Note that the debenture interest is allowed before assessing profits for taxation.

Performance Analysis (Book Values)

Return on total capital employed (gross) $\frac{£154{,}200}{£850{,}000} = 18{\cdot}1\%$

Return on total shareholders' equity (net) $\frac{£62{,}500}{£650{,}000} = 9{\cdot}6\%$

Gear Ratio

Fixed interest capital as proportion of total
200,000:850,000 = 1:4·25

Fixed interest capital relative to equity funds
200,000:650,000 = 1:3·25

Most accountants are familiar with this type of analysis but its use for any practical purpose, particularly in terms of financing requirements, is negligible. If market values are utilised instead then the information can be of more use:

Performance Analysis (Market Values)

	Symbol	£
Market value of equity	MV_E	1,250,000
Market value of debt	MV_D	184,000
Total earnings gross	P	154,200
Interest for debentures	I	24,000
Earnings for equity shares gross	P_g	130,200
Earnings for equity shares net of tax	P_n	62,500

(*a*) Return on total market value $\dfrac{P}{MV_E+MV_D} = \dfrac{154{,}200}{1{,}434{,}000} = 10{\cdot}75\%$

(*b*) Cost of debentures (gross) $\dfrac{I}{MV_D} = \dfrac{24{,}000}{184{,}000} = 13.04\%$

(*c*) Return on equity shares (gross) $\dfrac{P_g}{MV_E} = \dfrac{130{,}200}{1{,}250{,}000} = 10.42\%$

(*d*) Return on equity shares (net) $\dfrac{P_n}{MV_E} = \dfrac{62{,}500}{1{,}250{,}000} = 5{\cdot}00\%$

(*e*) Gear ratio: Market value of debt capital as proportion of total market value of firm = 184,000:1,434,000, or 1:7·8

The average cost of capital (*a*) represents the minimum rate of return which must be earned by any increment of capital if the existing position is to be maintained. Strictly this will only be true if the additional sum is raised in the same gearing ratio as that in equation (*e*). If the sum required is comparatively small relative to the existing structure, then if it is raised exclusively by one method or the other it will not unduly affect the ratio. If, however, it should be a substantial amount then the effect of the change in proportion must be examined. The general relationships can be expressed as follows:

Let K equal the relevant rates either being paid, earned or required; then it can be shown that it is the proportion of equity to debt capital and their respective rates which are significant, not necessarily the absolute amounts.

Let the proportion of total market value of debt capital to total value of the firm be represented by W_1; then

$$W_1 = \frac{MV_D}{MV_E+MV_D} = \frac{184{,}000}{1{,}434{,}000} = 0{\cdot}13$$

Let the proportion of total market value of equity capital to total value of the firm be represented by W_2; then

$$W_2 = \frac{MV_E}{MV_E+MV_D} = \frac{1{,}250{,}000}{1{,}434{,}000} = 0{\cdot}87$$

(i.e. the difference between 13 per cent and 100 per cent). Then if K_A is the average cost of capital in market terms, K_D the cost of debt capital in market terms, and K_E the cost of equity capital in market terms

$$\begin{aligned} K_A &= W_1K_D + W_2K_E \\ &= (0{\cdot}13 \times 13{\cdot}04\%) + (0{\cdot}87 \times 10{\cdot}42\%) \\ &= 1{\cdot}69\% + 9{\cdot}06\% \\ &= 10{\cdot}75\% \end{aligned}$$

This is the gross rate. The basic formula applies even if a net rate is required but because equity earnings are usually considered post-tax by the potential investor, then an after-tax average may be required. In this event the interest on debt capital must be expressed at its net, i.e. after-tax, cost:

	£
Cost of debentures (gross)	24,000
Taxation (at 52%)	12,480
	11,520

$$\therefore \text{ Cost of debentures (net)} = \frac{11{,}520}{184{,}000} \times 100 = 6{\cdot}3\%$$

$$\begin{aligned} K_A &= W_1K_{D_1} + W_2K_{E_1} \\ &= 0{\cdot}13 \times 6{\cdot}3\% + 0{\cdot}87 \times 5{\cdot}0\% \\ &= 0{\cdot}82\% + 4{\cdot}35\% \\ &= 5{\cdot}17\% \end{aligned}$$

This net figure of 5·17 per cent is equivalent to the average gross rate of 10·75 per cent reduced by taxation at 52 per cent. However, the major point is that to pay interest of £1 on debentures the firm needs to earn £1, but to have distributable profit of £1 the firm must earn £2·08.

Note that in this particular example gearing is low, i.e. the proportion of debt capital at market value to the total market value of the firm is small and therefore the average rate (gross) of 10·75 per cent is near to the return of 10·42 per cent on the ordinary shares. If twice the amount of debt is assumed to be outstanding and the rest of the data remain unaltered, the revised figures would be:

	£
Market value of equity	1,250,000
Market value of debt (£400,000 × 92)	368,000
Total earnings (gross)	154,200
Interest for debentures (£400,000 at 12%)	48,000
Earnings for equity shares (gross) (balance)	106,200

then $W_1 = \text{Weighting of debt capital} = \dfrac{368{,}000}{1{,}250{,}000 + 368{,}000} = 0{\cdot}23$

$$W_2 = \text{Weighting of equity capital} = \frac{125{,}000}{1{,}250{,}000 + 368{,}000} = 0{\cdot}77$$

$$K_D = \frac{48{,}000}{368{,}000} = 13{\cdot}04\%$$

$$K_E = \frac{106{,}200}{1{,}250{,}000} = 8{\cdot}5\%$$

$$\begin{aligned} \therefore K_A &= W_1K_D + W_2K_E \\ &= 0{\cdot}23 \times 13{\cdot}04\% + 0{\cdot}77 \times 8{\cdot}5\% \\ &= 3{\cdot}0\% + 6{\cdot}54\% \\ &= 9{\cdot}54\% \end{aligned}$$

This is a reduction of 10·75% − 9·54% = 1·21% in the average rate and 10·42% − 8·5% = 1·92% in the return on equity caused by the larger debt. Assuming this was felt not acceptable the formula can be used to determine the average rate required under the new gearing to maintain the previous rate of return for the equity shareholders:

$$K_A = W_1 K_D + W_2 K_E$$

where
$$W_1 = 0{\cdot}23$$
$$W_2 = 0{\cdot}77$$
$$K_D = 13{\cdot}04\%$$
$$K_E = 10{\cdot}42\% \text{ (required)}$$

$$K_A = (0{\cdot}23 \times 13.04\%) + (0{\cdot}77 \times 10{\cdot}42\%)$$
$$= 3{\cdot}0\% + 8{\cdot}02\%$$
$$= 11{\cdot}02\%$$

The minimum acceptable rate for investment projects would therefore become 11·02 per cent.

		£
Check	Market value of equity	1,250,000
	Market value of debt	368,000
		1,618,000
	Average rate required	11·02%
∴	Profits required gross = 11·02% × £1,618,000 =	£178,303
		£
	Profit before tax and interest	178,303
	Debenture interest	48,000
	Balance accruing to equity	130,303

$$\text{Return on equity shares (gross)} \ \frac{\pounds 130{,}303}{\pounds 1{,}250{,}000} = 10{\cdot}42\%$$

Calculation of a weighted cost of capital for use as a minimum rate of return or cut-off rate is a complex procedure and there is no one satisfactory method but it should still be attempted. The method used above can be criticised on the grounds that:

(i) It does not differentiate between preference for distributed or retained profits by the investor.
(ii) There is no allowance for 'growth' expectations.
(iii) The current market price has been used—but what is current market price? This may deviate substantially over one day, much less a reasonable time-span.
(iv) Taxation has only been considered in relation to the company position and not from the view of investors.
(v) No reference has been made to inflation.
(vi) Maintenance of the existing earnings level is assumed.

All these points are valid but methods which take account of these factors can equally be criticised on other grounds. Some writers maintain that the amount of money distributed as dividends has less effect than growth of earnings but this is in turn dependent upon the liquidity preference of investors, which changes over time. If the current market price, however modified for trends, is not used, then estimates of the rate of growth must be made before such prediction models can be used.

Taxation relief on debentures has been considered to the exclusion of other taxation because its effect is so fundamental and calculable as to make it particularly relevant. The practice of giving tax relief on loan interest payments but not on preference share interest payments has led to virtually a complete cessation of the issue of the latter form of security. No other taxation aspect, as yet, is likely to be so fundamental in affecting a general approach to the problem and therefore it requires special mention.

Finally, in respect of inflation, if it considered that a general rate of inflation will apply to all aspects of the investment appraisal then generally speaking the decision will not be affected. If, however, some elements of the project are considered to be subject to inflation at a different rate to others then these differentials can be subject to adjustment before discounting—a process considered in more detail in Chapter 9.

The word earnings has been used throughout but the symbol P is used, signifying profit. In computing the figures above it is implicit that the profit or earnings is represented by cash flow. Normally when one uses published information or conventionally prepared profit and loss accounts for analysis, the depreciation figure can be extracted and dealt with as required. The earnings figures used should be those after a sufficient provision has been made to maintain the existing earning capacity of the business. To the extent that the depreciation provision is not sufficient to do this, the earnings must be reduced by any further amount required merely to maintain the existing rate of return. If this is not done the rate will be too low for use as a cut-off rate on new projects.

Another factor should be considered when using the approach illustrated above. Reference to example 3 shows that the gross cost of debt was computed at 13·04 per cent, because no reference was made to redemption. This would be reasonable if the period to go to redemption was very long or the debentures were irredeemable. If as was demonstrated in example 1, however, the redemption period is near then this becomes a factor of significance as the rate computed of 15 per cent with four years to go indicates. The latter rate would, therefore, provide a better guide to the current cost of debt to the firm than that used in example 3 and should be substituted for the lower rate.

The Capital Asset Pricing Model

Traditional methods were based largely on an extension of securities analysis, described as the process of estimating risk and returns of alternative investments in relation to the time-span concerned. This is fundamental to each particular choice so the problem of **portfolio management** is to combine the best of these alternatives into a selection which will meet the needs and objectives of particular investors. The process is similar to that used when making a particular choice for expenditure of capital within the firm and similar unsophisticated techniques can be used. However, in the same way as the econometric techniques of risk analysis and discounted cash flow were applied to the investment decision within the firm, similar quantitative techniques were developed for use in the optimisation of portfolio selection.

In the now standard work *Portfolio Selection: Efficient Diversification of Investments,* Harry M. Markowitz advocated a more mathematically biased approach. His contention was that the investor is 'risk-averse', a term implying that investors are reluctant to invest and must be tempted to part with their money by the offer of a risk premium. At the other end of the scale is the gambler or risk seeker who looks for opportunities involving risk or chance. Markowitz suggested that the investor would seek to maximise the expected return and minimise the variance from it. The expected return is computed, as is any other expected value, statistically; it is the weighted average of the expected return of each security in the portfolio. The weighting factors here are in respect of risk and this raises issues as to how risk can be satisfactorily measured. In common with game theory, it assumes that rational behaviour is to minimise the risk.

This brief summary is much simplified as the whole theory is highly complex and the subject of special texts and studies. As with the Modigliani–Miller thesis (page 104), it may be criticised as being impractical by virtue of the assumptions made, but the same arguments used in defence of that approach apply here. Theories of this nature and the empirical studies used to support or condemn them, force the advocate or critic to isolate the variables, identify the constraints and clarify thinking and practice on the subject. This invariably has some practical side benefits at least.

In order to minimise risk, most investors—individuals or institutions—do not have all their funds in one investment. Attempts are made to create a portfolio or selection of alternatives that will maximise the objective of the investor with the minimum risk of loss. The portfolio will in particular cases depend upon the objective as previously described—i.e. do we wish to maximise current income, ultimate growth or maximum capital profits. Attempts to formulate a general approach to portfolio construction along lines suggested by Markowitz were developed by W. F. Sharpe ('Capital Asset Prices—A Theory of Market Equilibrium under Conditions of Risk', *Journal of Finance*, September 1964).

The basic premise was that subject to certain constraints the expected return from an individual equity investment incorporates a measure of its own risk when compared with overall market performance.

The main constraints or assumptions were:

(*a*) *Perfect capital market*—no transaction costs or taxes and all investors had access to relevant information.

(*b*) *Homogeneous Expectations*. The view of all investors on expected rates of return, degree of variation and relationship between differing securities was identical.

(*c*) *The time horizon* was identified for all investors—that is the time span considered relevant for decisions was the same for all investors.

These assumptions would appear very unrealistic but work done to date by institutions such as the London Business School suggests that the model works even when they are withdrawn.

The measure of risk of an individual share when assessed against the overall market performance is termed a Beta (B) coefficient.

The theory of the CAPM states that the return on an investment R is equal to the risk free rate of interest plus a risk premium multiplied by the Beta coefficient. When depicted graphically it produces a straight line known as the SML (Security Market Line)—see Fig. 8—and the basic equation becomes:

$R_j = R_f$ plus $(R_m - R_f)B_j$

where R_j = return expected on investment

R_m = return expected on the market portfolio$_m$

R_f = risk free rate of interest

B_j = the Beta coefficient measuring systematic risk for investment$_j$ relative to risk for the market as a whole

Rates of return in general can be thought of as comprising two elements—a reward for *time* and a reward for *risk*:

R_f is the pure interest (time) rate

R_m is the total return on the *overall* stock market

Thus the term $(R_m - R_f)$ represents the risk premium, i.e. the difference between the pure interest (time) rate and the average return on the market as a whole.

The Beta coefficient of an individual security measures the riskiness of the share relative to the overall stock market risk being measured by whether the share price rises or falls more or less than proportionally to changes in the overall stock market.

Securities having risk characteristics equatable to the market as a whole have a Beta coefficient of 1·0. If they are susceptible to greater risk the coefficient will be greater than 1·0, whilst if they are subject to a lower degree of risk the coefficient will decline until the return equates with the risk free rate, i.e. Beta will be zero. This can be represented graphically (see Fig. 8).

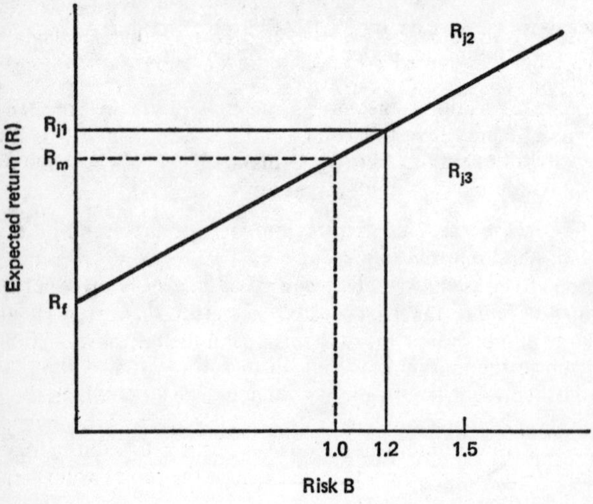

Fig. 8

On the graph the single line (SML) connects and rises through the points R_f and R_m. The minimum return equates with a portfolio comprising all risk free securities and R_m corresponds to a portfolio having risk characteristics equatable with the market as a whole, e.g. *The Financial Times* All Share Index. At this point B would be equal to 1·0. A security or portfolio having a B factor less than 1·0 would be less risky than the market as a whole whilst a security or portfolio having a B factor in excess of 1·0 would be subject to higher risk and raise the required rate of return.

Expected Rate of Return

A simplified formulation for computing the required rate of return would be:

Expected Rate of Return = Short term interest rate
plus risk premium
(both net of personal taxes)

thus if:
(i) 15% is the Treasury Bill rate.
(or similar rate such as Gross yield to redemption on long dated securities)
(ii) standard rate of personal taxation is 30%
(iii) market risk premium $R_m - R_f$ is 10% net
(iv) B equals 1·0

then

$$\text{Required Return} = 15\ (1 - 0{\cdot}30) + 10$$
$$= 10{\cdot}5 + 10 = 20{\cdot}5\%$$

B is equal to 1·0

If a *particular* security had a B factor of 1·2 then required rate of return

$$= 15\ (1 - 0{\cdot}30) + 1{\cdot}2\ (10)$$
$$= 10{\cdot}5 + 12 = 22{\cdot}5\%$$

and this would be the equity rate to be used in investment calculation. In situations involving a weighted cost of capital (as discussed from page 102 onwards) it would provide a value for K_E.

For Investment appraisal

R_{j1} Indicates the expected return for utilisation in projects as computed (22·5%).

For market use

R_{j2} Would represent the position of an actual security which the analyst expects to be on the SML with a Beta of 1·5. Since it is above the line its return is *higher* than anticipated suggesting a buying situation. If a large number of buyers take this action the return will fall bringing R_{j2} on to the market line.

R_{j3} Could represent the position of an actual security which the analyst expects to be on the SML with a Beta of 1·5. Since it is below the line its return is lower than anticipated suggesting a selling situation. If a large number of sellers take this action the return will rise pushing R_{j3} up to the market line.

This is only the first stage in the development of the model. Important modifications have to be made in respect of corporate (i.e. company) taxation since we need to know what returns companies have to earn (gross) on their assets in order to satisfy shareholders. Under the UK imputation system the amount of payout (i.e. dividend policy) will also affect the issue. Secondly most companies are not entirely equity financed—loan capital is a regular part of the financing structure. The cost of this and the different taxation treatment require that a weighted cost of capital be taken into consideration when considering hurdle rates for particular projects.

The above paragraphs represent a minimum outline of the final conclusions. Students preparing for professional accounting examinations will require more extensive knowledge for which a prerequisite would be the economic and statistical studies carried out earlier. The remaining paragraphs and examples are primarily for the benefit of readers so qualified.

The extent to which an investor is risk averse can be represented by indifference curves. These show the various combinations of risk and return at which the investor is indifferent to choice and are illustrated graphically in Fig. 9.

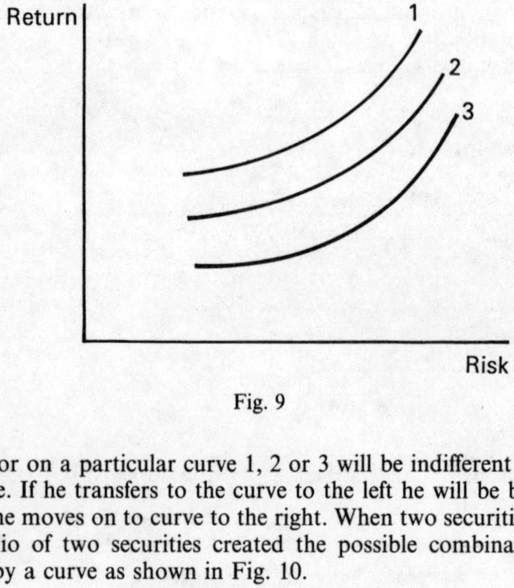

Fig. 9

The investor on a particular curve 1, 2 or 3 will be indifferent to any move on that curve. If he transfers to the curve to the left he will be better off and vice versa if he moves on to curve to the right. When two securities are mixed, i.e. a portfolio of two securities created the possible combinations can be represented by a curve as shown in Fig. 10.

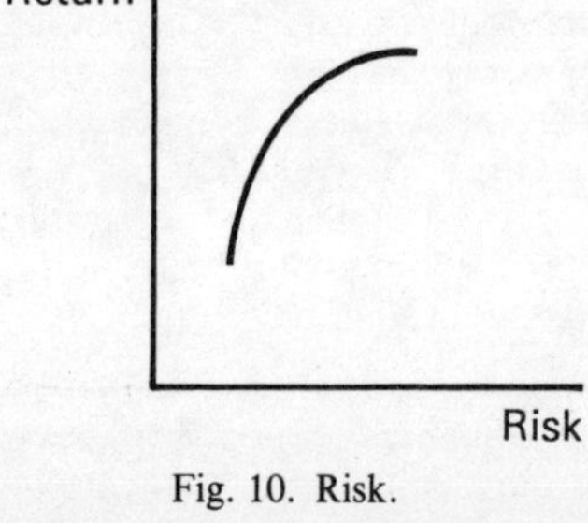

Fig. 10. Risk.

As the number of investments in the portfolio is increased the possible combinations are greater but if all the opportunities relative to the size of fund and time horizon are considered they are limited. In Fig. 11 the shaded area represents the potential choices in the Markowitz model.

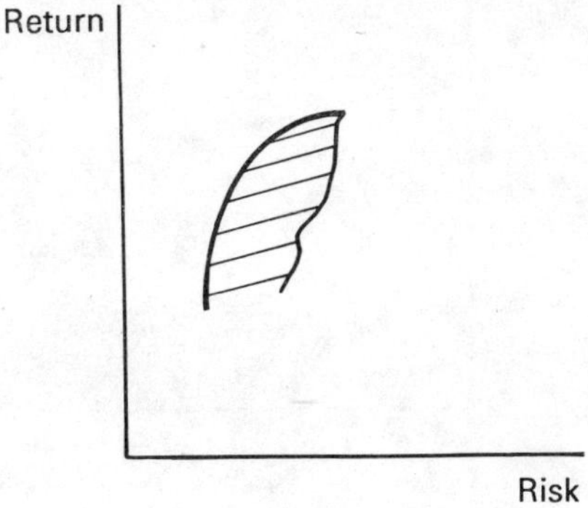

Fig. 11

For any situation, and as specified above in the model constraints, an investor who is risk averse will choose the portfolio offering maximum return for minimum risk. This is termed the **efficient frontier**. Any move to the right will produce higher risk and/or lower returns, and combinations to the left do not exist. If Fig. 9 and Fig. 11 are combined the optimal portfolio can be identified as shown in Fig. 12.

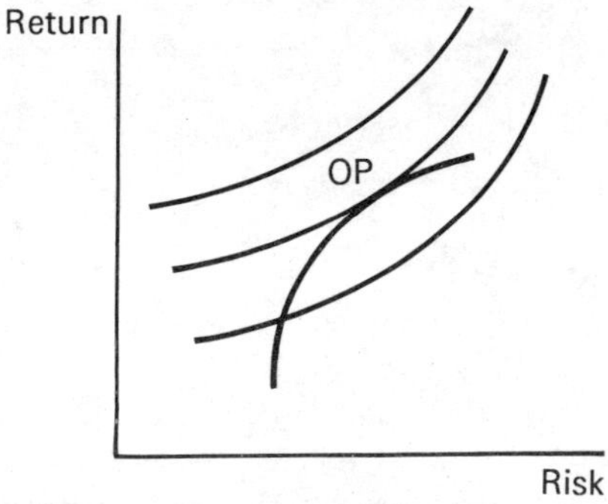

Fig. 12

The point OP on an indifference curve which corresponds to an identical point on the line of the efficient frontier will represent the optimal portfolio but only if fixed interest risk free securities are excluded. In Fig. 13 Rf represents the risk free rate of lending (and theoretically borrowing). If an investor puts part of his funds into these investments it will reduce his overall risk. This will enable him to move to a higher indifference curve. Since the point on the return line Rf is determined by the rate applicable at the time of choice the best portfolio combination will be that which joins the risk free rate Rf tangentially to the maximum point on the efficient portfolio curve (M). This gives a similar graph to that shown in Fig. 13.

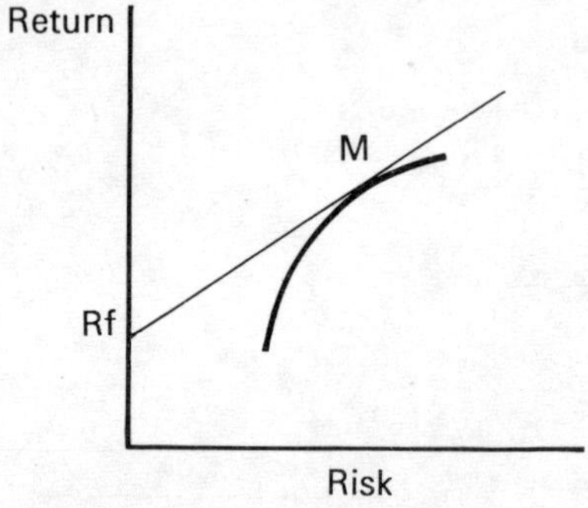

Fig. 13

We have seen above that the risk premium in the capital asset pricing model CAPM is designated the Beta factor (symbol B or β). Calculus and statistics can be used to show that:

(*a*)
$$\beta = \frac{\text{Covariance pf,i}}{\text{Variance pf}}$$

where Covariance pf,i is the covariance of expected returns of existing portfolio (pf) and the returns of the new investment (i) or (in the case of investment appraisal) the new project. Variance pf is the variance of the returns of existing portfolio.

There is a convenient relationship between the variance and the standard deviation of a series and this provides an alternative way or means of expressing Beta.

(*b*)
$$\beta = \text{Correlation pf,i} \times \frac{\sigma \text{i}}{\sigma \text{pf}}$$

where Correlation pf,i is the correlation coefficient between the portfolio returns and the individual investment returns. σpf is the standard deviation of the portfolio returns. σi is the standard deviation of the individual investment. The correlation coefficient is usually designated by the Greek letter ρ (rho) but Corrpi is used here to provide guidance. Similarly pf has been used to identify the portfolio to avoid confusion with p (for probability) used below.

Example 4

The manager of AB plc has to decide on an investment proposal costing £100,000. The potential conditions have been reduced to four corresponding to forecast economic and other conditions. The probabilities stated below are associated with the conditions designated A, B, C and D together with expected returns. Evaluate the proposal using the CAPM method.

Situation	*Probability* p	*Return on existing portfolio* *Rpf* (%)	*Return on new investment* R_i (%)
A	0·4	18	13
B	0·3	20	14
C	0·1	12	8
D	0·2	30	22

The risk free rate is 7 per cent.

The problem can be solved using Formula (*a*) or (*b*). Since it requires additional computations to use (*b*) this is included only to show that they produce identical answers. The subsequent example gives data for the second formula already worked out hence the necessity to be aware of both formulae.

Workings

We need to compute the weighted averages for Rf and R_i before we can compute deviations:

$$\bar{R}_{pf} = (0{\cdot}4 \times 18) + (0{\cdot}3 \times 20) + (0{\cdot}1 \times 12) + (0{\cdot}2 \times 30) = 20{\cdot}4$$

$$\bar{R}_i = (0{\cdot}4 \times 13) + (0{\cdot}3 \times 14) + (0{\cdot}1 \times 8) + (0{\cdot}2 \times 22) = 14{\cdot}6$$

Situation	p	*Rpf*	R_i	$Rpf - \bar{R}pf$	$R_i - \bar{R}i$	*Variance*	*Covariance*
A	0·4	18	13	−2·4	+1·6	2·304	−1·536
B	0·3	20	14	−0·4	−0·6	0·048	+0·072
C	0·1	12	8	−8·4	−6·6	7·056	+5·544
D	0·2	30	22	+9·6	+7·4	18·432	+14·208
						27·840	+18·288
a	*b*	*c*	*d*	*e*	*f*	*g*	*h*

Column e = Difference between 20·4 and column c
Column f = Difference between 14·6 and column d
Column g = Variance of returns on existing portfolio $= \sum (b) \times (e)^2$
Column h = Covariance of expected returns on the existing portfolio and those of new investment $= \sum (b) \times (e) \times (f)$

$$\text{Beta} = \frac{\text{Covariance pf,i}}{\text{Variance pf}}$$

$$= \frac{18{\cdot}288}{27{\cdot}84} = 0{\cdot}657$$

R_i = Required rate of Return = Rf + β(Rpf − Rf)

$$R_i = 7 + 0{\cdot}657(20{\cdot}4 - 7)$$
$$= 15{\cdot}8$$

Situation C shows a return less than this.

Using Formula (b)

$$\text{Correlation } \rho \text{ (rho) pfi} = \frac{\text{Covariance pf,i}}{\rho\sigma\text{pf}, \sigma_i}$$

Covariance pf,i is computed as in Column *h* above $= +18{\cdot}288$. σpf is equal to $\sqrt{\text{Variance pf}} = \sqrt{27{\cdot}84} = 5{\cdot}276$.

We need to compute the variance of i in order to compute σ_i:

p	R_i	pR_i	$R_i - \bar{R}_i$	$p(R_i - \bar{R}_i)^2$
0·4	13	5·2	−1·6	1·0240
0·3	14	4·2	−0·6	0·108
0·1	8	0·8	−6·6	4·356
0·2	22	4·4	+7·4	10·952
	$\bar{R}_i =$	14·6	$\bar{R}_{pf} =$	16·44

$$\sigma_i = \sqrt{16{\cdot}44} = 4{\cdot}054$$

$$\text{Correlation pf,i} = \frac{18{\cdot}288}{5{\cdot}276 \times 4{\cdot}054} = 0{\cdot}855$$

$$\text{From } (b) \text{ Beta} = \text{Correlation pf,i} \times \frac{\sigma_i}{\sigma \text{pf}}$$

$$= 0{\cdot}855 \times \frac{4{\cdot}054}{5{\cdot}276}$$

$$= 0{\cdot}657 \text{ as before}$$

It may not be necessary to prove the above relationships but knowledge of the formulae and ability to transpose them would be required from final professional students. Frequently the statistical factors given above will be given and the student will be expected to work out the conclusion. A typical problem including gearing and the aspects already illustrated is given in example 5 as a consolidating exercise.

Example 5

A colleague has been taken ill. Your managing director has asked you to take over from the colleague and to provide urgently needed estimates of the discount rate to be used in appraising a large new capital investment. You have been given your colleague's working notes, which you believe to be numerically accurate.

Working notes

Estimates for the next 5 years (annual averages)

Stock market total return on equity	16%
Own company dividend yield	7%
Own company share price rise	14%
Standard deviation of total stock market return on equity	10%
Standard deviation of own company total return on equity	20%
Correlation coefficient between total own company return on equity and total stock market return on equity	0·7
Correlation coefficient between total return on the new capital investment and total market return on equity	0·5
Growth rate of own company earnings	12%
Growth rate of own company dividends	11%
Growth rate of own company sales	13%
Treasury bill yield	12%

The company's gearing level (by market values) is 1:2 debt to equity, and after tax earnings available to ordinary shareholders in the most recent year were £5,400,000 of which £2,140,000 was distributed as ordinary dividends. The company has 10 million issued ordinary shares which are currently trading on the Stock Exchange at 321 pence. Corporate debt may be assumed to be risk free. The company pays tax at 35 per cent and personal taxation may be ignored.

Required:

(*a*) Estimate the company's weighted average cost of capital using:
(i) The dividend valuation model.
(ii) The capital asset pricing model.

State clearly any assumptions that you make. Under what circumstances would these models be expected to produce similar values for the weighted average cost of capital?

(*b*) You are now informed that the proposed investment is a major diversification into a new industry, and are provided with the following information about the new industry.

Average industry gearing level (by market value) 1:3 debt to equity
Average payout ratio 55 per cent
Average Beta coefficient (β equity) 1·50

Using any relevant information from parts (*a*) and (*b*) prepare a brief report recommending which discount rate should be used for the investment. Any relevant calculations not included in your answer to part (*a*) should form part of your report.

(*c*) Discuss the practical problems of using the capital asset pricing model in investment appraisal. (CACA)

Solution

(*a*) (i) *The dividend valuation model (pages* 99 *and* 241)

If dividends are expected to grow at 11 per cent then the earnings required to meet this dividend would be:

$$\frac{\text{Dividend per share}}{\text{Current Market Price}} \times 100 + 11$$

$$\text{The dividend per share is } \frac{£2{,}140{,}000}{10{,}000{,}000} = 21{\cdot}4 \text{ pence}$$

This is the current year (0) so that predicted dividend for first year of forecast with 11 per cent growth rate will be $(D_1) = 21{\cdot}4 + (11\% \times 21{\cdot}4\%) = 23{\cdot}75$.

$$\text{Cost of Equity } K_e = \frac{D_1}{p} \times 100 + 9\ (\%) \text{ (See pp. 99–102)}$$

$$= \frac{23{\cdot}75}{321} \times 100 + 11 = 18{\cdot}4\%$$

Since the cost of debt capital is not given it must be assumed to equate with the Treasury Bill yield of 12 per cent. However, Corporation Tax is allowed against this so that after tax cost is $12(1 - 0{\cdot}35) = 7{\cdot}8$ per cent. The ratio of debt to equity is 1:2 ∴ $\frac{1}{3}$ of the total capital is debt and $\frac{2}{3}$ equity.

The weighted cost of capital (WACC) is therefore equal to (7·8 per cent $\times \frac{1}{3}$) + (18·4% $\times \frac{2}{3}$) = 14·87 per cent.

(ii) *The Capital Asset Pricing Model*

$$\beta e = \text{Coefficient of Correlation e,m} \times \frac{\sigma e}{\sigma m} \quad \text{(As equation } (b) \text{ page 117)}$$

where Coefficient of Correlation e,m is the correlation coefficient (ρ – rho) between total own company return on equity (e) and total stock market return on equity (m).

σ_e is the standard deviation of own company return on equity.
σ_m is the standard deviation of total stock market return on equity.

Cost of Equity $r_e = r_f + \beta(r_m - r_f)$

$$\beta e = \frac{20 \times 0{\cdot}7}{10} (\%) = 1{\cdot}4$$

$$r_e = 12 + 1{\cdot}4(16 - 12) = 17{\cdot}6\%$$

$$\text{WACC} = 7{\cdot}8 \times \tfrac{1}{3} + 17{\cdot}6 \times \tfrac{2}{3} = 14{\cdot}33\%$$

They would equate when the stock market is in equilibrium and inputs to the model are correctly expressed.

(*b*) For a geared company (as above) the combined Beta is:

$$\beta_g = \beta_{\text{ungeared}}\left(1 + (1 - t)\frac{D}{E}\right)$$

For the industry β_g is equal to β for the equity as the Treasury yield is assumed to be risk free, producing zero for the expression $\frac{D}{D+E} \times$ zero, since any expression multiplied by zero is zero. The Beta factor for the asset is initially as for an ungeared company so substituting above: 1·5 represents β_g for the average gearing ratio of all companies combined:

$$1{\cdot}5 = \beta_{\text{ungeared}}(1 + (1 - 0{\cdot}35)\tfrac{1}{3})$$

$$1{\cdot}5 = \beta_{\text{ungeared}}\ 1{\cdot}217$$

$$\therefore \beta_{\text{ungeared}} = \frac{1{\cdot}5}{1{\cdot}217} = 1{\cdot}233$$

Beta for the asset is therefore 1·233.

The asset Beta now has to be regeared in line with the gearing of the particular company:

$$\beta(\text{geared for company}) = \beta_{\text{asset}} \times \frac{E + D(1 - t)}{E}$$

$$= 1{\cdot}233 \times \frac{2 + 1(1 - 0{\cdot}35)}{2}$$

$$= 1{\cdot}233 \times \frac{2{\cdot}65}{2}$$

$$= 1{\cdot}634$$

Finally the adjusted Beta factor must be incorporated into the basic model:

$R_i = R_f$ plus $(R_m - R_f)\beta_i$
$= 12 + (16 - 12) = 1{\cdot}634$
$= 18{\cdot}54\%$

The weighted average cost of capital for the project is therefore:

$7{\cdot}8\% \times \frac{1}{3} + 18{\cdot}54\% \times \frac{2}{3} = 14{\cdot}96\%$

Suggested rate is 15%.

Long-Term Sources of Capital

The Market for Long-Term Funds

New issues of capital are made either when a company is getting a public quotation for its shares—i.e. transferring its status from a private company—or when large amounts of additional capital are required by an existing quoted company. The motives which encourage the change of status from a private company are usually:

(i) The company has outgrown the ability of the existing owners either to finance it or control it effectively.

(ii) Major shareholders may have died or a scheme is being devised to reduce the effect of taxation when this occurs. Alternatively, the existing shareholders may not have the ability or the interest of the founder of the company in its continuance or may simply require liquid funds for themselves.

The various national and localised stock exchanges provide facilities for the continuous marketing of new and existing securities. Most new issues even for large firms are handled by intermediaries acting on behalf of the vendor. These include specialist issuing houses, merchant banks and, more recently, departments created for this purpose by the clearing banks.

They offer advice on alternative methods, timing, price and promote confidence in the issue by virtue of their status and reputation.

The issues of securities is made in one of the following ways.

Offer for Sale

This is the most popular form for medium-sized companies or those changing status to quoted companies for the first time. Under this method the issuing house purchases the shares and then issues them to the public. It has the merit that the amount that will be received by the company is known—the issuing house fixes a price sufficiently above the price it has itself paid to cover its own expenses and charges. The offer for sale includes full details of the company in a similar form to that prescribed for a prospectus when a public issue is made. Since it is the document used to promote the effective sale of shares it should present all the facts about the company as clearly and attractively as possible.

Public Issue

This is another form of offer for sale but in this case it is made directly by the company concerned to the potential investors. The expenses of printing, advertising and complying with Stock Exchange requirements for this type of issue are high. To be successful and economic the amount required must be substantial and the reputation of the firm considerable. Because of these factors the large established company is more likely to raise money by means of a rights issue, i.e. by direct appeal to its existing shareholders.

Tender

This form of offer is less common than either of the above. The public are invited to subscribe for shares at a price above a stated minimum. The shares are then offered at one price above this minimum at which sufficient bids have been received for all the shares on offer. The company, therefore, receives the benefit of any premium which is created should the issue be successful.

Placings

These can be either private or public depending on the circumstances. A **private placing** is achieved by negotiation between a company which is too small to achieve a quotation and investment trusts or other institutions which are prepared to invest in the company. Thus the shares of the placed company became part of the investments of the quoted company purchasing them, but are not quoted directly on the Stock Exchange.

A **public placing** is one in which shares to a value not in excess of £350,000 are placed—up to 75 per cent of the value may be placed directly with selected institutions but at least 25 per cent must be available to jobbers to create a market for dealings in the normal way.

Introduction

A company may desire a public quotation for its shares primarily to assess their value rather than to raise new capital. The Stock Exchange may in this event permit shares to be 'introduced' provided there are a minimum of 50 shareholders and existing shareholders are prepared to make sufficient shares generally available if necessary to create a market. This method may also be used where the shares concerned are already quoted on another stock exchange.

Strictly speaking the stock exchange is not a source of finance as it does not itself provide the required money. Savings of individuals or firms are the source and these are invested via the stock exchange in a form of security which the particular investor finds attractive. The importance of individuals has tended to lessen with the growth of institutional investment. By institutions in this sense is meant enterprises which first collect individual savings and then become a major subscriber to be reckoned with. The large insurance companies and pension funds in particular have taken on a dominant role, channelling a multitude of small incomes into equity investment. This does not mean that other investors will necessarily follow the lead of the institutions—although these are advised by professionals, but since such advisers are not risking their own funds their attitudes to risk may be different from that of the single investor. Over the last three decades the performance of the market has been erratic. The boom (so called go-go) period of the 1960s was replaced by severe reluctance on the part of small investors to subscribe. This was due to a large variety of reasons such as high inflation, high taxation and limitation of dividends compared with interest rates on fixed interest stocks which offered better returns for less risk. The rate of economic—particularly industrial—growth was small in mid-1976, for example, a major issue of shares in one company attracted fewer than 500 applications from the public and three-quarters of the shares were left with the underwriters in spite of being promoted by several issuing houses. Contrary to this a large number of rights issues were successful. It would appear that investors were prepared to respond to requests from existing companies, with a demonstrated history of performance and in which they already had an interest but the appeal of a newcomer was restricted.

This situation gradually changed and in the next ten years an almost permanent 'bull', i.e. continuously rising market, emerged. The general public became aware, through large share issues such as TSB, British Telecom and British Gas, of the attractions or otherwise of shareholding. Most subscribers were able to make profits on the new issues if they did not wish to retain them and prices generally showed continuous growth. Facilities for share dealings were gradually widened culminating in the so called 'Big Bang' bringing British practice more into line with other international stock exchanges. Financial institutions were permitted with effect from 1st March 1986 to own Stock Exchange subsidiaries resulting in easier buying and selling for the small investor. This was followed on 27th October 1986 by the abolition of the segregation between the duties of brokers and jobbers, and changes in the methods of computing charges and commissions.

There was a huge jolt to this situation when the international stock markets collapsed on 19th October 1987, the so-called 'Black Monday'. During the following week the American Dow Jones and British Financial Times share indexes fell below their year's levels by 36·1 per cent and 32·1 per cent respectively. A major issue of shares by BP planned for this time became overpriced and subscribers anticipating a 'stag' profit found themselves in a loss situation. The unprecedented step was taken of the government intervening and offering to buy back the shares at a guaranteed price. This is dealt with more fully in Chapter 10. A brief exposition is given here to indicate the volatility of local and world markets and to demonstrate that **Timing** of an issue is the most important factor in getting the best deal. The irrelevance and unreality of the theoretical and practical techniques used for pricing and forecasting, and the credibility of the experts to guarantee the accuracy of their advice has not been more effectively brought into question than by these events of late 1987.

Admittedly the stock exchange exists to allow the normal levels of supply and demand to operate and if confidence is not forthcoming then the logical result would be that firms concerned would not be able to raise money and continue in existence, as demonstrated by the demise of some previously established firms in certain industries such as Rolls-Royce, BSA and others. In other instances, because of political policies concerned with maintenance of employment and other factors, the government has intervened as a major supplier of funds. Whether this is desirable in the particular industries concerned is a matter for debate elsewhere but it is important that these influences should be recognised and borne in mind when working through the examples which follow later. These merely illustrate the conventional approach to analysis of the data primarily for demonstration purposes. The data for a practical exercise will be available in similar form though in greater detail, but the skill lies in relating the figures computed to the situation prevailing at the time.

In addition to insurance companies and pension funds the other major institutional investors in equities are the investment trusts and unit trusts. The two should not be confused. **Investment trusts** are companies formed for the collective investment of money subscribed by shareholders. They can acquire unquoted securities, underwrite quoted securities and subscribe for capital issues including those they underwrite. They also subscribe to the specialised institutions listed later. **Unit trusts** are similar in operation but minimum subscriptions are lower, there are legal differences and restrictions on the type of shares in which it can invest. A holder wishing to relinquish his holding can sell it back to the unit trust whereas a share in an investment trust is negotiable on the stock exchange in the normal way.

Venture Capital

The repetitive criticism by various parties of the failure of the banking and financing sector to provide the required type or amounts of money for industrial investment and expansion, led to the creation, after the Second World War, of various **special financial institutions** to assist or supplement government intervention. Although the objectives were roughly the same the methods adopted tended to vary with the political party in power. An early example was the ICFC (Industrial and Commercial Finance Corporation) established in 1945. This incorporated certain specialised groups such as EDIT (Estate Duties Investment Trust), AMC (Agricultural Mortgage Corporation) and TDC (Technical Development Capital). This prospered, became FFI (Finance for Industry) and all the activities were ultimately incorporated into the 3i group which is described separately below.

The National Enterprise Board (NEB) was the controversial brainchild of the 1974 Labour government. Funds were provided directly by the government and went to support mainly firms such as British Leyland (Austin Rover) and the reconstructed Rolls-Royce. In most instances the objective was to maintain employment which invited criticism that there was little long-term gain in employing people if their output had no market or the firm could not compete effectively in it. Under successive Conservative governments of the 1970s and 1980s it has gradually been eroded.

Most established companies have little difficulty in obtaining finance from the market, banks or other institutions. It is small and medium-sized organisations which have problems. The original Radcliffe Committee of 1958 produced a report emphasising the lack of availability of finance for this section of the business community and spawned a variety of agencies such as those above, primarily through cooperation between the government and institutions such as commercial banks and insurance companies. A similar committee was set up in 1977 headed by ex-prime minister Sir Harold Wilson. Its brief was similar to that of the previous committees—the MacMillan Committee on Finance and Industry (1931) and the Radcliffe report on the working of the monetary system (1959). The former identified a need for financial sources for small and medium companies (the so-called MacMillan Gap) and the latter the extent to which that gap had been filled. The Wilson Committee concluded that it was the **price** of finance rather than the lack of sources which rendered this section of the financial market difficult.

Venture capital can be defined as providing capital to individuals, partnerships and (mostly) non-public companies. All capital is in a sense 'venture' capital since returns are not absolutely certain but it is the higher degree of risk carried by the projects concerned which justifies the adjective being used in this sense. Similarly, most venture capital implies equity (ordinary) shares investment although the investors may frequently come up with combined packages of loans, debt capital and equity. Where capital is supplied to larger businesses with an established track record the risk is lower and the term 'development capital' is frequently used. The early 1980s saw a large increase in the number and style of institutions prepared to supply venture capital. The Stock Market was buoyant, the public had been made more aware—by various privatisation issues of large undertakings such as British Telecom and British Gas of the existence and function of the Stock Market. This culminated in an increase in the outlets for sale and purchase of shares the so called 'Big Bang'. Subsequently events of October 1987 tended to create a more pessimistic outlook but this is more related to investment and is described in Chapter 10.

Banks, insurance companies and other groups are now much more interested in competitive supply of venture capital, frequently operating through specialised subsidiaries. Nevertheless, any project is subject to rigorous vetting and criteria.

Details of the tasks and functions for which the investment is required would be very similar to those described below for Investors in Industry. A detailed description of their range of activities therefore provides an indication of the range and function of the totally private sources.

Investors in Industry (3i) plc

The functions of the original ICFC and its subsidiaries were subsequently incorporated into a holding company—Investors in Industry plc or 3i. The shareholdings are restricted at present to the Bank of England and the major clearing banks. The make-up of the shareholding according to the accounts for the year to 31st March 1987 was as follows:

Shareholders		%
Bank of England		14·98
Bank of Scotland		3·11
Barclays Bank plc		18·80
Lloyds Bank plc		13·66
Midland Bank plc	16·13	
Clydesdale Bank plc	1·84	17·97
The Royal Bank of Scotland plc		7·56
National Westminster Bank plc	22·93	
Coutts and Co	0·70	23·63
Waterloo Trustee Co Ltd		0·29
		100·00

The group provides permanent and long-term investment capital as well as advice to businesses of all types. It can provide amounts up to £50m for all types of projects and operates through a network of twenty-five regional offices plus City connections. It has a special reputation for helping Britain's small and medium-sized businesses via loans, shares, hire-purchase, leasing and financial guarantees. The company has no government subsidy and is a profit-making concern. It therefore adopts the same approach as other commercial institutions and makes around 1,000 investments a year. It has a good pedigree and has been instrumental at some stage in the development of some internationally known companies such as the Trusthouse Forte Group. The method and sphere of operations in common with other venture capital suppliers is to work along the following guidelines.

The company recognises four main 'product' streams according to the chief executives' review of 1987. These are as follows:

(i) **Start ups.** This is where an individual (or several individuals) have a new product or service they wish to launch. Such an undertaking is likely to be too risky for local bank managers. The risks are high as possibly no more than 10 per cent are successful but the present climate is to encourage such innovation.

(ii) **Management Buyouts.** There was a spate of takeover activities in the 1970s and 1980s. Frequently when the mergers were completed the enlarged company found itself with some activities which did not fit in with the major objective of the new group or were unwanted for other reasons. Managers of these activities are increasingly seeking the assistance of 3i (and similar institutions) to take over the companies in which they have their experience and expertise. Sometimes it is not only management but workers as well who combine and companies are not always particularly small. National Carriers is a good example of how an undesired activity owned by British Rail was bought out and developed in this way. Frequently debt capital, rather than equity, forms a substantial part of the package in order to leave the locus of managerial control undisturbed.

(iii) **Private Placements.** This is more likely in a growth, development or retirement situation. An established business may need to find a partner for expansion or to realise partial holdings in order to pay death duties or provide for retirement of a partner. In this case a proportion of the equity shares are placed with individuals or institutions leaving controlling interest with the existing ownership.

(iv) **Development Capital.** These are funds required for financing major projects or reorganisations. The company is probably medium sized and this will enable growth to join the Unlisted Securities Market (USM) or ultimately to become a public limited company (plc). The following figures extracted from the report of 3i plc (for year to 31st March 1987) are included here as an indication of the scale of its operations:

New investment £368m (£61m from retained profit).
£198m raised worldwide in five different currencies bringing total to £267m invested in 1,400 companies over five years.
£101m invested in 109 management buy outs.
13 companies joined the USM.
15 companies obtained full market status.

The company has several subsidiaries specialising in consultancy, 'High Tech' companies, property portfolio management and corporate finance. Together with banks, pension funds, insurance companies and the BES scheme it is a major contributor to venture capital.

Government Sources and Assistance

The government acts as it sees fit to create a balanced climate for all activities. This may be carried out through direct and indirect fiscal and other policies. The government may change tax rates, ceilings and allowances for investment but successive governments of either political belief have created some institutions and a brief history of the major activities has been given on page 124. The following is a list of some of the forms of assistance available, particularly to small companies and distressed areas at the time of writing.

Business Expansion Scheme

This scheme was designed to channel funds directly from higher rate taxpayers into approved schemes. It was introduced in 1981 and by 1986 was estimated to have raised £700m for venture capital. Significant tax advantages are granted to the investor. Investment of sums up to £40,000 per annum are allowable against an individual's higher rate tax. The original termination date of 1986/7 has now been extended. To qualify for the tax concessions a large number of conditions must be complied with, the salient ones being:

(i) The shares must be in an unquoted UK trading company.
(ii) No individual must own more than 30 per cent of the equity of the company.
(iii) Shares must be held for five years and subscribed for by the investor.
(iv) The investor must not be connected with the company.
(v) Such holdings cannot be used to create losses.

The 1988 Budget proposed a limit of £500,000 on the amount which could be raised by any one company under the scheme in any one year.

Finance for Assisted Areas

Areas with high unemployment or higher than average unemployment are designated **assisted areas**. These areas are mostly in the coastal parts of Wales and Cornwall, the West Coast of Scotland and other selected areas. There are two grades which determine the assistance available.

Development areas: These are eligible for regional development grants and regional selective assistance (see below).

Intermediate areas: Eligible for selective assistance only.

Development areas are mainly around Glasgow, Newcastle, North and South Wales and the extreme west of Cornwall. Intermediate areas include the West coast of Scotland, coastal areas of Wales, the Midlands and around Lands End. Status is determined by the time taken for potential employees to travel to work.

(i) *Regional Development Grant:* This applies only to development areas and as such the project must:

(*a*) Provide assets and/or create jobs in the area.
(*b*) Either create new or expand existing capacity.
(*c*) Result in a material change to a product or process.
(*d*) Relate to a qualifying activity. (This is a list of manufacturing and service activities compiled by the Department of Trade and Industry.)

There are limits and conditions but a general level of assistance is 15 per cent of approved capital expenditure or £3,000 per new job created. This is being phased out in 1988 in favour of Regional Selective Assistance.

(ii) *Regional Selective Assistance:* These are discretionary grants available to both grades of assisted area:

(*a*) The project must have potential to achieve viability in three years.
(*b*) The Department of Trade and Industry must be satisfied the project will not take place without the grant on the basis proposed.
(*c*) Existing employment must be safeguarded and/or additional employment created.
(*d*) The project must contribute to regional or national benefit.

There are two main forms of assistance:

(*a*) *Project Grants:* These are negotiable and based on eligible costs of capital expenditure—fixed or working capital; or the number of jobs created or maintained.
(*b*) *In-Plant Training Schemes:* These provide finance for essential training costs forming an integral part of a project which qualifies for Regional Selective Assistance. It may cover up to 80 per cent of such costs.

Business Improvement Services

These are supported by the UK government and the European Regional Development Fund. The objectives were to help new firms to start up and existing small firms to expand, particularly in areas affected by job losses in shipbuilding, textiles, steel manufacture, mining and fishing. This effectively means mainly North England, East Midlands, South West England and Wales. Scotland has similar facilities. A total of £100m was made available for assistance in starting up a business or paying consultants. To assist the start up funds are provided for:

(*a*) Business check up.
(*b*) Management and financial services.
(*c*) New product studies.
(*d*) Computer applications.
(*e*) Other consultancy.
(*f*) Common services (groups of small firms sharing facilities).
(*g*) Investment projects.

In addition finance can be obtained to engage Providers of Services (indirect consultants). These can be engaged for such investigations as:

(*a*) Market research.
(*b*) Risk appraisal.
(*c*) Common services.
(*d*) Advisory and counselling.
(*e*) Databases.
(*f*) Employing enterprise personnel.

In all the above activities the firm concerned has to provide part of the costs varying between 30 per cent and 50 per cent. There is a maximum grant under each heading and the scheme is being modified from 1988.

Support for Innovation

Finance is available to encourage firms to undertake research and development projects of an innovative nature. Sums available are between £100,000 and £5m and the proportion varies between 25 per cent and 50 per cent of the total.

Small Firms Loan Guarantee Scheme

This was a scheme started in 1981 whereby the government did not provide the money directly but 70 per cent of any loan obtained from any bank under the scheme was underwritten by the Government. Small sole traders, partnerships or limited companies were eligible with a maximum amount of £75,000 and time span of 2–7 years.

Enterprise Zones

The Department of Environment set up special areas to encourage industrial and commercial activity in areas of opportunity. Sites were usually land left derelict by unrequired facilities such as surplus steel manufacture (Dudley). There were over twenty such areas in July 1987. They do not receive finance directly but are granted benefits extending up to ten years. These include exemption from local authority rates and up to 100 per cent allowances for Corporation Tax and Income Tax for expenditure on Plant and Machinery, Land and Buildings, Non-financial inducements such as speedier planning approvals are also included.

There are other direct sources of finance in addition to the above. A full list is available from the Department of Trade and Industry. Applicants should, however, note the timescale for approval and also 'cash limits' imposed by the government at a particular time may delay receipt of agreed payments. There are also a great variety of small firms advisory services run by the appropriate departments of universities, polytechnics, banks and other institutions. While not providing funds they may provide free, or at subsidised rates, the expertise essential in the early stages of the birth of a business.

Ordinary Shares

Ordinary shares are valued either on an earnings basis or an assets basis. In a going concern one would expect the earnings basis to predominate since if the net assets per share were worth more than the market price it would be better to sell up and reinvest in other activities. As the ordinary shares normally carry control through their voting power, a fight for control may force up the market price of the share temporarily and thus introduce a factor other than the anticipated earnings. There are ordinary shares without voting powers and there are also deferred ordinary shares which are usually issued to the original vendors as part of a settlement.

New Issues

In determining a price for a new issue, the price is set within a range left open as long as possible until the actual timing of the issue. The factors to be considered in assessing the range are:

(*a*) Market rating of similar quoted shares.
(*b*) General state of the economy and political and international issues at the time.
(*c*) State of the particular industry concerned.
(*d*) The size of the issue relating to the total investment in similar securities already quoted.

(*e*) Yield required by investors in similar companies in terms of dividends and earnings.

This can be illustrated by considering the following tabulation. Assuming that investors expect an earnings yield of 8 per cent net of tax, the maximum amount of capital which can be supported at this rate can be computed by dividing the maintainable average annual net earnings by the earnings yield. The estimated price per share will then depend on this figure and the number of shares issued.

	A (£)	*B* (£)	*C* (£)
Average maintainable earnings	20,000	30,000	40,000
Taxation at 52%	10,400	15,600	20,800
	9,600	14,400	19,200
Earnings capitalised at 8%	120,000	180,000	240,000
	$\left(£9{,}600 \times \frac{100}{8}\right)$	$\left(£14{,}400 \times \frac{100}{8}\right)$	$\left(£19{,}200 \times \frac{100}{8}\right)$
Price per share:			
40,000 shares	£3·00	£4·50	£6·00
80,000	£1·50	£2·25	£3·00
100,000	£1·20	£1·80	£2·40

If dividend yields are used these will be adjusted by means of the cover sought and the tax rate applicable to give the gross earnings required. A dividend yield of 4 per cent, twice covered, will correspond to a required earnings yield of 8 per cent since both are net of corporation tax. If the value of a share and number of shares are known or predetermined then a required earnings level can be computed.

Dividend yield required	4%
Cover	2
∴ Earnings yield	$= 2 \times 4\% = 8\%$
Taxation rate	52%
∴ Gross earnings rate required	$= 8 \times \frac{100}{48} = 16{\cdot}6\%$
Number of shares	= 40,000
Market price per share	= £3·00
∴ Market value of capital	= £120,000
Earnings level required	$= £120{,}000 \times 16{\cdot}6\% = £20{,}000$

Rights Issues

A rights issue is an offer for sale of shares to existing shareholders, such shares being offered in the proportion that the shareholders' existing holdings bear to the existing total number of shares issued. A range of prices can be assessed. It is usual for the offer price to be pitched below the current market price in order to provide some incentive for subscription. The extent of the gap will be determined by the increment of profit the new capital is expected to contribute. It must at least maintain parity with the existing rate otherwise the market price of the existing shares will be pushed below their current level and the value of the rights jeopardised.

Factors to consider are the existing share price, the forecast earnings level, the number of shares already in issue and the minimum capital required.

Example 6

Issued ordinary share capital	
1,000,000 shares of 50p (nominal value)	£500,000
Market price per share	£2·50
Existing earnings after tax per annum	£180,000
It is anticipated that this will increase after the rights issue to:	£200,000
Amount required (exclusive of expenses)	£400,000

It is therefore necessary to consider:

(i) What additional amount must be added to the £400,000 required to cover expenses of issue.

(ii) What number of shares are to be issued.

(iii) At what price they will be issued.

Determining the Ratio

For the reason stated (i.e. there would be no rights value attached) the price must be below £2·50. The number of shares required at this price to raise £400,000 would be

$$\frac{£400{,}000}{£2{\cdot}50} = 160{,}000$$

This means that 16 shares would be offered for every 100 held. Should we wish to raise a larger sum than £400,000 and keep the price below £2·50 we can determine upper and lower limits of share price for any particular ratio. More shares than the above 160,000 are required to be issued, so try 20 shares for each 100 existing, i.e. 1 for 5, which would indicate 200,000 additional shares.

Assuming expenses are expected to amount to 10 per cent of the sum required, the total requirements are £440,000.

One for five (200,000 shares)

Minimum sum required is £440,000

Lowest price is therefore $\frac{£440{,}000}{200{,}000} = £2{\cdot}20$

The average value per share after the issue would be determined as follows:

5 existing shares at £2·50	£12·50
Add 1 additional share at £2·20	£2·20
	£14·70

New market price per share $= \frac{£14{\cdot}70}{6} = £2{\cdot}45$

Value of rights per old share:

$$= \frac{\text{New market price} - \text{Cost of new share}}{\text{No. of shares required to purchase one new share}}$$

$$= \frac{£2{\cdot}45 - £2{\cdot}20}{5} = £0{\cdot}05\text{, or 5p per share}$$

One for four (250,000 shares)

Minimum sum required is £440,000

$$\text{Lowest price is therefore } \frac{£440{,}000}{250{,}000} = £1{\cdot}76$$

The relevant data at a variety of prices could then be tabulated:

Possible price (£)	*Amount raised* (£)	*Ex rights price* (£)	*Rights per old share* (£)	*Earnings per share* (£)	*Earnings Earnings* (%)	*p/e ratio*
1·76	440,000	2·35	0·1475	0·16	6·81	14·68
1·80	450,000	2·36	0·14	0·16	6·78	14·75
2·00	500,000	2.40	0·10	0·16	6·67	15·00
2·10	525,000	2·42	0·08	0·16	6·61	15·13
2·20	550,000	2·44	0·06	0·16	6·56	15·25
2·30	575,000	2·46	0·04	0·16	6·50	15·38
2·40	600,000	2·48	0·02	0·16	6·45	15·50
2·50	625,000	2·50	—	0·16	6·40	15·63
a	*b*	*c*	*d*	*e*	*f*	*g*
	$(= a \times 250{,}000)$	$\left(= \frac{£10 + a}{5}\right)$	$\left(= \frac{c - a}{4}\right)$		$\left(= \frac{e}{c} \times 100\right)$	$\left(= \frac{c}{e}\right)$

The relationships are linear and can be determined from graphs as indicated in later examples. The figures produced for this and other ratios would provide only indications of the possible alternatives. The dividend rate was not given, but assuming a rate of 20 per cent on the nominal value of the share this also could be worked out on the proposed prices and compared with existing and projected figures. It would normally be stated whether or not it was expected that present dividend rates would be maintained and the following tabulation assumes a constant dividend.

Dividend rate = 20% of nominal value (50p) = £0·10 per share

$$\text{Existing dividend yield} = \frac{£0{\cdot}10}{£2{\cdot}50} \times 100 = 4\%$$

Since the average (ex-rights) price is now lower the dividend yields on the ex-rights prices are in excess of 4 per cent. The dividend yield on the new share is higher still as it is related to the price paid for this share.

Price		Dividend yield on	
New shares (£)	Ex-rights (£)	New shares (%)	Ex-rights (%)
1·76	2·35	5·68	4·26
1·80	2·36	5·56	4·24
2·00	2·40	5·00	4·17
2·10	2·42	4·76	4·13
2·20	2·44	4·54	4·10
2·30	2·46	4·35	4·06
2·40	2·48	4·17	4·03
2·50	2·50	4·00	4·00
a	*b*	*c*	*d*
		$\left(= \frac{10p}{a} \times 100\right)$	$\left(= \frac{10p}{b} \times 100\right)$

Column *c* indicates the dividend yield on the new or marginal investment. Since it is at a rate determined by the nominal value it is a fixed amount per share of 10p and average rate of dividend yield on the new market price is represented by column *d*.

If the rights issue is anticipated, dealers on the stock exchange may have marked the price down in anticipation that some of the existing shareholders will either not wish to take up the rights or may not have the liquid resources to do so.

Under favourable conditions this would be compensated by the fact that firms making rights issues are normally expanding and the downward movement will quickly be arrested if evidence of good performance is forthcoming. Again for reasons stated previously, the attitudes of investors may be completely misjudged and the issue fail or be taken up by underwriters.

Preference Shares

Preference shares were originally a popular form of long-term security with a variety of types. They could be preferential as to payment of dividends and repayment of capital, with or without participating or cumulative rights. Since the introduction of the corporation tax system, however, which allowed interest on debt capital for relief against profits but did not extend this concession to preference holders, their appeal has declined to the extent of being a rarity among new issues.

With a high taxation level the advantage to the firm is obvious. If the corporation tax rate is 50 per cent, earnings required to pay 8 per cent on preference shares would be 16 per cent of the sum concerned whereas earnings required for debenture interest payments would equate with the coupon rate.

Debentures, Convertible Loan Stock and Share Warrants

The characteristics of the pure debenture have already been described on page 98. A firm can, however, issue convertible loan stock, which is a form of security that combines the appeal of fixed interest securities with an opportunity to change into an equity holding at a later stage, if desired. The terms and dates of possible conversion are stated at the time of issue, the holder acquiring a right to substitute ordinary shares at a fixed ratio to his holding of stock. The value of the conversion rights can be ascertained by comparing the value of the security as a pure debenture at contract terms with the market value of the shares at the conversion date.

The cost of such capital to the firm will be the interest payment on the debt. An issue of convertibles is likely to be successful in a period when the investor is fairly confident of growth, thus making the later possible conversion a profitable operation to him. This accounts for the high volume of such issues in the late 1960s and early 1970s. Firms can use this method when they either require money for particular capital expansion or alternatively when short-term borrowing has become excessive and it is desired to make the capital structure more permanent. The subscription money raised would be utilised in paying off overdrafts, etc. Such a firm could still trade on the equity, i.e. the existing equity holders would benefit from the growth generated until such time as conversion was made, when benefits would have to be shared.

The coupon rate paid on convertibles would be lower than offered on the straight debenture since the investor is being given the option of an alternative future form of investment. If the company fails to make progress the maximum cost to the company is known—it equates with the interest costs plus any redemption commitments. It is the investor who will lose as the anticipated favourable increase in share price will fail to materialise and he will decline to take advantage of the conversion possibilities but can still obtain his interest and return of the capital sum.

Example 7

Offer price per £100 nominal value =	£100, i.e. par value
Coupon rate	12%
Period to redemption	20 years
Convertible after 5 years	
Conversion rate	60 ordinary shares per £100 nominal value
Share price at time of issue	£1·30
Current cost of fixed interest finance for similar companies	15%

If it is desired to compare the likely position in five years' time a growth rate for the shares must be predicted. This could be based on earnings forecasts at the time of the issue or the investor's assessment by reference to the variables affecting growth. Suppose this is estimated at 6 per cent p.a.; then using the compound interest formulae:

$$\begin{aligned}\text{Projected share price} &= P(1+r)^n\\ &= P(1+0{\cdot}06)^5\\ &= 1{\cdot}30(1{\cdot}3382)\\ &= £1{\cdot}74\end{aligned}$$

where P is the present price, r the growth rate, and n the number of years.

In five years' time the stock will have 15 years to run as a straight fixed-interest investment. Assuming the cost of finance is still 15 per cent, the value of the investment at that time can be computed as equivalent to an annuity of £12 p.a. and a single repayment of £100 in 15 years' time when the current cost of money is 15 per cent.

	Present value of £1 *at* 15% *of*: Annuity	Single repayment	Total
Interest receipts £12	5·847		£70·2
Redemption £100		0·123	£12·3
			£82·5

The projected share price in five years is £1·74 and the holder entitled to 60 shares in total; therefore the exchange value would be 60 × 1·74 = £104·4. If the forecast rate of growth has been achieved, conversion is acceptable at this point. If the growth rate had been only 1 per cent p.a. then the share price would be £1·30 × $(1{\cdot}01)^5$ = £1·30 × 1·051 = £1·366, and exchange value would be 60 × £1·366 = £81·6. This is almost equal to the value of the security as a pure debenture. In five years, however, the fortunes of the firm in particular or the economy in general may have completely changed and, if due to depressed conditions the market price of the share had fallen to £1, then the exchange value is only £60 and the investor will retain the fixed interest stock.

Share Warrants

A share warrant is a document that entitles the holder to subscribe at some future period and at a predetermined price to an issue of shares in a company. They carry no interest and may entitle the holder to one share or more per warrant. When the warrant is for more than one share any quoted figures are given per share. Warrants are variously described as **subscription rights** and **options**, and the latter term more clearly describes their intent. They are usually offered as an *added* inducement to subscribe for loan stock: thus a company might issue 12 per cent unsecured loan stock with option to subscribe for 50 shares at 80p per share for every £100 of loan stock held during the years 1985–1990. The distinction between this and the convertible loan stock should be clear. In the case of the convertibles the investor subscribes his initial investment as a loan and sometime in the future either *exchanges* his loan certificate for a share certificate or the company redeems the debenture—there is no additional capital provided. In the case of a warrant the investor has the option to subscribe *additional* funds to the company at some future date.

The warrant holders may exercise the option on their own behalf or they may—in the case of a quoted company—sell their options on the stock exchange. Most warrants are issued in settled periods and when indications of growth are good. The investor anticipates that the share price will move upwards during the period in which he may exercise his option. He will then be able either to purchase a share well below the market price at the time or sell the option—the greater the gap between the fixed price at which he can buy a share and the market price of the warrant the greater will be his gain. If things have not gone well with the company the market price per share could be below the fixed subscription price. In this event there would be little point in exercising the option at that time as the shares concerned could be bought cheaper on the open market. Any investors purchasing the warrants at this stage are gambling on a recovery in the fortunes of the company. Warrants are negotiable so that the initial holder can transfer his option at its own market price.

From the point of view of the company it is the dilution effect on earnings per share when the new shares are issued which is of importance. The market price is related to earnings per share by means of the price/earnings ratio. Analysts will always compare the performance on an actual basis and also on the position if and when all the options were taken up. Unless the growth in profits is sufficient to match the increased number of shares partaking in it then earnings per share will reduce and market price will be affected accordingly.

Retained Earnings

A firm may decide to use the surplus cash generated from its operations for reinvestment rather than in payment of dividends. Generally the factors which determine the decision to invest or distribute are:

(i) The level of dividends previously paid and currently expected by investors in the class of share concerned. This level may be artificial in the sense that it may be legally determined or restricted (dividend restraint); therefore it is necessary to consider carefully the extent to which this factor is free to operate.

(ii) The effects of the personal taxation systems on the dividends received. Comprehensive analyses have been prepared to assess the effect on investment motivation of the differential tax rates affecting investors with differing incomes. From the point of view of assessing cost of capital to the company it is reasonable to ignore these on the grounds that the market price effectively represents the weighted views of all investors in the demand price.

(iii) The distinction made by the taxation system as to the rate to be applied to distributed as opposed to undistributed profits. If there is no distinction then choice is not affected. If there is a considerable difference—as where taxation policies are designed to encourage reinvestment rather than distributions—then this must be taken into account.

(iv) Retained earnings are normally considered in the accounting sense as profit available after distributions and provisions have been made. This is net of a figure for depreciation, usually on historical cost. In the sense in which the term is used here it should be further adjusted to represent the actual cash surplus available after all distribution and after making suitable provision at current prices to maintain the existing earnings position.

If the firm is able to use the surplus funds to increase the rate of return on the capital as a whole then retention is justified. This means that the project for which the funds are required must be tested to see if the rate of return is higher than that existing at present. But the question arises yet again as to which rate, i.e. determined on what basis. A start can be made by using market price and existing earnings per share but the cost of capital computed on this basis could be amended by any significant factors known to the firm or adjusted in accordance with one of the formulae incorporating growth. The one essential is that genuine effort is made to ensure that projects potentially financed from internal sources are assessed on as intensive a basis as those for which extra funds are required from external sources.

Share Issues not Providing Additional Funds

A company may on occasion issue shares which do not result in the raising of additional finance. Originally known as **bonus issues** or **capitalisation issues**, other terms now used are **free** or **scrip issue** since the word 'bonus' in particular implies the giving of something extra when this is in fact not so. A scrip issue may be made in lieu of paying a cash dividend, in which case obviously there is no monetary payout by the company but the shareholder has the opportunity of selling the shares should he prefer cash.

Alternatively, an issue may be made to bring the nominal share capital more into line with market values. This may be desirable on the one hand because the market price per share is high and inhibiting dealings or because the dividend *rate*—related to the nominal value—is high although the *yield*—related to the market value—is only reasonable.

Example 8

Balance sheet of AB Ltd as at 30th September

Issued share capital	£
50,000 ordinary shares of £1	50,000
Revenue reserves	25,000
	75,000
Represented by	
Net tangible assets	75,000
Market value per share	£2·00

It is proposed to make a scrip issue of one £1 nominal value ordinary share for every two now held.

Show the effect of the proposals on the balance sheet of AB Ltd after the scrip issue and indicate the position of the holder of 100 shares, before and after the issue.

On a balance sheet basis each share is worth $\frac{£75,000}{50,000} = £1{\cdot}50$ before the issue. After the issue the balance sheet will appear as:

Issued share capital	£
75,000 ordinary shares of £1	75,000
Represented by	
Net tangible assets	75,000

On a balance sheet basis each share is now worth $\frac{£75,000}{75,000} = £1{\cdot}00$.

Before the issue the shareholder had 100 × £1·50 = £150 equity interest. After the issue the shareholder has 150 × £1·00 = £150 equity interest, i.e. his position is unaltered.

Market Values

Total market value before scrip issue = 50,000 × £2·00 = £100,000

Total market value after scrip issue = £100,000

But since there are now 75,000 shares each share is worth $\frac{£100,000}{75,000} = £1{\cdot}33$.

Market value of 100 shares before scrip issue = 100 × £2 = £200

Market value of 150 shares after scrip issue = 150 × £1·33 = £200.

The above figures demonstrate how *theoretically* the financial position of the shareholder is unaffected in terms of total valuation. In *practice*, his total value will probably be affected since the market may take the view that the dividend rate (in the absence of legal restraint) may be maintained at the same level on the new nominal holding. Thus if a rate of 10 per cent was being paid before the issue, the dividend due on a holding of 100 £1 shares would be £10, but after the issue the entitlement with a *maintained* rate of 10 per cent on a holding of 150 shares would be £15. In view of this increased distribution the share price may move upward. Conversely, if existing and potential investors take a pessimistic view of the company's potential then the share price will move downward.

For similar reasons a company may decide to split its shares, i.e. to reduce their nominal value. If each £1 nominal value share is converted to two 50p shares then the market value of each original share will be halved. The distinction between this and the operation described in the previous paragraph is that there would be no movement out of reserves to nominal capital on the balance sheets. The total nominal share capital would remain unaltered and only the quantity and par value of the shares would be affected; a maintained dividend of 10 per cent would provide only the same sum in dividends as previously.

Short-Term Sources of Capital

Term loans are postponements of financing; they must be paid back out of future earnings. The short-term needs of a business will be of a temporary nature, when it has good expectations that its future cash flows will improve sufficiently to repay the loan within a period of about one year. Factors giving rise to such needs will include:

(*a*) Seasonal trade fluctuations.
(*b*) A trade surge or an unusual marketing opportunity.
(*c*) An unusual transaction.
(*d*) A circumstance peculiar to the business, such as the failure of a debtor or a contract loss.
(*e*) Particular expectations not realised.

Such conditions can linger and give rise to medium-term measures, especially when the circumstances are not immediately recognised and it is discovered that the condition is a general shortage of money rather than one particular to the business.

Sources of finance for relatively short periods—up to one year—are:

Trade suppliers
Bank overdraft
Acceptance credits
Factoring

Trade Suppliers

This is probably the first source to which a business turns when negotiations are formally made to defer payments or when accounts are not paid on due date. Businesses generally resort to this method in times of finance shortages with everyone tending to lean on everyone else, i.e. delayed receipts from debtors leading to reciprocal treatment to the creditors. When it would be normal practice to take discounts for prompt payment the cost of deferring settlement will be the lost discounts. Success will depend much upon the strength of the parties and care is needed to avoid a cutting-off of essential supplies or precipitative action by a creditor in taking legal recourse for settlement. Safeguarding liquidity by deferring payments does not introduce new funds into the business.

Bank Overdrafts

Banks lend on overdraft by permitting a business to overdraw its account up to a specific limit. This facility should ideally be used for temporary situations, often being kept in reserve for unusual events. The big advantage to the borrower is its flexibility, particularly in that interest is charged on the daily balances. However, disadvantages can arise in its uncertainty of tenure and the variability of the interest rate. In times of general shortage of money or enforced measures to reduce lending initiated through the Bank of England, banks reduce overdraft facilities and as the interest rates are based upon the minimum lending rate controlled by the Bank of England the costs of borrowing can fluctuate detrimentally. In October, 1976, for example, a then record minimum lending rate of 15 per cent was enforced with consequential rates of 16–20 per cent for overdrafts, depending upon the type of borrower.

Overdrafts are granted on the personal judgment of the bank manager, who will consider the trade and economic climate operating at the time. He bases his judgments on his knowledge of the company and its management and he would require an evaluation of the needs for the loan and the forward prospects against a background of its past performances. He will be sensitive to the current value of the assets, the funds invested by the proprietors and the ultimate situation in the event of a liquidation. The bank will invariably insist on a first charge and may require specific collateral security on the fixed assets, or specific realisable assets or a floating charge on the business as a whole. In the event of apparent deficiencies of cover or abnormal risk the directors may, individually and collectively, be required to enter into contractual guarantees.

Acceptance Credits

A bill of exchange for a specific period is drawn upon a merchant bank who accepts it, either against securities or some other proof of ability to honour at due date such as a particular trading transaction. The business discounts the bill with a discount house at rates usually lower than overdraft rates. The discount house recoups its advance at due date either from the drawer or the merchant banker who was virtually guaranteeing the bill by his acceptance.

The bill can be drawn on a customer and discounted after acceptance but the reactions of the discounting house will be governed by its knowledge of the acceptor, or drawee, and it may be necessary to obtain the further acceptance of a merchant bank by way of guarantee.

Acceptance credits in the form of documentary credits operate more widely in the export market.

Factoring

A factor advances sums to a business in need against the specific security of its debtors. The advance is usually 80–90 per cent of selected debtors, for which an interest charge is made for the period. The business assigns the indebtedness to the factor, who sometimes intervenes to collect the debts direct or, if it is wished that their participation be kept confidential, then the business collects and transfers the receipts to the factor acting as his agent.

Additional and optional services are offered by factors to control administratively the debtors of the business. This will involve the sales ledger accounting, order approvals and payment control. A service fee is charged by the factor.

The intervention of the factor will focus upon the risk of bad debts which he will seek to safeguard against by his selection of specific debtors against which to make his advance or by credit control at the order stage, in which event the business may find itself under constraint in its marketing efforts.

Medium-Term Sources of Capital

Medium-term requirements of funds can be interpreted as from one to five years or so, and each of the sources mentioned above for short-term temporary requirements can often be extended for longer periods: trade suppliers for as long as their patience will last, the overdraft at the bank manager's judgment, acceptance credit by the use of the revolving credit, and the factor's advance by contractual arrangement. Additional sources for the medium-term will include:

Bank loans
Finance house loans
Hire purchase
Leasing

Bank Loans

These differ from overdrafts in that they are negotiated agreements for the advance of particular sums for stated periods at a stable interest rate over the life of the loan, which may depend upon the economic climate when the loan is contracted. Periods are negotiable but banks usually operate upon a maximum term of 10 years. Such loan agreements will be specific as to cover, the payment of the interest and the capital redemption which may commence after, perhaps, the initial two years. The borrower will therefore incur defined commitments and failure to meet them can incur recourse to the remedies defined in the agreement, including liquidation.

Finance House Loans

Loans are available from finance institutions in a similar way as from banks. Some may be prepared to accept higher degrees of risk than others but this will be reflected in higher interest rates.

Hire Purchase

Purchases of most commercial and industrial fixed assets can be obtained through hire purchase from finance companies who specialise in this type of facility, with repayments spread over periods of 2–3 years. Usually the seller is a party to the transaction—in fact, the availability of hire purchase may comprise an element in his own marketing strategy to attract his customer. The finance house usually prefers to remit the purchase price direct to the seller and negotiate the hire purchase agreement direct with the purchaser. There are mutual benefits to both the buyer and the seller; the latter receives prompt payment in full and the former the relief from finding the purchase price in full by paying interest and capital over the prescribed period while taking immediate delivery of the asset and, in effect, paying out of earnings.

Acquisition of buildings is not suitable for hire purchase because of the limited repayment period.

Leasing

Leasing of industrial plant and equipment is more readily available than at first seems apparent and applies to specific requirements in a manner similar to hire purchase. A leasing agreement is entered into with a finance house for specific periods or the life of the equipment, which remains the property of the finance house which obtains the appropriate tax allowance as owners. The leasing charge ranks as an allowed expense for tax for the lessee, who although never owning the equipment is required to keep it maintained and who is able to meet the leasing charge out of the new marginal earnings.

Leasing does not bring in new money to the business but it obviates finding the capital sum and introduces additional earning capacity. Leasing agreements will often permit withdrawal after one year but this will depend on the versatility of the equipment.

Hiring performs a similar service, but whereas leasing applies to plant of specific requirements of a business and is covered by a formal agreement, hiring applies to equipment of common appeal for casual periods of time, sometimes inclusive of operator. It is particularly attractive where the hirer has too little need to justify purchase. Hiring operates extensively in the field of contractors' plant and there are hiring businesses who acquire plant solely for the purpose of hiring.

Worked Examples

1. Assessing Merits of Alternative Forms of Issue

The following data relate to B Ltd:

Issued capital 500,000 ordinary shares of £1 each
No fixed interest capital

	£
Earnings before tax	120,000
Corporation tax (assumed at 45%)	54,000
Earnings after tax	66,000
Price/earnings ratio: 16	

It is intended to raise further capital amounting to £600,000 by one of the following methods:

(i) an issue of 20-year debenture stock at 6 per cent per annum;
(ii) a one-for-one rights issue priced at £1·20 per share;
(iii) a three-for-four rights issue priced at £1·60 per share;
(iv) a three-for-five rights issue priced at £2·00 per share.

You are required to answer the following questions:

(*a*) For a shareholder who had purchased his existing holding at the current market price, at what level of earnings before interest and tax would a rights issue be more beneficial than the debenture issue?

(*b*) Assuming the price/earnings ratio remained unchanged, what level of earnings before tax would be needed to ensure that the shareholder did not suffer a capital loss?

(*c*) What factors would be taken into account in deciding which scheme of rights issue should be adopted? (CIMA)

This problem, although set from the point of view of the investor, nevertheless illustrates some of the factors to be considered by the firm if any of the alternatives are to be successful as an issue.

Part (*a*)

The factor that relates the data given to the existing market price is the earnings yield and this is determined as

$$\frac{\text{Earnings per share after corporation tax}}{\text{Market price of share}} \times 100$$

or

$$\frac{\text{Total earnings available to equity}}{\text{Market value of equity}} \times 100$$

If a debenture issue is made then there is an immediate commitment (prior charge) to pay the interest before any earnings are available at all to existing shareholders.

If a rights issue is made the earnings yield will be determined by the level of profits available to the existing market value of the equity plus the total additional capital subscribed.

The requirement is therefore that the return on investment after the new capital injection must be greater than that at present being employed. We can first establish then the point at which either alternative is equal. The answer can be determined graphically or algebraically.

Solution by graph: If a debenture issue is made there is a commitment to pay £36,000 p.a. of the earnings before anything is available to shareholders. The existing earnings before tax are £66,000 + 54,000 = £120,000.

Debenture Issue: At this level the earnings yield can be computed as follows:

	£
Pre-tax profits	120,000
Debenture interest gross	36,000
	84,000
Taxation (45%)	37,800
	46,200

$$\text{Earnings yield} = \frac{£46{,}200}{16 \times £66{,}000} \times 100 = 4{\cdot}375\%$$

Minimum gross earnings of £36,000 must be achieved before any earnings are available for equity interests; therefore, when earnings are £36,000 with a debenture issue the earnings yield will be zero. The relationship between gross earnings and earnings yield in this instance is linear and we can therefore indicate this by joining the two values as indicated in the graph (Fig. 14).

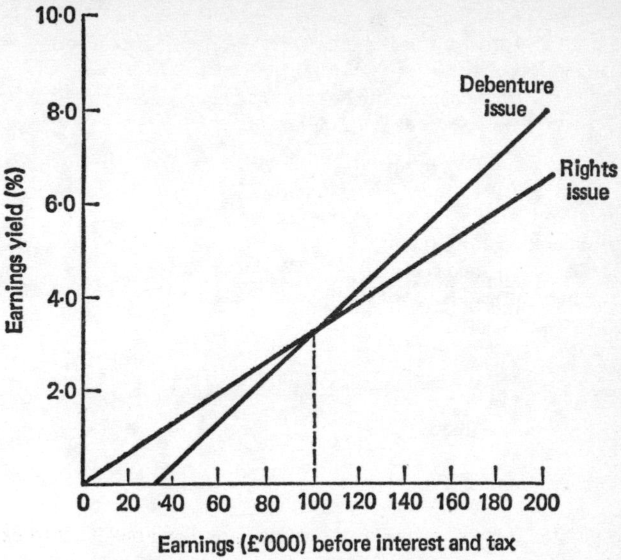

Fig. 14. Relationship between earnings yield and pre-tax earnings.

Rights Issue: When gross earnings are zero the earnings yield on all shares is zero. At the existing level of earnings of £120,000 the earnings yield is computed thus:

	£
Pre-tax profits	120,000
Taxation (45%)	54,000
	66,000

	£
Market value of existing shares (£66,000 × 16)	1,056,000
Additional subscription	600,000
	1,656,000

$$\text{Earnings yield} = \frac{66{,}000}{1{,}656{,}000} \times 100 = 3{\cdot}99\%$$

These two values can also be plotted on the graph in Fig. 14 as indicated.

Deductions from graph:

(i) At gross earnings of approximately £100,000 the earnings yield is the same with either form of issue. Below this figures the earnings yield is *higher* with a rights issue than with a debenture issue. Above the figure of £100,000 the fixed charge for interest has a lessening influence and therefore the debenture issue is to be preferred. A rights issue would therefore be more beneficial for earnings between zero and £100,000.

(ii) This does not mean that the shareholder will be as well off as before the investment. The words 'more beneficial' are interpreted as meaning which is the better position at the level of earnings concerned.

(iii) The break-even position can be predicted algebraically by simply relating the two positions. Let x equal gross earnings:

(1) Earnings for equity interests = 55% $(x - 36{,}000)$
Market value of equity = £1,056,000

(2) Equity issue
Earnings for equity interest = 55% x
Market value of equity = £1,656,000
Dividing both sides by 1,000 then at break-even

$$\frac{0{\cdot}55(x - 36{,}000)}{1056} = \frac{0{\cdot}55x}{1656}$$

$$580{\cdot}8x = 910{\cdot}8x - 32{,}788{,}800 \text{ (by cross-multiplying)}$$

$$330x = 32{,}788{,}800$$

$$x = \frac{32{,}788{,}800}{330}$$

$$x = £99{,}360$$

$$\text{Earnings yield} = \frac{\text{Profit after tax}}{\text{Market value of equity}}$$

$$= \frac{0{\cdot}55(£99{,}360)}{£1{,}656{,}000} \times 100$$

$$= 3{\cdot}3\%$$

If this is the break-even it can be confirmed by checking with the debenture alternative and the same earnings yield of 3·3 per cent:

Required earnings after tax = 3·3% × £1,056,000	= £34,848
∴ Earnings before tax	= £34,848 × $\frac{100}{55}$
	= £63,360
Add debenture interest	= £36,000
Total pre-tax earnings	£99,360

Note: (1) The number of shares does not affect the conclusion if earnings yield is used as a criterion. (2) No provision is made for redemption of debentures. If this were done it would overstate the cost since it is a repayment of the original capital. The additional provision required can be computed as an annual provision for 20 years out of taxed earnings or the lower annual provision required if such provision is specifically invested in interest-earning securities.

Part (b)

Here the requirement is that the shareholder does not make a capital loss.

Debenture Issue: The current market price has been determined by pre-tax earnings of £120,000. The additional earnings required if the £600,000 is raised by a debenture issue is equal to (£600,000 at 6 per cent) £36,000; therefore the minimum earnings to maintain the share price would be the sum of these, i.e. £156,000.

Rights Issue:

Existing market value =	£1,056,000
Additional investment =	£600,000
New market value	£1,656,000

The existing p/e ratio of 16 must be maintained if the shareholder is to suffer no capital loss.

$$\therefore \quad \text{Required earnings after tax} = \frac{£1,656,000}{16}$$

$$\text{and required earnings before tax} = \frac{£1,656,000}{16} \times \frac{100}{55} = £188,181$$

Part (*c*)

Factors to be taken into account in deciding which scheme of rights to be adopted include:

(i) The state of the market and the relative value of the rights as inducement to subscribe.

(ii) Rating and trends of B Ltd shares and that of similar companies.

(iii) The dividend yield and cover in B Ltd and related companies.

(iv) The success or otherwise of recent rights issues.

(v) The extent to which growth of earnings per share is diluted by the increased number of shares.

(vi) Assuming shares carry voting rights, the extent to which change in ownership could affect change in control. This could be the case if a large number of existing shareholders sold or assigned their rights.

Alternative Solution

Earnings yield was taken as the criterion in the first approach but *earnings per share* could also be used. This would result in an extreme answer with a one for one rights issue since to maintain the existing earnings per share the additional £600,000 capital would have to generate the same earnings as the existing market value of £1,056,000. The figures can, however, be produced for illustration:

	Debenture	*Rights issue*
	£	£
Existing pre-tax earnings	120,000	120,000
Debenture interest	36,000	—
	84,000	120,000
Taxation at 45%	37,800	54,000
	46,200	66,000
Earnings per share	*pence*	*pence*
with debenture issue—500,000 shares	9·2	—
with rights issue—(1 for 1) making 1,000,000 shares		6·6
(3 for 4) making 875,000 shares		7·54
(3 for 5) making 800,000 shares		8·25

Again we can establish alternative points on the earnings per share graph (Fig. 15) either by assuming another earnings level or considering the condition for the earnings per share to be zero. With a debenture issue £36,000 will still be required, whereas with a rights issue of any ratio earnings per share will be zero when gross earnings are zero. From Fig. 15, a rights issue would be more

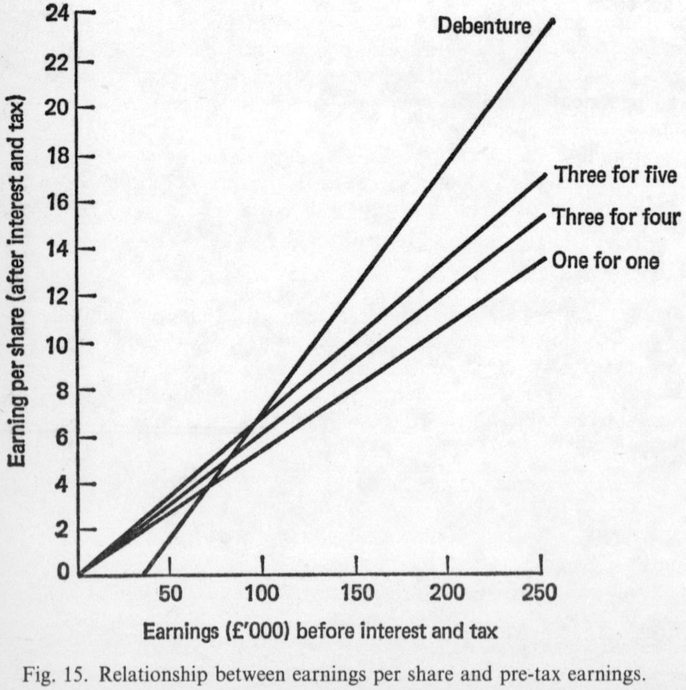

Fig. 15. Relationship between earnings per share and pre-tax earnings.

beneficial than a debenture issue only up to the following earnings levels:

Rights issue of one for one	£72,000
Rights issue of three for four	£84,000
Rights issue of three for five	£97,500

2. Preparing Forecast and Testing Borrowing Power

(*a*) Borrowing is said to add to the risks of a business. You are required to outline and comment on the normal methods of risk measurement by the borrower.

(*b*) The table below summarises the accounts of A Ltd for the year ended 30th June 19x8.

The company proposes to raise £750,000 by means of a 6 per cent debenture issue during the current year ending 30th June 19x9, to cover an expenditure of £300,000 on land and buildings and £400,000 on plant and machinery.

Sales and profits in the current year are expected to be the same as those for year ended 30th June 19x8, and thereafter to increase significantly. However, this expectation must be qualified by the possibility of a business recession arising shortly. It is thought that this recession, if it materialises, could commence during the two years January 19x9 to December 19y0, but during the year ending June 19y0 is regarded as the most likely time. The likely pattern of sales and expenses during the possible recession is given in the notes which follow the accounts.

You are required to:

(i) Prepare a forecast to indicate A Ltd's capability of supporting the proposed new borrowing in the event of such a recession.

(ii) Outline your strategy for dealing with any financial problems which may be indicated.

Profit and loss account for year ended 30th June 19x8

	£000	£000
Sales		5,600
Cost of Sales		4,340
Gross profit		1,260
Expenses:		
Fixed	300	
Variable	448	
Depreciation	140	
		888
Profit before tax		372
Corporation tax (45%)		167
Profit after tax		205
Dividend (7%)		140
Retained profit		65

Balance sheet as at 30th June 19x8

	£000	£000
Fixed assets, at cost less depreciation:		
Land and buildings	250	
Plant and machinery	700	
		950
Trade investments		100
Current assets:		
Stock and work-in-progress	1,085	
Debtors	1,120	
Cash	200	
		2,405
		3,455
Less Current liabilities:		
Creditors	585	
Current taxation	167	
Dividend	140	
		892
Net assets		2,563
Represented by:		
Share capital		2,000
Retained profits		396
Future taxation		167
		2,563

Notes on possible recession:

1. It is considered that sales, in relation to those of year ended 30th June 19x8 would be:

First year:	25% lower
Second year:	50% lower
Third year:	30% lower

During the above years it is thought that gross profit would probably fall to 15 per cent of sales value; but that after this period sales and gross profit would be as in year ended 30th June 19x8.

2. Fixed expenses are unlikely to change in total. Variable expenses should remain at the percentage of sales in the accounts given above.

3. Depreciation of plant and machinery is calculated at 20 per cent of written down book value each year.

4. For simplicity, Corporation Tax may be calculated at 45% of the relevant accounted profit.

5. In the absence of positive action, year-end stocks and creditors would vary in proportion to cost of sales for the year while debtors would vary in proportion to sales. (CIMA)

Notes

1. The difference between the example and the one on page 141 is that a tentative amount and form of financing is introduced from the start, i.e. the proposal is that fixed assets of £700,000 be financed entirely by a debenture issue of £750,000, the balance of £50,000 being utilised for working capital. It is necessary, therefore, to predict the profit figures and check by means of balance sheets and funds flow whether the particular means of financing is acceptable.

2. The question states that the recession is most likely to commence 'during year ended June 19y0'. The worst situation will therefore be if sales start to decline immediately at the commencement of this accounting year. The full reduction of 25 per cent has therefore been applied to the forecast volume of sales for year ended 30th June 19y0, i.e. this is the first year of the recession periods.

3. Ratios deduced from the question are:

$$\text{Present gross profit} = \frac{£1,260}{£5,600} = 22{\cdot}5\%$$

but for years ended 30th June 19y0 to 19y2 inclusive it is to be 15 per cent. The cost of sales figures is therefore deduced *after* inserting the gross profit calculated at 15 per cent of sales.

Variable expenses are $\frac{£448}{£5,600} = 8\%$ of forecast sales.

Since no specific date is given a full year's depreciation has been charged in respect of the year ended 30th June 19x9 although the plant was purchased 'during the year'. Similarly, a full year's interest has been charged as payable on the debentures.

4. Taxation at 45% is not applicable after 19y0 since this is the last year in which a profit has been made. It has been assumed in the answer that the company paid the tax when due. By the end of June 19y2 the company has accumulated tax losses of (227 + 290 + 184) = £701,000 and the profit of £377,000 realised in the year to 30 June 19y3 would be offset against this, resulting in no assessment in respect of that year. The taxation treatment suggested is a little unrealistic. Taxation allowances in respect of capital expenditure would be substituted for depreciation and also the firm could opt for repayment of taxation paid earlier in lieu of offsetting against future profits. It is also assumed that no dividends are paid in view of the anticipated recession. The company could, however, decide otherwise for one or more of the years concerned and this could be discussed in part (ii).

5. Stocks $\frac{£1,085}{£4,340} = 25\%$ of cost of sales

Creditors $\frac{£585}{£4,340} = 13{\cdot}5\%$ of cost of sales

Debtors $\frac{£1,120}{£5,600} = 20\%$ of sales

6. The balance sheet is computed and items fitted in excluding the cash figure. Since subject to the above assumptions this will be the only missing

item, the cash balance becomes the figure it is necessary to insert in order for assets to equate with liabilities. Should the figure be negative it indicates the overdraft balance or cash deficit at end of period.

(a) Normal Methods of Risk Measurement by the Borrower

Types of Risk

1. Effects of the loan interest on profits:

Loan interest is a priority charge; retained profits and dividends take what is left.

In times of recession the loan interest can seriously erode earnings or completely eliminate them.

2. Effects of loan interest on the cash flow:

Failure to pay interest and redemption when due could bring about foreclosure by the lender.

This may cause selling of essential assets, seriously affecting earning power and confidence in the business or a complete liquidation.

Measuring Risk

1. Ratios of profits before tax and interest—past and present.
2. Times dividend is covered by net earnings.
3. Gearing ratio—the lower this, the lower is the risk.
4. Estimate of break-up value of the business and the ranking of the liabilities and lenders.
5. Ratio of fixed assets to total assets—as a basis of security.

Some businesses by their nature and/or asset structure may affect interpretation of this data. (Other features from the text could amplify these points.)

Solution to (b) (i)

Forecast Profit and Loss Accounts (£000) Year ended 30th June

	19x9	*19y0*	*19y1*	*19y2*	*19y3*	*Question notes*
Sales (% of 19x8)	100	75	50	70	100	
	(£000)	(£000)	(£000)	(£000)	(£000)	
Sales	5,600	4,200	2,800	3,920	5,600	1
Cost of sales	4,340	3,570	2,380	3,332	4,340	
Gross profit	1,260	630	420	588	1,260	1
Expenses Fixed	300	300	300	300	300	
Variable	448	336	224	314	448	2
Depreciation	220	176	141	113	90	3
Profit before interest and tax	292	(182)	(245)	(139)	422	
Interest	45	45	45	45	45	3
	247	(227)	(290)	(184)	377	
Tax @ 45%	111					4
	136	(227)	(290)	(184)	377	
Dividend	—	—	—	—	—	4
Retained profit	136	(227)	(290)	(184)	377	

Forecast Balance Sheets as at 30th June (£000)

	19x9		19y0		19y1		19y2		19y3		*Note*
Fixed assets											
Cost less depreciation											
Land and buildings	550		550		550		550		550		
Plant and machinery	880		704		563		450		360		
		1,430		1,254		1,113		1,000		910	
Trade investments		100		100		100		100		100	
Current assets											
Stock	1,085		892		595		833		1,085		5
Debtors	1,120		840		560		784		1,120		5
Cash	410		560		717		314		328		
		2,615		2,292		1,872		1,931		2,533	
		4,145		3,646		3,085		3,031		3,543	
less Current liabilities											
Creditors	585		480		320		450		585		5
Current tax	167		111		—		—		—		4
Dividend	—		—		—		—		—		4
		752		591		320		450		585	
		3,393		3,055		2,765		2,581		2,958	
Represented by											
Share capital		2,000		2,000		2,000		2,000		2,000	
Reserves											
Balance b/f	396		532		305		15		(169)		
Profit and loss	136		(227)		(290)		(184)		377		
		532		305		15		(169)		208	
		2,532		2,305		2,015		1,831		2,208	
Debentures		750		750		750		750		750	
Future tax		111		—		—		—		—	
		3,393		3,055		2,765		2,581		2,958	

(b) (ii) Outline of strategy for dealing with any financial problems

Initially it is a matter for the management of A Ltd to form a judgment on the basis of the prepared forecast as to whether its strategy will survive the possible recession and achieve the long-term objectives of the business. In the light of the impact of the recession upon profits and liquidity a fundamental decision will be needed as to whether to proceed with the debenture-raising and capital investment.

The effect upon trading results is to incur a loss in 19y0, 19y1 and 19y2, resuming a profit in 19y3. The subsequent benefits may justify this.

The forecast of cash flow suggests that the company could avoid serious embarrassment to its liquidity:

	19x8	*19y2*	*19y3*
Quick ratio assessment			
Debtors + Cash	£1,320	£1,098	£1,448
Creditors	£585	£450	£585
Ratio	2·25:1	2·4:1	2·5:1
Cash percentage to creditors			
Cash	£200	£314	£328
Creditors	£585	£450	£585
Percentage	34	70	56

However, the company should consider a further element of risk to which it is exposed—namely, whether its interpretation of events is sufficiently accurate—and to what extent other influences could arise which separately or collectively could bring added strain. Such possibilities could include:

1. The recession could be more severe and/or extend over a longer period.
2. No redemption payment or period for the debenture is given.
3. Pressure for dividends could develop, particularly in 19y3 when profits resume.
4. Effects of inflation could affect trading and costs.
5. Aspects of industrial relations under the pressures of the recession could retard recovery.

It would, therefore, be wise for the company to have some contingent policies in case the position worsens from that depicted by the forecast of trading. Such contingent policies could include:

1. With the debentures being about 50 per cent of the fixed assets upon implementation of the expansion, a second loan would be difficult. Therefore, should further funds be needed, an internal generation of funds would be needed from:

(*a*) Stocks at three months of usage.
(*b*) Debtors at $2\frac{1}{2}$ months of sales.
(*c*) Deferment of creditor payments.
(*d*) Sale of fixed assets or any 'sale and lease back' arrangements could meet with a bar from the debenture holders.
(*e*) Sale of the trade investments.

2. The taxation system operative at the time or anticipated over the period of the forecast may be critical to the strategy on cash flow. By claiming maximum capital allowances and carry-back facilities, the company will receive the benefit of earlier injection of cash than would be the case in the more simplified version of the forecast as presented.
3. The crucial feature of the whole strategy, however, could be reconsidered—namely, whether to proceed with the debenture and expansion in 19x9. The extra productivity does not seem to be required until after 19y3 and the uncommitted £50,000 of the debenture is not specifically needed for working capital in the recession years; the interest of £45,000 p.a. would not need to be paid—in the five years of the forecast this amounts to £225,000 less tax, of course.
4. If some interim improvements in efficiency were needed consideration could be given to hire purchase or renting any assets needed and so relieve any immediate drain on cash resources.

On the other hand, if it was felt that the forecasts had been prepared on an over-interpretation of events and that the most likely difference would be for an improvement upon the forecasts then the company would wish to proceed with its strategy to be ready for any uplift in demand as soon as it became apparent. It could then rely upon steps for the internal generation of extra cash to cover for any minor adverse contingencies.

Questions

1. E plc, an engineering component manufacturer, intends to acquire five numerically-controlled machining centres. The cost of the equipment and installation will amount to approximately £400,000. E plc's management is convinced, after a detailed comparison of the existing and proposed production methods, that the investment is likely to provide savings and/or additional earnings over the next five years as follows:

Financial year	*Prospective gain at current prices* £
1987/88	28,000
1988/89	84,000
1989/90	135,000
1990/91	150,000
1991/92	200,000

It is company policy to write-off its plant and machinery on a straight-line basis over ten years and this has been allowed for. The prospective gains from 1992/3 onwards are thought to be uncertain due to probable import penetration by third world countries adopting appropriate technology. The forecasts take into account the assumption of marketing specialists that the new production methods will enable E plc to attract some business from its competition. The figures take forecast taxation into account.

E plc's advisors have suggested that an equity flotation for the required funding would not be practicable and also that a rights issue or the holding back of normal dividend payments would be inappropriate.

The company has therefore approached PF plc and obtained a promise of finance on the understanding that payment of a £40,000 'deposit' and 60 monthly payments of £10,000 would be guaranteed by a charge both on the plant and on E plc's working capital. After payment of the final £10,000 PF plc has agreed to sell the centres to E plc for £40,000 cash. Interest charges are expected to be tax allowable.

E plc's directors are concerned that compliance with Statement of Standard Accounting Practice No. 21 will affect the company's gearing ratio. They wonder whether any further flotation of debt or equity, required to counter inflation or to assist in aiding the directors' strategy of developing the business 'one step at a time', would be likely to cost five percentage points over and above what would otherwise have to be paid in interest charges or dividend payments, if the securities are to be made sufficiently attractive to prospective investors.

You are required to:

(*a*) Suggest and evaluate an appropriate financial strategy for E plc's directors to follow.

(*b*) Suggest the economic considerations of which the company has to take account.

(*c*) Recommend whether E plc should proceed with the installation of the proposed machining centres.

Note: Assume a corporation tax rate of 35 per cent.

(CIMA)

2. The annual reports of commercial corporations increasingly contain details of share option schemes.

You are required to:

(*a*) Discuss whether share option schemes, for either directors or employees generally, can benefit the interests of the shareholders in the company.

(*b*) Contrast share option schemes with other schemes for relating managers' rewards to the financial performance of the company.

(*c*) Describe the treatment of share option schemes in calculations of earnings per share.

(CIMA)

3. (*a*) Coppice plc plans to obtain a listing on the United Kingdom Stock Exchange. The company wishes to raise approximately £3 million, and the Stock Exchange authorities have informally indicated that either an offer for sale or a placing would be permitted. Coppice's finance director has obtained information about the costs associated with new issues. This information is detailed below.

Issuing house commission (not including underwriting)	½%
Underwriting commission*	1½%
Accounting and legal fees: Offer for sale	£40,000
Placing	£15,000
Capital duty payable to the government on the proceeds of the issue	1%
Advertising: Multiple page advertisement in a national newspaper	£50,000
Small advertisement in a national or regional newspaper	£3,000
Share registration costs: £1,000 plus £1 per shareholder	
Stock Exchange initial fee: Offer for sale	£4,000
Placing	£2,000
Other costs: Offer for sale	£25,000
Placing	£10,000

The company pays tax at a rate of 35%

* In an offer for sale, underwriting commission will effectively be deducted from the issue price in determining the price that the company receives.

Required:

(i) Discuss how an offer for sale differs from a placing.

(ii) Estimate the total after tax issue costs if Coppice plc uses:

1. an offer for sale;
2. a placing.

(iii) If Coppice plc decided to seek a listing on the Unlisted Securities Market (USM) what difference would this make to the method of issue and to the costs involved?

(*b*) Coppice eventually decides to enter the stock market by using an offer for sale. Its merchant bank considers that the issue should comprise two million shares at a price of 145 pence per share. The two million shares will form half of the company's issued ordinary share capital. As an alternative, the merchant bank suggests an offer for sale by tender. The merchant bank is willing to underwrite a tender issue of two million shares with a minimum price of 140 pence per share. Coppice agrees to the issue by tender and receives the following tenders:

Price tendered (pence)	*Number of applicants at the price*	*Number of shares applied for at the price*
175	2	22,000
170	84	74,000
165	127	192,000
160	410	724,000
155	1,123	928,000
150	2,254	1,324,200
145	3,520	4,956,000
140	6,410	12,230,000

The company decides to allocate the same percentage of the number of shares that were requested to all successful tenders.

Required:

(i) Estimate the amount of funds that the company will raise from the tender, net of issue costs, and the average size of shareholding that will result.

(ii) Suggest reasons why tenders are not the most frequently used method of raising equity finance.

(*c*) One year later the after tax earnings of Coppice plc are £1 for the year just ended and the company's PE (price/earnings) ratio of 9 is relatively high for the industry. Coppice decides to expand, and to raise further funds by means of a rights issue of 500,000 shares at eight per cent discount on the current market price.

Required:

Estimate the value of a right prior to the shares being traded ex-rights and the theoretical ex-rights price.

Under what circumstances would the market price be likely to move exactly to the theoretical ex-rights price? (CACA)

4. The following Appendix gives extracts from the annual report of X plc for the three years ended 31st December 19x4, 19x5 and 19x6.

You are required to:

(*a*) Explain and justify the calculation of capital gearing given by the company.

(*b*) Contrast this calculation with *two* other possible methods of expressing relationships between shareholders' funds and other sources of capital.

(*c*) Set out the possible advantages and disadvantages of the company's method of financing its major acquisition in 1986.

(*d*) Analyse the changes in the company's working capital over the three years and suggest possible explanations for those changes. (CIMA)

Appendix to Question 4

Extracts from the Annual Report of X plc

Group Balance Sheet at 31st December

Notes		*19x6* £000	*19x6* £000	*19x5* £000	*19x5* £000	*19x4* £000	*19x4* £000
	Fixed assets						
	Tangible assets		330,530		284,499		255,235
	Investments		11,295		9,778		11,558
			341,825		294,277		266,793
	Current assets:						
1.	Stocks	25,254		21,599		16,998	
2.	Debtors	25,341		23,040		18,759	
	Cash	3,482		3,488		1,280	
			54,077		48,127		37,037
3.	Current liabilities		101,970		70,723		51,503
	Net current liabilities		47,893		22,596		14,466
	Total assets *less* current liabilities		293,932		271,681		252,327
4.	Creditors falling due after more than 1 year		(53,450)		(56,379)		(55,436)
	Provision for deferred taxation		(1,366)		(1,942)		(1,962)
	Net assets		239,116		213,360		194,929
	Capital and reserves						
5.	Called-up share capital		47,472		24,307		24,179
	Share premium account		5,474		5,405		4,774
	Revaluation reserve		111,653		112,384		102,691
6.	Other reserves		—		5,669		9,256
7.	Profit and loss account		74,517		65,595		54,029
			239,116		213,360		194,929

Notes to the balance sheet	*19x6*	*19x5*	*19x4*
1. Stock	£000	£000	£000
Raw materials	2,988	2,472	2,118
Work-in-progress	1,736	974	929
Finished goods	18,982	17,038	13,054
Consumable stores	1,548	1,115	897
	25,254	21,599	16,998

2. *Debtors*	£000	£000	£000
Trade debtors	17,609	13,196	12,990
Others, including prepayments	7.732	9,844	5,769
	25,341	23,040	18,759
3. *Current liabilities*	£000	£000	£000
Short-term loans	35,279	18,946	368
Overdrafts	3,875	2,265	7,062
Trade creditors	27,893	17,723	13,811
Other	34,923	31,789	30,262
	101,970	70,723	51,503
4. *Creditors falling due after more than one year*	£000	£000	£000
Debentures and loan stock	8,014	11,605	11,999
Unsecured bank loans	39,439	39,617	38,466
Corporation tax	5,997	5,157	4,971
	53,450	56,379	55,436
5. *Called-up share capital*			
Authorised	£000	£000	£000
9% cumulative preference shares of £1 each	4,652	4,652	4,652
5% cumulative redeemable convertible preference shares of £1 each	23,520	—	—
Ordinary shares of 25p each	27,828	23,348	23,348
	56,000	28,000	28,000
Called up and fully paid	£000	£000	£000
9% cumulative preference shares of £1 each	4,652	4,652	4,652
5% cumulative redeemable convertible preference shares of £1 each	23,137	—	—
Ordinary shares of 25p each	19,683	19,655	19,527
	47,472	24,307	24,179

The 5 per cent cumulative redeemable convertible preference shares of £1 each were issued during 19x6 in respect of the acquisition of a company engaged in manufacturing activities.

6. Goodwill on acquisitions was written off against other reserves in 19x5 and 19x6 and against the profit and loss account in 19x4.
7. The directors hold 22 per cent of the ordinary share capital.

	19x6	*19x5*	*19x4*
Supplementary information			
A. The company discloses the following 'gearing percentage', calculated by expressing 'total net borrowings' as a percentage of shareholders' funds excluding the 9% preference shares:	35·5%	33·0%	29·7%
B. The group turnover was as follows:	£000	£000	£000
Manufacturing and merchandising businesses, largely on credit terms	241,058	214,276	177,711
Service business, mainly on cash terms	44,782	40,018	25,192
	285,840	254,294	202,903

5. (*a*) What is meant by business risk? Outline the major factors that determine a company's business risk and comment upon how controllable these factors are by a company.

(*b*) Discuss to what extent business risk is of relevance to an investor owning a well diversified portfolio.

(*c*) Huckbul Ltd plans to purchase a new machine in the near future which will reduce the company's direct labour costs, but will increase fixed costs by £85,000 per year. Direct labour costs are expected to fall by 20 per cent per unit of production. The new machine will cost £820,000 and will be financed by a five year fixed rate term loan at an interest cost of 15 per cent per year, with the principal repayable at the maturity of the loan. The company normally pays half of after tax earnings as dividends, subject to the constraint that if after tax earnings fall the dividend per share is kept constant.

Huckbul expects its volume of sales to increase by 15 per cent during the current financial year.

Summarised extracts from the company's most recent financial accounts are detailed below.

Profit and loss account	£000	£000
Turnover		3,381
Operating expenses		
Wages and salaries	1,220	
Raw materials	873	
Direct selling expenses	100	
General administration (all fixed)	346	
Other costs (all fixed)	380	
		2,919
Profit before interest and tax		462
Interest		84
Profit before tax		378
Corporation tax		151
Profit available to ordinary shareholders		227

Balance sheet	£000	£000
Fixed assets		1,480
Current assets	1,720	
Less current liabilities	1,120	
		600
		2,080
Long term debt		570
Net assets		1,510
Capital and reserves		
Ordinary shares (25p)		800
Share premium account		320
Other reserves		390
		1,510

The company is subject to taxation at a rate of 40 per cent.

Required:

State clearly any assumptions that you make.

(i) Evaluate the effect of the purchase of the machine on both the degree of operating gearing and the financial gearing of Huckbul Ltd, comparing the position at the start of the current financial year with the expected position at the end of the current financial year.

(ii) What are the implications for the ordinary shareholders of Huckbul as a result of the purchase of the machine:

1. If turnover increases by the expected 15 per cent.
2. If turnover falls by 10 per cent. (CACA)

6. The board of directors of Rickery plc is discussing whether to alter the company's capital structure. Corporate legislation permits Rickery plc to repurchase its own shares and it is proposed to issue £5 million of new debentures at par, and to use the funds to repurchase ordinary shares.

A summary of Rickery's current balance sheet is shown below:

	£000
Fixed assets (net)	24,500
Current assets	12,300
Current liabilities	(8,600)
	28,200
Financed by	
25p Ordinary shares	4,500
Reserves	14,325
	18,825
5% Debentures redeemable at par on 31st December 1997	9,375
	28,200

The company's current ordinary share price is 167p, and its debenture price £80. Rickery's finance director does not expect the market price of the existing ordinary shares or debentures to change as a result of the proposed issue of new debentures. The risk free rate of interest is estimated to be 5·5 per cent per annum.

Rickery's equity beta is estimated by a leading firm of stockbrokers to be 1·24, and the estimated market return is 15 per cent. Debenture interest is payable at the end of the year. Issue costs and transactions costs may be assumed to be zero.

Required:

(*a*) Evaluate the likely effect on the weighted average cost of capital of Rickery plc if the company restructures its capital:

(i) If the company pays tax at the rate of 35 per cent.
(ii) If the company does not expect to pay corporate taxes for the foreseeable future.

All the relevant calculations must be shown. State clearly any assumptions that you make.

(*b*) Rickery's finance director believes that the market price of the company's existing ordinary shares and debentures will not change. Explain why he might be wrong in his belief and suggest what changes might occur. (CACA)

7. (*a*) In recent years there has been a large increase in the number of management buy-outs, often when a company is in financial distress. What are the possible financial advantages of a company's shares being sold to a group of managers relative to liquidation of the company?

(*b*) Five managers of Leivers Ltd are discussing the possibility of a management buy-out of the part of the company that they work for. The buy-out would require a total of £700,000, of which £525,000 would comprise the purchase cost, and £175,000 the funds for a small expansion in activity, and for working capital. The managers believe that they could jointly provide £70,000.

Required:

(i) Discuss possible sources of finance that the managers might use to raise the required funds.

(ii) What are likely to be the major factors that a potential supplier of finance will consider before deciding whether to offer finance? What type of security or other conditions might providers of finance specify? (CACA)

8. (*a*) The table below sets out the year-end levels of the price of ordinary shares in W plc and of a representative Stock Exchange index.

Year	*W plc* £	*Index*
1	2·40	1280
2	2·50	1350
3	2·30	1500
4	1·80	1480
5	2·55	1510

You are required to use this information to calculate the beta coefficient of W plc ordinary shares, ignoring any dividend payments.

Work to four decimal places only at each stage of calculation.

(*b*) Assume an approximate beta coefficient of 1·5, a risk-free rate of 5 per cent per annum and an expected return from equities generally of 8 per cent per annum.

You are required to calculate the expected rate of return on W plc ordinary shares.

(*c*) W plc has just paid a dividend of £0·30 per share and the market expectation is that this dividend will grow at a constant rate of 5 per cent per annum. The 'cost of capital' for W plc may be taken as 10 per cent.

You are required to calculate a market value for W plc ordinary shares using a dividend valuation model and assuming a perfect market.

(*d*) You are required to discuss whether it would have been correct in part (*c*) to use as the 'cost of equity capital' the expected rate of return computed in part (*b*).

(CIMA)

9. What are the differences between a finance lease and an operating lease? Outline the advantages from leasing equipment rather than purchasing it. (CACA)

10. (*a*) You are required, in connection with the selection and holding of investments, to discuss each of the following points of view.

(i) An investor holding only one security need be concerned only with the unsystematic risk of that security.

(ii) An investor who holds a number of securities should take account of total risk.

(iii) An investor should never add to a portfolio an investment that yields a return less than the market rate of return.

(*b*) The following data relate to four different portfolios of securities:

Portfolio	*Expected rate of return* %	*Standard deviation of return on the market portfolio* %
K	11	6·7
L	14	7·5
M	10	3·3
N	15	10·8

The expected rate of return on the market portfolio is 8·5 per cent, with a standard deviation of 3 per cent. The risk-free rate is 5 per cent.

You are required to identify which of these portfolios could be regarded as 'efficient'.

(CIMA)

11. A local authority uses borrowed funds for many of its major capital projects. At present, it has under consideration a project for which additional borrowing will be required. The project will involve an initial outlay of £5 million. Apart from social benefits, positive cash flows are expected from it at the rate of £850,000 per annum between years 3 and 15 inclusive. The DCF rate of return from the project has been calculated as approximately 10 per cent.

(*a*) You are required to explain briefly and comment on *six* factors that might be taken into account by the Authority in deciding whether its initial borrowing for this project should be short-term or long-term.

(*b*) The Authority has a choice between the following methods of servicing the debt related to the above project:

(i) By equal annual payments, incorporating varying amounts of interest and capital repayments. If this method were adopted, there would be a 'grace period' of two years during which interest would be added to the loan but no payments would be made of interest or capital.

(ii) By equal annual repayments of capital, plus interest on each year's outstanding amount.

(iii) By paying interest on the capital sum advanced, but repaying capital in one lump sum at the end of the loan period.

Assuming a 15-year loan with interest at 10 per cent, you are required to calculate the total debt service costs (interest plus capital repayments) under each of these three methods and to comment on the results.

(*c*) If method (iii) were selected, you are required to summarise the means by which the Authority could ensure that funds were available to make the terminal repayment of loan capital. (CIMA)

12. (*a*) At a time of historically high interest rates, the treasurer of W plc explains to you that any acquisitions or other new investments by the company are required to yield a rate of return at least as high as that from any alternative uses to which the money could be put.

You are required to explain the implications of this policy.

(*b*) X plc has large liquid resources, currently invested at an average interest rate of $10\frac{1}{2}$ per cent. The company's latest annual accounts have just been published, showing pre-tax earnings of £120 million on 470 million ordinary shares. Immediately following publication, the Stock Exchange price of the shares stands at 213 pence. The company decides to repurchase 37·5 million of its own shares for cash at that price.

You are required to comment on the likely financial implications of this decision.

(*c*) Y plc, in its annual report, has announced the following financial policies:

(i) To increase earnings per share by 5 per cent per annum.
(ii) To achieve an annual return on assets of 25 per cent.
(iii) Dividend cover to be not more than three times.
(iv) The ratio of debt to equity not to exceed 50 per cent.
(v) Interest charges to be covered six times by trading profit.

During the year covered by the report, assets totalling £1,200,000 were financed by debt £400,000 by ordinary shareholders' funds £800,000. There were 500,000 ordinary shares in issue. Profit before interest was £300,000 and dividends were covered exactly three times.

You are required to review the operation of policies (i) to (v) above from the points of view of their desirability, practicability and internal consistency, illustrating your answer with reference to the data given, where appropriate.

Note: Where appropriate, the rate of corporation tax may be assumed to be 35 per cent. (CIMA)

13. Answer any *two* parts of this question. Each part carries equal marks.

(*a*) Explain what is meant by venture capital. Give examples of the main providers of venture capital in the United Kingdom and assess the importance of venture capital to small companies.

(*b*) Within a financial management context discuss the problems that might exist in the relationships (sometimes referred to as agency relationships) between:

(i) shareholders and managers, and

(ii) shareholders and creditors.

How might a company attempt to minimise such problems?

(*c*) Outline the main differences that exist between the financial systems of the United Kingdom and *one* of France, West Germany and Japan.

(CACA)

14. A study of 136 institutions offering venture capital in the UK was reported in the financial press during 1985.

Some aspects of that study are summarised below.

Venture Capital Institutions Classified by Amount of Finance Offered

Minimum investment £000	*Total number*	*Maximum investment £000*				
		Under 100	*100–500*	*500–1,000*	*Over 1,000*	*'Open'*
Under 50	46	8 (*a*)	14 (*a*)	13 (*b*)	4 (*c*) (*d*)	7
50–100	59	1 (*a*)	13 (*a*)	28	11	6 (*c*)
Over 100	31	—	3	9 (*e*)	11	8 (*c*)
Total number	136	9	30	50	26	21

Notes:

(*a*) More than half the institutions in these categories offered equity capital only. In all other categories loan capital, either alone or with equity, was more significant.

(*b*) Enterprise Boards and Development Agencies were mostly in this category.

(*c*) Venture capital subsidiaries of clearing banks were in these categories.

(*d*) Investors in Industry plc included here.

(*e*) Equity Capital for Industry included here.

You are required to:

(*a*) Describe *four* circumstances under which a business might seek venture capital.

(*b*) Comment generally on the availability of venture capital for various sizes of investment.

(*c*) Describe the constitution and particular features of:

Investors in Industry plc;
Equity Capital for Industry;
Development Agencies.

(*d*) Explain why certain major industrial enterprises might undertake the provision of venture capital and suggest what special advantages this might have for the business receiving the investment.

(*e*) Solve the following problem:

An entrepreneur has formed a company to undertake an innovative activity and has taken up 37,500 shares at £1 each. He has also persuaded an investor to invest £112,500 for a further 37,500 shares. He forecasts that in the fifth year of operation the company will generate earnings of at least £800,000 after tax, at which stage he hopes to bring the company into the Unlisted Securities Market. A price/earning ratio of about 12 is anticipated. No dividends will have been paid up to that time.

At the end of the first year the company needs to raise a further £400,000 to complete the development of its product and commence production. A venture capitalist is found who will invest this amount, but is seeking to get back six times his investment in four years, from the sale of shares allotted to him.

You are asked:

(i) What proportion of the total share capital would the venture capitalist require and what number of shares would this represent?

(ii) What amounts of capital gain would be made by the entrepreneur, the initial investor and the new venture capitalist respectively if the price/earnings ratio of 12 were achieved? (CIMA)

5

ANALYSIS AND DIAGNOSIS OF PERFORMANCE

Business Performance

Performance is synonymous with achievement—the results obtained from endeavour. Business endeavour is concerned with fulfilling a need of the community and the first essential measure of achievement will be that sufficient numbers of the community find the service acceptable at the price so that the total income will exceed the financial outlay in providing the service—namely, operating at a profit. Profit therefore becomes the first indicator of the combined operations of all those functions which make up the business, and the amount of profit will begin to quantify this combined effort.

The amount of profit will not in itself demonstrate the level of achievement until a form of comparison is introduced, and judgment from a comparison will firstly depend upon the acceptability of the base against which the comparison is being made. The first requirement is to ensure that the profits being compared are relevant to each other and similarly constituted. Internal comparisons will best ensure this and may relate current achievements of the amount of profit with:

(*a*) *Past achievements:* This will demonstrate whether business is better or worse than previously, and the degree of change. It does not necessarily define whether the past achievements were acceptable or adequate.

(*b*) *A defined target of achievement:* This will represent the outcome of a forecast of sales and costs under the circumstances expected in the form of a budget. It also need not necessarily define the adequacy of the profit target.

Comparisons can also be made against the achievements of other businesses where available. It is difficult to be sure that such comparisons are on a like for like basis, even if operating in a similar market or industry, partly as to the composition of the profit, but more particularly concerning the scope of the businesses under comparison. A small business making £10,000 profit with 2 per cent of the market will not meaningfully relate to the giant with £2 million profit with 30 per cent of the market, with several spin-off benefits in other market sectors.

An interpretation of adequacy of the amount of profit for one business may not be similar to another, even if closely related as to product and market. Adequacy is related to the needs of the business, which in turn are governed by its objectives and composition. Thus the amount of profit must be adequate to provide for:

(*a*) The cost of the capital—
  The reward expected or demanded by different classes of shareholder and providers of long-term capital.

(*b*) The investment needs of the business—
  (i) The costs of replacing assets, which in inflationary circumstances will be at prices in excess of the normal depreciation provided in casting the profit.

(ii) The costs of additional assets for growth.
(iii) The working capital requirements for changing circumstances and growth.

(*c*) The reserves and contingencies deemed necessary as protection against expected or unexpected circumstances.

Adequacy of profit needs will therefore be peculiar to each business and perhaps to different phases of the evolution of each. A family-owned business may require a lower dividend commitment than one whose shareholders include the range of professional investors; the pedantic, cautious business will have lesser profit needs than its dynamic, extrovert counterpart straining to expand; and the business operating in a safe, essential commodity market will need less cover for contingencies than the one subject to sudden changes of whim by a fickle market.

The business which is able to interpret these factors and define its profit needs and then match them to the market conditions of volume and price against its own cost expectations, will provide a very adequate basis against which to compare its actual amount of profit in due course. A comparison along these lines tests the adequacy of the amount of profit only against the needs of the business—what the profit can be made to do—and it is essentially introspective in that it is the business looking at itself. Management will not learn from this about the capabilities of the business to earn profit unless and until the target is more definitive as to the profit of the business ought to be making. Comparisons can be made outside the business with others of a like product or service, but judgments will be inconclusive without some interpretation of the scope or potential of each business. A form of common factor is needed by which to align each business.

A review of the above factors which regulate the profit needs of a business will reveal that the focus is upon the capital of the business; how much capital can be supported by the profit and leave some over for expansion and safety. Conversely, the view can be taken as to how much profit can be earned by the capital when converted into the specific resources required by the business. Different businesses require a different pattern or emphasis of resources, but they can all have a common interpretation of value.

Two businesses can market similar products. One may manufacture throughout and therefore require appropriate resources and the other may factor the product and only require storage facilities. Comparisons of the profit by reference to their resources need not take into consideration the identity of those resources—their total value provides a common factor between them.

Physical and financial resources remain just resources until they are operated or put to work by people, so that the human resources of a business are absolutely essential. They will comprise the operating skill and physical muscle and the whole range of management skills. These people collectively govern the profit by their diligence and application and the manner in which they make use of the resources at their disposal, commencing, of course, with deciding the precise physical resources required for the task. An acceptable manner of financially interpreting the value of a business's human resources has yet to be found, but research has been proceeding for several years and may yet conclude in acceptable concepts and methods. Suffice it at this stage to reflect that the cost of supporting the human resources must be met before the amount of profit is cast.

A further test of adequacy of profit or level of achievement of the business becomes apparent in relating the profit to the measurable resources, which then, in effect, reflects the competence or performance of the human resources—the people comprising the business—in making use of the physical resources at their disposal. In this manner the performances of different businesses can be compared. Those of a similar product or market will be the more directly comparable but the method can be accepted as a general basis for comparing businesses of unlike characteristics in that focus is upon the common factors of the people of the business and the resource funds at their disposal.

Profit and Capital Employed

The relationship between profit and capital employed has become an accepted general reflection of business performance. A business is said to be more efficient when the ratio of profit to the capital employed is higher. As this ratio is affected by changes in both or either of the profit and the capital employed, management needs to focus upon the composition of each. Thus a business may have achieved the best profit it deems possible from the capital employed at its disposal, but it may also be possible to achieve that degree of profit with less capital employed, or greater profit still if more capital were available and converted into specific resources.

This gives rise to a differentiation in the meaning of terms used to describe meritorious performance.

A business is said to be **efficient** when the ratio of the profit to the capital *at the disposal of the business* is above a given normal level.

The business is described as **effective** when the ratio, being similarly above the given normal level, reflects the profit to the ideal or *desirable level of capital needed to operate the business*.

The objectives of management thus are to become ever more effective, so in optimising the profit and finding whatever extra capital may be needed for the task within the bounds of the highest ratio possible.

Measurement of performance by relating profit to capital employed needs to be undertaken with some care in regard to:

(i) Interpretation of the level of the ratio.
(ii) Content of the profit.
(iii) Nature of the capital employed.

The ratio itself, as with the amount of profit previously discussed, will not reflect adequacy until compared with another ratio and the basis of this will be significant for worthwhile judgments. The base for comparison may be:

(*a*) Internal past performance to demonstrate trends.
(*b*) The best past performance.
(*c*) The budgeted performance.
(*d*) Other business of a like nature.
(*e*) A combination of other like businesses to reflect the weighted average of, say, an industry.
(*f*) The best of such performances.
(*g*) The return judged possible from alternative uses of the capital, i.e. the current cost of capital in safe or risk loan situations.

It is important that the context of the comparison should be clear.

The term 'profit' has the generally accepted interpretation of the surplus of sales revenue over the cost incurred in its achievement, and although accountancy practice has evolved standards of treatment and interpretation as to what constitutes income and costs, there can be differences of degree that could affect the content of the profits under comparison. For example, allowances for depreciation basically depend upon a judgment of what the life-span of an asset will be and this can vary between companies. In the case of identical aircraft one airline may consider that the £5m asset will serve them for five years and another only three years; the difference upon their respective profits for this single aircraft will be £666,666 p.a. (£5m ÷ 5 = £1*m* p.a.; £5m ÷ 3 = £1,666,666 p.a.).

The objectives of the business being compared may also be different in key respects so as to affect the content of the profits. The one may seek to reward its people more generously, to provide more acceptable conditions of work, to maintain its assets more diligently and ensure a greater degree of continuity by spending on market research about its future markets and the evolution of product improvements and new products. Such a company may therefore be setting itself more comprehensive objectives than the making of profit, which a form of measuring the profit itself will not necessarily reflect. Stability reflected in constancy or improving trends of profit coupled with the public image of the company, may be involved in coming to a judgment about its performance.

Unusual circumstances may have affected the content of profit in any particular period so as to make it unrepresentative—such as a stock write-off due to design change, a buying risk which did not succeed, an adverse effect of rates of exchange, or the fortuitous 'once-off' contract. The accountancy profession, through its recommended standards of accountancy, recognises this and suggests that the effects of abnormal circumstances be separately demonstrated in published accounts so when thus treated adjustments for comparison purposes can be made. Care should be taken to ensure that profits and ratios used as a base for the comparison are similarly adjusted.

Capital employed has various interpretations, some more generally accepted than others, much depending upon the precise interpretation and judgment that is intended.

Net Capital Employed

This is generally accepted as interpreting efficiency in the use of funds by managements. Published comparisons between companies tend to use this basis, as do managements when making judgments about themselves. The constituents are:

Ordinary and preference paid-up share capital Revenue and capital reserves Long-term loans Deferred liabilities	*equivalent to*	Intangible assets, e.g. goodwill, formation expenses Fixed assets less depreciation Net current assets

Total Assets Employed

This is used when more pertinent judgments are required about the use of funds, in that current liabilities are included as capital leaving the current assets at gross. Advocates suggest that gross current assets more appropriately reflect the total funds being put to use irrespective as to the manner in which the funds are made available. They arise either out of cash paid out or commitments incurred which have to be met and represent ownership.

The exclusion of the current liabilities is claimed on the basis that if debtors, as sums owing to the business, are included then the creditors, being sums owing by the business, should also be taken into consideration. More particularly the creditors demonstrate the degree to which actual cash has not yet been needed in the funding of resources. This can more particularly be recognised in the view that as creditors will largely constitute suppliers of materials, then the stocks included in the current assets will—to the extent of the creditors—not yet have required cash funds to be found.

The interpretation thus rests on whether 'funds' should be confined to the cash funds only or not.

Proprietors' Capital Employed

This excludes the long-term loans, confining the capital to that supplied and appertaining to the shareholdings, namely the net worth. The shareholders' interest is what has been achieved with the capital they have provided. Where loan capital has been made available this has, of course, been put to work in the business additionally, so from a management's point of view the extent to which the earnings from this loan capital exceed its cost will enhance the profits of the business and become interpreted as an improved ratio on a stable shareholder's capital. Such a ratio does not necessarily interpret acceptable levels of use of the loan or share capital and it may disguise inefficiencies elsewhere in the business.

It is essential that the profit and the capital employed are properly related, being compared on a 'like for like' basis. If, for example, the total profit includes earnings from investments, then the capital needs to include the value of the investment. The profits from such investments will not appertain to the business operations of the company under review; they in effect reflect the use of any capital surplus to these operations so that judgment about the internal management of the business should exclude the investment income and also the amount of the investment from its capital employed. On the other hand, however, any capital supplied by minority interests will have been put to general use in the business and contribute to the profits inclusive of that deemed applicable to minority interests. Shareholders more concerned about the profits applicable to themselves and therefore 'after minority interests', will need to relate that profit to the capital exclusive of the minority holding.

This feature particularly appertains to any adjustments that are made in the content of the profit of an unusual nature, so that a comparable adjustment is made in the balance sheet values of relevant assets. Thus if an abnormal stock write-off is added back to the profit for comparison purposes, then the adjusted profit must relate to a capital employed similarly increased because the stock valuation on the balance sheet would have been abnormally reduced by the write-off. If a business revalues its fixed assets then the inference is that the depreciation reserve has been proved to be inaccurate under whatever factors have developed. The depreciation and thus the profit of the year under comparison will need to be adjusted so as to be based upon the new valuation of the assets before a comparison is made to the newly constituted capital employed.

Performance measurement is not necessarily confined to businesses as a whole. Management control is constantly seeking to evaluate the performances of the separate responsibilities, and where divisions of profit can be made directly attributable to a decentralised area of control, then care should be taken to relate the profit to the capital under the control of the particular responsibility which directly produces the profit. Product divisions and separate factories are often conceded decentralised responsibilities to the extent of being primarily judged against target ratios of profit to capital employed. In other respects it becomes a matter of relating a profit to an appropriate capital employed as will fulfil the objective of the judgment. For example, judgments about a general manager will exclude income and capital related to investments and to surplus cash retained in the business, these being deemed to relate to the financial control responsibility; the factory responsibility may be segregated from sales and confined to the factory profit only, measured on transfers into warehouse, and its own fixed assets, exclusive of debtors with creditors confined to suppliers of materials and factory expenses.

Where manufacturing is separated from sales in this way, care is needed in comparing the individual responsibilities with each other—even sales divisions or outlets with each other—because of any artificial inborne biases in fixing the internal selling prices and thus the profits. Also, the capital employed may be so much less within the sales function and indeed provide a far inferior contribution where selling expertise may more directly belong to the individual through his flair, skill and application. Here it is important then to provide targets of performance peculiar to each sector of the business rather than compare them with each other.

The general practice is to use the balance sheet valuations for the capital employed deemed to be relevant for any particular purpose, but variations in these bases can render comparisons doubtful in value and may sometimes be downright misleading. Depreciation allowances can be crucial in this respect, particularly when assets are elderly but maintained in good condition so as to retain their productivity and thus ensure that the value produced consistently exceeds the variable cost of production. Thus a consistent marginal return from any piece of plant which is reducing in value each year throughout its depreciation will show an increasing ratio of return, and this in itself will discourage its replacement or its scrapping. A manager, on the ratio judgment, will not wish to bring in a new replacement at an undepreciated enhanced value, for only a marginal increase in contribution, because it will show a worsening in his overall return on capital employed. Thus there is a danger that managers will be discouraged to replace assets until a serious deterioration in output becomes apparent and necessitates a high cash outlay when the majority of the plant may need replacing at once, producing a catastrophic deterioration in the return on capital employed as it will then virtually all be at new cost.

To avoid this situation, advocates suggest a valuation of assets on an original cost basis, but extremes of judgment can still be found. With a constant valuation of a particular item of plant on this basis, any fall in contribution will worsen the ratio of performance even if it is in itself generally acceptable. The manager can be placed in a position that to avoid any deterioration at all in his overall return, he is constantly scrapping and replacing and squandering the resources of his business.

It becomes necessary to ensure that assets are not over-depreciated, which would depict a low book value and an artificially high rate of return, and that returns on individual items of plant are studied on suggestions of replacement in conjunction with the return on the whole manufacturing unit.

Further complications arise when as prices rise two machines of similar output, purchased at different times, have different historical costs and thus reflect different returns on capital employed about which judgments may be made. The aggravation of a high degree of inflation in recent years highlighted this problem for profits will be measured in terms of a current level of selling prices, but assets will be represented by values on former levels of price as interpreted by their historical costs. Increasingly it is felt that the whole of the capital employed should be reflected in terms of their current values and the accountancy profession, accepting the need, have been attempting to create a common practice to calculate and present this information. This aspect is dealt with in some detail in Chapter 9.

The Use of Ratios

Although there are many ways of expressing a ratio, it remains a means of demonstrating a relationship between two factors and this presupposes that the factors have a relationship—that they have a bearing upon each other. The ratio itself is inadequate for a judgment in isolation when it is solely communicating a fact—it needs to be compared, and the value of such a comparison will greatly depend on the basis and acceptability of the ratio against which comparison is made. This may be a target or ideal of performance, or it may trace a sequence through time when the value may lie in the trends revealed rather than the isolated unusual occurrence. One of the skills of management is the anticipation of events and the wise interpretation of trends is part of this skill, enabling early corrective action to be taken before adverse effects become serious or even irretrievable.

In that the relationship expressed is between two factors a change in the ratio can occur from a change in either of the factors or both, and a constancy in the ratio may not necessarily reflect constancy in the two factors: they may vary in direct relation to each other. Because of this and also because ratios do not reflect volume in themselves, it is often desirable to review and compare the absolute values of the factors comprising the ratio.

A single ratio may provide only a limited view of a situation so that there is often the need to use several ratios in the one context to provide cross reflections and depth to the interpretation.

As discussed earlier in this chapter, in the private sector profit is the accepted basis of interpreting business performance. Measuring the degree or level of this performance can call for the use of a range of ratios.

The Primary Ratio—Profit: Capital Employed

This is probably the most widely used financial interpretation of performance in business and has been extensively reviewed earlier in the chapter for this reason. When comparisons are made outside the particular business care is needed that the factors of profit and capital employed are commonly based; in the case of profit the chief variants can be the treatment of interest and tax and with capital employed the treatment of long-term loans. Fundamentally this ratio reflects efficiency in the use of the capital resources of the business.

Secondary Ratios

Profit: Sales

Sales: Capital Employed

Profit to sales gives guidance to the adequacy of the profit from the customer. It shows how much each customer or each £100 of sales is contributing by way of profit.

Sales to capital employed demonstrates the productivity of the capital or the combined effort generated. It is advisable to compare within similar industries because of differences in the nature of assets.

Skill is involved in the ability to interpret the message contained within the comparisons of the absolute data and the associated ratios, but of course the range of knowledge to be extracted will be limited by the information available.

It is not unusual for interpretations from the primary and secondary ratios to be imprecise so that some expansion of the comparisons becomes advisable to add depth and understanding (see Table 9 for some examples).

Supplementary Ratios Reflecting the Efficient Use of Resources

Profit: Fixed Assets

Sales: Fixed Assets

This specifically examines efficiency in the use of fixed assets. The sales ratio interprets the effort and productivity and if all other things are equal improvements here should reflect better profit, but of course, this need not be so as profit will depend on other factors than volume. Reference to the profit sales ratio will give the first clue on this.

Interpretations in this area should have regard to 'time-lag'. This is a term which depicts the time interval between investment in fixed assets and the actual generation of the intended profit. Complicated processes or manufacturing cycles with integrated sequences or with long time-cycles can be some time in working up to the additional volume and resulting profits, and again the early periods of new methods can carry undue starting expenses which affect the first profits. Some reference to the industries can give guidance in this.

The extent of any new investment or more particularly the proportions of the new investment, could also lead to an extension of this time-lag. If, for example, a manufacturing business increases its fixed assets by 50 per cent in one year and has disposed of a block of wholly depreciated and thus old assets, it would seem to be involved in a major reorganisation which could undoubtedly disturb the rhythm, volume and profitability of the enterprise before the benefits appear.

Profit: Plant and Machinery

Sales: Plant and Machinery

Profit: Buildings

Sales: Buildings

These ratios are a matter of breaking down the fixed assets into the constituents. It helps where new investment has been made in any single direction and it certainly helps where the fixed assets are predominantly plant or buildings. Intensive manufacture will look to the use of the plant for its volume and profit, and retailers and wholesalers will be vigilant about their

Table 9. Some Interpretations from the Primary and Secondary Ratios and Absolute Data

	Target	*Actual*	*Interpretations*
	Performance No. 1		
Profit	£150,000	£150,000	Adequate volume of profit but inadequate performance level from the capital; either too much capital or insufficient use of it.
Capital	£1m	£1·2m	
Sales	£1·5m	£2m	Inadequate margin from the customer—could be costs up or selling price reductions.
P:CE	15%	12½%	Effort and productivity raised to match the reduction from the customer. Raises possibility of profit improvement if this activity can be maintained with more efficient use of the capital.
P:S	10%	7½%	
S:CE	150%	166%	
	Performance No. 2		
Profit	£150,000	£120,000	Efficient use of resources but inadequate volume of profit.
Capital	£1m	£0·8m	
Sales	£1·5m	£1·5m	Inadequate margins from the customer—could be costs up or selling price reductions.
P:CE	15%	15%	Sales volume maintained from increased productivity from the lower capital. This is a 25% increase in rate and raises the question whether the productivity standard is low or can be maintained at this level.
P:S	10%	8%	
S:CE	150%	187%	
	Performance No. 3		
Profit	£150,000	£160,000	A favourable improvement in all-round performance—namely additional profit from increased efficiency on lower capital and extra volume of sales.
Capital	£1m	£0·89m	
Sales	£1·5m	£1·6m	Maintaining the sales increase on the lower capital meant a 20% improvement in productivity.
P:CE	15%	18%	
P:S	10%	10%	
S:CE	150%	180%	

use of buildings. The latter group will tend to express the ratios in terms of area for greater clarity.

Profit: Working Capital
Sales: Working Capital

In cases of large retailers, supermarkets and wholesalers the working capital may be the predominant resource at their disposal and therefore focus will be upon its efficient use, especially as it is more difficult to control investment in this type of asset.

Profit: Stocks
Sales: Stocks

The ratio of sales to stocks is extensively used in manufacturing and also the distributive industries as a guide and means of evaluating the control of this item of working capital, so vital in the struggle to maintain adequate cash flow. It must be appreciated, however, that sales value of the product is not a like-for-like comparison with the purchase price of materials and that changes in sales mix with different materials content can provide misleading comparisons, as can the introduction of new products or new methods, especially those which involve a change of manufacturing and purchasing policy whereby wholly finished parts are acquired in lieu of manufacturing from raw materials or vice-versa.

Supplementary Ratios Reflecting the Use of Manpower

Remembering that it is people who put the fixed assets to use, it is really they who produce the profit and sales from the resources at this disposal so that performance relative to manpower can be a further ingredient for assessment.

Profit: Total Employees
Sales: Total Employees

These are general ratios for monitoring trends and when used outside the business should be confined to comparisons of like products or industries, because of fundamental differences of context which can occur. Only if the other ratios are maintained can the profit ratio be representative because of the wide range of other factors which can affect the profit.

Fixed Assets: Total Employees
Plant and Machinery: Total Employees

A review of the performance of people is not wholly meaningful without some consideration of the amount of assets as resources put at their disposal, and ratios expressing value per person should be interpreted together with the productivity per person. It may be, of course, that higher productivity need not arise from extra direct employee effort, rather the maintenance of normal effort from improved resources.

Finer judgments can be made by making use of a breakdown in the functions of the manpower, particularly separating:

Works personnel—direct workers
indirect workers
Administrative personnel
Sales personnel

Where information is available to measure production and sales separately, then the former is more accurately related to the works personnel and the latter to sales personnel. If output is interpreted in units or standard hours, then the ratios are more precise and if the time worked by personnel is available then the ratio becomes more definitive in terms of effort.

Ratios of Performance of Decentralised Responsibilities

Each of the preceding ratios as measures of performance can be used to assess subdivisions of the enterprise, providing the information is available and their performance can be interpreted in terms of profit. Such divisions can include:

Products and product groups.
Divisions—sub-groups of companies often concerned with product grouping.

Individual factories or companies.
Departments.
Sales territories or geographical areas.

In decentralised companies control will be exercised from the centre chiefly on performance measured through a range of selected ratios, and responsibilities will be absolute in that the objectives and parameters of responsibility will be clearly defined and then appropriately measured and judged.

The Use of Ratios in the Control of Resources

Investment in fixed assets can be controlled up to the commitment stage by the use of disciplined procedures whereby projects are evaluated for the added profitability they are expected to provide for the enterprise. Criteria are established for judgments about acceptability and a formal authority is given for those approved and desirable. The discipline further ensures that the subsequent expenditure conforms to the approval. There is thus a specific act of commitment and a prescribed decision-making process—control of the expenditure is therefore assured.

In due course it should be possible to measure the actual performance related to a particular investment and relate this to the results forecast upon which the decision was made and for which the proposer firmly holds the responsibility for the outcome. Alternatively, should this measurement not be possible in isolation the intended change upon the overall results will have been registered at the appropriate stage and actual performance will be related to the new expected level. Responsibility may not be so absolute, but a functional responsibility there certainly should be.

Whereas it is possible to control the initial expenditure upon new fixed assets, once the expenditure is made and the assets are in existence, the enterprise, as the adjective to the assets implies, is committed so that it is difficult to convert back into cash should the circumstances change. Even if conversion is possible a loss may be inevitable.

With falling demand a reduced ratio of profit to the fixed capital employed will be inescapable and primarily the business will need to establish the basic cause; that it is the demand and not the efficiency of the fixed assets. Where possible it is advisable to identify unused assets and segregate their value as such so as to relate performance to the assets actually in use in order to localise their efficiency rating.

Current assets are the more vulnerable because control of their creation can not be formalised as in the manner for the fixed assets. They arise, as the title implies, from the current or day-to-day operations of the business from events, local decisions and omissions of management and also from circumstances outside the business itself. If a supplier improves upon his lead-time the stock investment will rise; if an anticipated product demand does not materialise work-in-progress and finished stocks can rise; if a customer is short of cash and delays payment of his account, then the investment in debtors will rise.

A saving grace of current assets is that, whereas control of the initial expenditure is more difficult than for fixed assets, management action is possible subsequently to correct the position. Control first is at operational level with disciplined procedures and criteria for judgment in the spheres where circumstances are within the control of management. These will include stores control for reorder levels of materials; production control for ensuring adherence to work cycles; and the disciplines of granting credit terms on sales.

Next it is a matter of demonstrating, accurately, regularly and quickly, the expenditures in current assets through the control accounting in sufficient detail for the position to be clearly appreciated. It is admittedly a process of surveying what has actually happened and since this is past tense, no amount of management action will change it—only correct it afterwards.

Since current assets are of a variable nature it becomes necessary to establish standards of acceptability between the related factors—the 'caused' and the 'causing'—and to monitor the actual ratios against the standards and observing the trends. Management should then be alerted to early anticipating action to prevent advance effects from becoming really harmful.

The use of ratios in this way falls into two spheres according to the purpose and objective of the control: **efficiency ratios** and **liquidity ratios**.

Efficiency Ratios

The following ratios are particularly relevant to control of Working Capital.

Stockholdings to Usage

The purpose of holding stocks is to ensure continuity of operations and so avoid the cost penalties of running out of stock, such as machine and manpower standing time and the delayed delivery to the customer with its possible permanent harm. The chief factors governing the amount of stock to hold are the rate of usage and how long it takes for replacements to arrive, and particularly the extent that these factors may vary. At the same time, this continuity of operations, ensured through the holding of stocks, needs to be undertaken efficiently—that is, at the lowest combined cost of the investment and the administrative cost of replacing the stock. This will determine the maximum stock and in turn the average stock. The formula is

$$\text{Average stock} = \frac{\text{Maximum stock} - \text{Minimum stock}}{2}$$

Effective control will first require a standard or target against which to compare the actual stockholding. An acceptable common factor can be the time content—how long it will take to exhaust the stock. The variable factor to convert a stock valuation will be the rate of usage expressed in value terms. The standard time content can be one established by custom and practice or be that of a known efficient business in the same industry, or the previous best attained by the particular business; but the best origin should be through its own budget control data, namely:

(*a*) Calculation of maximum and minimum stock of each item stored from newly expressed economic order quantities.

(*b*) Evaluation of these maximum and minimum stocks at standard prices.

(*c*) Calculation of the average stock value per formula.

(*d*) Interpretation of the average stock value into a usage time factor by relating it to the budget value of production materials required for the ensuing budget period.

Thus	Calculated average stock:	£99,200
	Value of budgeted production materials:	£256,800
	Budget period	8 weeks
	Ratio of usage =	

$$\frac{\text{Valuation of stockholding}}{\text{Value of budgeted production materials}} \times \text{Budget period}$$

$$= \frac{£99{,}200}{£256{,}800} \times 8 \text{ weeks}$$

$$= 3{\cdot}1 \text{ weeks}$$

The actual stockholding is also converted into a ratio of usage requiring an appropriate measure to interpret the level of usage which the stockholding is in existence to service and a prerequisite will be for this and the stock to have a common basis of valuation. The ability to ensure this will depend upon the information available, and where the study is internal to the business, this should present few problems. External assessments depend upon the published information, some of which is more detailed than others. If a general heading of 'stocks' is used to describe the stockholding, it becomes a matter of deciding upon the probable content of the valuation, bearing in mind the type of company and product, and extracting a usage indicator of similar content and the relative period of time. Thus if the title in its context is taken to imply that the stocks consist of materials only, the content of the valuation would be expected to be 'at cost' and the usage indicator could be the purchases of materials for the accounting period under review. If the interpretation was total stocks inclusive of materials, work-in-progress and finished products, then the content of valuation would be expected to be direct materials, direct wages and total factory overheads. The usage indicator here could be the cost of production comprising the same contents for the accounting period under review.

The information available should always be used to the very best advantage to interpret the situation for right judgments to be made. Strictly, stockholdings exist to meet the next immediate demand, so if information on this from the budgetary control data is available, then a more accurate interpretation is possible. The next best information will be for an immediate past actual period on the assumption that this reflects the latest known level of activity. In the case of manufacturing concerns it will be the data reflecting production activity rather than sales activity, which would reflect the environment in which the stockholdings are operating.

In the case of a materials stockholding, the following presentation illustrates the alternative use of information that may be available. The order conveys the preference subject to availability of the data.

Actual stock-holding of materials:	£147,500
Budget of material requirements from production budget:	£256,800
Duration of new budget period:	8 weeks
Value of material cost of production for previous year:	£1,237,100
Value of material purchases for previous year:	£1,310,000

Usage ratio related to budget $= \dfrac{£147{,}500}{£256{,}800} \times 8$

$= 4{\cdot}6$ weeks of usage

Usage ratio related to cost of production $= \dfrac{£147{,}500}{£1{,}237{,}100} \times 52$

$= 6{\cdot}2$ weeks of usage

Usage ratio related to cost of purchases $= \dfrac{147{,}500}{£1{,}310{,}000} \times 52$

$= 5{\cdot}85$ weeks of usage

The above are alternative interpretations of the period of time the actual stocks in hand will last according to which of the information happens to be available. The period of usage appropriate to the basis chosen should be compared with the policy target which the business sets itself that stocks should be sufficient to minimise the cost of providing them and ensure continuity of operations, and earlier demonstration of how this could be calculated is relevant to use here—namely, 3·1 weeks.

When information of stockholdings is detailed, providing separate valuations for materials, work-in-progress and finished products, then separate ratios reflecting efficiency in the investments become possible, providing opportunities for more precise control and the more specific segregation of the respective responsibilities. In the case of work-in-progress the ratio standard can be extracted from the budget control data or from the manufacturing time-cycle of the particular business, thus reflecting the nature and complexity of the product. Guidance is needed as to the content of the stock value and this can often be discerned from the manner of presentation of the data. It is then necessary to interpret the usage or rate of throughput in the same content terms to ensure a like-for-like relationship. Appropriate interpretations could be:

Basis of stock valuation	*Throughput interpretation*
Prime cost	Direct wages and materials cost of production for an accounting period.
Variable cost	Direct wages, materials and variable overheads cost of production for an accounting period.
Works total cost	Direct wages, materials and total overheads absorbed cost of production for an accounting period.

If the budgeted costs of production were available for the next accounting period, then these would be preferable, and if costs of production were not apparent, then budgeted cost of sales would suffice. In standard costing the stock valuation of work-in-progress would be at a standard cost and therefore the throughput valuation would also be at standard cost.

Care should be taken when progress payments apply that the net stock valuations after progress payment deductions are used.

Calculation of the usage ratio is as previously demonstrated:

$$\text{Usage ratio} = \frac{\text{Value of WIP stock}}{\text{Value of cost of production}} \times \text{Weeks of accounting period}$$

$$= \frac{£367{,}800}{£455{,}370} \times 13 \text{ weeks (Specimen figures)}$$

$$= 10{\cdot}5 \text{ weeks}$$

Finished product stocks exist to serve the sales demand and therefore the activity or usage level will be reflected by the cost of sales and similarly to work-in-progress; it is necessary to discern the content of the stock valuation and evaluate the throughput in the same cost terms, but the stress here is that it is the cost of sales which is most relevant. The same comments about the use of budget information and the application of standard costs apply.

It should be emphasised that efficiency of investments in stockholdings is highlighted through the use of usage ratios. They can give indications about a business and the way it is run, whether it seems to have management competence and whether a sense of control is apparent. For internal use these ratios are only the first level in the sequence of control in that they alert and give warning about the degree of efficiency, the general area of responsibility and where correction is required. It is the action taken by management arising from this information that is important in the process of control and especially the effectiveness of such action; it is one thing deciding upon a course of action or even next giving the necessary instruction to subordinates about what they are required to do, but it is then necessary to ensure that their interpretation of the instructions and the effectiveness of their performance brings about the results intended. Where there is little or no stores control at all investments in stocks will almost certainly adversely increase. This can also apply when the control procedures are not being revised to accord with the present circumstances, particularly in regard to demand and usage levels. Discipline and responsibility are the bases of effective control.

Debtors to Sales

The investment in debtors is governed by the interplay of sales and payments, these being the basic ingredients and therefore the essential factors contributing to the investment. Thus the focus for control will be the value of sales, the credit terms operating and the degree to which the customers honour the credit terms.

The credit terms may be an important feature of the marketing competitiveness, custom and practice in the trade or industry, or subject to the negotiating strengths of the buyer and seller. With mixed products or different sectors of the market differing credit terms may apply, but on the whole one business may have basic terms which they apply. Ensuring payment within the credit terms is a matter for specific control, keeping in mind that the transaction is not completed until this is ensured, and an early prerequisite is to make a judgment about a customer's ability to pay before the commitment is made, i.e. at the order placing stage.

With reasonably stable conditions of credit operating, the prime influence upon debtors will be the volume of sales in a direct relationship. A ratio interpreting this relationship can be a straightforward percentage of debtors to sales, but the more self-explanatory will be the time-ratio reflecting the period of sales which is comparable, as a measure of efficiency, with the effects of the conditions of credit. Debtors will consist of the most recent sales and therefore the time content will be based on these, especially in seasonal and variable circumstances. Generally it will be necessary to use sales for the most recent prior period as representing the sales level influencing the debtors' investment under review.

The standard against which to compare the actual time-ratio will be based upon the terms of credit operating, and a certain amount of care will be needed as to the date when the debtor balance is struck and the normal settlement period operates. If four-weekly accounting periods operate, the closing date can occur at different times in a calendar month, so that if the settlement period is based upon calendar months there could arise occasions when the debtor balance operating date falls just before or just after the settlement date. Where a standard period of credit is allowed—say, 'payment one month'—then this will be the base for reflecting a standard time ratio against which to make comparisons and judgments. If varying terms of credit apply then it is a matter of calculating a weighted average from the sales mix of credit terms.

Under credit terms of 'payment one month' the debtor is required to pay for all the sales of one month at the end of the following month, by which time a second month's sales have been made. Even if he pays promptly the payment will not be received until the early days of the next following month, and the business can be pleased if settlement is received in the first two weeks of that month. In effect, therefore, 10 weeks of new sales could occur and the creditor still be content, so the standard could be at eight weeks of sales (ideal) or 10 weeks of sales (practical expectation). The period of credit is not necessarily reflecting the *average* investment in debtors, but the investment at a particular time, i.e. at the end of the calendar month when the accounts are struck.

The time-ratio of an actual debtor balance is obtained by relating it to an appropriate sales level for a period of time as nearly preceding the date of the balance as to reflect the rate of sales which would have influenced it. When intervals are used the two months' preceding sales will be known as being wholly contained in the end-of-the month debtor balance (in the example of Fig. 16) and it will then be a matter of interpreting to what extent the third preceding month's sales remain in the balance. Otherwise it is necessary to use the best prior information of sales available, and if only annual sales are given, then this will be used.

Control of debtors will be through the medium of an efficient credit control system which keeps every account under surveillance, initiating pressures for payment up to litigation stages if necessary although in times of general cash shortages considered judgments will be required about taking steps to initiate a liquidation. Subdivisions of the debtors' balance in age groups are helpful and can form the basis of the pressure procedures; other subdivisions will come from separate ledgers for areas and perhaps thus focusing upon sections of the sales force or of market sectors—separating wholesalers from retailers, for example. The most effective contribution of the credit control system will often

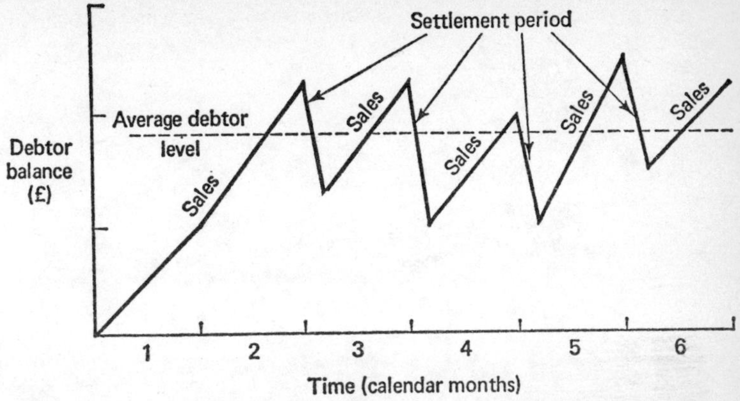

Fig. 16. The sales content of debtors under 'payment one month' terms of credit.

Notes

1. In the first month and second month no payment falls due.
2. Payment for month 1 sales is received in the early days of month 3; for month 2 in month 4, and so on.
3. In calendar-month accounts the review is always made of the peaks of debtor investment and therefore the standard time ratio must reflect this, i.e. min. 8 weeks; max. 10 weeks of sales content.
4. The average debtor level is obtained by taking the cumulative balance each day or week in the period under review averaged over the number of days or weeks, which could be six or seven weeks' sales content in the above example.
5. The 'snapshot' date of the debtor balance can thus be seen to be important to the settlement period.

be the knowledge built up about the creditworthiness of customers to ensure that they do not build up indebtedness beyond their ability to pay; this means a control at the order acceptance stage which can only be properly undertaken by the credit controlling function. The risk of bad debts must always be assessed against the extra volume and contribution possible from a freer atmosphere—it will be a matter of degree, relating the cost of the risk with the contribution, and this will need to be kept under constant review.

Examples of Debtor:Sales Time Ratios

Debtor balance	£175,600
Preceding month's sales	£85,000 in 4·1 weeks
Second preceding month's sales	£50,000 in 4·3
Third preceding month's sales	£35,000 in 4·6
Last quarter's sales	£170,000 in 13·0
Four preceding month's sales	£25,000 in 4·2
Annual sales	£820,000 in 52·0

Using preceding month's sales: $\frac{£175,600}{£85,000} \times 4{\cdot}1 \quad = 8{\cdot}47$ weeks of sales

Using preceding two months' sales: $\frac{£175,600}{£135,000} \times 8{\cdot}4 \quad = 10{\cdot}93$ weeks of sales

Using preceding quarter's sales: $\frac{£175,600}{£170,000} \times 13 \quad = 13{\cdot}43$ weeks of sales

Using annual sales: $\dfrac{£175{,}600}{£820{,}000} \times 52 = 11{\cdot}14$ weeks of sales

Using sales in monthly steps:

Preceding month 1	£85,000	= 4·1 weeks of sales
2	£50,000	= 4·3
3	£35,000	= 4·6
4*	£5,600	= 0·94
	£175,600	= 13·94 weeks of sales

Month 4 $= \dfrac{£5{,}600}{£25{,}000} \times 4{\cdot}2$ weeks

* Balance of £5,600 necessary to equate with stock capital of £175,600.

Creditors to Purchases

As an item of net current assets the balance of creditors needs to be kept under control in terms of a ratio of time, the method being similar as for debtors. In the absence of any information about credit purchases of expense items, it will be necessary to assume that the creditors' balance is derived from material purchases. The standard for comparison will be based upon the terms of credit agreed on purchases and should this be 'payment one month' it should be realised that payment is usually at the end of calendar month, which would reduce the creditors' balance as at that time, so this should then only comprise the last month's purchases.

When the accounting presentation of the P. & L. account shows the purchases with the opening and closing stocks, then the purchases for the period are readily available for the ratio calculation. Should the presentation be in the form of costs of production, then it will be necessary to calculate the purchases from the material cost of production and the opening and closing stocks of material—in the manner of a material control account:

	£
Material cost of production for the year	1,237,100
Add—Closing stock of materials	147,500
	1,384,600
Less—Opening stock of materials	74,600
	£1,310,000
Creditors' balance at the end of the year	£161,230

Time ratio $= \dfrac{161{,}230}{1{,}310{,}000} \times 52$

$= 6.4$ weeks

The presentation may, however, give the production costs of the sales, which is the next step in the cost accounting. It will be necessary to use the opening and closing material content of work-in-progress to calculate the material cost of production and then proceed as above. Alternatively, and for preference, the two steps can be made in one by combining the opening stocks of material in work-in-progress and the material stocks and similarly for the closing stocks:

		£
Material cost of sales for the year		1,172,820
Add—Closing stock:		
Material content of WIP	216,492	
Material stocks	147,500	363,992
		1,536,812
Less—Opening stocks:		
Material content of WIP	152,212	
Material stocks	74,600	226,812
Purchases for the year		£1,310,000

The constituents of the work-in-progress are not always shown, in which case the material content will not be available; it becomes a matter then for discernment as to what this could be. If the materials cost of production predominates it would be logical to substitute the opening and closing total work-in-progress values; should this not be so, the proportion of material comprising the total cost of production could be assumed to apply to both the opening and closing stocks of work-in-progress. To be really precise in assumptions of this context it would be more logical to assume that as the work-in-progress is only part finished, then only half the labour and production overheads have been expended and all the materials issued.

Examples

		£
Cost of production—	Materials	1,237,100 = 60%
	Direct Wages	371,130 = 18%
	Production Overheads	453,603 = 22%
		£2,061,833

Increase in WIP (total cost)	£96,500
assumed material content 60% =	£57,900

Alternatively:

Material	60% = 60/80 = 72,375
Direct wages ($\frac{1}{2}$ of 18)	= 9%
Production overhead ($\frac{1}{2}$ of 22)	= 11%
	80%

Actual ratios in time will interpret the extent the credit terms are being exceeded and thus the degree to which finance is being extracted from the suppliers. Here there is danger of any single creditor taking extreme action to obtain payment, but before this many suppliers will, through their own credit control, put a stop on further supplies.

Fixed Assets and Total Assets to Sales

Control in this sphere is essentially that of measuring efficiency as to the work generated by the assets rather than effectiveness in the adjustment of the asset to a level more competent to support the effort. The use of ratios in this context has been dealt with earlier on pages 172–4.

Liquidity Ratios

Managing the finances of a business can often call for careful judgment in striking the right balance between an outwardly aggressive policy of making the resources work energetically, and rewardingly, and retaining enough in liquid cash to satisfy the outgoings that arise. Ideally the plan is to maintain a constant turn-round of the funds so that enough arrive to satisfy the next immediate demand.

Good financial management is based upon cash flow forecasts, regularly revised, which reflect the plans of the business and the amendments to it which arise from the pressures operating upon the business. Keeping an eye upon what is next likely to happen is essential for good control. Next in importance is to ensure that the turn round in funds is keeping a proper equilibrium between the incomings and the outgoings, which can be demonstrated by a few strategic ratios supported by other pointers by way of classification or emphasis.

Control through knowledge of liquidity is not only an internal matter. The liquidity of suppliers is important to the buying function, who have the responsibility of ensuring continuity of supplies, and therefore overcommitment and possible liquidation needs to be taken into account. The marketing function also needs to be sensitive about the liquidity of customers to ensure that contracts are eventually closed with payment; consideration of this aspect before contracts are entered into can often be rewarding.

Current Assets to Current Liabilities

This ratio reflects the potential incoming funds related to liabilities arising for payment. It is usual for bank overdrafts to be included in the current liabilities on the grounds that this would be a loan of a short-term nature and certainly the lending of funds by banks in this way can be a fluctuating policy, depending upon the economic climate, so that a call-in of overdrafts can occur at the very times a business is expecting difficulties from other spheres. However, bank overdrafts can rotate over extended periods and become of a semi-permanent nature, when they might more properly be considered to be of a capital nature, rather than as a current liability. A generally accepted level for this ratio is 2:1 but this can be subjected to further considerations outlined later.

Quick Assets to Current Liabilities

This is a more precise measure in that it seeks to relate the next immediate accessible sources of cash available with the liabilities to be met. The assets will comprise debtors, marketable securities and cash, and the liabilities those for current settlement, and would thus exclude a bank overdraft as this would not rank for immediate settlement—stocks are excluded. A generally accepted ratio is 1:1.

Other Supporting Considerations

The creditor's balance reflects the extent to which either goods or services have been received—concluded orders and contracts—but the business may have entered into commitments of an aggravated or abnormal nature which should be taken into consideration as forthcoming creditors. These could be capital commitments, buying commitments or other circumstances such as heavy advertising or high research expenditures. Most of these would be knowledge of an internal nature, but for external judgments capital commitments need to be declared in published accounts. Chairmen's reports are often revealing about intentions and good sensitive observances of outward manifestations of a company's plans can be helpful.

The maturing of long-term loans can be an important forward commitment. Internally this would be known and plans laid accordingly; in external situations the fact of maturability needs to be disclosed under the Companies Act.

A fast turnover of stocks will excuse a lower ratio of current assets to current liabilities and a fast ratio of debt collection would explain low debtors and the resulting similar lower ratio, and also above average credit taking will also depress this ratio. These factors are therefore worthy of further examination in such a circumstance.

Knowledge of the business and particularly the extent it is subject to seasonal changes may be of help in considering what a business's next immediate prospects are likely to be. Internally these would be known and planned for and externally they can be discerned. Businesses within industries of known cycles invariably tailor their credit terms within the known pattern; the agricultural industry is probably the best known in this respect.

Businesses subject to spontaneous circumstances and therefore more risks need to be judged by their need for more generous cover to weather adverse effects upon their affairs. Vulnerability to loss of profits can here be a helpful guide, reflected by the ratio of fixed costs to total costs. A high ratio of this type should require a high ratio of current assets to current liabilities to tide over a period of depression when the break-even point induced by the high fixed costs would be more quickly under pressure and cash flow challenged.

In times of inflation liquidity becomes a special problem because investments in higher costs of supplies and pay increases to workpeople occur some time prior to the receipt of cash from their earnings. Where the business is unable to pass on all or any of such increases to its customers, or when this is subject to protracted delay, the outcome can become serious. A liquidity ratio increasingly used under such circumstances is:

(Stock + Debtors − Creditors) ÷ Long-Term Capital

This relates those current assets which reflect the existing level of inflation to the stable valued long-term sources of capital. The higher this ratio the greater will be the pressure to raise more finance or retain more profits within the business, either by an overall increase in net profits or at the expense of the profits distributed.

Diagnosis and Conclusions about Performance

The practice of using numerals to communicate about events, happenings and achievements in business is quite old. As business affairs have become more complex so has this form of presentation developed and because it is really a coded communication particular skills are needed to decode the messages and extract the full value of the knowledge conveyed. Accountants rank highly among those capable of using this form of code, but the training of any manager is not complete without attention to it.

Notwithstanding the need to acquire some degree of skill in this sphere, a large proportion of managers either do not achieve sufficient skill or remain uncomfortable and unsure in the use of the numerate code, so that there is a great need for a more comprehensible translation into words in order to:

(i) Make the communication better understood.
(ii) Save the time of the receiver of the communication in translating and extracting the meaning of the message.
(iii) Ensure there is minimal possibility of the message being misunderstood.
(iv) Ensure the appropriate emphasis or clarification is communicated.

The more comprehensive the information the greater the need for this translation into words. Where the information is internal to the business managers will be better aware of the context, and supporting data are usually available to supplement, amplify and clarify, but external information is invariably without this support, so that a translation is dependent upon the limited communication available and the skill of the translator becomes even more important. Business is also entering an era of greater dissemination of information about performance to its employees, who generally have still less skill in understanding the numerate code or the vocabulary of business and accounts so that presentation and translation will become of greater importance.

The first stage of translation is the observation or comment about performance arising from the comparisons of absolute data and ratios such as:

'Improved profit volume but ratio of profit to capital employed is marginally below target.'

'The ratio of profit to capital employed is only fair compared to the average of the industry.'

'The ratio of profit to capital employed is much inferior to the previous year.'

There is, however, a considerable difference between comment and diagnosis. Comment amounts to a direct translation of the figures into words; diagnosis calls for the identification of an opinion or a conclusion from the symptoms which must be recognisable from the data presented. Diagnosis thus seeks firstly to extract the key data and interpret their significance and then to explain the reasons why the situation is such as it is. From this more comprehensive knowledge the manager will know what decision and action to take. Diagnosis thus requires knowledge about causes and effects in the business scene and an ability to recognise relevant and associated data with the capability of interpreting it. This will entail the use of ratios and absolute data of a sample of the key facts in a cross-checking pattern. Experience can supply a valuable contribution in forming possible and logical explanations for changes and differences observed.

The process of diagnosis then proceeds to examine each explanation for justification from whatever supporting data are available on a simple 'go' or 'no go' conclusion. The depth of the study and often the conclusiveness of the judgment will thus be limited by the volume and nature of the information to hand—apart from the skill of the diagnostician. This limitation may leave the final conclusion as a choice between two or more alternatives supported by the most practical reasoning in the context in which the information is set. In an internal business situation, supplementary information may be needed; it will be necessary to define precisely what data are required and should they not be readily available, then consideration will need to be given to the cost of obtaining the information against the importance of the judgment to be made. In an external situation the diagnosis is a prisoner of the information supplied and therefore the conclusions may be less precise.

The process of diagnosis is largely one of posing the challenge as to why, and then seeking the answers from the data. If, for example, profit is found to be lower than expected it is inadequate to comment:

'The profit under review is £10,500, or 5·7 per cent below target.'

This is only a direct translation of the numerate code. Diagnosis seeks an answer as to how this has come about and will offer explanations and from this suggest courses of action to correct the situation.

Where profit is under review in this way, and especially if the ratio to capital employed is significant, then the inadequacy can be the profit itself, or the capital employed or both. If the amount of profit seems adequate but the return on capital employed inadequate, then inquiries will proceed into the capital content for efficiency in the use of the capital or the control of capital investment along the lines outlined earlier in the chapter. Suggestions as to inadequacy of the amount of profit will lead to an examination of the factors which control this—namely, selling prices, volume and costs. In external situations it is rare for information to be available about volume in terms of product units and therefore changes in selling prices are not easily discernible. Volume of sales or production then needs to be measured in terms of value. Recourse to the rate and amount of contribution will give valuable clues, as a stable profit/volume ratio will suggest that selling prices and variables are unchanged. Should an examination of the rates of individual items of variable cost reveal some inconsistencies, then there arises the possibility of compensating changes in selling prices or other of the variable costs. A further search of the data could disclose a higher proportion of wholesale or export sales with their keener prices and higher discounts; thus where an analysis of sales or production is available, this may provide data about selling prices or contribution changes as the result of a change in mix. Any inconsistencies in the variables will need to be pinpointed and here, of course, in times of inflation the direct material content will be very vulnerable.

Thus it will be seen that diagnosis is a matter of posing the appropriate questions and when the answer is unsatisfactory ('no go') the questions proceed along that avenue on a similar basis. If there is more than one acceptable answer, cross-checks are sought to eliminate some in favour of others until the most likely one is apparent.

By way of further explanation and guidance we take the following questions from examinations in Financial Management. Any diagnosis will be limited by the data presented.

Worked Examples

Example 1

Fig. 17 relates to a major development project on one of your company's products.

(*a*) Interpret the significance of the information conveyed by the chart.

As financial controller, safeguarding the finances and profitability of the company, state:

(*b*) What further information you would require.

(*c*) What action you would take.

(CIMA)

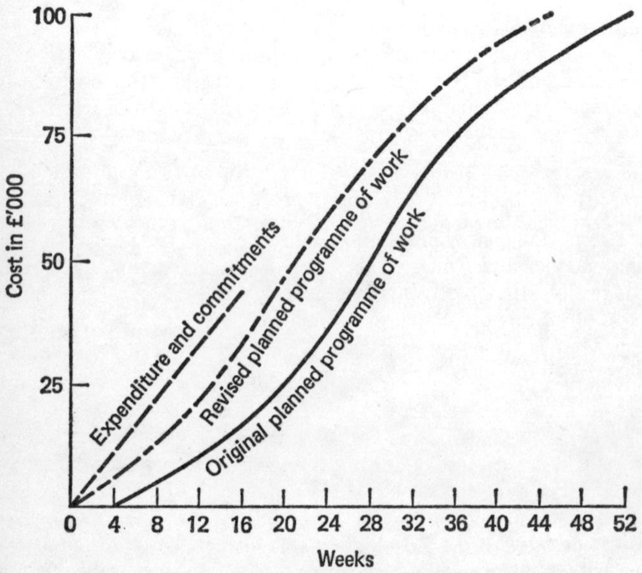

Fig. 17. Details of development project for Example 1.

Interpretation

The information expresses costs and time.

The programme of work, being expressed in costs, represents expenditure in salaries and direct variables if internal, or regular progress charges if wholly external.

The straight line to week 16 purports to show actual expenditure to that date and as such it would appear to demonstrate about £8,000 overspending. However, as this includes 'commitments', the planned expenditure may include these later in the programme when the commitments are expected to mature into payments.

The revised total cost is the same at £100,000.

Commencement of the project is brought forward four weeks and the conclusion eight weeks, thus compressing the time period into 44 instead of 48 weeks.

Funds to meet the expenditure will now be required earlier than planned, ranging from four weeks to eight weeks earlier—for example, the first £50,000 will be required by week 20 instead of week 28.

The project will thus be earlier and quicker in its completion and there is some doubt as to whether there is overspending. It is a matter of ensuring that the funds can now be available for the revised timing, what effects the change in programme can have, and to ascertain whether overspending is taking place and, if so, what the final effects of this could be.

Further Information Required

Identity of the commitments and identification of where they are allowed for in the programme. The aim is to check whether the expenditure and commitment are comparable as plotted with the revised programme, and at the same time to evaluate any actual overspending that is occurring. Overspending will affect the eventual profitability of the product.

Identify the reason for revising the time-scale of the programme with a view to establishing whether it will similarly affect the subsequent pre-production stage and in due course production, deliveries and the receipt of funds.

Establish whether and which project was deferred to permit the earlier start on this project; the objective is whether any expenditure is deferred to make the funding of this project easier to finance.

Establish what is to happen in weeks 44 to 52, with a view to discovering whether any standing costs, salaries, etc., of the department—if the expenditure is internal—will be continuing without any subsequent project, or whether another can be brought forward in time to take up the facilities.

Action by the Financial Controller

Evaluate the effects of the earlier requirement of funds for the project upon the cash flow of the company and ensure cash will be available by either:

(*a*) Deferring other expenditure if difficulties appear likely.
(*b*) Arranging temporary facilities with the bank.

Reappraise likely revised cost of project if some overspending has been established, particularly should this appear to affect the product profitability and any decisions that we made upon it.

Report and advise of the facts and the reappraisal to chief designer, marketing director and managing director.

Ensure a revised sanction is authorised for any reassessed level of spending apparent.

Example 2

The following information relates to an engineering company making consumer durables:

	Actual		*Budget*
	19x4/x5	*19x4/x5*	*19x5/x6*
	£	£	£
Sales	214,000	235,000	275,000
Production cost:			
Materials	79,180	82,250	96,250
Direct labour	34,240	32,900	37,125
Indirect labour	34,240	38,775	44,000
Other costs	26,322	28,670	35,750
	173,982	182,595	213,125
Administration	21,400	25,850	33,000
Selling	5,992	7,050	7,150
Distribution	2,568	2,820	3,850
	203,942	218,315	257,125
Net profit before tax	10,058	16,685	17,875
	214,000	235,000	275,000
Balance sheet at year-end:			
Fixed assets at cost	120,000	155,000	175,000
Less depreciation	65,000	65,000	80,000
	55,000	90,000	95,000
Stock and work in progress	55,112	62,452	67,808
Debtors	35,178	32,192	33,904
Other current assets	4,210	3,500	2,750
	149,500	188,144	199,462
Less current liabilities	17,500	12,512	15,184
Total capital employed	132,000	175,632	184,278
Number of people employed (Average during year)			
Direct	43	41	47
Works indirect	31	35	40
Administration	30	37	36
Sales	6	7	7
	110	120	130
Floor space occupied (square feet)	30,000	30,000	32,000

Give your interpretation of the production, commercial and financial management of the company over the period shown, illustrating your answer with a tabulation of selected key ratios.

(CIMA)

Evaluation of Performance

	19x3/4	*19x4/5*	*Budget 19x5/6*
	£	£	£
Sales	214,000	235,000	275,000
Profitability			
Profit amount	10,058	16,685	17,875
Profit:Sales	4·7%	7·1%	6·5%
Profit:Capital employed	7·6%	9·5%	9·7%
Sales:Capital employed	162%	134%	149%

1. The improvement in 19x4/5 has the appearance of a determined effort—the profit is increased by 66 per cent against a sales increase of 10 per cent.
2. This has been achieved from a marked improvement in the profit contribution from the customer.

   This could be from increased selling prices or reduced costs.

   Increased selling prices with increased sales may be a little doubtful.

   As the ratio of profit to capital employed indicates more efficient use of capital, the improvement is more likely to be coupled with efficiency in reduced costs.

   The achievement has been from a reduced degree of volume effort from the capital employed—134 per cent against 162 per cent—which suggests there is capacity in hand if even better sales can be found.
3. The budget for 19x5/6 appears to be a consolidating effort on the 19x4/5 achievement. A better throughput of effort is planned at 149 per cent and the efficiency in use of capital improved marginally.

   With a decided further increase in sales (17 per cent) budgeted at the expense of the profit-sales margin, this suggests the company may be bidding for volume from a reduction in selling prices.

Evaluation of Production Performance

	19x3/4 Percentage of works cost	*19x4/5 Percentage of works cost*	*Budget 19x5/6 Percentage of works cost*
Cost structure			
Materials	45·5	45·1	45·2
Direct labour	19·7	18·0	17·4
Indirect labour	19·7	21·2	20·6
Other costs	15·1	15·7	16·8
	100·0	100·0	100·0
Use of Labour			
Indirect:Direct (£)	100%	118%	119%
(numbers)	72%	85%	85%
Labour rates:			
Direct (p.a.)	£796	£802	£790
Works indirect (p.a.)	£1,105	£1,108	£1,100
Profit per direct worker	£234	£407	£380
Profit per indirect worker	£324	£477	£447

1. 19x4/5 is emphasised as the much improved year.
2. There was a significant change in tactics in that more indirect workers were introduced in this year at the expense of the direct workers who were reduced in numbers.
3. The materials content keeps quite stable.
4. There is a rising trend in other expenses which offsets the gains in direct labour content.
5. With the labour rates holding quite constant the conception is that the improvement in volume did not arise from the effort per person, otherwise an improvement in earnings could have been expected.

   The improvement could therefore have been in methods—namely, improved productivity of the plant.
6. It is significant that the wages rates of the indirect workers are considerably in excess of those for the direct workers.

   This suggests that the indirect workers are more highly skilled and as this is an engineering company they could largely comprise tool-setters and tool-makers.

   This would confirm the impression that the improvements have come from better or enhanced methods.

Evaluation of Commercial Performance

	19x3/4	*19x4/5*	*Budget 19x5/6*
Selling costs	£5,992	£7,050	£7,150
Sales	£214,000	£235,000	£275,000
Selling costs: Sales	2·8%	3·0%	2·6%
Sales per sales staff	£35,666	£33,570	£39,285
Profit per sales staff	£1,675	£2,383	£2,555

1. The increase in sales cost in 19x4/5 reflects the extra effort required for the increase in sales; for one extra staff this is a good achievement.

   The volume benefits are reflected in the production performance.
2. The increase in the budget sales for no extra staff is clearly demonstrated, adding some confirmation to the suggestion that this volume increase is likely to be achieved from reduced selling prices.

   It is possible that the further improvement in sales is expected partly to be assisted by improved deliveries from the production efficiencies.

Evaluation of the Financial Control and Efficiency of Assets

Fixed Capital

1. The depreciation reserve in 19x4/5 is the same as 19x3/4, on increased fixed assets at cost of £35,000.

   This hardly means that there was no depreciation charged in 19x4/5; if this was so it would have been apparent in 'Other costs', which presumably must include depreciation.
2. The probability is that assets were disposed of during 19x4/5 necessitating the writing out of Costs and Depreciation from each account. As there is no profit or loss on sale of assets shown this would imply that they had been disposed of at book value, or that their life had exceeded the time-span covered by the depreciation, so that the net book value was nil and they had been scrapped and not sold.

The net effect therefore is that the depreciation reserve written out equated to the annual depreciation charge. This further means that the new additions were much in excess of the £35,000 asset value increase between the two years.

This suggests a major overhaul of the fixed assets in an aim for greater productivity, which bears out the possibilities expressed under the review of employee performance.

3. This diagnosis is borne out by the budgeted increase in Other costs, which undoubtedly reflects the higher depreciation on the 19x4/5 and the 19x5/6 increases in assets.

Working Capital

	19x3/4	*19x4/5*	*Budget 19x5/6*
Stocks @ WIP usage ratio (Stocks: Total production costs)	16·5 wks	17·8 wks	16·5 wks
Debtors' time ratio (Debtors: Sales)	8·5 wks	7·1 wks	6·4 wks
Liabilities time ratio (Current liabilities: Materials)	11·5 wks	7·9 wks	6·2 wks
Quick liquidity ratio (Debtors: Creditors— Composition of other current assets not clear)	2·0:1	2·6:1	2·2:1
Basic liquidity ratio (Current assets: Current liabilities)	5·4:1	7·8:1	6·9:1

1. The cash flow is very good with both liquidity tests better than double the normal expectation. This should give rise to considerations of holding excess cash and improved utilisation of these resources. The stockholding ratio each year is quite good for an engineering manufacturing business and the debtors' collection as good as could be expected.
2. Considering 19x4/5 was a big effort year the company did well to improve its liquidity ratios.
3. The expectation of increased higher sales in 19x5/6 on reduced credit to debtors seems optimistic; but this gives further support to the probable reduction in selling prices in that year.

Evaluation Summary

1. There was a successful drive for all round improvement in 19x4/5 comprising:

   (*a*) New plant and turn-out of old plant.
   (*b*) Change in the use of labour and methods.
   (*c*) Improved use of labour and plant.

2. A consolidation is planned in 19x5/6; the efficiencies gained permit some lower selling prices with an expected further increase in volume which the company is now able to handle.
3. There is good cash flow control and an improving efficiency in the use of resources generally.

Questions

1. Mansfield plc is a major manufacturer of confectionary and other food products. The company has recently embarked on a major acquisition programme to increase the sales of its products throughout the world. For example, in 19x6 the company acquired a major American potato crisp company, Ben's Foods Inc. Presented below are extracts from the Group's financial statements for 19x7, together with several financial ratios that have been derived from those statements.

Mansfield plc Group Balance Sheet on 31st December 19x7

	19x7 £m	*19x6* £m
Fixed Assets		
Tangible assets	408·5	359·7
Current assets		
Stocks	172·9	159·1
Debtors	171·1	145·9
Cash at bank and in hand	55·7	25·1
	399·7	330·1
Creditors: Amounts falling due within one year		
Bank overdrafts and loans	47·7	54·3
Other creditors	181·6	163·5
	229·3	217·8
Net current assets	170·4	112·3
Total assets less current liabilities	578·9	472·0
Creditors: Amounts falling due after more than one year	16·0	13·5
Loan capital	148·6	99·9
Provisions for liabilities and charges	21·6	9·5
	392·7	349·1
Capital and reserves		
Called up share capital	83·0	82·0
Share premium account	75·0	73·4
Revaluation reserve	47·3	47·5
Profit and loss account (including currency translation differences)	187·4	146·2
	392·7	349·1

Mansfield plc Group Profit and Loss Account for the Year Ended 31st December 19x7

	19x7 £m	*19x6* £m
Turnover	1156·5	951·9
Cost of sales	739·0	617·1
Gross profit	417·5	334·8
Distribution costs	48·3	39·1
Marketing, selling and administrative expenses	280·0	226·5
Other operating income	(4·6)	(4·2)

Trading profit	93·8	73·4
Interest	19·3	12·2
Profit on ordinary activities before taxation	74·5	61·2
Taxation on profit on ordinary activities	16·5	14·9
Profit on ordinary activities after taxation	58·0	46·3
Extraordinary items	11·5	13·5
Profit attributable to ordinary shareholders	46·5	32·8
Dividends	18·4	15·7
Added to reserves	28·1	17·1
Earnings per ordinary share	36·0p	30·9p
Calculation based on following number of ordinary shares	160·6m	149·5m

Selected notes to the accounts

1. *Geographical analysis of sales and trading profit*

	19x7		*19x6*	
	Sales	*Trading Profit*	*Sales*	*Trading Profit*
	£m	£m	£m	£m
UK	470	39	444	36
Europe	227	5	198	3
N America	309	31	175	17
Australasia	58	2	48	1
Rest of World	93	17	87	17
	1157	94	952	74

2. *Trading profit*

	19x7	*19x6*
	£m	£m
Trading profit is after charging the following:		
Depreciation on owned assets	34	27
Depreciation on assets held under finance leases	2	2
Hire charges under operating leases	7	6

3. *Acquisitions*

	19x7	*19x6*
	£m	£m
Tangible assets	2	72
Net current assets	1	36
Net borrowings	—	(4)
	3	104
Goodwill on acquisition	—	53
Purchase consideration	3	157

The purchase consideration was financed in part by the issue of shares (£36m) and in part by loan capital and cash (£121m).

Based on the above financial statements the following ratios have been calculated:

	19x7	19x6
Profit on ordinary activities after taxation / Capital and reserves	14·8%	13·3%
Turnover / Capital and reserves	2·95	2·73
Profit on ordinary activities after taxation / Turnover	5·0%	4·9%
Current assets / Creditors—amounts falling due within one year	1·74	1·52
Interest / Trading profit	20·6%	16·6%
Profit attributable to ordinary shareholders / Dividends	2·53	2·09

You are required to write a report to a potential individual investor comparing the financial performance and business strategy of Mansfield plc in 19x6 and 19x7. Your report should state clearly the assumptions upon which your analysis has been based and indicate, with reasons, any additional information that would be useful.

(ICAEW)

2. Duit plc, a builders' merchants/DIY company is building up its national coverage of outlets. Regional companies have been set up, each with its own board of directors responsible to the main board situated in London. It is expected that eventually each regional company will have between ten and twenty outlets, each under the control of an outlet manager.

The outlet managers will be allowed to hire and fire whatever staff they need and the introduction of a head count budget is being considered by Head Office. Each outlet manager is responsible for his or her own sales policy, pricing, store layout, advertising, the general running of the outlet and the purchasing of goods for resale, subject to the recommendations below. Duit plc's policy is that outlet managers have to apply to the regional board for all items of capital expenditure greater than £500, while the regional board can sanction up to £100,000 per capital expenditure project.

Outlet sales are made to both retail and trade on either cash or credit terms. Debtor and cash control is the responsibility of regional office. Cash received is banked locally, and immediately credited to the Head Office account. Credit sales invoices are raised by the outlet with a copy sent to regional office. Within each outlet it is possible to identify the sales origin, e.g. timber yard, saw mill, building supplies, kitchen furniture, etc.

Timber for resale is supplied to an outlet on request from stocks held at regional office or direct from the ports where Duit (Timber Importers) Ltd has further stocks. Duit Kitchens Ltd provides kitchen furniture that the outlets sell. Duit plc also has a small factory making windows, doors and frames which are sold through the outlets. When purchasing other products for resale, the outlet is requested to use suppliers with which Head Office has negotiated discount buying arrangements. All invoices for outlet purchases and overheads are passed by the respective outlet manager before being paid by regional office. In existing Duit outlets a perpetual inventory system is used, with a complete physical check once a year.

Information concerning last year's actual results for one of Duit plc's outlets situated at Birport is given below:

Birport DIY Outlet

Trading and Profit and Loss Account for Year to 31st March 19x8

	£	£
Sales—note (1)		1,543,000
Less Cost of Sales		1,095,530
Prime gross margin (29%)		447,470
Less		
Wages—note (2)	87,400	
Salaries—note (3)	45,000	
Depreciation: equipment—note (4)	9,100	
buildings	3,500	
vehicles (4 cars)	6,500	
Vehicle running expenses	6,170	
Leasing of delivery lorry	6,510	
Lorry running expenses	3,100	
Energy costs	9,350	
Telephone/stationary	9,180	
Travel and entertaining	3,490	
Commission on sales	7,770	
Bad debts written off	9,440	
Advertising	25,160	
Repairs	6,000	
Rates, insurance	13,420	
Sundry expenses	10,580	
Delivery expenses	7,400	269,070
	Net profit (11·56%)	178,400

Position at 31st March 19x8

	£
Debtors	100,900
Stock	512,000

Notes:

1. Sales can be identified by till code—cash/credit, trade/retail, timber, kitchen furniture, frames, heavy building supplies, light building supplies, sawmill, etc.
2. Workforce of 15 distributed as follows: timber yard—3, sawmill—1, sales—7, general duties—1, administration—3.
3. Paid to 3 sales representatives and the manager.
4. Equipment used in sales area, sawmill, yard.

The manufacturing companies and the importing company report directly to the main board.

You are required to suggest key performance indicators which could be used in a responsibility reporting system to evaluate the performance of the outlet managers and the regional board management. Include in your answer a justification for each performance indicator that you select.

(ICAEW)

3. (*a*) A company manufacturing agricultural machinery is faced with the possibility of a strike by its direct production workers engaged on the assembly of one of its machines.

The trade union is demanding an increase of 7 per cent back-dated to the beginning of its financial year (1st January), but the company expects that if a strike does take place, it will last four weeks after which the union will settle for an increase of 5 per cent similarly back-dated.

The machine whose production would be affected by the strike is sold to distributors at a discount of 20 per cent from the current recommended selling price of £3,000.

Estimated costs for the machines are:

	Fixed per year £000	*Variable per machine* £
Production	16,000	1,800
Distribution	1,000	100

Direct labour costs comprise 40 per cent of the variable production costs.

The budgeted output is 27,500 machines in fifty working weeks per year.

If the strike takes place the following events are expected by the company:

(i) Maintenance staff, whose wages are included in the fixed production costs, would be used to carry out an overhaul of the conveyor system using £25,000 worth of materials. This overhaul would otherwise be undertaken by an outside contractor at a cost of £100,000 including materials.

(ii) Sales of 650 machines would be lost to competition. The balance that would ordinarily have been produced during the strike period could, however, be sold, but these machines would have to be made up in overtime working which would be at an efficiency rate of 90 per cent of normal. This would entail additional fixed costs of £10,000 and wage payments at time and one-half.

You are required to:

(i) State, with explanations and full supporting data, whether from a purely economic point of view you would advise the management to allow the strike to go ahead, rather than agree to the union's demand.

(ii) Explain briefly *three* factors, not considered in your above evaluation, that may have adverse financial effects for the company if the strike were to take place.

(*b*) Assume that the strike goes ahead, and that it lasts three weeks, after which agreement is reached between the company and the union for a 6 per cent pay increase back-dated to 1st January. Assume also that the anticipated loss of sales to competitors of 650 machines occurs and the balance is made up by overtime working.

A newspaper reports that the cost of the strike to the company was £5 million. The trade union counters this claim by insisting that the strike was contrived by the company, to its benefit, as the machines were selling at a loss.

You are required to:

(i) Comment on the statements made by the press and the trade union.

(ii) State, with supporting calculations, whether the company was justified in using overtime working to produce the balance of machines saleable but not produced during the strike.

(CIMA)

4. (*a*) Discuss the uses and limitations of accounting ratios to measure the viability and performance of a business. (Use suitable ratios to illustrate your answer.)

(*b*) Explain any further benefits of ratio analysis which may be gained within a scheme of inter-firm comparison.

(SCCA)

5. The summary forecast profit statement and balance sheet of the AB Company Ltd for the next 12 months is as follows:

Summary Profit Forecast for Next 12 months

	£	£
Sales income (100,000 units)		1,200,000
Less: Variable costs	900,000	
Fixed costs	150,000	
		1,050,000
Profit		£150,000

Summary Balance Sheet

Investment in fixed assets		1,500,000
Investment in working capital—Debtors	200,000	
Stock	80,000	
Cash	24,000	
	304,000	
Less: Creditors	60,000	
		244,000
Total Investment		£1,744,000

Profit as return on investment = 8.6%.

The directors are concerned about the low return on investment, particularly because of the under-utilisation of the investment in fixed assets. There is little likelihood of significant alterations to selling prices and costs and the only apparent way of improving the situation is increased sales. All sales are on credit and the company operates a very strict control procedure which has virtually eliminated bad debts. Because of this a number of potential customers have had to be refused and some existing customers have taken their business elsewhere. The suggestion has been made that a relaxation of the credit control policy could increase sales substantially. Specifically, if the company were to introduce a scheme whereby a 2 per cent discount—at present no discount is given—were given on accounts paid within ten days, and if the company were willing to accept 'riskier' customers, the sales would increase by 40 per cent. Probably 65 per cent of the customers would avail themselves of the discount and the average collection period of the remainder would be half of what it is at present. Bad debts would be of the order of 2 to 6 per cent on total sales.

Comment on the above situation, making full use of the information given and highlighting any matters which should be brought to the attention of the directors.

(CACA)

6. The financial year of Flatearthers Ltd ends on 30th September and year-end balance sheets are summarised below for the last three years.

	19x6 (£000)	19x7 (£000)	19x8 (£000)
Fixed assets:			
Land and buildings	260	255	250
Plant and machinery	200	210	220
Vehicles	40	41	43
Furniture and fittings	35	31	27
Current assets:			
Stocks and WIP	200	280	400
Trade debtors	400	560	800
Prepayments	5	6	8
Cash at bank	20	—	—
	£1,160	£1,383	£1,748
Financed by:			
Ordinary shares (fully paid)	600	600	600
General reserve	100	100	100
Profit and loss account	17	77	197
12% debentures 19y2	200	200	200
Current liabilities:			
Trade creditors	100	150	230
Accrued expenses	8	10	12
Proposed dividend (gross)	60	60	80
Tax payable @ 50%	75	120	200
Bank overdraft	—	66	129
	£1,160	£1,383	£1,748
Sales turnover (£000)	2,000	2,800	4,000
Pre-tax profits (£000)	150	240	400

You are required to discuss the position disclosed by the above data together with the calculation of such ratios and other figures as you think will help you. What advice, if any, would you give to the management of Flatearthers Ltd? (SCCA)

7. Your managing director has seen a statement in the financial press which suggests that at all times, but particularly when liquidity is a problem, management should pay particular attention to the cash operating cycle—that is, the time between paying for your raw materials and recovering this from your own customers.

Using the following information, prepare a memorandum for your managing director commenting on the cash operating cycle and suggesting how it might be improved.

	Year 1 £	Year 2 £
Stocks—Raw materials	20,000	27,000
Work-in-progress	14,000	18,000
Finished goods	16,000	24,000
Purchases	96,000	130,000
Cost of goods sold	140,000	180,000
Sales	160,000	200,000
Debtors	32,000	48,000
Creditors	16,000	19,500

(CACA)

8. Discuss the problems to be faced in the valuation of fixed assets for the purpose of determining the return on capital employed as a business performance indicator. (SCCA)

6

MEANS OF CONTROLLING CAPITAL AND SPECIAL EXPENDITURE

The Capital Budget

The capital budget will have defined the physical resources required to implement the marketing and manufacturing plan for the business. The new resources will be needed either from the expected profits and cash flow derived therefrom or from new sources of funds which have been adjudged as being available.

These new physical requirements will have incorporated not only those seen to be necessary for the new manufacturing programme, but also those seen from the forecast as being needed in the years ahead of the budget year which will have been decided upon sufficiently in advance to allow for the appropriate time-span for their availability. The capital budget will therefore include:

(*a*) Major projects—long term.
(*b*) Minor projects—short-term.
(*c*) New resources for volume growth.
(*d*) New resources for cost reduction purposes.
(*e*) New resources for quality requirements.
(*f*) Replacement by planned programmes or seen to be imminent.
(*g*) New or improved resources to fulfil statutory requirements.
(*h*) New or improved resources for facilities to improve or sustain working conditions for personnel.
(*i*) Attendant related features to support the consequences of the capital development such as waste facilities, environment protection measures and general services of heating, power, access, etc.

The formal approval of the master budget, which incorporates the capital budget, represents authority to proceed with the company plan thus defined with its objectives of attainment and limitations of time and expenditure. However, the expenditure on capital is usually excluded from this authority to proceed on the grounds that circumstances may change; that the very latest information is required before actual commitment; that changes of opinion may arise as to what is best to acquire; that priorities as to the use of the cash resources may alter; and that insufficient time was available at the budget setting stage to obtain precise information and to evaluate the acceptability of the proposals. When these reservations do not apply, and particularly when proposals are adequately evaluated, then expenditure may be automatically authorised at the budget stage.

Most usually the acceptance of the capital budget implies one of principle, the precise authorisation being reserved for a subsequent formal application and review procedure on each separate project.

Capital Expenditure Approval

An early requirement will be to define who is empowered to give the necessary authority for capital expenditure. This will vary with the type of business, but more particularly with the responsibilities enshrined within the functions of the particular business. It may be a single person such as the chief executive, managing director or the financial director as head of the finance function, but in the larger companies a Capital Expenditure Committee may be invested with the authority. This relieves the individual when there are numerous projects to consider and as it usually comprises the heads of the main functions, it can relieve any tendency for undue bias.

Some clarification may also be necessary as to who may request the approval for capital expenditure. This may be more obvious in some businesses than others, depending upon the specification of the responsibilities appropriate to each function. Certainly the applicant must be one who has the prime responsibility for the accuracy of the information submitted on which the decision will be made, and also for the performance in due course derived from the investment.

The authorising body will need to define the criteria and standards of performance on which their decisions will be based, and it is advisable for these to be communicated to prospective applicants to permit evaluation to be made beforehand and thus avoid unnecessary requests. Approval decisions will also take into consideration:

(i) Whether the request was originally incorporated in the capital budget.
(ii) The changing priorities of the business.
(iii) The ranking factors currently applicable.
(iv) The business performance to date in relationship to the budget and changes in available cash flow.
(v) The impact of other demands upon the available cash flow, particularly from the working capital.
(vi) Any new facts available likely to affect the future performance of the business.
(vii) Any new developments affecting the outside sources of finance.

Some businesses, depending upon their circumstances, may insist upon formal approval for every single item of capital expenditure, regardless of value; others confine the approval to items above a certain amount, such as £100. Larger businesses may delegate a block of funds, say £1,000, for authorisation at functional level for minor projects. Control of this is then exercised through appropriate classification codes of expenditure against this limit. The limit may be absolute for the whole budget period, or it may operate upon an indent system whereby itemised past expenditure of this nature is submitted for retrospective approval by the authority and the sum thus approved reinstated in the limit. In this way the functional head can be kept under surveillance about his expenditure decisions and a ceiling maintained to limit his scope, but at the same time extending a degree of discretion.

For those projects requiring formal approval prior to commitment the authority will require the appropriate information on which to base its decision—it having already decided the criteria for this decision-making. The most acceptable way of ensuring this is in the form of a document drawn up for the purpose incorporating the information requirements. Such information would normally include:

1. The general purpose or objective of the project.
2. The precise description of the capital items required.
3. The supplementary service facilities as a consequence of installing the capital items.
4. The estimated cost of each item required (firm quotations are usually insisted upon).
5. The payment terms applicable.
6. The expected date of delivery and subsequent payment based upon the above terms (this information gives guidance of the cash flow implications of the transaction).
7. The economic justification, either in terms of new income and new costs or in terms of net savings in comparison to existing methods. The information is best arranged to demonstrate the economic returns in the context of the judgment criteria, i.e. profit/savings percentage to initial capital expenditure. Where judgment criteria are based upon present values then the data need to be arranged in annual divisions to permit discounting.
8. The functional justification as an alternative when the proposal is not of an economic nature.

See Fig. 18 (page 202) for typical application format.

In the case of major projects such as the introduction of an important new product involving buildings, extensive plant and services with an impact upon profits of some consequence, then this will have figured in the company's forecasts from its early conception when research and development grants were first required. The decisions would have been progressive at each stage with all the chief functions involved. The eventual and final decision to proceed will therefore not be a sudden acquaintance with the bare facts of the project, but nevertheless the project application will need to be formalised and a single sheet as illustrated in Fig. 18 will be inadequate. It is customary for such applications to be made more extensively and they may even run to a small brochure consisting of a review of the physical and performance capabilities of the product, a survey of the market, the competition and the market share, a comprehensive list of requirements with the best estimates of cost available at the time, and a forecast of the net returns. Some reference to alternative courses of action may be included and mention of any special problems involved such as government or legislative conditions, building site alterations, etc.

An approval of such an application would be on the basis that the overall total was closely approximate in view of the lack of preciseness in some estimates; it could be in the nature of a limit of commitment. Sections of such an approved project could be included in any new capital budget according to its date of requirement and it is most usual that as each item falls due for implementation, an individual application is required for allotment out of the global sanction.

Control of Authorised Capital Expenditure

Once the application for the capital expenditure has been authorised it becomes a matter of ensuring its faithful implementation, which falls into two categories:

Application for capital expenditure sanction	Ref. No. Date

Category: (a) (b) (c) Company/Division:
Proposer:
Project description:

Assumed life years
DCF yield %
Taxation rate %
Payback years from

	Amount (000's)			Currency	
	19	19	19	19	19
Proposed new investment					
1 Land					
2 Buildings and services					
3 Plant and machinery					
4 Fixed assets at cost (1 + 2 + 3)					
5 Capital grants or deductions					
6 Net fixed assets (4–5)					
7 Working capital (Net)					
8 Total assets					
To be financed by:					
9					
10					
11 Total sources (9 + 10)					
Performance:					
12 Addition from proposal					
13 Profit before tax					
14 Profit after tax					
15 Sales					
16 Cash flow					
Returns	%	%	%	%	%
To Total Assets					
17 Profit before tax 13:8					
18 Profit after tax 14:8					
19 Sales 15:8					
To Sales					
20 Profit before tax 13:15					
21 Profit after tax 14:15					

Notes:

Signed: ....

Fig. 18. Application for capital expenditure sanction.

1. Category:
   (*a*) Applications for items costing less than £10,000 submitted through local signatories.
   (*b*) Applications above £10,000 but less than £100,000 submitted through local board procedure.
   (*c*) Applications above £100,000 to be submitted through main board procedure.
   Delete categories not applicable.
2. Proposed New Investment: Supporting schedules for all items 1—8 to be included in submission.
3. Sources of Finance (9–11):
   Details of sources proposed—e.g. equity, loan or other capital, bank overdraft or central group financing—must be included.
4. Performance (13–21): The basis of computation of anticipated returns must be included, with particular reference to treatment of depreciation, inflation and exchange rates where items are relevant.
5. Labour: Changes in labour force as result of implementing decision must be indicated.
6. Where the cost of capital is known or considered predictable with reasonable accuracy the net present value should also be indicated in the submission.

Execution—under the responsibility of the applicant and

Control—under the responsibility of the finance organisation to ensure that the execution is fulfilled within the terms of the authorisation.

It is imperative that absolute discipline is exercised throughout the organisation, and to ensure that all parties are fully aware of the requirements. The issue of a formal procedure becomes a necessity. This will lay down the sequence of steps to be followed, the appropriate forms to be used and how they should be completed and who has authority to do what with particular stress as to what may not be done. The foremost of those things which may not be done will be:

(*a*) Exceeding the limit of expenditure authorised. Some businesses may allow a defined marginal excess, but usually any need for more funds requires a supplementary formal application for the extra expenditure.

(*b*) The spending of the sum authorized in a manner other than specified by the authorisation. A change of opinion may subsequently occur or new circumstances may arise, but these should require a new application and authorisation. There is a great temptation if the project is underspent for an extraneous item to be acquired to use up the approved sum.

(*c*) The entering into commitments other than those verified by the controller and identified by him as falling within the scope of particular authorisations.

As may be expected, the control procedure will pivot around the controller, who is usually operating within the finance responsibility. He may be the chief accountant or the budget officer, and he would normally fulfil the role of secretary to the capital expenditure committee, marshalling the applications for consideration, ensuring all the applications were appropriately completed and keeping the minutes of the meeting, particularly maintaining the records of the authorisations granted.

Control should be maintained in three phases:

1. The sanction application related to the capital budget. This will be one of the factors taken into consideration by the authorising body. Should an application not have featured in the capital budget it may be that approval can only be considered if a like amount is removed from the capital budget.

2. The sanction approval related to the commitments entered into either through the buying or works functions. The key feature is to control at the commitment stage: the expenditure stage is after the event and therefore too late to be influenced.

3. The actual expenditure related to the commitment. Commitment amounts may comprise some element of estimate, but these should be well formulated. The final actual expenditure should be closely related to this and demonstrated through the control data.

Procedural steps (see Fig. 19)

Step 1

The applicant submits his request to the **capital expenditure authority** for approval upon the appropriate documents.

Step 2

Approval of the application is communicated to the applicant via the **controller**, who prior to the onward transfer first identifies the approval with

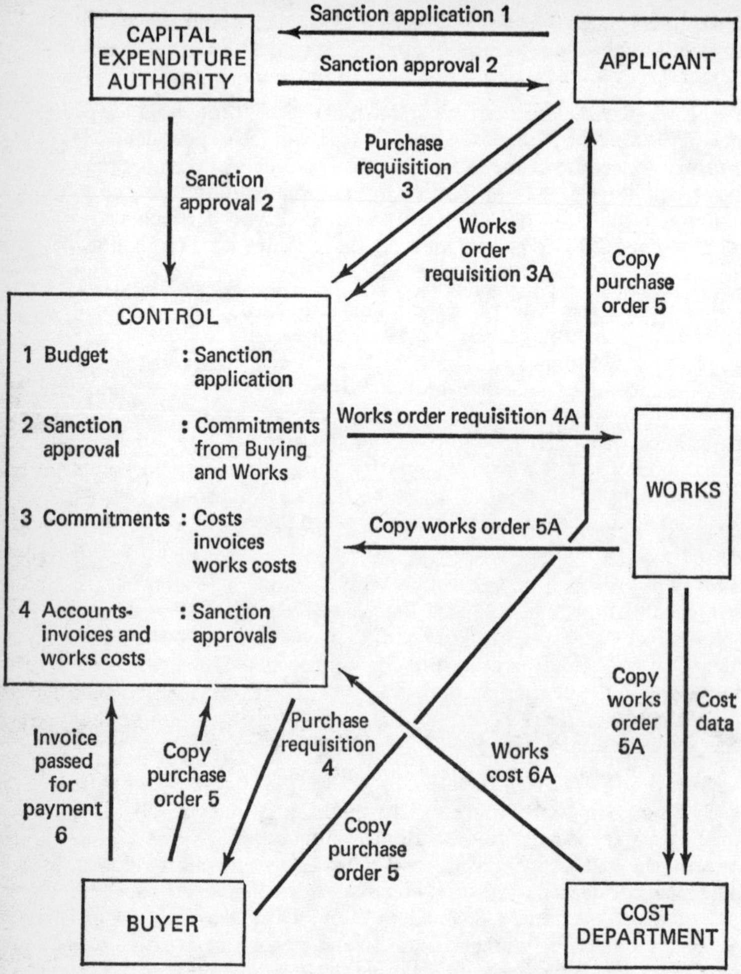

Fig. 19. Procedure for capital expenditure control.

an appropriate control number within a prescribed classification containing suitable subclassifications for large projects. (When the controller is also secretary to the approving authority this operation is made more simple.) The onward communication to the applicant will now signify its control number with subclasifications if applicable. The application documents are often in multi-set form to permit copies for all subsequent purposes.

Step 3 + 3A

The applicant subsequently raises a **purchase requisition** for an outside purchase or a **works requisition** for an internal manufacture, bearing the approval number, but sending these first through the controller. This is the first stage in the commitment process.

Step 4 + 4A

The controller checks the items and amounts with his own copy of the approval, records the allocation and sends the requisitions either to the purchase or production control departments, whichever is appropriate, suitably **verified**. The procedure will be quite clear that no commitment is made without this verifying formality.

Step 5 + 5A

Upon receipt of the verified purchase requisition the buyer will initiate the **purchase order**, quoting the approval control number, sending a copy to the controller and applicant to indicate the formal commitment of the company.

On the authority of the verified works requisition the production control department will raise the appropriate **works order** upon the manufacturing or service departments with a copy to the cost department and also a copy to the controller and applicant. The works order will carry the approval control number and the sum allocated for the task.

The receipt of the copies of the purchase order and the works order confirms as a formal commitment the allocation previously recorded by the controller from the requisitions. Justification in using the requisition and the orders for control is that if only the requisition is used, it becomes a matter of assumption that the buyer implemented it faithfully; there may be some final aspects of the order remaining for the buyer to conclude. If reliance were wholly upon the purchase order, then the commitment is made before the controller sees the copy.

Step 6

When the outside order is concluded the passed invoice is forwarded to the controller from the accounting function. The controller records the **actual cost** against the commitment he has already established.

In the case of the internal work the costs incurred are collected by means of the established system with the cost department controlling the actual cost progressively against the authorised amount communicated to them upon their copy of the works order.

The accounting function will advise the controller of the actual expenditure upon each order, either progressively for each accounting period or at the close of each order, according to the system in operation.

The controller should automatically ensure that the actual costs he records each accounting period are in accord with the capital expenditure revealed in the accounts of the company.

Where, as is often the case, the controller is a member of the accounting function, this liaison is simplified and the control data form an analysis of the capital expenditure for the period under the authorisation classification references.

Management Advice

The data collected by the controller form the basis of two control reports: one to the capital expenditure authority and the other to the successful applicants, who have the responsibility for fulfilling their respective projects.

The capital expenditure authority needs the assurance that its decisions are being faithfully implemented and the applicants need guidance progressively that their implementing decisions are in line with the constraints imposed upon them.

The regular control returns to the capital expenditure authority will comprise comparisons of:

(*a*) *Authorisations against capital budget*. This could be sub-analysed under responsibilities or departments, or under project classifications. The aim is to relate decisions to the original plan which may need variations according to the progress of the business and new circumstances which arise.

(*b*) *Commitments against authorisations*. The commitment is the vital stage in the implementation process and brings more preciseness to the values.

(*c*) *Actual expenditure against commitments*. This provides the valuable data of commitments outstanding and in the process reveals under- and over-expenditure against commitment. Explanations of unusual variations will be important, although expected overspending should be subject to special application at the time.

Control information to applicants will follow similar lines, but in more detail with data provided for each item of an authorised project.

The Monitoring of Subsequent Results

Considerations of applications and the decisions made as to approval must, by the very nature of the situation, be based upon a forecast of future events. It is highly likely that definitions of the capital expenditure can be quite precise—even based upon firm quotations from outside suppliers—but the gains by way of extra profits or savings will depend upon estimates of what is expected to happen. It will be the task of the secretary of the authorising body to make inquiries about the origins of the data submitted, so that some guidance can be brought to bear on the risk element contained within the data.

Once the decision is made to approve there is an element of trust that the expenditure will produce the returns that were forecast. An extension of the control procedure takes the form of auditing the results when the project is in operation. This can be undertaken on a sampling basis or on all projects as a matter of routine. The objective of audits of this kind is not to interfere with the project once in operation because the fixed nature of the investment expenditure makes it almost impossible to undo once in progress. In an extreme case it would be a matter of considering the extent to which the outlay could be restricted. The objective is more to validate the judgments and data which originally prompted the application and approval so that it becomes more a management audit than an investment audit. The applicant is being called upon to justify the performance promised in his application.

The value of these control audits lies in the revelation of factors which arise in due course that were not anticipated and the extent to which there was inadequate preparation by the applicant. In this way over-optimism, bias, carelessness or inadequacy becomes revealed in respect of those who are in a position to make investment applications and decisions.

Controls Applied to Special Expenditure

There are categories of special expenditure—which include tooling, maintenance, research and development, and marketing projects—that call for a form of control at the commitment stage similar to that used for capital expenditure because the value concerned can be high and often crucial to profitability and also because of a latent time-span between commitment and completion.

In all cases where control is exercised from the budget statement by comparing actual expenditure with budget it is really too late for action because actual expenditure demonstrates what has already happened. Control cannot be exercised upon past happenings; only future compensatory decisions can be made and these may not be possible, advisable or sufficiently timely. Over-expenditure with a good explanation is not control.

The key for effective control is for the decisions to be made at the time of commitment because commitments inevitably result in the actual expenditure appearing some time later—often much later. A commitment decision therefore needs to take into consideration the impact upon expenditure some time in the future and the planned expenditure for the particular category of expense within the same time period.

Tooling

In industries such as engineering and plastics tooling may form part of a capital project or arise because of changes in methods or product in the course of normal business development. In the former case control will be exercised as part of the capital expenditure control. In the latter case control will be exercised in relation to the estimated cost undertaken when the appraisal of the project was made. There is here a two-step form of control; first of the actual cost of the tool against estimate, and secondly of the effect of this upon the expenditure budget of the manager concerned. If the tool is to be made outside then control is off the quotation; if it is to be made inside then progress comparisons of actual cost throughout manufacture are necessary.

Part of the problem in control is again the time-lag between commitment and recording of the actual expenditure so that it becomes difficult to relate the timing of the expenditure incurred with the accounting period of the operating department's budget carrying the allowance for the tool. It is often advisable to compare the cumulative totals of actuals and budgets and ignore the individual accounting periods.

Maintenance

Maintenance expenditure is notoriously difficult to control through conventional budgetary control methods because of the incidence of projects at high cost and the frequent time delays between the event and the charge being processed into expenditure.

The manner in which the budget is formulated and concentration upon the commitment stage can together provide the key for control, although much will depend upon the extent a manufacturer uses internal staff compared with subcontractors. Internal staff can be adequately controlled at the source against the key elements of the budget—namely, through numbers and overtime work with responsibility resting with management as to adequacy of the work performed. Major subcontract work can best begin at the budget planning stage from a list prepared of all the things seen by the maintenance engineer as being necessary. Budget estimates are made of each project and arranged in descending order of priority of importance to the operation of the business.

In general, the cut-off point in the ranking will be what the business feels it can afford that year, although conditions of working and legislation requirements may sometimes over-ride this. The budget will thus not be just a global sum for the year but an itemised list of the projects to be done for that sum of money, having made some allowance for unexpected factors which may arise.

Subsequently projects are put in hand and committed only after strict reference to this budget list and the latest data. Should a project arise not on the list it is either monitored from the contingency allowance or introduced at the expense of a project dropped from the list. In the extreme event that this is not possible or advisable a conscious decision to overspend the budget is made in full cognisance of the facts rather than discovering this some time afterwards from the operating statements. Projects dropped from the list will usually head the next year's budget list and joining them will be items committed too late in the year for expenditure to actually accrue that year.

The final step is to relate the actual expenditure on each project against its committed estimate and any net overspending must be considered as new commitment decisions arise progressively throughout the year. This again may call for the cropping of projects to ensure an annual expenditure within budget.

Research and Development

One of the best forms of control for research and development budgets is for them to comprise individual projects relating to the plan for the department. There are similar features here as for maintenance in the degree of work undertaken by the internal staff or by subcontractors, including any special purchases. Internal control can be made, through numbers of staff, appropriate grades and overtime. Maintaining of performance becomes a local management matter. Subcontract work and special purchases can be itemised under projects and reviewed at the commitment stage.

However, research and development work has a high degree of imponderables and the accuracy of estimates can be difficult. Subsidiary control is under projects comparing actual expenditure against the project budget progressively as the work proceeds. This needs to be undertaken in conjunction with interpretations of the proportion of the work completed at the budget review stages. Illustrations of impending or actual over-expenditure will cause considerations about deferring or dropping other projects to compensate. Decisions to proceed and thus cause over-expenditure of the budget must be consciously made upon the facts and especially upon the effects of the added expenditure upon the economics of the project itself.

Decisions to drop research projects are among the more difficult to make but abortive projects are inevitable in this sphere. Keeping this cost to a minimum calls for decisions early in the time-scale of the project.

Marketing

Similar problems arise in controlling marketing expenditure under formal budgetary control methods as have been mentioned earlier, such as the call for control at earlier stages.

The importance of marketing to particular businesses varies enormously and although the control processes outlined below are based upon the methods employed by a large, highly market-orientated company, the methods can be applied in principle to most other businesses where the marketing expenditure justifies some extra effort to control. A budget of the total marketing expenditure is divided under:

(*a*) Account manager responsibility
(*b*) The product lines under each account manager
(*c*) Heads of expenditure
(*d*) Accounting periods

The apportionment throughout the accounting periods gives effect to strategies, seasonal variations, new product promotions with overall coordination between the product lines to avoid any self-provoked competition between them and to maintain consistency of total sales. The apex of the control is the adherence to the total marketing expenditure budget; managers have discretion to amend their own details but must adhere to their own totals, so changes must be self-correcting. Lead times are worked out between commitment and the actual charge date but in due course the recorded actual expenditure may differ from budget due to under- or over-expenditure or because charges have turned up more quickly or later than anticipated, changes in tactics or in the timing of some projects.

Effective control is by means of a reconciliation along the following lines:

Product X—Period 6
Classification 651—Special Discount Offers

			£
Actual expenditure			16,510
Add—Invoices not received for printing			1,050
dies			275
Late discount claims from traders, accrued			3,500
			21,335
Less—Expenditure included in respect of previous periods:			
Invoices for period 5		842	
” ” 4		210	
Discount claims from traders for period	5	1,260	
” ”	4	815	
” ”	2	462	
” ”	1	105	
			3,694
Expenditure for this period only (carried forward)			17,641

Expenditure for this period only (brought forward)		17,641
Original budget	18,300	
Less project withdrawn to counter over expenditure on TV in period 3	1,200	
		17,100
Variation		
Overspending—Project 27/1	176	
32/1	253	
35/4	432	
	861	
Underspending project 26/2	320	
Total—Adverse		£541
Corrective action		
Reduce period 9 budget		200
10		350
		£550

This process exposes the variance and provides the means of adjusting the forward budgets which then control the new commitments. A stage may be reached towards the end of the year when there are insufficient months to absorb the corrections brought forward. Commitments then have to be deferred and become the nucleus of the new year's budgets. In the event that expenditure which seems absolutely vital but which would exceed the budget becomes necessary then application has to be made to the top authority of the company for a concessionary grant to exceed the original budget.

Case Study of Decision-Making in Capital Investment

An Account of the Meeting of the Board of Directors of Trojan Ltd held on Wednesday, 22nd September, 19x6

Present:

Chairman—A. J. Rearsby (Managing Director)
R. E. S. Brown (Finance and Secretary)
N. C. Butterworth (Research)
A. J. K. Formby (Non-executive)
P. E. Goode (Production)
C. T. Jones (Marketing)
P. Wilkins (Non-executive)

After considering the Accounts for August, which showed a marginal improvement over the expectations of the budget and the satisfactory indications of the forward order position, the meeting received a report from the Marketing Director upon his recent tour of Holland and Germany and approved his recommendations for the appointment of sole agencies in these countries.

In introducing the last agenda item 'The Capital Budget for 19x7', the Chairman explained that he had reserved the majority of the time of the meeting for this item to permit adequate discussion. He reminded the meeting of the minutes of the previous meeting which referred to a report of a post-project audit which had highlighted apparent exaggerations in values provided in the application for the project.

Dealing with the considerations before them, the Chairman explained that normal procedure had been followed in that the various departmental managers had tabled their requirements and at this stage the Capital Expenditure Committee had only verified the basic facts and calculations. In due course this Committee would consider every capital expenditure application in the light of the approved budget and any change in the company's financial position at the time.

The Applications

The applications were listed under Appendix 1 (see page 215), grouped into categories A, B and C according to the nature of the projects.

Category A consisted of a single project which was unavoidable to prevent proceedings against the company by the local authorities (Appendix 2—see page 215).

Category B consisted of two alternatives available to implement a single replacement project (Appendix 3—see page 215).

Category C consisted of five projects for consideration on their merit (Appendix 4—see page 220).

Discussion of Category A

The Production Director, observing that the investment of £5,000 would earn no profit, asked what effect this would have on the average return on the company's capital employed. The Finance Director pointed out that he had ascertained that an adverse decision if proceedings were made against the company—and this seemed quite certain if the necessary plant amendments were not undertaken—would incur a minimum fine of £1,000 and maybe more. He felt that, although of a negative kind, the investment would be safeguarding the profit to this extent. He accepted the point that a zero rate of return would adversely affect the average return on capital employed and conceded that there were occasions when this was used as a minimum required of revenue-earning projects. He gave the assurance that any assessment of an average rate of return for comparison purposes made due allowance for a proportion of zero-rated investments such as the one under consideration.

Decision Concerning Category A: That the expenditure be approved for inclusion in the budget.

Discussion of Category B

The Production Director explained that the existing machine was virtually worn out and would need replacing within one year. It had already exceeded its life span by two years and had been an excellent investment.

The work performance was related to the company's main product and as the sales of this seemed assured for the next five years—reference 'Five-year Sales Forecast', minute 4:776—it had been deemed prudent to assess the project on this period only, although the machines themselves were assessed as having a life-span of 15 years. The salvage values shown in Appendix 3(*a*) were therefore of a very conservative nature. There was thus a contingency of further use of both machines, which although specialised, could later be adapted should this be required. The company could accept, therefore, that ensuring the continuity of the work was imperative: the decision required of the meeting was which replacement machine would serve the company the better.

Both machines would competently perform the work required but with technical advances over the years one was more highly developed than the other, reflecting in more favourable operating performances but at a higher initial investment cost. Only two companies could provide the equipment required; the investment costs were in each case based upon quotations which were held firm for six months—five of which still remained open. The engineering department had had access to the performance data of both machines and to similar machines on the manufacturers' sites and other users had been contacted. Satisfaction has been expressed about maintenance, quality and technical factors.

As a choice of this nature had not been before the Board since the present assessment procedure had been introduced the Finance Director explained that he had taken the liberty of presenting the financial data in some detail, namely:

Appendix 3: Project Appraisal Computation Summary (see page 215)

(*a*) Basic data.
(*b*) Comparison of Annual Cash Gains.
(*c*) Total cash flows from proposed investment.
(*d*) Computation of internal rate of return.

After an examination of the data presented the Marketing Director inquired why a provision for general administration overhead had not been included in the costs before the cash flow and profit were computed.

The Finance Director replied that whereas general administration overheads were included in the price fixing structure in the long term it was considered more appropriate to exclude them in comparisons of this nature when the amount of such general administration overheads was unaffected by either of the machine alterations. The comparison was confined to the actual expenditure influenced by each machine. Fortunately in this case the parts to be manufactured were wholly complete off these machines; with no other machines involved in the cycle it made the omission even more appropriate.

The Chairman commented that there did not appear to be much difference in the internal rate of return for each of the machines, notwithstanding the cost savings of B2. The Finance Director accepted this but pointed out the higher investment cost of B2 by way of compensation in the rate. He suggested that very different rates would have suggested that one machine was vastly superior and then the case need not necessarily have been submitted to the Board for decision.

The decision concerning Category B: Resolved that notwithstanding that machine B1 carried the slightly higher rate of return, machine B2 would be accepted for inclusion in the budget, because it appeared:

(*a*) To be technically more reliable.
(*b*) To have the greater surplus capacity, should this be needed.

(*c*) That under inflationary conditions common to both sets of circumstance the gain in cost savings could widen in favour of B2 and reduce its present unfavourable comparison in the internal rate of return.

Discussion of Category C

The Production Director emphasised that whereas the category A project did not involve a choice because it was legally required and the category B project, as a necessary replacement, was unavoidable, the category C projects involved a choice: to invest in any, all or none.

The proposals were from various departments and in their preliminary review the Capital Expenditure Committee had assured themselves of the need and viability of each of the projects. The essential data for each was summarised under Appendix 1 in accordance with the newly revised procedure now in operation but supporting data were included for more detailed reference under:

Appendix 4 (see page 220)

(*a*) Proposal summaries
(*b*) Computation summary
(*c*) Ranking summary

The non-executive director, Mr. P. Wilkins, opened the discussion by commenting that the rates of return on all the category C projects seemed so much better than project B (Appendix 1). The Finance Director replied that this was because the rates of return for category C were before tax and those for category B were after tax at 35 per cent. He pointed out that whereas this may seem inconsistent, categories B and C were not related as to the decisions required of the board and it had seemed more appropriate to take the after-tax results for category B because whichever machine was chosen the replacement would take effect within the next six months, for which period it was known that the present taxation procedure would apply. All of the category C projects, however, were optional or subject to deferment. It was felt more appropriate to take the gross rate as a starting point to demonstrate the respective outcomes on a common basis.

The Chairman observed that category C required an investment of £120,000 and with A and B this called for £137,500 in total. He expressed some doubt as to whether the company could afford this amount, inquiring of the position should it be desirable to limit investment to a lower sum.

Making use of the detailed information of the appendices, the Finance Director extracted and circulated the following, with category C projects, in descending order of rate of return:

Project	*Internal rate of return* %	*Capital cost* £	*Cumulative investment* £
A	—	5,000	5,000
B2	6·9 net	12,500	17,500
C5	26·4 gross	10,000	27,500
C4	21·8	20,000	47,500
C1	21·0	50,000	97,500
C3	19·9	15,000	112,500
C2	17·2	25,000	137,500

He went on to reveal that from the draft revenue budget figures available it seemed highly likely that virtually all the internally generated profit that could be retained for 19x7 would be required for the extra working capital of the growth they were expecting together with the expected impact of inflation on it. He suggested that the Board ought to consider financing the fixed capital requirements from borrowing. The availability of such funds was not too difficult but borrowing rates were somewhat high. There would be some net return provided the pre-tax cost of borrowing did not exceed the internal rate computed and as demonstrated. His preliminary inquiries in anticipation of this problem suggested that borrowing rates would be below the lowest rate of return of C2 at 17·2 per cent.

The Chairman felt that the company would not be able to borrow at a multiplicity of rates and that the total commitment sum needed to be examined most carefully. He inquired about the effects upon their deliberations if loan facilities could only be negotiated between £90,000 and £110,000.

The Finance Director explained that this in technical terms raised two points:

(i) What was the capital cut-off rate for the company?
(ii) What was the best way of investing a restricted amount when the cut-off rate was known?

He explained further that the cut-off rate was normally the average rate of return already being made by the company or the cost of obtaining finance from an external source. As he felt confident that the latter would not exceed 15–16 per cent then if this became the cut-off rate then the whole of the £120,000 of category C would qualify. He stressed that on the other hand the Board had been disappointed in the decline of the overall rate of return over the last two years and if the last year's rate was used as a cut-off then the task of improving upon it is made more difficult. He reminded them that, in effect, the Board had already determined a cut-off rate of 20 per cent gross in that all discussions on the subject had brought them back to this objective. He added further that the projects to qualify for approval could also be influenced by the amount and manner of raising the funds. If, for example, a cut-off rate of 20 per cent was decided upon then projects C2 and C3 would be eliminated and the investment would become £97,500. If the funds were raised on a variable basis such as bank overdraft the limit could be fixed at this figure, but if a fixed sum—say, £110,000—was raised it would become a matter of ensuring how best to spend all of it to ensure maximum benefit to the company. This latter course would require a different approach and a revised presentation of the information.

Appreciating these points, the Chiairman referred to his opening remarks and inquired whether and to what extent the cash flow data of the projects under consideration could be accepted as reliable.

The Marketing Director replied that they had always accepted that elements of risk operated in forward estimates and he had been glad of the opportunity to collaborate in the preparation of the paper on the subject. In particular the Project C3 had been used as the example in the paper and after some discussion at the time a preference was expressed for adopting the 'most probable' method. All other projects had been reviewed and based upon 'most probable' criteria.

Decision concerning Category C: That the company adopt a cut-off rate of return of 20 per cent in deciding acceptability of investments; that Projects C1,

C4 and C5 be approved for inclusion in the budget for 19x7, the total investment becoming £97,500; that the Finance Director investigate sources and costs for borrowing the necessary funds with preference being expressed for a variable sum basis.

It was recorded that consideration was given to project C3 which returned a rate of 19·9 per cent, but a desire to limit investment in the one year to a maximum of £100,000 caused its deletion.

Postscript

In due course project B2 was authorised through the Capital Expenditure Committee and was installed on 31st March 19x7.

Six months later, on 1st October 19x7, in the normal course of the procedures a post-installation audit was undertaken into the project.

The findings and the report appear under Appendix 5, together with a desk memorandum made by the Production Director (Fig. 20).

Appendix 1. Summary of Capital or Special Revenue Applications (Year 19x7)

Project category	*Title*	*Classification*	*Cost (£)*	*Life (years)*	*Internal rate of return (%)*	*Cash payback period (years)*	*Remarks*
A	Dust extraction plant	Statutory	5,000	15	—	—	
B1	New moulding machine—	Replacement	10,000	6·9	2·85		
B2	Alternatives	Replacement	12,500	8·1	3·18		
C1	Additional product line	Additional capacity	50,000	10	21·0	4·29	
C2	Additional product line	Additional capacity	25,000	10	17·2	5·17	
C3	Revised inspection sequence	Cost reduction	15,000	5	19·9	3	
C4	Modifications to existing product resulting in increased sales	Quality improvement	20,000	3	21·8	1·5	
C5	Substitution of existing plant with more profitable alternative	Cost reduction	10,000	4	26·4	2·25	

Appendix 2. Project Appraisal Computation Summary (Category A)

Class: Statutory

Purpose: To provide more effective dust extraction facilities in Grinding Department. The factory inspector stated on a previous visit that conditions should be substantially improved and suggested a maximum period of one year to get the necessary conversions done.

Data: Three quotations had been received and amounts quoted were £4,800, £5,000 and £6,000 respectively. The lowest quotation could not be faulted in respect to the specification but the contractor concerned was not prepared to guarantee completion with the next six months. As six months had already elapsed since the inspection it was felt that the £200 additional cost required by the second supplier was justified in view of the fact that the guaranteed completion in three months from placing contract. In any event, from the point of view of employees' health and welfare the quicker the job was completed the more satisfactory the position would be. Both potential suppliers said the equipment would be good for a minimum of 15 years.

Appendix 3. Project Appraisal Computation Summary (Category B)

(a) Basic Data

Class: Replacement

Purpose: To provide essential replacement of existing plant. Completely identical replacement is not available so that choice is between two machines capable of doing the job.

Data:

	Alternative		
	B1	*B2*	*Remarks*
Capital cost	£10,000	£12,500	
Salvage value	£1,000	£2,000	
Estimated life: Maximum per supplier	15 years	15 years	
Projected write-offf period	5 years	5 years	
Production capacity			
Units per annum (maximum)	720,000	900,000	Normal shift
(required)	600,000	600,000	
Units produced per hour	400	500	
Sales value of product per 1,000 units	£12·50	£12·50	
Production costs			
Variable			
Direct material per 1,000 units	£2·60	£2·00	
Direct wages (per hour)	£1·50	£1·50	
Overhead			
Machine (per hour)	£0·30	£0·60	
Others (per 1,000 units)	£1·00	£1·00	
Fixed			
Routine maintenance per annum	£100	£250	

Taxation: Capital allowances were at the rate of 25 per cent per annum on reducing balance and it is anticipated that there will be profits from other sources against which these can be claimed. Tax allowances are assumed to lag by one year and the assumed rate is 35 per cent over the relevant period.

(*b*) *Comparison of Annual Cash Gains*

	Alternative			
	B1		*B2*	
Output and sales (units)	600,000		600,000	
	per 1,000 units (£)	*Total* (£)	*per 1,000 units* (£)	*Total* (£)
Sales	12·50	*7,500*	12·50	*7,500*
Less				
Direct material	2·60	1,560	2·00	1,200
Direct wages	3.75	2,250	3·00	1,800
Variable overhead				
Machine	0·75	450	1·20	720
Other	1·00	600	1·00	600
Fixed				
Routine maintenance		100		250
		4,960		4,570
Annual cash gain before tax		2,540		2,930

Remarks:

(c) Total Cash Flows from Proposed Investment

Year	Capital Allowances		B1 Year £	B1 Cumulative £	B2 Year £	B2 Cumulative £
0	Cost of plant		10,000		12,500	
	Writing down allowance		2,500	2,500	3,125	3,125
	Written down value	c/f	7,500		9,375	
1	Allowance		1,875	4,375	2,344	5,469
		c/f	5,625		7,031	
2	Allowance		1,406	5,781	1,758	7,227
		c/f	4,219		5,273	
3	Allowance		1,055	6,836	1,318	8,545
		c/f	3,164		3,955	
4	Allowance		791	7,627	989	9,534
		c/f	2,373		2,966	
5	Realisation		1,000		2,000	
			1,373		966	
	Balancing allowance		1,373	9,000	966	10,500
			(a)	(b)	(a)	(b)

Column a: This represents the annual allowance for the period concerned at 25 per cent on reducing balance. The c/f figure provides the basis for the following year's allowance. The annual figure is incorporated into the next tabulation.

Column b: This is the cumulative allowance (sum of the annual figures) granted by the end of that period. Since they do not equal the set expenditure—original cost less salvage value—a balancing allowance is due at the end of Year 5 in lieu of the 25 per cent figure.

B1

Year	Investment £	Income £	Allowance £	Net £	Taxation delay 1 year £	Net cash flow £
0	−10,000		2,500	−2,500		−10,000
1		2,540	1,875	665	+875	3,415
2		2,540	1,406	1,134	233	2,307
3		2,540	1,055	1,485	397	2,143
4		2,540	791	1,749	520	2,020
5	+1,000	2,540	1,373	1,167	612	2,928
6					408	+408
	−9,000	12,700	9,000	3,700	1,295	2,405
a	*b*	*c*	*d*	*e*	*f*	*g*

B2

a	*b*	*c*	*d*	*e* = *c* − *d*	*f* = 35% of *e* delayed	*g* = *b* + *c* − *f*
0	−12,500		3,125	−3,125		−12,500
1		2,930	2,344	586	+1,094	4,024
2		2,930	1,758	1,172	205	2,725
3		2,930	1,318	1,612	410	2,520
4		2,930	989	1,941	564	2,366
5	+2,000	2,930	966	1,964	679	4,251
6					688	−688
	−10,500	14,650	10,500	4,150	1,452	2,698

(*d*) *Computation of Internal Rate of Return*

Project B1 *Capital cost £10,000*

Year	*Cash flow* (£)	9% *Factor*	9% *Present value* (£)	8% *Factor*	8% *Present value* (£)
0	−10,000				
1	3,415	0·91	3,108	0·93	3,176
2	2,307	0·83	1,915	0·86	1,984
3	2,143	0·76	1,629	0·79	1,693
4	2,020	0·70	1,414	0·74	1,495
5	2,928	0·64	1,874	0·68	1,991
6	−408	0·58	−237	0·63	−257
			9,703		10,082

Approximate rate of return 8%

$$\text{Correction to rate} = \frac{10{,}082 - 10{,}000}{10{,}082 - 9{,}703}$$

$$= \frac{82}{379} = 0{\cdot}22$$

Corrected rate = 8·22%

The rate of 8·2 per cent is accepted for practical purposes.

Project B2		*Capital cost £12,500*			
		7%		6%	
Year	*Cash flow* £	*Factor*	*Present value* £	*Factor*	*Present value* £
0	−12,500				
1	4,024	0·93	3,742	0·94	3,783
2	2,725	0·87	2,371	0·89	2,425
3	2,520	0·80	2,016	0·84	2,117
4	2,366	0·75	1,775	0·79	1,869
5	4,251	0·70	2,976	0·75	3,188
6	−688	0·65	−447	0·70	−482
			12,433		12,900

Approximate rate of return 7%

$$\text{Correction to rate} = \frac{12{,}900 - 12{,}500}{12{,}900 - 12{,}433}$$

$$= \frac{400}{467} = 0{\cdot}86$$

$$\text{Corrected rate} = 6\% + 0{\cdot}86\% = 6{\cdot}86\%$$

The rate of 6·9 per cent is accepted for practical purposes.

Summary

Project	*Capital cost* (£)	*Internal rate* (%)	*Cash payback* (*years*)
B1	10,000	8·1	4·04
B2	12,500	6·9	4·20

Assumptions made above:

1. Taxation credits or charges are assumed received or paid one year after transactions giving rise to them.
2. All payments and receipts are deemed to occur on the last day of the year concerned.
3. Year 0, etc. are used in preference to the actual calendar year of the budget period in order that the timings can be more clearly illustrated.
4. The cash payback period represents the time taken for cash flows to equate with the original cost and is given to indicate the length of time taken for a project to pay for itself in conventional monetary terms.

Appendix 4. Capital Expenditure Proposal Summary

(a) Proposal Summaries: Category C

Project	*Initiator*	*Capital cost (£)*	*Life (years)*	*Anticipated cash flows*
C1	Marketing	50,000	10	£10,000 in Year 1 growing at increments of £1,000 p.a. for 4 years; then regular at £14,000 p.a.
C2	Marketing	25,000	10	£5,000 p.a. for first 3 years, £6,000 p.a. for next 3 years, £8,000 p.a. for next 2 years, and £2,000 p.a. for final 2 years
C3	Quality control	15,000	5	£5,000 p.a. in equal annual cash flows
C4	Marketing	20,000	3	£10,000 in first 2 years and £5,000 in Year 3. In addition £5,000 out of the original cost of £20,000 is working capital assumed to be self-liquidating at the end of Year 4
C5	Production	10,000	4	£4,000 p.a. in equal annual cash flows. In addition the plant will be sold at end of Year 4 for a lump sum of £2,000

(b) Computation Summary

Project	*Capital cost (£)*	*Life (years)*	*Cash flow (£)*	*Years*	*Internal rate of return (%)*	*Cash payback (years)*
C1	50,000	10	10,000	1		
			11,000	2		
			12,000	3		
			13,000	4		
			14,000	5–10	21·0	4·29
C2	25,000	10	5,000	1–3		
			6,000	4–6		
			8,000	7–8		
			2,000	9–10	17·2	4·67
C3	15,000	5	5,000	1–5	19·9	3
C4	20,000	3	10,000	1–2		
			5,000	3		
			5,000	4	21·8	1·5*
C5	10,000	4	4,000	1–4		
			2,000	4	26·4	2·25
	£120,000					

* This is the period required for recovery of the original fixed capital cost. If the working capital is included the payback period is extended to just two years.

(c) *Ranking of Investment Proposals*

Internal rate of return			*Payback*		
Project	*Capital cost* (£)	*Internal rate* (%)	*Project*	*Capital cost* (£)	*Cash payback* (*years*)
C5	10,000	26·4	C4	20,000	1·5
C4	20,000	21·8	C5	10,000	2·25
C1	50,000	21·0	C3	15,000	3·0
C3	15,000	19·9	C1	50,000	4·29
C2	25,000	17·2	C2	25,000	4·67

Assumptions and comments:

1. All capital costs and revenues are deemed to arise at the end of the period concerned.
2. The estimated cash flows are 'most probable' incomes after assessing alternatives in the manner described in Chapter 3. Apart from this the data have not been subject to any form of sensitivity or statistical analysis.
3. The internal rate of return has been computed on a pre-tax basis. It is considered that this is to be preferred for this preliminary analysis as doubt exists as to the likely continuation of either the rate or the system over the maximum range considered, i.e. 10 years.
4. Where items of plant are being replaced any credit due in respect of sale of this has been accounted for in producing the above figures.

Appendix 5. Project Appraisal—Post-Installation Audit

Project description:
Replacement of outworn and outdated plant for production of Component 138.

Project Ref.: B2
Authorised: 1/11/x6
Installed by: 31/3/x7
Audit date: 1/10/x7

	Unit	*As stated on application for approval*	*Actual to date*	*Remarks*
Statistics				
Area occupied	square feet	400	400	
Power rating	h.p.	50	50	
Capacity	per hour	500	480	Teething problems.
Life of plant	years	15	15	Anticipate should reach
Life of project	years	5	5	rated output by 31/12/x7

(*contd over*)

	Unit	*As stated on application for approval*	*Actual to date*	*Remarks*
Capital				
Cost		£12,500	£12,600	Extra expenditure sanctioned for improved safety feature
Salvage value		£2,000	£2,000	
Revenue				
sales	per 1000	£12·50	£12·70	Government sanctioned price increase
Costs				
Direct materials	per unit	0·20p	0·22p	Extra wastage on running in
Direct wages	per hour	£1·50	£1·70	Regrading necessary. See variance report
Overhead				
Machine	per hour	£0·60	£0·70	Increased cost of power.
Others	per unit	0·10p	0·11p	High national insurance cost
Routine maintenance	per annum	£250	£200	Annual rate based on first 6 months actual

Comparison of Cash Gains: Project B2

	Capital expenditure application		*Annual rate of first half-year (actual)*	
Output and sales (units)	600,000		600,000	
	per 1,000 units (£)	*Total* (£)	*per 1,000 units* (£)	*Total* (£)
Sales	12·50	7,500	12·70	7,620
Less				
Direct material	2·0	1,200	2·2	1,320
Direct wages	3·0	1,800	3·54	2,124
Variable overhead				
Machine	1·2	720	1·46	876
Others	1·0	600	1·10	660
Routine maintenance		250		200
		4,570		5,180
Annual cash gain before tax		2,930		2,440

Responsibility Analysis

Analysis of Variations from Estimate:

				£	£
Favourable:	Sales Department				
	Price increase			120	
	Operating Department				
	Maintenance			50	
				—	170
Adverse:	Operating Department				
	Capacity—wages		84		
	—power		36	120	
	Material usage		—	120	
	Engineering Department				
	Operator rating			240	
	Price increases				
	Power			120	
	Nat. Ins.			60	660
Net deficit per annum					£490

Comments

Price increases. It is company policy to exclude anticipated price increases from forecasts of results. It is noted that the cost increases have exceeded the sales price increases but these are not necessarily related as the latter are retrospective to cover last year's cost increases and the former are current cost changes.

Operating Department. The maintenance saving is based upon the first year actual and, being a new machine, this is to be expected. It is possible for this gain to be offset by heavier costs in later periods. The capacity deficit of 20 units per hour represents the average for the six-month period. The teething troubles are due to operator inexperience and failure of the auto-switching gear, requiring unusual attention from the supplier's engineers. Both factors are showing improvement: output for the last four weeks was

480 per hour
500
488
494

Material usage was directly affected by the above factors.

Engineering Department. With the machine being so far advanced in design compared with the replaced machine an operator of greater skill than had been foreseen was required. The old machine used a Grade 4 operator. The new machine was assessed for a Grade 5 operator. It was found necessary to use a Grade 6 operator. The Engineering Department had access to all the technical information necessary to assess operator grading when the replacement machine was under consideration. This should have been demonstrated as a cost difference between B1 and B2 at the time of the project submission.

Conclusions. The capacity and material usage adverse costs of £120 p.a. should be eliminated within the next six weeks. Progress reports are required weekly until further notice. The price increases and adverse operator rating costs amounting to £420 are permanent.

Questions on Case Study

1. Was the company correct in using a zero rate of return for the statutory project? What are the alternatives and their relevant advantages and disadvantages?

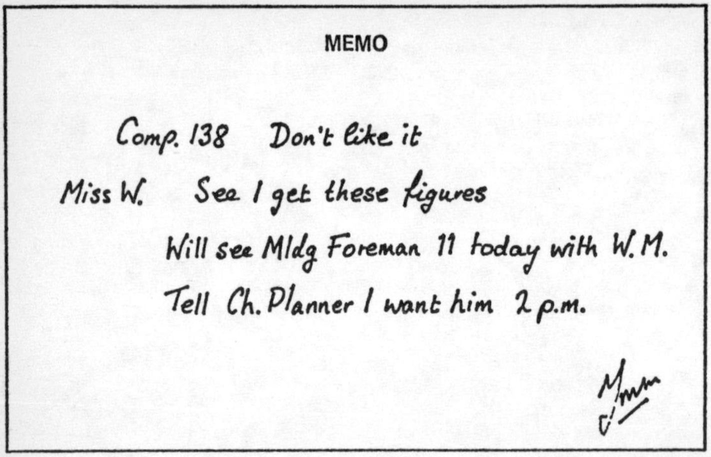
MEMO

Comp. 138 Don't like it

Miss W. See I get these figures

Will see Mldg Foreman 11 today with W.M.

Tell Ch. Planner I want him 2 p.m.

Fig. 20. Desk memo from the production director to his secretary—post audit: component 138.

2. What do you consider to be the 'relevant cost factors' when making a choice between two machines capable of doing the same job? Rearrange the data for projects B1 and B2 on this basis and ascertain which investment produces the more favourable result.

3. On the basis of the information given do you consider that the Board was correct in recommending B2? What further information would you request if you did not agree with the decision?

4. Do you agree with the argument put forward for using a 'gross' rate of return, i.e. before taxation, for projects in category C as opposed to a 'net' rate of return, i.e. after taxation, for projects in category B?

5. Compute the net (after tax) rate of return for projects in category C using the same assumptions as were used for group B and compare the results for ranking.

6. (i) How valid are the two measures used—i.e. payback period and internal rate of return—as criteria for decision making?

7. Recompute the data for the decision process on at least three alternative bases: (i) net present value; (ii) discounted profitability index; and (iii) uniform annual cash flows.

8. Describe and illustrate the application of the following techniques used where probability of future outcomes is not quantified: (*a*) game theory; (*b*) various criteria of optimism.

9. What contribution can we make use of from the disciplines of (*a*) statistics and (*b*) sensitivity analysis in checking the significance of movements of particular variables in the final estimate?

Questions

1. Sotherton plc has an extensive research facility involved in the research, development and promotion of various projects. The managing director wishes to maximise Sotherton plc's reported earnings per share figure for the year while still complying with the requirements of SSAP13. Therefore, he seeks your advice as financial director.

Information regarding the research department's activities for the year ended 31st July 19x6 is given below:

(*a*) £750,000 spent on a new gas ionising plant. Such plant is highly specialised and has minimal scrap value due to contamination. It has an expected life of ten years and came into use from 1 July 19x6.

(*b*) A contract was entered into with a cosmetics group on a cost plus 25 per cent basis to develop a kissproof lipstick. So far Sotherton plc has incurred costs of £90,000 and has received £25,000 on account. Further costs of £35,000 to complete the contract are expected before 31st July 19x7. The balance of the contract price is to be settled on completion.

(*c*) Dr Lacey, a nuclear physicist, was employed at a cost of £25,000 to conduct investigations into sub-atomic wave motions. This work is vital to the future success of several current projects.

(*d*) £250,000 has been spent on the research and development of a new audio product. 40 per cent is attributable to development. The product will not be marketable until 19x8. Further total costs of some £400,000 are estimated, but financial backing is available from institutions and there are no doubts over the technical feasibility of the product. It is expected to have the same impact on home entertainment as television.

(*e*) A new low alcohol beverage was launched on 1st February 19x6 with an expected market life of four years. During the year £20,000 was spent on advertising. Development expenditure brought forward amounted to £300,000.

You are required to prepare a memorandum for the managing director of Sotherton plc recommending how items (*a*) to (*e*) above should be reflected in the statutory accounts. You should take account of the requirements of SSAP13 and the managing director's wish to maximise reported earnings per share. Your memorandum should indicate any assumptions you have made and any additional information that would be useful to your analysis. (ICAEW)

2. Describe and discuss the important stages that should be followed when a company wishes to develop and implement a new programme of capital investment. Do *not* confine your discussion to the nature and use of evaluation techniques in the appraisal of capital investments. (CACA)

3. One of the most important decisions which concerns financial management is the decision to incur capital expenditure. Discuss the information which is required in a system for the planning and control of such expenditure. (CACA)

4. Describe a system for ensuring the effective control of capital expenditure, including verification of the performance of projects after approval. (SCCA)

5. 'Because of the difference in emphasis and variations in procedures it is fruitful to distinguish between capital allocation decisions at the design level and the capital budgeting level.' Discuss what you consider this statement means, and list the procedure you suggest might be followed in considering a project *either* at design level *or* at capital budgeting level. (SCCA)

6. A company prepares annual budgets of capital expenditure for approval by the board, as part of the master budget for the year ahead. The chief accountant complains that he is not able to give the board adequate information because he is not able to evaluate individual projects (including replacement projects) before they are included in the budget.

(*a*) To what extent do you consider this complaint might be justified and what action, if any, do you think might be taken to remedy the position?

(*b*) You are required to design a comprehensive form for use in capital expenditure authorisation requests, making provision for the information which might be required for DCF evaluation. (CIMA)

7. The financial director of a holding company calls for budgets of capital expenditure for the forthcoming year from each subsidiary company. At the same time he points out that expenditure on approved projects will be rationed in proportion to the profits made by the various subsidiaries in the current year.

The managing director of a subsidiary which has incurred a loss objects. This he considers is tantamount to saying that because a company has not made a profit in the past, it shall not be given the opportunity to do so in the future. He suggests that it is probably the unprofitable company which requires the biggest infusion of new finance.

Do you agree? (CIMA)

8. The ABC Company has an annual expenditure of over £2 million on research and development, equivalent approximately to 6 per cent of sales turnover. The system applied in the past for dealing with this has been to determine at the beginning of the financial year the total amount to be spent on research and development, and then to leave to the research and development director the decision as to how this should be spent. Total expenditure is reported on a monthly and cumulative basis and no action is taken provided this indicates that the annual expenditure will not exceed the amount provided for. The managing director, while appreciating the risk attached to research and development and also not wishing to interfere with the right of the research and development director and his colleagues to determine research policy, nevertheless feels that a more purposeful approach to planning and control of research and development expenditure should be considered.

Prepare a memorandum outlining a suggested system which might achieve what the managing director desires. (CACA)

9. D Ltd manufactures and markets household durables. All recommendations for the acquisition of fixed assets by the company have to be supported by a financial justification statement. The three examples given below have been taken from past justification applications.

You are required to:

(*a*) Comment on whether each presentation is correctly categorised and whether the information given justifies the investment.

(*b*) Suggest some basic rules for future financial evaluation of such projects.

(i) Paint Spraying Plant

Category: Replacement.

Purpose: To provide cleaning and painting facilities for product DS27, the new waste disposal unit.

Proposal: To purchase electrostatic spray painting plant at a cost of £40,000.

Reasons: (*a*) Existing hand-spray equipment has not sufficient capacity to handle the increased volume of expected production.

(*b*) Hand-spraying would be uneconomical.

(ii) Threading Machine

Category: Cost saving.

Purpose: To provide facilities for threading components hitherto profile-turned on lathes.

Proposal: To purchase a high-speed threading machine at a cost of £9,000.

Reasons: (*a*) Cost savings are estimated at £1,950 p.a., as follows:

	Setting-up		Operating		Total
Per year	70 times		150,000 components		hours
Method	Hours each		Hours per 100		
Present	$1\frac{1}{2}$	105	$2\frac{1}{2}$	3,750	3,855
Proposed	$2\frac{1}{2}$	175	$1\frac{1}{4}$	1,875	2,050
		Hours saved per annum			1,805

	£
Annual cost savings:	
Labour 1,805 hours at £0·60 per hour	1,083
Overhead 80% of labour cost	867
Total	£1,950

(*b*) The existing equipment does not produce components of acceptable accuracy.

(iii) Jig Boring Machine

Category: Development.

Purpose: To provide the tool-room with up-to-date means of jig boring.

Proposal: To purchase one Model 999 jig boring machine at a total cost of £20,000.

Reasons: (*a*) The existing machine, even if it was not beyond economical repair, is now 40 years old.

(*b*) The new machine would continue the present trend towards more sophisticated machinery in the tool-room with a consequent large reduction in the high volume of work subcontracted which often incurs costly delivery delays.

(*c*) Unfortunately, no new machine has the same capacity as our existing machine and a smaller replacement might not handle the volume of jig boring expected to be needed over the next 25/30 years, though this is difficult to assess. The machine proposed is the best in the world, and would release recently acquired milling and drilling machines for other work.

(*d*) The existing machine has a resale value of £2,000.

(CIMA)

7

VALUATION OF A BUSINESS

Introduction

The concept of value is difficult to define because it must of necessity be subjective. Quite frequently the term value is automatically equated with cost or monetary equivalent. This is incorrect and an illustration can be drawn from the technique of value analysis which usually differentiates at least four types of value: use value, exchange value, esteem value and cost value. Water in the UK has, comparatively, a low cost value but its use value is extremely high. In a time of shortage or drought the exchange value and cost value increase rapidly. In times of plentiful supply most people would put a relatively low figure on the value of water. This would reverse as water became scarcer, and a higher price or cost would be quoted. This is a confusion between value and cost. We can easily increase the cost of an item without adding one penny to its use value.

There exist similar difficulties in trying to create one basis by which a business may be valued. Granted that it is necessary to value the business in monetary terms, the purpose for which the valuation is required will determine the subjective assessment ultimately made, as will the relative status of the parties concerned—i.e. although the purpose may be the same (say liquidation), the views of the owners and creditors on a 'reasonable' valuation of the company will differ considerably. Business and share valuations are carried out primarily for one or more of the following purposes.

Sole Traders, Partnerships and Unquoted Shares

(i) For taxation and estate duty settlements.

(ii) Determining a selling price for the business as a going concern.

Quoted Shares

(i) By the firm to confirm the realism or otherwse of its own market valuation.

(ii) Determining the price at which new shares or rights issues may be made.

(iii) By one firm, of the shares of another with a view to purchase as an investment or takeover proposition.

Although the purpose of the valuation may be similar, the objective may be different, and this too will affect the ultimate valuation. For example, the purpose may be for A Ltd to purchase B Ltd but the objective would be, among other things, either protective, i.e. buying up a competitor, or expansive, i.e. increasing production facilities. Thus although one of the techniques of share valuation described subsequently may be adopted to the exclusion of others, the final figure will be a subjective one and will be determined by interaction of the parties concerned in terms of strategy, management strengths or weakness, accuracy of predictions in terms of numerical results and behavioural responses and other factors discussed in later chapters.

Valuation Techniques

The type of company, the purpose and the objective of the valuation will influence both the choice of technique and the final figure. Nevertheless, the basic approach to valuation is by reference to one of two bases either as to what the business owns, i.e. the assets, or as to what the business can create, i.e. earnings.

Asset Basis

Fixed assets are brought into a company's books at purchase price and normally reduced over time by some conventional depreciation provision made on original cost. Current assets are usually reflected in the accounts at current values—subject to any specific adjustment such as bad debts. In respect of a going concern, so long as these figures are 'reasonable' on an historical cost basis then—until compulsory updating in respect of inflation is introduced in published accounts—the figures in respect of fixed assets do not represent what the assets are worth, either (*a*) on a going concern basis, or (*b*) on break-up value.

If the expenses of a survey—which could be considerable—are ignored, then a revaluation would be achieved by substituting revised estimates for the book figures and reconstructing the accounts on that basis. The spate of takeover bids occasioned by the 'go-go' companies of the 1960s made directors more aware of the danger of understating the value of assets. Around this time bids were quite frequently made—or a sufficient holding of shares built up to go forward with proposals—whereby the company taken over virtually financed the operation. Companies having large cash and investment holdings or substantial freehold interests in land and building were particularly vulnerable. The majority of shareholders or potential investors relying on published accounts and the financial press for their information were quite frequently unaware until it was too late of the substantial undervaluation.

Example 1: Valuation of a Business on an Assets Basis

The following data are representative of the latest accounts of B Ltd. The additional information has been made available by the company and you are requested to complete a valuation figure on an assets basis for the company and report to the board of directors upon the implications of the figures.

Balance Sheet of B Ltd as at 30th June, 19...

	(£000)	(£000)	(£000)
Fixed assets			
Land and buildings at cost			1,380
Plant and machinery at cost		6,550	
Less depreciation		(2,330)	
			4,320
Fixtures and fittings at cost		60	
Less depreciation		(20)	
			40
			5,740
Trade investments at market value			2,520

Current assets			
Stocks		900	
Debtors		850	
Cash and short-term deposits		380	
		2,130	
Less Current liabilities			
Current taxation	(240)		
Creditors	(850)	(1,090)	
Net current assets			1,040
			9,300
Represented by:			
Future taxation			200
Shareholders' funds:			
5% Cumulative preference shares			350
Ordinary shares of 50p issued and fully paid	2,380		
Reserves and share premium b/fwd	3,600		
P & L account balance	460		
			6,440
Loan capital:			
10% debentures			2,310
			9,300

After detailed investigation, the following information comes to light:

	(£000)
(*a*) Present value of land (freehold)	1,200
(*b*) Present value of buildings: at disposal prices	500
at current values	1,700
(*c*) Present value of plant: at disposal prices	2,000
at replacement cost	9,000
Average life expectancy of plant—5 years	
(*d*) Present value of fixtures and fittings: at disposal prices	5
at replacement cost	100
Average life expectancy—4 years	

(*e*) The stocks included items valued at £40,000 which have been declared redundant after the balance sheet date and which are now worth £15,000 at scrap prices. The balance of the stock is at cost but present replacement cost is estimated at £1,000,000, though it would realise only 70 per cent of this in a forced sale.

(*f*) Of the debtors, it is estimated £16,000 is sufficiently doubtful to be written off and since the date of the balance sheet a debtor with outstanding debts of £20,000 has been declared ankrupt and the expected dividend will be 30p in the £.

(*g*) Trade investments comprise five separate holdings. The total cost was

£4,800,000. The best estimate of future value is 10 per cent p.a. compound growth rate from the present market value. The market value stated does not allow for realisation expenses of £320,000 if sold.

Valuation of B Ltd—Assets Basis

Item	*Book value* (£000)	(£000)	*Going concern* (£000)	(£000)	*Break-up* (£000)	(£000)
Fixed assets						
Land		1,380		1,200		1,200
Buildings				1,700		500
Plant		4,320		9,000		2,000
Fixtures and fittings		40		100		5
		5,740		12,000		3,705
Trade investments		2,520		2,520		2,200
Net current assets						
Stocks	900		1,015		715	
Debtors	850		820		820	
Cash	380		380		380	
	2,130		2,215		1,915	
Less Creditors	240		240		240	
Current tax	850		850		850	
		1,040		1,125		825
Total assets		9,300		15,645		6,730
Less Amounts due to:						
Future taxation	200		200		200	
Debenture holders	2,310		2,310		2,310	
Preference shareholders	350		350		350	
		2,860		2,860		2,860
Attributable to ordinary shares		6,440		12,785		3,870
Number of ordinary shares (000s)		4,760		4,760		4,760
Value of one share		£1·35		£2·69		£0·81

Treatment of the Items

Book value: This column represents, without amendments, the value per share on the figures recorded in the historical accounts. Its use for any financial management purposes is restricted, but it may form either a starting point for computation and discussion or may be required—particularly in purely academic examples—as confirmation of the procedure and methods subsequently adopted.

Going concern basis: This column produces a result which is the outcome of revaluation in accordance with the notes to arrive at the value of the business in terms of present prices if all assets are to be relinquished by the company. It would be comparatively easy, for example, to establish a figure for land but buildings would require separate valuation. Alternatively, indices could be used but are not so satisfactory. If any item of plant or fixture were not required this would be separately valued since in the case of a sale they could either be sold after purchase or deducted from the offer price and left in the hands of the vendor. The valuation of plant is particularly difficult in practice since:

(*a*) Quite frequently a machine, when worn out, is not replaced or cannot be replaced by an identical or even similar model. Methods and design improvements, a great degree of automation, and other similar technological changes prevent this identical replacement.

(*b*) The various items of equipment are usually too numerous to evaluate separately or there may not even be a reliable plant register. In this event plant and machinery items are quite frequently grouped into categories and evaluated by reference to an index obtained from government or trade sources. An example of machine groups would be:

(i) Heavy plant—slow speed (e.g. presses).
(ii) Medium duty (e.g. capstan lathes, drillers).
(iii) Precision—high-speed (e.g. precision grinders).

The value of the machines would be recomputed using a replacement cost index and adjusted for condition in terms of numbers of years life expectancy. Disposal values are simply what could be obtained on a second-hand or purely scrap basis.

Trade investments: The general practice is to show these in the historical accounts at cost or market value, whichever is lower. The value taken in this example ignores the growth prediction and assumes that the investment is being liquidated. It could be argued that this is a very conservative approach on a going concern basis and this is true. If one were fairly confident that the growth rate would be achieved then this figure could be recomputed for as many years into the future as might be considered relevant or agreed between the parties.

Current assets: The figure of £1,105,000 is the present worth of the stocks retained if the business continues, i.e. the replacement cost of usable stocks plus revenue from scrap sales of redundant stocks. Similarly, debtors represent the best estimate of the actual realisable cash figure. The bank and cash balances are not, of course, subjected to any amendment.

Current liabilities: These are not normally adjusted since in the case of creditors they represent known sums due and similarly current taxation and dividends due.

A subtotal is normally computed at this point as this represents the total assets available to long-term creditors and ownership interests. The provision for future taxation is included with other claimants, usually because the amount is subject to agreement with the taxation authorities and the credit period is in excess of one year. The amounts due to debenture and other mortgage holders are also deducted and similarly preference shares in accordance with the terms concerned. The asset values are then computed in terms of per-share holding according to the classification and ranking of the shares—a simple matter if there is only one category of ordinary shares and they all rank equally in terms of claim.

Break-up basis: The results in the final column of the example are arrived at in a similar manner to the above but by inserting the figures relevant to a break-up basis, i.e. discontinuing the business. Buildings, plant, fixtures and stocks are revalued and the amounts reflect the changed situation. The other items are unaffected but the resultant figure is obviously very much lower.

The range on an assets basis is therefore between a high of £12,785,000 and a low of £3,870,000.

If the business could be purchased at a price below £3,870,000 then it would obviously be advantageous to the buyer, since irrespective of figures produced by alternative evaluation methods the buyer would make a profit even if the entire enterprise was subsequently resold.

The book value of the assets in the above example lies somewhere between the two extremes. For some years up to 1985 larger public companies were required to supply information on current costs to indicate the effects of inflation. The SSAP concerned (see Chapter 9) was No. 16 but the mandatory status of this standard was withdrawn in July 1985 and the position is under review. Obviously if any revaluation figures are supplied for this or other purposes they can be utilised. Such information obviously goes part of the way towards preventing a completely misleading impression conveyed by the historical data alone. The valuations produced on a break-up value are completely independent of the ability or otherwise of the assets concerned to generate earnings. Figures on a replacement cost or going concern basis are not so independent because they are related to the ability of the company carrying on at the existing earnings capacity. This provides the link between the assets and earnings bases discussed in the following section.

It was further stated above that the average life expectancy of the plant and machinery was five years. This would require breaking down in detail to be of real help since one major item may be expired next year. The anticipated life of the assets is required in order to ascertain potential capital expenditure in terms of amount and timing of replacements to maintain or improve future profits and cash flow.

Earnings Basis

An alternative approach to assessing the value of a business is to assess the 'sum it is worth' paying now for the future earnings of the business. There is a variety of ways of doing the computation. The major alternatives are discussed below.

Capitalisation of Earnings Basis

This method was introduced in Chapter 4 and requires the computation of an expected rate of return and projection of future cash flows or adjustment of past results to reflect anticipated trends. If a pre-tax rate of return of 20 per cent is required and a firm has expected future cash inflows of £10,000 p.a. then the value of the firm on this basis is that sum which when invested at 20 per cent p.a. would produce an income of £10,000 p.a., i.e. £50,000. The factors determining the rate depend upon which approach is being used. Usually the 20 per cent would represent either the rate of return expected for firms in that particular industry—it may not represent the cost of capital to the buyer—or it could represent a return on capital employed (ROCE) computed on a conventional historic accountancy basis, thus

$$\text{Minimum target ROCE required} = 10\% \text{ after tax}$$
$$\text{Corporation Tax rate} = 35\%$$
$$\therefore \text{ Gross earnings rate required} = 10 \times \frac{100}{100-35} = 10 \times \frac{100}{65}$$
$$= 15{\cdot}38\%$$

B Ltd

Assume the average maintainable earnings of the company used in the asset valuation example was £1,200,000 p.a.; then

$$\text{Capitalised value of B Ltd} = \frac{1{,}200{,}000}{15{\cdot}38} \times 100$$
$$= £7{,}802{,}340$$

The important phrase in this context is 'average maintainable earnings'. This can be expressed as—in the above example—15·38 per cent gross or 10 per cent net of Corporation Tax. The net earnings are also referred to as average maintainable distributable earnings since this is the rate which governs the maximum dividends payable and retained profits. If a rate is used which is representative of that expected from all equity-financed firms in an industry with a similar degree of risk then this is usually obtained from information published about the performance of public, i.e. quoted, companies. Provided the average maintainable distributable earnings can be forecast for a period and combined with a realistic rate the method is simple to understand and easy to apply. In terms of a value put on a purchase price it corresponds to a payback type of assessment since it does not account for benefits arising after the payback period, i.e. if the rate of return is 10, then after 10 years the original cost has been recouped by the purchaser of the business.

This method can be adapted for use where earnings are growing to give some emphasis to the latest performance or forecast by weighting the average, thus:

The most recent three-year profits of AB Ltd are as follows:

19x4 £11,500, 19x5 £14,000, and 19x6 £16,000.

In this case the weighted average could be computed as:

			£
19x4	£11,500 ×	1 =	11,500
19x5	£14,000 ×	2 =	28,000
19x6	£16,000 ×	3 =	48,000
		6	87,500

$$\text{Weighted average} = \frac{£87{,}500}{6} = £14{,}583, \text{ say } £14{,}600.$$

If the required capitalisation rate were 12 per cent the derived capital value would be $\frac{£14,600}{12} \times 100 = £121,666$.

The weighting factors of 1, 2 and 3 are purely arbitrary in this case and would in practice be selected according to the degree of emphasis one desired to attach to the data concerned.

A further requirement, whether historical or projected figures are used, is to establish that the earnings figures used are adjusted to reflect the correct resultant cash flow anticipated into the business. In this respect profit and loss accounts figures would have to be adjusted in respect of depreciation, non-recurring and extraordinary items in the data for a particular period. Guidance is available from the various Statements of Standard Accounting Practice, but these are primarily intended to provide published data on a comparable basis. They are not to be interpreted as the only ways in which items can be viewed when actually assessing a valuation since this will always be subjective to an assessment on each individual item. On the other hand, in dealing with theoretical examples or problems requiring treatment in published accounts (dealt with more fully later) then if a different approach is used the reason for such an approach should be stated. Furthermore, if capital investment is being made by the company in new projects there is invariably a delay between the timing of the investment and the receipt of regular cash inflows from it. If this is not adjusted in the earnings computation the result would be, on a long-term basis, to understate the current worth of the business concerned.

Goodwill and Super-Profits

These words are used to describe adjustments to basic figures produced when historically based earnings computations have been used. In most elementary exercises **goodwill** is computed either on a basis of *n* years times the average profits or inserted as a figure necessary to produce a balance sheet which agrees after all revaluations have been made, i.e. merely the difference at a specific date between the purchase price paid and the values at which related assets and liabilities have been taken into the accounts.

In financial management we are less concerned with traditional accounting treatments and more concerned with the basis of computation. In this respect the term **super-profits** may be more representative. In assessing an acceptable rate of return a prospective business purchaser has at least one alternative in that he can put his capital into a comparatively risk-free investment. The addition to this rate in a particular case will represent the increased return relevant in respect of average performance for that particular risk class. If the return actually being earned or forecast is in excess of the figure derived then the difference represents 'super-profits'. In any problem it must be made clear whether one is interpreting 'super' as the incremental profits over and above a 'reasonable' or risk-free rate or whether they are being interpreted as the return over and above that expected for an average performed in the industry or type of business concerned.

Example 2

1. Coracles Ltd build boats, all of the same class. The summarised accounts for the year 19x8 are as follows:

Trading and Profit and Loss Accounts

	£	£
Sales (20 boats)		80,000
Cost of sales:		
Materials	48,000	
Labour	8,000	
		56,000
		24,000
Fixed overheads	11,600	
Office salaries	2,000	
Directors' remuneration	4,000	
		17,600
Net profit		6,400
Losses brought forward		4,900
Profit carried forward		£1,500

Balance Sheet—31st December, 19x8

	£	£
Share capital:		
1,000 shares of £1 each		1,000
Undistributed profits		1,500
		£2,500
Fixed assets:		
Plant and machinery	2,500	
Vehicles	1,500	
		4,000
Current assets:		
Stock	11,000	
Debtors and bank	9,500	
	£20,500	
Current liabilities:		
Creditors	17,000	
Directors' account	5,000	
	£22,000	
		(1,500)
		£2,500

Upton is offered all the issued shares at their net asset value on 31st December, 19x8, subject to the addition of goodwill valued at four times the projected earnings before taxation for 19x9 and the lease valued at £1,500. For the purpose of computing the 19x9 earnings, you ascertain that:

(1) Based on firm orders, 25 boats should be sold in 19x9 at the 19x8 price.

(2) The percentage costs of production based on sales should remain steady, apart from an anticipated increase in the labour rate to 12½ per cent.

(3) Fixed overheads will increase by £1,700 and office salaries by 10 per cent.

(4) A fair managerial remuneration for the directors is £3,000 p.a.

You are required to: (*a*) compute the price at which the shares are being offered to Upton, and (*b*) list the matters which require consideration to enable you to form an opinion of the reasonableness of the offer price. (ICAEW)

Goodwill in this example is required to be computed on a straightforward basis subject only to adjustment in respect of the projected earnings. The first step is to prepare this forecast as a basis for computation of goodwill.

(*a*) *Computation of price at which shares are being offered to Upton*

Projected Earnings for year ended 31st December, 19x9

	£	£
Sales (25 boats at 19x8 prices)		100,000
Cost of sales		
Materials (60% of sales)	60,000	
Labour (12½% of sales)	12,500	
		72,500
Gross profit		27,500
Fixed overhead (£11,600 + £1,700)	13,300	
Office salaries (£2,000 + £200)	2,200	
Directors' remuneration (£4,000 – £1,000)	3,000	
		18,500
Profit (before tax)		9,000

Computation of Price

	£
Goodwill (4 × £9,000)	36,000
Lease	1,500
Net assets at 31st December, 19x8, as per the offer	2,500
Total valuation	£40,000
Value per share (1,000 shares)	£40

(*b*) *Matters requiring consideration*

(i) Realism of the value attributed to fixed and current assets: are they worth more or less than book value?

(ii) How much of the combined debtors and bank figure is hard cash?

(iii) What is the explanation for the losses brought forward?

(iv) Are the increases forecast in fixed overhead and labour costs reasonable?

(v) The liquidity position is critical. We have £9,500 worth (maximum) of quick assets and owe £17,000 to creditors, exclusive of directors account.

(vi) Are there any contingent liabilities and does the existing position justify any goodwill?

Example 3

The summarised balance sheet of a private limited company, as on 31st December, 19x9, is as follows:

	£
Share capital:	
Authorised, issued and fully paid	
10,000 6% preference shares of £1 each	10,000
30,000 ordinary shares of £1 each	30,000
Profit and loss account	50,000
5% debentures	20,000
Sundry creditors	15,950
	125,950

	Cost £	*Depn.* £	£
Fixed assets:			
Goodwill	10,000	—	10,000
Freehold property	25,000	—	25,000
Plant, etc.	20,000	10,000	10,000
	55,000	10,000	45,000
Quoted investments			20,000
Current assets:			
Stocks		18,000	
Debtors		19,950	
Bank balance (Current account)		23,000	
			60,950
			125,950

The profits of the three years 19x7, 19x8 and 19x9 were £14,700, £21,500 and £16,000 respectively, after charging debenture interest but before providing for the preference dividends.

The sole shareholder has agreed to sell all the preference shares, which are repayable at par in a liquidation, to a purchaser for 75p a share. He has also agreed to sell all the ordinary shares to another purchaser. The price of the ordinary shares will be calculated so that the purchaser will obtain a return of 10 per cent on the net physical assets attributable to the ordinary shares, as on 31st December 19x9, and in addition pay an amount for goodwill of three times the average super-profits (i.e. the profits over the 10 per cent) of the previous three years.

The purchase consideration is to be based on the figures shown in the balance sheet as on 31st December 19x9, and on the profits of the previous three years' accounts, subject to relevant adjustments in respect of the following matters:

(1) The vendor, with the consent of the purchaser, has agreed with the holder of the debentures that the company will purchase these for cancellation at a discount of 25 per cent.

(2) It has been ascertained that the current rental value of the freehold property is £3,360 and that it could be sold on the basis of an 8 per cent return. It is agreed to substitute the relevant value for the book value.

(3) A revenue creditor of £550 had been omitted from the balance sheet as on 31st December, 19x9.

(4) The market value of the quoted investments was £25,000.

(5) 10 per cent of the profit shown in the accounts for 19x8 arose from a non-recurring item, which it is agreed should be eliminated.

(6) A general provision of 5 per cent had been made in 19x9 against the debtors, which it is agreed is not now required.

You are required to compute the purchase price of the ordinary shares. Ignore taxation.

(ICAEW)

Here the adjustments more closely follow the varied type of adjustment given earlier in the text and the question is more practical. The first stage is again to compute the goodwill:

	£	£
Profits 3 years to December 19x9 (£14,700 + £21,500 + £16,000)		52,200
Add:		
Debenture interest not required if redeemed (3 × 5% × 20,000)		3,000
Provision for bad debts no longer required $\left(\frac{5}{95} \times 19{,}950\right)$		1,050
		56,250
Less: Non-recurring income 19x8 (10% × 21,500)	2,150	
Revenue creditor omitted 19x9	550	
		2,700
3 years' total adjusted profits		53,550
Average annual profit $\frac{£53{,}550}{3} =$		17,850
Less annual preference dividend		600
Profit available to ordinary shareholders		17,250

It is now necessary to compute the value of the net physical assets attributable to the ordinary shares in order to establish whether the return of 10 per cent on this figure is above or below the £17,250 p.a. computed above.

	£	£
Net Physical Assets		
Freehold property $\left(£3,360 \times \frac{100}{8}\right)$		42,000
Plant		10,000
		52,000
Quoted investments		25,000
Net current assets		
Stocks	18,000	
Debtors $\left(£19,950 \times \frac{100}{95}\right)$	21,000	
Bank (£23,000 – £15,000 deb. redemption)	8,000	
	47,000	
Creditors (15,950 + 550)	(16,500)	
		30,500
		107,500
Less Attributable to preference shareholders		10,000
Attributable to ordinary shareholders		97,500
Profits required for 10% annual return on £97,500 =		9,750
Annual profit anticipated as above =		17,250
∴ Annual 'super-profits' =		7,500
Goodwill = 3 years at £7,500 p.a. =		22,500
Physical assets		97,500
∴ Total valuation of 30,000 ordinary shares =		£120,000
Value per share		£4

Modifications to the Basic Methods

A variety of valuations can be arrived at using earnings in some form or other. These vary from the simple *n* years purchase of adjusted profits typified in the computation of sale values of sole traders, professional and business partnerships, to complex mathematical assessments of potential earnings of multinational companies. One thing they have in common, however, is the limitation of data derived from the past as an accurate indicator of future worth. Methods relying primarily on historical analysis have been discussed in the previous section. Alternatives to this historical approach are now considered.

Discounted Cash Flow

The proponents of this method argue that buying or investing in another company is no different from any other capital investment project and any proposition can, therefore, be evaluated by one of the methods using the DCF principle described in Chapter 3. This would mean determination of either:

(*a*) The internal rate of return for the investment or purchase, and a comparison to see whether this is greater than the present return or one capable of being obtained by the prospective purchaser elsewhere.
(*b*) Using the net present value method to determine whether the present value of the future cash flows at some cost of capital is greater or less than the purchase price contemplated.

In order to use either of these methods we would require data in respect of the business purchase corresponding to that required for the investment problems described in Chapter 3. This would comprise:

(i) Net cash flow projections for the future period. These would be after tax but with depreciation added back and with any anticipated growth or decline in the specific annual figures built into the forecasts.
(ii) Adjustment in respect of any capital expenditure anticipated at future dates should the cash flow in (i) be in respect of wholly revenue items.
(iii) Similarly, if it is anticipated that any assets purchased are or will become surplus to requirements then allowance should be made for the amounts and timing of cash receipts in respect of these.
(iv) Information on any capital repayments which may fall due at a future date—e.g. redeemable debentures—and estimated scrap value of the business at the end of the contemplated time-span, should this be anticipated.
(v) In cases where it is proposed to use the net present value method a rate for the cost of capital must be specified. Similarly, rates and bases of taxation assessment must be predicted.

Earnings, Dividends and Retained Profits

A great deal has been written and many mathematical models developed in efforts to formulate a general theory. The basic premise is comparatively simple. The purchaser of a business or share in a business is buying the right to the total or proportional earnings either for a specified or anticipated time period or, if the time-span is unknown, then theoretically to perpetuity. In the latter case this would formally be represented by the mathematical notation

$$P_0 = \sum_{n=1}^{n=\infty} E_1 + E_2 + E_3 \cdots E_\infty$$

i.e. the total cash inflows for all time will equal the sum of the inflows in the individual periods. If we combine this with the cost of capital we are saying yet again that money received in the future is not worth as much as that received now by virtue of the interest forgone. If we know or estimate that the expected rate of return for a given industry (risk class) is r then we must discount at this rate to get the present value of the future cash flows. The formula then becomes

$$P_0 = \sum_{n=1}^{n=\infty} \frac{E_n}{(1+r)^n}$$

i.e. the price now is equal to the sum of the future individual cash flows discounted at the appropriate rate of return. In Chapter 4 the general symbol

K was used for the cost of capital and an appropriate suffix used for which cost of capital was concerned, e.g. K_e represented the cost of the equity. In this case the formula might be stated

$$P_0 = \sum_{n=1}^{n=\infty} \frac{E_n}{(1+K_e)^n}$$

Earnings, by definition, have been restricted to what would be considered average maintainable distributable earnings. Most writers on the subject of valuation, however, confine the variable for consideration to anticipated dividends rather than earnings. In this case the formula would become

$$P_0 = \sum_{n=1}^{n=\infty} \frac{D_n}{(1+K_d)^n}$$

In this case D represents dividends as opposed to earnings, and P is the discounted value of the right to receive such dividends to perpetuity or for a given number of years (n) and the terminal value expected at year n. The ratio between E (earnings) and D (dividends) represents the cover—the number of times such dividends would be paid out of the earnings concerned. Since the price/earnings ratio, as explained in Chapter 4, indicates that earnings, distributed or not, are the unit to which stock market indices are basically related, then it is suggested that for most practical purposes earnings will be the more useful. Without earnings no dividend can be paid and dividend payments are affected by so many other factors—legal restraint, taxation, retentions policy of the particular company concerned, to name but a few—that for calculation purposes they are the more relevant variable. In historical terms the p/e ratio represents the latest known market price as a multiple of published or modified earnings per share. In theoretical terms the p/e ratio represents the present value of the future stream of earnings discounted at the appropriate cost of capital. It is, however, precisely the difficulties encountered in deciding what the appropriate value of this rate is which tend to be make practitioners look to the market figures for guidance. Rates can be computed starting with a rate such as government or local authority bonds and adding a premium for risk related to the element of risk anticipated in the project concerned.

Finally, there is the modification made to the basic models in respect of growth. To recapitulate the approach referred to in Chapter 4, if the dividend base is used, then

$$P_0 = \frac{D_0(1+g)}{(1+r)} + \frac{D_0(1+g)^2}{(1+r)^2} + \cdots \text{ to infinity}$$

where P_0 represents the present value, D_0 the dividend in Year 0, g the annual growth rate of dividend, and r the return anticipated by purchaser or investor.

If r is greater than g (which is likely), this simplifies to

$$P_0 = \frac{D_0(1+g)}{r-g}$$

A similar expression could be derived using earnings, provided these were at a constant annual rate, but this is less predictable than with dividends since growth rates are less likely to be at constant annual rates and there will probably be adjustments in respect of extraordinary items which will give a random distribution of earnings figures. The Capital Asset Pricing Model discussed in Chapter 4 may also be used to provide a basis of valuation.

Summary

1. There are two major groups of techniques of valuation: one based upon assets and one on earnings.
2. The principles and theories are common to quoted and unquoted companies.
3. Historical analysis is restricted in use but so are the theories of valuation by virtue of the unknowns which have to be estimated or assumed.
4. There may be a single true valuation in theory but in practice the purpose and circumstances of the transaction and the bargaining strengths of the relevant parties will result in a subjective assessment different from this. The motivations likely to be involved in this subjective assessment are dealt with more fully in the following chapter.

Worked Examples

Solutions to Questions on Valuation

Valuation of a Business for Marketing on the Stock Exchange

The shares of Z Ltd, an existing private company, are to be marketed on the stock exchange. You are required to suggest, showing the basis of your calculations:

(*a*) What the market value of the company should be.
(*b*) A recommendation for the aggregate flotation value.
(*c*) How many shares should be issued, and in what denominations, having regard to the required dividend yield and dividend cover.
(*d*) The 'offer for sale' price per share.

A Ltd, B Ltd, and C Ltd are engaged in the same type of business as Z Ltd. Recent information of all four companies is given below:

	A Ltd (£000)	*B Ltd* (£000)	*C Ltd* (£000)	*Z Ltd* (£000)
Profit after loan interest and before tax, Year 1	1,360	1,120	508	1,170
2	1,500	960	529	1,080
3	1,910	1,140	507	1,090
Net capital employed, end of Year 3:				
Loan	1,500	390	500	—
Equity:				4,700
Ordinary share capital	2,000	1,540	994	
Reserves	2,310	4,260	1,656	
Total	5,810	6,190	3,150	
	£	£	£	
Nominal value per share	0·10	0·25	0·25	
Current share price	0·80	1·40	0·90	
	%	%	%	
Last dividend	19·5	17·3	16·0	

A Ltd appears to have secure and advancing dividends, supported by gradually growing earnings, B Ltd shows solid dividends, although earnings have failed to make progress. C Ltd's dividends and earnings have shown negligible movement in recent years. Z Ltd has a sound record, although it has made little headway in recent years. Its own forecast of profits before tax for Year 4 is £1,200,000; although in view of its past record this forecast should be treated with caution. The company has adequate liquid assets.

The rate of Corporation Tax may be assumed as 45 per cent throughout.

(CIMA)

(a) Suggested Market Value of Z Ltd

Since no information is given about the value and condition of assets, the market value estimates will need to be related to earnings. Two fundamental factors have to be estimated: average maintainable distributable earnings and an appropriate p/e ratio for Z Ltd. Figures are computed in respect of the other three companies for comparison purposes.

A Ltd: Suggest that a weighted average of the last three years is used by virtue of the steady upward trend:

i.e.

	(£000)
1 × 1,360 =	1,360
2 × 1,500 =	3,000
3 × 1,910 =	5,730
	10,090 ÷ 6 = £1,681,000

B Ltd & C Ltd: Suggest a simple average since both companies have shown little movement:

$$\text{B Ltd (£000)} \ \frac{£1{,}120 + £960 + £1{,}140}{3} = £1{,}073$$

$$\text{C Ltd (£000)} \ \frac{£508 + £529 + £507}{3} = £515$$

Z Ltd: 'Treating the estimate with caution' could mean ignoring it or giving it equal weighting. Alternatively, a weighting factor could be applied using the reverse effect to that adopted for A Ltd. However, a simple average of Years 1, 2 and 3 would produce (£000)

$$\frac{(£1{,}170 + £1{,}080 + £1{,}090)}{3} = £1{,}113$$

This compares with a forecast of £1,200,000 for Year 4, and using the aveage will produce a more conservative valuation.

Average earnings after taxation will therefore be:

	A (£000)	B (£000)	C (£000)	Z (£000)		*Origin of data*
Earnings before taxation	1,681	1,073	515	1,113		
Less taxation (45%)	756	483	232	501		
	925	590	283	612	1	
Number of shares	20,000	6,160	3,976		2	$\frac{\text{Equity cap.}}{\text{Nom. value}}$
Earnings per share	£0·046	£0·096	£0·071			3 = 1 ÷ 2
Price per share	£0·80	£1·40	£0·90			4 given
p/e ratio	17·4	14·6	12·7			5 = 4 ÷ 3
Market value of equity (£000)	16,000	8,624	3,578			6 = 2 × 4 or 1 × 5
Book value of equity (£000)	4,310	5,800	2,650	4,700		7 given
Return on equity (book)	21·5%	10·2%	10·7%	13·02%		8 = 1 ÷ 7
Earnings yield	5·78%	6·8%	7·9%			9 = 1 ÷ 6

The earnings yield (9) is equitable with the return on equity except that it is post-tax profit related to market value as opposed to return on book value (8). The variation in the book return indicates its restricted use for valuation purposes and we look to the return being earned on the market value. This varies only between 5·78 per cent and 7·9 per cent and since the p/e ratio is the reciprocal of the earnings yield it could have been computed from this. The range of p/e ratios is between 17·4 and 12·7 and if the midway point is taken it becomes $\frac{17{\cdot}4 + 12{\cdot}7}{2} \simeq 15$. This would give a market value for Z Ltd of £612,000 × 15 = £9,180,000, say £9,200,000, or in round terms £9,000,000.

(*b*) *Aggregate Flotation Value*

The aggregate flotation value would be somewhat less than the above figure. In the same way as rights issues are offered at a price designed to offer some advantage to existing shareholders, so the flotation value will be pitched normally somewhere below the anticipated market value to create a market demand and attract investors away from alternative investments. This is the area where the expertise of the professional advisers would be put to the test. If the reduction is too great then the company loses the benefit of the higher worth of the shares. If it is too little shares may not be taken up or extra underwriting commission incurred.

Company B is more nearly comparable with Z Ltd, but with Z being a new entrant some premium on B's p/e ratio would probably be expected and pitching the required ratio arbitrarily 10 per cent below that of B would give 90% × 14·6 = 13·14, say 13.

The aggregate flotation value would then be 13 × £612,000 = £7,956,000, say £8,000,000.

(*c*) *Required Number and Denomination of Shares*

Here the objective is to make share prices, yields and cover comparable with similar risk and size companies. The two items are entirely interdependent. Increasing the number of shares will automatically offset the amounts per share but the dividend yield and cover are effectively related to the total amounts concerned.

	A	B	C	Origin of data
Last dividend rate (gross)	19·5%	17·3%	16·0%	1 given
Nominal share capital (£000)	2,000	1,540	994	2 given
Cost of dividends (£000)	390	266	159	3 = 1 × 2
Post-tax profits (£000)	925	590	283	4
Dividend cover	2·4	2·2	1·8	5 = 4 ÷ 3
Market value of company (£000)	16,000	8,624	3,578	6
Dividend yield	2·4%	3·1%	4·4%	7 = 3 ÷ 6

The average dividend cover is about 2·0. Z Ltd has available earnings of £612,000. With a target cover of 2, dividends would be restricted to

$$\frac{£612,000}{2} = £306,000.$$

The flotation value (part *b*) was £8,000,000. Therefore

$$\text{Dividend yield} = \frac{£306,000}{£8,000,000} \times 100 = 3{\cdot}83\%$$

This would appear comparable. It now remains to determine whether this could be related to the nominal dividend rates and share prices existing at present in the other companies. The nominal dividend rates are between 19·5 and 16·0 per cent. If the flotation value is raised in 25p shares sold at £1·00, nominal value will be £2,000,000 and the dividend rate $\frac{£306,000}{£2,000,000} \times 100 =$ 15·3 per cent—comparable with the other companies.

(*d*) *The offer for sale price would be:*

$$\frac{£8,000,000}{8,000,000} = £1 \text{ per share}$$

Note. The above scheme is only one of a large number of possibilities. Any alternatives which provided something similar would be acceptable as a tentative solution in theory or in an examination and as a starting point in practice. Strictly speaking, the relationships between earnings and dividend would be expressed differently by virtue of the applications of ACT (Advance Corporation Tax). It is considered, however, that the principles are best illustrated as above and the treatment of ACT left until later, since its effect upon the wider issue involved and demonstrated above is restricted.

Comparison of Statistics for Valuation of a Private Company

At a meeting of the directors of the Alpha Company Ltd—a privately owned company—in May 19x8 the recurrent question is raised as to how the company is going to finance its future growth and at the same time enable the founders of the company to withdraw a substantial part of their investment. A public quotation was discussed in 19x7 but because of the depressed nature of the stock market at that time consideration was deferred. Although the matter is not of immediate urgency, the chairman of the company—one of the founders—

produces the following information which he has recently obtained from a firm of financial analysts in respect of two publicly quoted companies Beta Ltd and Gamma Ltd, which are similar to Alpha Ltd in respect to size, asset composition, financial structure and product mix:

		Beta Ltd	*Gamma Ltd*
		£	£
19x7	Earnings per share	1·50	2·50
19x3/x7	Average earnings per share	1·00	2·00
19x7	Average market price per share	9·00	20·00
19x7	Dividends per share	0·75	1·25
19x3/x7	Average dividends per share	0·60	1·20
19x7	Average book value per share	9·00	18·00

The chairman asks on the basis of this information what you think Alpha Ltd was worth in 19x7. The only information you have available at the meeting in respect of Alpha Ltd is the final accounts for 19x7, which disclose the following:

Share capital (no variation for 8 years)	100,000 ordinary £1 shares
Post-tax earnings	£400,000
Gross dividends	£100,000
Book value	£3,500,000

From memory you think that the post-tax earnings and gross dividends for 19x7 were at least one-third higher than the average of the previous five years.

You are required, making *full* use of the information above, to:

(*a*) Answer the question of the managing director.

(*b*) Discuss the factors to be taken into account in trying to assess the potential market value of shares in a private company when they are first offered for public subscription. (CACA)

Summary of Data

	Beta Ltd	*Gamma Ltd*	*Alpha Ltd Basis*		*Origin of data*
	£	£	£		
19x7 Earnings per share	1·50	2·50	4·00	$\frac{£400,000}{100,000}$	1
19x3/x7 Average EPS	1·00	2·00	3·20	$\frac{(4 \times 3) + (1 \times 4)}{5}$	2
19x7 Dividends per share	0·75	1·25	1·00	$\frac{£100,000}{100,000}$	3
19x3/x7 Average dividends per share	0·60	1·20	0·80	$\frac{(4 \times 0·75) + (1 \times 1)}{5}$	4
19x7 Average market price per share	9·0	20·0	?		5
p/e ratio on 19x7 earnings	6·0	8·0			6 = 5 ÷ 1
p/e ratio on 19x3/x7 average	9·0	10·0			7 = 5 ÷ 2
19x7 Dividend cover	2·0	2·0	4·0		9 = 1 ÷ 3
19x3/x7 Dividend cover (average)	1·6	2·0	4·0		10 = 2 ÷ 4

Valuation of Alpha Ltd

		£	
Based on p/e ratio of Beta Ltd	19x7 only	2,400,000	(6 × £400,000)
	19x3/x7 average	2,880,000	(9 × £320,000)
Gamma Ltd	19x7 only	3,200,000	(8 × £400,000)
	19x3/x7 average	3,200,000	(10 × £320,000)

Conclusions

1. Value of Alpha Ltd on an earnings basis would appear to lie between a low of £2,400,000 and a high of £3,200,000.

2. There is little guidance from the dividends information except that assuming cash resources and freedom of choice in dividend policy, the cover is ample to improve present dividend policy in line with examples from outside.

3. Comparison on a book value of assets basis is undesirable in view of the limited amount of information available. At present the book valuation is in excess of that produced by highest earnings figures but the book value per share of £35 compares more than favourably with the £9·00 for Beta Ltd and £18·00 for Gamma Ltd.

Questions

1. The board of directors of Oxclose plc is considering making an offer to purchase Satac Ltd, a private limited company in the same industry. If Satac is purchased it is proposed to continue operating the company as a going concern in the same line of business.

Summarised details from the most recent financial accounts of Oxclose and Satac are shown below:

	Oxclose plc Balance sheet as at 31st March (£ millions)		*Satac Ltd* Balance sheet as at 31st March (*£000s*)	
Freehold property		33		460
Plant and equipment (net)		58		1,310
Stock	29		330	
Debtors	24		290	
Cash	3		20	
Less: Current liabilities	(31)	25	(518)	122
		116		1,892
Financed by				
Ordinary shares*		35		160
Reserves		43		964
Shareholders' equity		78		1,124
Medium term bank loans		38		768
		116		1,892

* Oxclose plc 50 pence ordinary shares, Satac Ltd 25 pence ordinary shares.

	Oxclose plc (£ millions)		Satac Ltd (£000s)	
Year*	Profit after tax	Dividend	Profit after tax	Dividend
$t-5$	14·30	9·01	143	85
$t-4$	15·56	9·80	162	93·5
$t-3$	16·93	10·67	151	93·5
$t-2$	18·42	11·60	175	102·8
$t-1$	20·04	12·62	183	113·1

* $t-5$ is five years ago, $t-1$ the most recent year etc.

Satac's shares are owned by a small number of private individuals. The company is dominated by its managing director who receives an annual salary of £80,000, double the average salary received by managing directors of similar companies. The managing director would be replaced if the company is purchased by Oxclose.

The freehold property of Satac has not been revalued for several years and is believed to have a market value of £800,000.

The balance sheet value of plant and equipment is thought to fairly reflect its replacement cost, but its value if sold is not likely to exceed £800,000. Approximately £55,000 of stock is obsolete and could only be sold as scrap for £5,000.

The ordinary shares of Oxclose are currently trading at 430 pence ex-div. It is estimated that because of difference in size, risk and other factors the required return on equity by shareholders of Satac is approximately 15 per cent higher than the required return on equity of Oxclose's shareholders (i.e. 115 per cent of Oxclose's required return). Both companies are subject to corporate taxation at a rate of 40 per cent.

You are required to:

(*a*) Prepare estimates of the value of Satac using three different methods of valuation, and advise the board of Oxclose plc as to the price, or possible range of prices, that it should be prepared to offer to purchase Satac's shares.

(*b*) Briefly discuss the theoretical and practical problems of the valuation methods that you have chosen.

(*c*) Discuss the advantages and disadvantages of the various terms that might be offered to the shareholders of a potential 'victim' company in a takeover situation.

(CACA)

2. Allote plc is proposing to obtain a listing on the Stock Exchange. The company wishes to raise £4 million of usable funds through an offer for sale of new ordinary shares. The £4 million will be invested in new projects. Administration and issue costs are expected to be $7\frac{1}{2}$ per cent of the gross receipts from the offer for sale.

Allote plc wishes to estimate the number of shares it should issue and the price at which the shares should be issued. For the issue to be successful the company has been advised that it should make the issue at a discount of 15 per cent on whatever share price is estimated as appropriate when comparisons are made with a similar listed company (or companies) in the same industry.

Summarised financial details of four listed companies in the same industry are shown below:

	Company			
	Benate	Cebate	Delate	Effate
Share price	195p	278p	46p	526p
Earnings available to ordinary shareholders	£3m	£1·01m	£1·09m	£6·17m
Dividend paid	£1·43m	£0·66m	£0·57m	£2·86m
Net book value	£31m	£9m	£8·6m	£58·5m
Market capitalisation	£39m	£12·51m	£12·604m	£75·218m
Gearing (total debt/total equity)	46%	36%	53%	31%
Equity beta	1·14	1·16	1·22	1·18
Growth rate in dividends; 5 years average	7%	7%	5·5%	5·5%

Allote plc summarised accounts for the latest financial year:

Profit and Loss Account

	£000
Turnover	31,894
Operating costs	28,284
Net interest payable	902
Profit before taxation	2,708
Taxation	948
Profit attributable to ordinary shareholders	1,760
Ordinary dividends	792
Retained profit	968

Balance Sheet

	£000
Fixed assets	7,430
Current assets	7,302
Less: Current liabilities	3,112
	11,620
Financed by:	
Ordinary shares (10p)	1,800
Reserves	6,620
Bank term loan	3,200
	11,620

Allote believes that the new investment will produce an initial post tax return of 14·5 per cent per annum and will allow the company to achieve an overall dividend growth rate, after the first year, of 6 per cent per annum for the foreseeable future. The company's proposed dividend policy is to maintain a payout ratio of 45 per cent. The company can borrow at 2 per cent above the Treasury Bill yield of 6 per cent per annum. This rate has not changed significantly for several years and is not expected to change in the near future. The return on the market is estimated to be 10 per cent per annum.

Required:

(*a*) Using *two* alternative valuation techniques advise Allote plc of the number of shares that the company might issue and the price at which the shares might be issued. (A range of values may be included if you consider this to be appropriate.)

(*b*) Give possible explanations why the share price of Delate and Effate differ by 480 pence although the companies have experienced similar growth rates in dividends during the last five years. Discuss how important this difference in share price is likely to be to investors.

3. The draft accounts of Crawford plc as on 31st March 19x7 disclosed net assets of £64 million, including distributable reserves of £12 million, and made a profit after tax of £2·7 million for the year ended on that date. It declared a dividend of £1·5 million for the year. During the year just ended the company made the following acquisitions, none of which had been accounted for in the books of the company at 31st March 19x7.

(*a*) 20th January 19x7, purchase for £6·9 million of 25 per cent of the equity capital, including voting rights, of Rushworth Ltd, a furniture company. The net book value of the assets of Rushworth Ltd at the date of purchase was £25 million. Rushworth Ltd reported profits after tax of £0·6 million for the year ended 31st March 19x7.

(*b*) 15th February 19x7, purchase of a loss-making chain of DIY stores in the Midlands for £2·8 million cash from Edmund, Tom and Maria, a partnership. The net book value of the assets at the date of acquisition was £3·7 million.

(*c*) 7th March 19x7, acquisition for £49 million of a 90 per cent interest in Bertram Carpets plc, a quoted company with 74 retail outlets in Scotland. The net book values of the assets of Bertram Carpets at the date of acquisition was £38 million. Post-acquisition profits for the year ended 31st March 19x7 were £0·3 million.

You are required to write a report for the directors of Crawford plc evaluating the methods of accounting for goodwill that are currently in common use by companies and groups, and advising them on the methods they should use in preparing the consolidated financial statements for the year ended 31st March 19x7 in respect of the above acquisitions.

(ICAEW)

4. The Massive Company Ltd was incorporated on 1st July, 19x7, for the purpose of acquiring North Ltd, South Ltd and West Ltd. The balance sheets of these companies as on 30th June, 19x7, are as follows:

	North Ltd £	*South Ltd* £	*West Ltd* £
Tangible fixed assets—at cost less depreciation	500,000	400,000	300,000
Goodwill	—	60,000	—
Other assets	200,000	280,000	85,000
	700,000	740,000	385,000
Liabilities	80,000	130,000	35,000
Issued ordinary share capital: shares of £1 each	400,000	500,000	250,000
Issued 10% loan stock	70,000	—	40,000
Unappropriated profits	150,000	110,000	60,000
	700,000	740,000	385,000
Average annual profits before loan interest (July 1972 to June 1977 inclusive)	90,000	120,000	50,000
Professional valuation of tangible fixed assets on 30th June 1977	620,000	480,000	360,000

1. The directors in their negotiations agreed: (i) the recorded goodwill of South Ltd is valueless; (ii) the ‘Other assets’ of North Ltd are worth £35,000; (iii) the valuation of 30th June, 19x7, in respect of tangible fixed assets should be accepted; (iv) these adjustments are to be made by the individual companies before the completion of the acquisition.

2. The acquisition agreement provides for the issue of 12 per cent unsecured loan stock to the value of the net assets of companies North Ltd, South Ltd and West Ltd, and for the issuance of £1 nominal value ordinary shares for the capitalised average profits of each acquired company in excess of net assets contributed. The capitalisation rate is established at 10 per cent.

You are required to:

(*a*) Calculate the amounts of Massive Company Ltd's loan stock and ordinary shares to be issued to the shareholders of North Ltd, South Ltd and West Ltd.

(*b*) Calculate the effect of the scheme on a holding of 1,000 shares in South Ltd if the profits before loan interest of Massive Company Ltd for the year ended 30th June, 19x8, are (i) £520,000 and (ii) £230,000 (ignore taxation).

(*c*) Suggest an alternative scheme explaining why it would be preferable.

(ICAEW)

5. The owner of ABC Ltd has established a business in the manufacture of high value-added parts for computer and office equipment systems. He is now looking for a buyer to take over the business. The plant site and building have been leased from the local authority, but all other assets have been acquired using a mixture of share capital and loans.

The price asked for the business is £280,000. The current balance sheet can be summarised as follows:

	£000	£000
Plant, machinery, fixtures and fittings at cost	400	
Less: Accumulated depreciation	100	
	—	300
Current assets:		
Stocks	100	
Debtors	200	
Cash	20	
	—	
	320	
Less: Current liabilities	180	
	—	
Net current assets		140
		—
Total assets *less* current liabilities		440
Less: Loans (short- and medium-term)		300
		—
Net assets		140
		==
Share capital and reserves		140
		==

The business has been in operation for four years. Its turnover and pre-tax earnings (after deduction of operating costs and interest) during this period have been:

	Year 1	*Year 2*	*Year 3*	*Year 4*
	£000	£000	£000	£000
Turnover	150	750	1,200	1,400
Earnings	10	40	65	70

You are required, as advisor to a potential purchaser, to give a *reasoned opinion* of the asking price, setting out relevant calculations. Explain clearly any assumptions used in this evaluation and state any further information you consider necessary.

(CIMA)

6. The directors of New Products Ltd are giving preliminary considerations to the making of an offer for sale of shares of the company. Summarised accounts for the last five years show (£000):

	19x6	19x5	19x4	19x3	19x2
Capital employed					
Share capital	340	340	340	340	340
Reserves	1,840	1,620	1,470	1,270	1,050
Loans	300	370	350	350	370
Deferred taxation	1,040	810	550	220	190
	3,520	3,140	2,710	2,180	1,950
Employment of capital					
Fixed assets	2,520	2,320	2,100	1,790	1,660
Associated companies	130	120	290	130	120
Net current assets	870	700	320	260	170
	3,520	3,140	2,710	2,180	1,950
Results					
Turnover	9,560	8,070	7,390	5,980	4,730
Trading profit	1,560	1,440	1,510	1,320	950
Profit before tax	670	530	590	580	510
Tax	368	298	320	300	280
Dividend	82	82	70	60	50
Retention	220	150	200	220	180

The share capital consists of fully paid ordinary shares of 25p and the current dividend represents a net amount of 6p per share. Two companies which are considered competitors in the major markets are already quoted and the most recent data from the *Financial Times* relating to them is shown below:

19x6 *High*	*Low*	*Stock*	*Price*	+ *or* −	*Div net*	*Cover*	*Yield Gross*	*P/E*
277	201	Company A 50p	202	−4	6·23	3·5	4·7	9·3
168	132	Company B 25p	132	−3	3·27	5·6	3·8	7·2

You are required to:

(*a*) Advise the directors on the possible price range that might be obtained showing clearly the alternative methods of calculation you have used.

(*b*) State the further information you would require to prepare the accountants report to be included in the offer for sale documentation.

(ICAEW)

7. The draft consolidated profit and loss account of G Group Ltd for the year ended 31st December, 19x6, was as follows:

	(£000)	(£000)
Operating profit		6,620
Share of profits less losses of associated companies		290
		6,910
Less Interest		1,507
Profit before taxation		5,403
Taxation:		
Parent company and subsidiaries	2,309	
Associated companies	140	
		2,449
Profit after taxation		2,954
Profit attributable to minority shareholders		309

Profit attributable to parent company shareholders before extraordinary items	2,645
Extraordinary items:	
Expenses of rights issue	103
Profit attributable to parent company shareholders after extraordinary items	2,542
Deduct Dividends paid or proposed by the parent company	1,012
Profit retained	1,530

A note dealing with parent company taxation explained that the charge of £2,309,000 included adjustments to prior years (credit of £274,000) and uncovered advance corporation tax on dividends of £56,000.

The issued share capital of the parent company was as follows:

	19x6	19x5
	£	£
£1,000,000 6% (now 4·2% plus tax credit) cumulative preference stock	1,000,000	1,000,000
Ordinary shares of £0·25 each	7,658,050	5,875,000

Changes in the ordinary share capital during the year were:

(i) On 5th May 816,000 shares were issued at a premium of £0·20 on the acquisition of H Ltd.

(ii) On 14th June the company made a rights issue of one share for every four held at a price of £0·35 per share.

(iii) On 11th November 237,200 shares were issued at a premium of £0·35 in part consideration for the acquisition of J Ltd.

Options to subscribe for 730,000 shares were granted to directors and senior executives on 31st March, 19x6. These options will be exercisable at £0·60 per share between 1st April, 19x9, and 31st March, 19y5.

The market price immediately before the rights issue was £0·45 per ordinary share.

You are required, having regard to SSAP 3:

(*a*) To calculate the appropriate figure of earnings per ordinary share for inclusion in the group annual report, giving reasons for your method of calculation.

(*b*) To outline the adjustments required to earnings per share (EPS) of previous years so that they can be compared with the EPS after the issue.

(ICMA)

8

GROWTH AND FAILURE

Acquisitions and Mergers

Purposes, Objectives and Reasons for Mergers

It is generally held that firms must grow in order to survive; that it is not possible to maintain a status quo indefinitely. The theoretical literature on this subject is allied with the twin concepts of value and objectives of the business. The concept of value has been dealt with in the previous section and most financial models are derived on the assumption that the objective of the business is maximisation of shareholders' wealth. This leads to the necessity to define shareholders' wealth, and this can be interpreted in two ways: (*a*) maximisation of profits, either distributed or earned; or (*b*) maximisation of the present value of the shareholding.

Developing social conscience and other factors have made such simple objectives difficult to follow and a considerable list of factors has emerged that require a business to modify such simplified constraints. Among these could be listed the following:

(i) The extent to which the government can, either by indirect or direct action, intervene to ensure that factors other than shareholders' wealth are given equal or priority treatment. These include:

- Location of industry
- Environmental factors
- Employment policies
- National economic interests
- Common Market and international trading
- Safety and welfare
- Government impact upon price and demand as a major purchaser
- Government financial assistance

(ii) The power and influence of trade unions and their ability to prevent or delay amalgamations in conflict with their own objectives.

(iii) The collective views of investors as represented through Stock Exchange reaction to the proposed deals.

Some Reasons for Mergers

These can be divided into a variety of groups, such as:

(*a*) *Economies of Scale*

This category consists primarily of firms which combine or are taken over in some form of **horizontal integration**, i.e. the firms' activities and interests are similar. Common examples of this type are the build-up of companies such as Austin-Rover, originally British Leyland, British Aircraft Corporation and Cadbury Schweppes. Motivation for this type of merger, particularly since the Second World War, has come from the need for larger groups in order to meet the increased competition and demand of integrated markets such as the European Common Market. Government policy, implemented through such organisations as the now defunct Industrial Reorganisation Corporation, encouraged similar movements into larger units by smaller firms. The major source of the economies of combinations in this form is expected to be in reduced costs of production, ability to finance joint research projects on a scale which would be outside the scope of the individual firm, and an integrated approach to selling and distribution of the end products. Such a combination would also be able to adopt a stronger bargaining attitude to suppliers of raw materials, eliminate unnecessary competition and close down excess capacity. The extent to which these advantages have materialised in practice, however, has been seriously challenged by the findings of empirical research such as that of Kitching, Hargreaves and Newbold.

Vertical integration is another way in which firms combine to achieve economies of scale. In this form of merger a firm combines with another at successive stages of production and/or distribution in the same industry. Such movement may be forward, as when one firm takes over another which is nearer the end of the finished goods cycle—e.g. flour millers taking over bakeries—or backward, as when a firm takes over a supplier of one of its major raw materials. Similar advantages would be expected to accrue in regard to production and research as those for horizontal integration. Motivation is primarily protectionist—to ensure regularity and quality of material supplies—or expansive, as when the more profitable stage may be later in the cycle of operations, e.g. breweries and petrol refiners securing their own retail outlets.

(b) Mergers involving Different Industries

These involve groups where firms acquire or merge with firms in unrelated product lines or spheres of activity. The objective may be systematic and gradual diversification of interest in order to strengthen the manufacturing, trading or financial base of the group. A company may begin to do this on its own initiative because it considers its existing structure to be too risky—too many eggs in one basket—or it may have had the change forced upon it. For example, when the private-sector mining interests were nationalised shareholders in the original companies were sometimes given the choice of either accepting a refund of capital or allowing the financial resources to be used by the company for different objectives. Some such firms therefore became holding companies predominantly providing finance to build up 'conglomerate' styles of investment. Generally the policy with this type of company would be consolidation before progressing on to other investments.

Another objective for the conglomerate type of growth is **diversification.** The stimulus for this may come from a variety of reasons. Firms may diversify to widen their trading base with the objective of reducing risk, as in the case of the tobacoo giants. It may be a desire to use excess capacity lying idle due to the seasonal nature of demand for a main product, or it may be an enforced technological change, as when a firm producing glass bottles moves into plastics as this material substitute becomes more popular.

The final form of combination which, in essence, is similar to the above is the **public investment company**. These have diverse interests but they are generally motivated by less conservative ambition than those mentioned above. Such companies see growth of earnings as the major target and in the boom period of the 1960s became known as the 'go-go' companies. As institutions they were not popular in government or employee circles. Since they were prepared to sell off any section of the company taken over—either for trading purposes or more frequently to realise the assets and provide a cash injection for the next takeover operation—such companies, it could be argued, were successfully following the policy of maximisation of shareholders' wealth. Any bid was preceded by close analysis of both earnings potential and asset worth. Quite frequently information possessed by the rank and file investor—obtained primarily from published accounts and chairman's statement—was totally inadequate. If the investor was convinced that assets were undervalued then a sufficient investment was obtained to get control and the assets stripped, i.e. the company ceased to trade. This meant unemployment and resentment in the labour forces of companies taken over. Employee resentment was further aggravated by bad management techniques, even where companies were allowed to remain operative. The major success of these companies occurred in a confident and responsive stock exchange atmosphere. The economic and political climate has changed since this date. Labour governments attempted to slow down such practice but a continuance of conservative governments in the 1980s has resulted in aggressive attempts at expansion by takeover bids. Following a slump in 1977 share prices rose almost continuously and expansion by acquisition became the order of the day. This went on until a number of factors including US imbalance of trade, economic policies and the continuing strength of Japan and West Germany in trade matters resulted in a reversal and collapse of the Stock Markets in the USA and the UK particularly in October 1987. See page 358, Chapter 10.

Acquisition Strategy

Some companies may be involved in only one merger or acquisition activity in the whole of their existence whereas others may have a definite policy for seeking out opportunities for investment. Whichever it is, a formalised programme of investigation, assessment and post-acquisition audit is desirable. The immediate objectives can usually be related to motives described above and summarised briefly below.

Motives for Mergers

Aggressive
- Buying up competition
- Buying for improved earnings per share
- Exploiting new products
  - new markets
  - technological innovation and research
  - under-utilisation of assets of potential subsidiary
  - management expertise

Defensive
- Buying up competition
  - better management
  - up supplier
  - to prevent takeover by others
  - for diversification
- Merging for mutual self-protection

The study team involved in preparing for a takeover or merger would have to investigate alternative possibilities, decide upon methods and suggest possible prices. The major problems requiring solution would differ according to the scale and type of acquisition but would be capable of being resolved into differing areas, some being common to all forms of acquisition. These areas and problems would include:

Personnel	Streamlining management structure of the group Retiring of surplus management and labour forces Integration of differing salaries, wages and welfare schemes Consultation with employee representatives
Production	Investigation of plant sizes, production methods, the rationalisation of production lines and sites
Marketing and distribution	Rationalisation of products, advertising, publicity, sales outlets and all aspects of the selling function
Research and development	Centralisation of common research and avoidance of duplication. Combination of resources to ensure essential research.
Administrative	Combination or otherwise of central functions, e.g. purchasing, data processing, accounting and management services
Financial	Best financial structure for the group; policies and pricing procedures for intra-company trading. Centralised cash management. Combined strengths to attract investment.

The solution to the above problems needs to be related to a time-base, and Kitching suggested in a report published in 1967 that only 20 per cent of mergers in the USA were successful and attributed a marked degree of success to those where the means of communication and channels of responsibility had been clearly established. It was further suggested that once the power structure had been decided, surplus managers should be retired and assets sold within three months, and the second three months be concerned with rationalising the new structure in depth.

Structure and Methods of Control

The terms used in discussing growth, takcovers and amalgamation are not standardised but some arbitrary distinction between the various forms of combination is desirable since it links up with accounting treatments and legal aspects of control. Some distinctions are:

(*a*) *Absorption:* One company acquires all the assets of another, the purchased company losing its individual identity.

(*c*) *Amalgamation:* Two or more companies sell their assets to a new company. This may involve dissolution of the original companies and distribution of proceeds to shareholders or they be offered interests in the newly formed company.

(*c*) *Takeover:* This is an emotive phrase but generally implies that control of the company taken over has passed to the purchaser. This is in contrast to an amalgamation, where ownership and control of the combined enterprise may remain in the hands of the original shareholders and directors.

Control Structure

There are varying degrees and types of control structure. They vary from 100 per cent or complete ownership, through a majority holding, down to minority control. The latter may be a small proportion of the total number of voting class shares but the remainder may be so widely dispersed as to enable effective control to be exercised by ownership of this comparatively small part of the equity. Large institutional investors contribute to this situation. Such institutions have over 40 per cent of their investments in quoted companies and they prefer the large companies since shares in these are more easily negotiable and holdings can be larger. On the other hand, they do not tend to take active participation in a company's affairs unless a very serious situation develops.

Decline and Failure

Reasons for Failure

A merger may be unsuccessful for the same reasons as an autonomous company may be unsuccessful and decline in performance. The most frequent causes, in common, may be listed as follows:

(*a*) *Failure of Management.* This may be general or in a specific area. The company may have outgrown the vision and ability of the individuals or team which created it. The financial control and direction may be weak while production and sales are satisfactory, or vice versa. Friction caused by personality clashes at top executive level may cause a chain reaction and affect cooperation and morale at all levels. In a sense one could say that all business failures are the result of inefficient management since it is their function to anticipate the reasons listed below and take alternative action. It is sometimes difficult to decide if a particular outcome has been outside management influence since there are limits to the extent that the most effective action could mitigate particular circumstances and to which executives could have performed better under adverse conditions than they did in good times. A fairly reasonable diagnosis and treatment which keeps a sick patient alive and ultimately enables the patient to recover is preferable to a completely accurate autopsy obtained after the patient's death. Similarly in business, lack of prompt action in response to effective control mechanisms can result in fatal delay.

(*b*) *Environmental Factors.* The climate in which the business operates is determined by a combination of national and international economic conditions, political situations and confidence of the business sector generally. In the UK in the 1970s and early 1980s there were serious rates of inflation allied with recurrent labour troubles. At the time of writing, inflation rates are lower but at the cost of high unemployment caused by the loss of manufacturing industries and the high level of imported goods. Ineffective control of cash flow has inevitably resulted in the highest incidence of bankruptcies recorded. Inevitably small businesses have suffered excessively—not least because of extended credit periods unjustly taken by large companies and groups to ease their own liquidity problems.

(*c*) *Specific Trade Conditions.* The above factors affect all companies to a varying degree. At any particular period of time one trade or company within a trade may be suffering badly. A lack of demand or confidence on the part of the final producers of consumer items will result in reluctance to invest in new production facilities and other forms of investment. This will result in lack of orders for capital equipment such as new factories, plant and machinery. There will, however, be a delay period before the effect of this works through the system. On any investigation therefore one might find economic indicators which show a degree of correlation between items but with a time-lag between them, as discussed in the chapter on forecasting. Recognition of this relationship could assist planning. The number of new car registrations in a period, for example, could be indicative of a trend in the motorcar servicing industry requirements.

(*d*) *Technological and Product Change*. This heading covers far too extensive a range of influences to be dealt with in detail here. It covers advances in manufacturing techniques of a revolutionary nature, the discovery of new or substitute basic materials, and prompted or involuntary changes in consumer preferences which render particular products obsolete.

(*e*) *Ineffective Financial Control*. It may be asked as to why this particular area should be singled out since the general responsibilities of other functions included in the management activities have been mentioned above and not developed. The answer is twofold: first, this book is directed towards financial management and therefore it is aspects of this that one would expect to be emphasised—a book on production management would emphasise other factors. Secondly, if the financial control system is weak other functions and line managers are either inadequately informed, misinformed, or informed too late for them to be able to use their abilities to the full. However brilliant the design and reliable the product or effective the marketing, the business survives or falls on its financial performance. The only exceptions are where certain companies or industries are supported by the government—which means ultimately the taxpayers—for a variety of reasons and even this cannot go on indefinitely.

(*f*) *Expansion beyond Optimum Size*. Industrial production in the UK has tended to become concentrated into a smaller number of larger groups. By 1970 the share of manufacturing net output controlled by the hundred largest enterprises had risen to about 40 per cent. A similar movement had taken place in other spheres such as banking, with no guarantee that such combinations were in the best interests of the country as a whole, or for that matter in the interest of a particular group, be it employee, management or investor. It is often claimed that the performance statistics of larger groups are artificial, particularly when ignoring the capital structure in financial analysis. Large groups are enabled by their size to use greater amounts of loan capital in the form of debentures and overdrafts. With favourable tax concessions on interest payments, they carry higher gearing ratios. A small firm wishing to borrow on loan or overdraft may have to pay, simply by reason of its smaller asset backing, a penal rate in comparison. This means that it must increase its operational efficiency if it is to show the same relative performance when measured by conventional financial yardsticks. This is why any purely theoretical references such as pyramids of ratios described elsewhere need to be tempered by the subjective skill of the assessor—the financial manager or equivalent.

(*g*) *Competition*. Competitiveness is an anchor-pin of a free enterprise society and constantly one business strives to outdo its competitors for the market they share so that growth to one can mean decline for another. Admittedly this can reflect upon the abilities of the management in decline as expressed in (*a*) above, but it may not always be because they are generally poor at managing—perhaps in one key respect another is sufficiently better in, say, marketing tactics, product performance or productivity. Here again the larger business has advantages. With a more extensive range of products it can forgo its contribution from any one effectively to outprice a business which is wholly dependent upon its single product. Inevitably success attracts competitors who will probe and exploit any weakness to obtain some level of submission or complete elimination.

At the beginning of this chapter the frequent claims for the benefits of mergers were repeated: the valuable 'synergy' released in combining productive, administrative, research and financial resources. As stated above, all too often the failure of at least one or more of these is concealed by the financial advantages gained, so that overall group performance, at least in the short or medium term, is implied to be satisfactory. This is being increasingly questioned and a number of investigations are now being conducted into the possibilities that in specific and general instances size has become an embarrassment. It may ultimately result in a reversal of the past trend or even to a break-up of some very large units into smaller, more manageable divisions.

Avoiding Failure

If the growth of an adverse position is to be avoided then continuing and vigilant action must be taken in response to the trends and conditions reported by the financial control. Among the means of revealing fields for potential action will be included:

(*a*) *Management Audit*. A continuing appraisal of the efficiency of the management processes and personnel. Such investigations may be done internally or by periodic investigations by outsiders or consultants. A rigid check on progress against original objectives must be made and in the case of mergers a post-acquisition audit should be conducted as described for alternative forms of investment on page 221.

(*b*) *Analysis of Products, Markets and Technical Change*. Management teams should make time to acquaint themselves with all factors likely to affect development or survival of the business. This means continuous reviews of product range, competitors' programmes, purchasing and stock policies.

(*c*) *Cash Flow Projections*. The frequency and depth of cash flow projections will depend upon the liquidity status of any particular business. The forecast and budget will provide a general control of the medium and long-term future, but any change of circumstance should promote a regular review. It is suicidal, for example, in the short term to control from the current bank balance; some means of foresight as to the next immediate future is important. The moment of commitment to any form of expenditure is the crucial stage for control, and this is best undertaken with a full knowledge of the implications upon future liquidity. Monitoring of performance and the projection of likely trends therefrom will provide guidance as to whether the planned cash inflow can support the outflows planned. Anticipatory action is one of the skills of successful management.

Recognition of Failure

As a result of failure to implement action as above or as a result of a combination of factors, a business may well be in a state of decline and failure. Such a business could still be the objective of a merger proposition—it may possess something of value to the bidder, such as trade name, technical 'know-how', tax losses or purchase of assets at a discount, i.e. all or some of its assets may possess a value in excess of the book values and purchase prices. If none of these applies, then there are various conditions which could exist. One such condition occurs when an immediate lack of cash to meet the debts incurred results in a situation of insolvency, and this may be technical in that the company could pay its way by realising its assets, but time is against it, or it may, more seriously, be legal as when the company is unable to pay its way, even if the assets were realised. The extreme consequences of this may be that action is taken by creditors and the company declared insolvent or the individual made bankrupt.

If the company does not enter this final phase, and thus virtually cease to exist, it may recognise the condition and endeavour to make a more realistic rearrangement of its capital structure to assist future development. This normally takes the form of writing off capital or similar schemes. This is usually the situation when a company has built up a large trading loss, when assets backing to the capital does not exist, or when the company is over-capitalised. Such over-capitalisation may have resulted from forming too favourable an estimate of potential cash flows from the original investment, or over-estimation of the cost of the original investment. The latter is less serious, since the surplus moneys could be invested elsewhere as an alternative to repayment by formal reconstruction, but the former situation would require more fundamental corrective action.

Capital Reduction Schemes

This is a means of writing off losses and correcting the recorded value of assets by reducing the amount of the share capital account. The balance created by the reduction is used to write off the adverse trading and other losses. Subject to satisfying the necessary legal requirements—which are authority in the articles, a special resolution and approval of the courts—the process is a pure book-keeping one. The primary objective is normally the elimination of debit balances (losses) on the profit and loss account to make practicable a resumption of dividend payments, and rejuvenate activity in the shares. The loss to the shareholder has already occurred: the reduction scheme, except in the one case of over-capitalisation referred to above, merely recognises this fact.

Example 1

Balance Sheet of XYZ Ltd as at 31st December, 19...

	£		£	£
Capital		Fixed assets		
Issued and fully paid up		Plant and machinery		14,000
20,000 ordinary shares		Current assets		
of £1	20,000	Stocks	3,000	
Current liabilities		Debtors	4,000	
Sundry creditors	4,000	Profit & loss account	3,000	
				10,000
	24,000			24,000

It is proposed that the profit and loss account balance be written off, that £1,000 be written off each of stocks and debtors and the figure for plant be reduced to its present valuation of £9,000. This is to be effected by reducing the capital to 20,000 shares of 50p each fully paid.

To effect this reduction in the books, the accounts representing plant and machinery, stock debtors and profit and loss account would all be credited with the sums listed above and the corresponding figures debited to the share capital account. The matter might be formally recorded as a journal entry as follows:

		£	£
Share capital account	*Dr*	10,000	
To sundries:			
Plant and machinery			5,000
Stocks			1,000
Debtors			1,000
Profit and loss			3,000

Assuming the scheme were formally approved the balance sheet would appear as follows:

Balance Sheet of XYZ Ltd as at 31st December, 19...

	£		£	£
Capital		Fixed assets		
Issued and fully paid up		Plant and machinery		9,000
20,000 ordinary shares of		Current assets		
50p	10,000	Stocks	2,000	
Current liabilities		Debtors	3,000	
Creditors	4,000			5,000
	14,000			14,000

The net worth of the business—total assets less liabilities—is now £14,000 − £4,000 = £10,000, and this more correctly reflects the real situation—namely, that the shareholders have interest in fixed assets and net current assets to the value of £10,000. As soon as the company begins to earn profits and cash flow becomes positive, it may be able to contemplate beginning to pay dividends again. In such a case the reduced nominal value of the shares enables a reasonable rate of dividend as a percentage to be declared even though the absolute profit distributed may be small.

Company Reconstruction

This term is used to describe a situation where the company concerned sells its net assets to a newly formed company. The consideration is usually by way of partly paid shares in the new company in exchange for the paid-up shares of the old company. The calling up of the unpaid part of the shares enables the new company to raise the necessary working capital to operate effectively. Such schemes may also be used to settle claims of major creditors, amalgamate two or more companies or change the relative rights of the various classes of shares. A special resolution is required authorising a liquidator to effect the proposals embodied in the scheme.

Example 2

A recent report recommended that a reconstruction be effected by forming a new holding company to acquire the whole of the issued share capital of Footpath Ltd. It has been decided to give effect to the reconstruction scheme by inviting holders of the fully paid shares and of fully paid convertible stock in Footpath to sanction a scheme of arrangement. The scheme will involve:

1. The acquisition by the new company of the fully paid shares in Footpath on the basis of one ordinary share of 50p in the new company for 10 fully paid shares of 25p in Footpath.
2. Arrangements whereby any holder of fully paid shares in Footpath may elect to sell his entitlement of shares in the new company at a price of £1·00 per share.
3. Provisions whereunder the convertible stock will cease to carry rights of conversion into ordinary shares in Footpath and will instead carry equivalent rights of conversion into ordinary shares in the new company. The conversion basis will be changed from one ordinary share of 25p in Footpath for 55p nominal of stock to one ordinary share of 50p in the new company for 550p nominal stock. The terms allow the holder of fully paid convertible stock to convert into shares of 25p in Footpath and accept the cash offer in respect of the fully paid shares arising on conversion.

There are in issue 148 million fully paid ordinary shares of 25p and £25m of fully paid 8 per cent convertible loan stock. The interest has been paid on the loan stock but no dividends have been paid on the ordinary shares for the last year, none is proposed and the directors do not foresee the likelihood of dividends for some years to come. The most recent middle market quotations were: ordinary shares—$7\frac{1}{2}$p; convertible loan stock—£40.

You are required to:

(*a*) Calculate the financial effects of the scheme on holders of fully paid ordinary shares in Footpath.

(*b*) Calculate the financial effects of the scheme on holders of fully paid convertible stock.

(*c*) Prepare the journal entries which would reflect in the books of the new company the acceptance by all ordinary shareholders of the offer.

(ICAEW)

The requirement here is to calculate the financial effects of the propositions in total as opposed to a holding of, say, 100 shares in similar examples.

(*a*) Fully Paid Ordinary Shares

Market value per share at present	$7\frac{1}{2}$p
Market value of 148 million shares	£11,100,000
Value of offer:	
One share of nominal value 50p for 10 existing shares	
∴ Total number of shares = 148 million ÷ 10	
= 14·8 million	
If opportunity is taken of cash offer at £1 each these are worth	£14,800,000
∴ Possible gain on sale	£3,700,000

No dividends are proposed or foreseeable by the existing company, so that any income prospects in the restructured company are likely to be more favourable than at present. The market value of $7\frac{1}{2}$p is only just over a quarter of the nominal value and this is the degree of deterioration so that the possibility of capital gain is attractive.

(*b*) Fully Paid Convertible Stock

Market value (per £100 Nominal) of nominal stock	£40
∴ Market value of £25 million of loan stock	£10,000,000
Value of offer:	
Number of ordinary shares offered—	
One ordinary share for 550p nominal	
∴ Total number of shares $= \dfrac{£25 \text{ million}}{550\text{p}}$	
$= 4{,}545{,}454$	
Cash value of offer at £1 per share	£4,545,454
Possible loss on sale	£5,454,546
Income	£
Interest at 8% on £25 million	2,000,000
*Yield at 20% gross on £4,545,454	909,090
Gain on income if capital gain is reinvested	1,090,910 p.a.

* This is assumed on the basis that the present yield on market value of the loan stock is (8% × £100) = £8 p.a. for an investment costing £40, i.e. the gross yield $= \frac{8}{40} \times 100 = 20\%$. If the return was higher than the average because of the unsatisfactory position of the company an equivalent investment would cost more and the yield would be correspondingly less. The gain of £1,090,910 therefore probably represents a minimum figure. The effects of taxation have been ignored as the attractions or otherwise of particular schemes would be influenced by the personal circumstances of the holders as discussed on page 34.

(*c*) The agreed value is £1 per 50p share in Footpath and the total holding is therefore worth £14,800,000 (part *a*). The entry required is to create at the same time the liability in respect of shares issued:

Books of Holding Ltd
Journal

	£	£
Investment in Footpath Ltd	14,800,000	
Share capital		14,800,000
Purchase of issued share capital of Footpath Ltd, 14,800,000 shares of nominal value 25p in exchange for £14,800,000 shares in Holding Ltd—nominal value 50p at £1 per share		

Valuation and Methods of Satisfying the Consideration

The basic methods for arriving at a valuation were discussed in Chapter 7. In merger battles or takeover bids the final price may be arrived at on much more subjective criteria. Among these may be behavioural factors such as the determination of the bidding participant not to surrender or lose face notwithstanding the cost, resulting in the apparent exploiting this weakness to exact a price in excess of the real worth. Similarly, the bidder may desire to be in charge of the largest company of a particular type for purely personal motives of prestige and power and again pay high for that privilege. In theoretical or case study examples this would not normally apply and what is primarily required is evidence of the ability to discern the major variables involved, quantify them and draw attention to any particular factors which would appear to require subjective assessment.

Methods of Satisfying Consideration

The acquirer of the business being absorbed or taken over will be obtaining control by purchasing either the assets of the vendor company or a shareholding which may be entire or partial. The consideration may be settled in the form of cash, securities or liabilities assumed and settled.

An offer to purchase for cash can be readily assessed in the short term in respect of a quoted company since to be effective it must be above the market price of the shares prior to the offer. This does not mean that determining the offer price that should be paid is made any simpler. Transactions prior to the bid may have been few and the price unrepresentative of a fair-sized market. Price movements may have been affected by all kinds of factors but in particular, if rumour or anticipation of the bid has been made, the price may have moved quickly upwards. The liquidity preference of investors in general and the opinion of the shareholders of the relative long-term prospects of the bidder will similarly affect the price.

In the case of unquoted companies the cash settlement will be negotiable as a straight sum or it may be a balance to be paid after the acquirer has assumed all or some of the existing liabilities. The acquiring company may use its own cash resources, making a direct offer to the shareholders of the company sought, or in order to reduce the strain on its own liquid resources and avoid the possible necessity for raising funds it may enter into an underwriting agreement whereby a cash alternative is made available to investors desiring it. The latter course also has tax advantages under the present UK system.

An alternative method of settling the consideration may be in the form of securities. These have all been described in Chapter 4 and the advantages and disadvantages of the various alternative forms summarised. To reiterate, they are likely to be either:

Ordinary shares
Debentures
Convertible loan stock
Share warrants

Preference shares have not been listed as they are now so rare that so long as present tax considerations apply the volume of issue is negligible. Indeed, companies endeavouring to take over another will probably offer straight debentures or convertible loan stock in exchange for the surrender of preference shares. They can offer a considerable financial incentive to the preference shareholder by paying higher interest than their existing dividend without having to increase earnings by virtue of the tax saving. At the same time the debenture offers a superior form of capital protection to the type of investor likely to have been attracted to preference shares in the first place.

In an actual business situation, once the total valuation has been agreed it is a matter of designing the way in which the consideration could be discharged in such a way as to tempt all parties to agree and simultaneously for the acquirer to achieve his objective. In theoretical and examination exercises it is usually only possible or practicable to suggest an initial course of action. In other words, it is impossible unless various participants simulate what they consider would be the continuing actions of the respective parties to follow the bargaining process all the way through. Theoretical exercises normally follow one of two or three methods in order to assess the degree of knowledge possessed by the participants in the exercise:

(*a*) A situation is given and instructions as to how the deal is to be constructed, proposed or completed. This is the easiest type of problem in so far as there will only be one answer.

(*b*) A situation is given as in (*a*) above but in addition there are requests for personal assessment on such matters as the merits or otherwise of a particular scheme and/or that a scheme of operations be proposed entirely by the reader or examine together with explanations or reasons why it should be considered practical and acceptable to all parties concerned. The examples which follow develop the technique therefore in this order of complexity and explanation is given where considered necessary if the course of action is arbitrary.

Example 3: A situation where details of a scheme are given and no comment required

The following information relates to an offer by Super Ltd to acquire the whole of the issued share capital of Roads Ltd. The terms of the offer were:

(i) For every 100 ordinary shares of 10p, each fully paid of Roads Ltd	13 ordinary shares of £1 each of Super Ltd 13 ordinary share warrants of Super Ltd £2 cash
(ii) For every 100 ordinary shares of 10p each 1p paid of Roads Ltd (a further 66p was payable on each share)	3 ordinary shares of £1 each of Super Ltd 3 ordinary share warrants of Super Ltd

The market price and dividends paid for the shares at the last practicable date were:

	Market price	*Dividend including tax credit*
Super Ltd ordinary shares of £1 each	480p	16·5p
Super Ltd ordinary warrants	150p	nil
Roads Ltd ordinary shares of 10p each fully paid	64p	13·5%
Roads Ltd ordinary shares of 10p each 1p paid	not quoted	nil

Financial information regarding Super Ltd:

Authorised £	*Share Capital*	*Issued and fully paid* £
19,000,000	Cumulative preference shares of £1 each	19,000,000
134,534,443	Ordinary stock units of £1 each	134,534,443
3,400,049*	Ordinary shares of £1 each	—
8,065,508	Unclassified shares of £1 each	—
£165,000,000		£153,534,443

* Reserved to satisfy in full the rights comprised in the company's existing ordinary stock warrants.

Super Ltd intends to increase its authorised share capital to £200,000,000.

Full implementation of the offer would result in the issue of 8,931,599 ordinary stock units and the same number of warrants. The warrants entitle holders to acquire ordinary stock on a basis of £1 stock unit for 1 warrant of Super Ltd at £4 per £1 stock unit for cash or by the surrender of £4 nominal value of Super Ltd's $8\frac{1}{2}$ per cent loan stock.

There is £80 million of loan stock outstanding at the present time.

Summarised latest profit and loss accounts:

	Super Ltd (£000)	*Roads Ltd* (£000)
Income from trading	58,000	2,141
Interest payable	10,000	—
	48,000	2,141
Taxation	19,000	899
	29,000	1,242
Preference dividends	2,000	—
	27,000	1,242
Ordinary dividends	16,000	455
Retained	£11,000	£787

Despite the existing low taxation charge it is estimated that any additional income will be taxed at 40 per cent.

You are required to calculate to one decimal place of a penny:

(*a*) The financial effects of the offer on a holder of 100 fully paid and 100 partly paid shares in Roads Ltd.

(*b*) The earnings per share of Super Ltd before and after the proposed acquisition.

(ICAEW)

(*a*) The financial effects upon a holder of shares in Roads Ltd.

100 Fully paid shares:		*Total*
	£	£
Existing holding is worth 100 × 64p		64·00
Offer is worth		
13 Super Ltd ordinaries @ 480p	62·40	
13 Super Ltd warrants @ 150p	19·50	
Cash	2·00	
		83·90
Capital gain at present market price		19·90
Existing income is 100 × 13·5% × 10p	1·35	
Potential income is 13 × 16·5p	2·145	
Income gain if dividend is maintained		0·795 p.a.
100 Partly paid shares:		
**Existing* holding is worth nominally		1·00
Offer is worth		
3 Super Ltd ordinaries @ 480p	14·40	
3 Super Ltd warrants @ 150p	4·50	
		18·90
Capital gain		17·90
Existing income	Nil	
Potential income is 3 × 16·5p	0·495	
		0·495

* This figure is arbitrary as it represents only what has been paid on the share. There is a contingent liability in respect of the unpaid calls of 66p each and this would represent a potential loss to the holder if the offer was not taken up. No one is likely to buy them merely to assume this responsibility and it would be equally or even more logical to say that they have no value at all. If this were the view taken then the figures summarised below would show an increase of £1.

Summary of Shareholders' Position

	Capital gain	*Income gain (p.a.)*
	£	£
In respect of 100 fully paid shares	19·90	0·795
In respect of 100 partly paid shares	17·90	0·495
Total	37·80	1·29

(*b*) Earnings per share

(i) *Before the offer*

Undiluted

Earnings available after tax and preference dividends	£27,000,000
Number of ordinary stock units	134,534,443
Earnings per share	20·1p

Fully diluted

	£	£
Basic earnings available		27,000,000
Add Interest saved on loan stock converted ($3,400,049 \times £4 \times 8\frac{1}{2}\%$)	1,156,016	
Less Corporation Tax now payable @ 40%	462,406	
		693,610
Earnings available		27,693,610
Ordinary stock units already issued		134,534,443
Add issue in exchange for loan stock		3,400,049
Total number of stock units		137,934,492
Earnings per share (stock units)		$\frac{£27,693,610}{137,934,492} = 20{\cdot}1p$

The above calculations show that before the offer and capital increase the maximum number of ordinary £1 stock units would be restricted to 137,934,492 and there would be no effect on the earnings per share if all the existing authorised share units were issued.

(ii) *After the offer*

Undiluted

Earnings available after tax and preference dividend:

Super Ltd	£27,000,000
Roads Ltd	1,242,000
	£28,242,000
Existing ordinary stock units Super Ltd	134,534,443
Issued in settlement on takeover	8,931,599
	143,466,042
Earnings per share (stock unit)	19·7p

	£	£
Fully diluted		
Earnings after tax and dividend at present		28,242,000
Add interest saved on loan stock converted		
(3,400,049 + 8,931,599) × £4 × $8\frac{1}{2}$%	4,192,760	
Less Corporation Tax at 40%	1,677,104	
		2,515,656
		30,757,656
Ordinary stock units issued as above		143,466,042
Add issued in exchange for loan stock (3,400,049 + 8,931,599)		12,331,648
		155,797,690

Earnings per share (stock unit) $\frac{30,757,656}{155,797,690}$ = 19·7p

Example 4: A situation where details of a scheme are given and a request is made for comment on its suitability or othewise and/or a request for an alternative scheme.

P Ltd and Q Ltd are public companies engaged in the same type of business. Following preliminary discussions at board level it has been decided to merge the companies. For this purpose a new company, PQ (19x5) Ltd, will be incorporated with an authorised capital of 7,800,000 ordinary shares.

A summary of the most recent data available about the two companies is given below. It is estimated that cost savings resulting from the linking of the companies would eventually be in the region of £200,000 per year.

You are requested to:

(*a*) Give calculations (with alternatives if necessary) of the equity value of the new company, and the proportions in which its shares should be allotted to the shareholders in P Ltd and Q Ltd respectively.

(*b*) Give calculations for an alternative scheme under which the maximum safe amount of loan capital would be issued and the proceeds used in part satisfaction of Q Ltd's shareholders.

(*c*) Comment on the benefits or disadvantages of each scheme for P Ltd's and Q Ltd's shareholders respectively.

(*d*) Advise the minimum period for which the offer to P Ltd's and Q Ltd's shareholders must be kept open, and what is the longest period it may be kept open without being declared unconditional.

Data relating to P Ltd and Q Ltd

	P Ltd *30th June* (£000)	*Q Ltd* *31st March* (£000)
Year end		
Profits before tax (Corporation Tax averages 52% on all profits)		
19x0	696	780
19x1	852	960
19x2	828	708

19x3		1,081		744
19x4		1,320		900
19x5		1,500		Not yet available
First half-year: 19x4		600		432
19x5		684		462
Latest balance sheet information (adjusted to comparable break-up values)				
Fixed assets		3,000		3,000
Current assets		3,360		3,600
		6,360		6,600
	(£000)		(£000)	
Current liabilities:				
Short-term loans	300		2,160	
Other	1,260		840	
		1,560		3,000
		4,800		3,600
Provisions and liabilities not currently due		600		360
Long-term loans		600		240
Ordinary shares of £0·20 each		960		600
Reserves		2,640		2,400
		4,800		3,600
		£		£
Current share price		0·90		0·60

(CIMA)

(*a*) (i) Assets basis

Note that the information given is stated to be 'adjusted' to comparable break-up values, i.e. they are *not* on balance sheet values or a going concern basis but represent the alternative value to the shareholders of liquidating their holdings.

	P Ltd		*Q Ltd*		*PQ Ltd*
	(£000)	(£000)	(£000)	(£000)	(£000)
Net assets		4,800		3,600	8,400
Less Liabilities not due	600		360		
long-term loans	600	1,200	240	600	1,800
Attributable to equity		3,600		3,000	6,600
Number of shares (000)		4,800		3,000	7,800
Value per share		£0·75		£1·00	£0·846

(ii) Profits basis (for workings see pages 272–4)

Profits after tax

	P Ltd	Q Ltd	PQ Ltd
Weighted average	£567,000	£394,000	
Annual rate of last $2\frac{1}{2}$ years	£592,000	£404,000	
Latest year's trading	£674,000	£446,000	
Annual rate of latest half-year	£784,000	£444,000	
Suggested profit forecast	£750,000	£450,000	£1,200,000
Earnings per share (forecast)	15·6p	15p	
Current price	90·0p	60p	
p/e ratio	5·8	4	

In addition to the £1,200,000 profit suggested for PQ Ltd there are anticipated cost savings of £200,000 p.a. These are presumably subject to taxation of 52 per cent as increased profits, so the net profit increase will be £96,000, making total profits for the group of £1,200,000 + £96,000 = £1,296,000 (say £1,300,000). At the p/e ratio applicable to P Ltd alone this would value the new company at (5·8 × £1,300,000) = £7,540,000. On the p/e ratio applicable to Q Ltd alone the valuation would be (4 × £1,300,000) = £5,200,000.

The value of the new company on an earnings basis would be between a low of £5,200,000 when using p/e ratio of Q Ltd and a high of £7,540,000 when using p/e ratio of P Ltd. The price settled would probably be between these two particularly as the total assets are worth £6,600,000.

Both companies' shares are 20p nominal and assuming a basis of exchange of one share in the new company for one in the old the following would be the position under three alternatives:

	P Ltd	Q Ltd	PQ Ltd
Number of shares (000s)	4,800	3,000	7,800
Valuation			
Pro rata to number of shares (£000)	4,062	2,538	6,600
Existing split	3,600	3,000	6,600
Earnings			
on Q Ltd p/e ratio (4·0)	3,200	2,000	5,200
on P Ltd p/e ratio (5·8)	4,640	2,900	7,540
Present market prices	4,320	1,800	6,120

It is suggested that the valuation be based on the assets basis of £6,600,000 as this is also approximately the figure produced by an unweighted average of the two earnings extremes, i.e. $\frac{£5,200 + £7,540}{2}$ (£000) = £6,370,000. The equivalent p/e ratio would be $\frac{£6,600,000}{£1,300,000} \simeq 5·1$.

Making the exchange on the basis of one for one means that P Ltd's stake in the assets of PQ Ltd will be £4,062,000 as against its existing worth of £3,600,000—an increase of £462,000. This is at the expense of shareholders in Q Ltd. On the other hand, it means that shareholders in P Ltd will face a reduction in their market value from £4,320,000 to £4,062,000 while Q Ltd have the value of their holding increased from £1,800,000 to £2,538,000. The range of alternatives, therefore, lies between these valuations and can be altered by changing the basis of the valuation, the basis of the split between the parties or both.

(*b*) The maximum amount of loan capital which could be issued will be governed by the ability of the combined group to provide an acceptable security in terms of asset cover and priority earnings. Q Ltd has substantially higher liability in relative and absolute terms in respect of short-term loans than has P Ltd, as can be seen from the relevant statistics:

	P Ltd	*Q Ltd*	*Total*	*Notes*
Current liabilities	£000	£000	£000	
Short-term loans	300	2,160	2,460	1
Other liabilities	1,260	840	2,100	2
	1,560	3,000	4,560	3 = 2 + 1
Long-term liabilities				
Provisions not current	600	360	960	4
Loans	600	240	840	5
Total liabilities	2,760	3,600	6,360	6 = {3 + 4 + 5
Total assets	6,360	6,600	12,960	7
Total liabilities: Total assets	43%	55%	49%	$8 = \frac{6}{7}$
Loans: net assets	14%	7%	13%	$9 = \frac{5}{7-3-4}$

The last two ratios are only two ways in which 'gearing' may be expressed. Any ratio which is accepted as normal must therefore be specified. Are we referring to a ratio computed on the basis of 8 or 9, for example? A reasonable ratio might be 60 per cent for the total liabilities: total assets ratio for this type of industry, in which case the maximum additional debt would be:

	(£000)	(£000)
60% × £12,960,000 =		7,776
of which existing commitments are		
Current liabilities	4,560	
Provisions	960	
Loans	840	
		6,360
Maximum additional debt		1,416

It must now be ascertained as to whether the group has sufficient earnings to support the above debt/equity structure.

Average maintainable distributable earnings as computed for (*a*) above were £1,300,000 p.a. Since these are after tax, gross earnings anticipated with taxation at 52 per cent would be $£1,300,000 \times \frac{100}{48} = £2,708,000$. Interest will already have been payable on short-term and long-term loans. These loans amount to £3,300,000 for the PQ Ltd (£2,460,000 + £840,000). Assuming an average interest rate of 15 per cent then earnings before interest would have to be increased by the interest paid on this sum, i.e.

		£
£3,300,000 × 15%		465,000
Add pre-tax profits above		2,708,000
Total pre-tax profits		3,173,000
Interest charges now due:	£	
Existing loans	3,300,000	
+ max. additional loans—	1,416,000	
	4,716,000 at 15%	707,400
		2,465,600

Cover: $\dfrac{£3{,}173{,}000}{£707{,}400} \simeq 4{\cdot}5$ times, i.e. adequate

Revised equity valuation	
Profits after interest	2,465,600
Taxation @ 52%	1,282,100
	1,183,500

p/e ratio from (*a*) above 5·1

∴ Anticipated market value = 5·1 × £1,183,500
= £6,036,000

The consideration due to Q Ltd shareholders as computed for (*a*) above was £2,538,000. If the full amount of extra debt of £1,416,000 is raised then this amount of the consideration would be discharged either by issuing loan stock to the original shareholders or paying them off with cash received from new loan holders. The equity holding would be reduced thus:

	£
Total sum due	2,538,000
Discharged by loan stock	1,416,000
Balance—shares in PQ Ltd	1,122,000

This figure is deducted from the £6,036,000 to arrive at the equity interest in PQ Ltd attributable to P Ltd.

Proportion of holding in PQ Ltd:

	P Ltd	*Q Ltd*	*PQ Ltd*
Value of holding	£4,924,000	£1,122,000	£6,036,000
Percentage of holding	81	19	100
Number of shares (000)	4,800	1,094	5,894*

* This would probably be adjusted in practice. The figure of 5,894,000 shares has been derived by maintaining the number of shares held by P Ltd shareholders as 4,800,000 and increasing the total equity in PQ Ltd pro rata.

(*c*)

	Pre-merger		*Post-merger*	
Scheme a	*P Ltd* %	*Q Ltd* %	*P Ltd* %	*Q Ltd* %
Number of shares of £0·20 each (000s)	4,800 62	3,000 38	4,800 62	3,000 38
	(£000)	(£000)	(£000)	(£000)
Asset worth	3,600 55	3,000 45	4,062 62	2,538 38
Earnings				
Forecast				
(without savings)	750 63	450 37		
(with savings)			800 62	500 38
Market value (current)	4,320	1,800		
(projected)			4,062	2,538
Scheme b	%	%	%	%
Number of shares of £0.20 each (000s)	4,800 62	3,000 38	4,800 81	1,094 19
	(£000)	(£000)	(£000)	(£000)
Asset worth				
Debt				1,416
Equity	3,600	3,000	4,200 81	984 19
Earnings				
Interest @ 15% on £1,416,000				212
Earnings for equity	750	450	959	225
Current market value				
Debt (on issue)				1,416
Equity	4,320	1,800	4,924	1,122

The advantage of scheme (*a*) is that the voting strength of the parties is the same after as before the merger, i.e. 62:38. There are compensatory features; P Ltd shareholders gain on asset backing at the expense of Q Ltd but Q Ltd shareholders gain on earnings and market value.

Under scheme (*b*) the market value of shares plus loan in Q Ltd is the same as (*a*) but the loan introduction has benefited the market rating of P Ltd shareholders by virtue of the increased earnings available to them. On the other hand, if the share distribution suggested is endorsed the control strength has moved to 81:19 in favour of the original shareholders in P Ltd.

(*d*) The bid must be open for acceptances for at least 21 days after the posting of the offer and any revised offer must be kept for at least 14 days. Unless there is a competing offer and the City Panel gives its permission, no offer may become or be declared unconditional more than 60 days after the offer is initially posted (Rule 22).

Workings

(*a*) Equity Value of New Company

(i) *Assets Basis*

	P Ltd	*Q Ltd*	*PQ Ltd*	
Attributable to equity (£000)	3,600	3,000	6,600	1
Existing shares (000s)	4,800	3,000		2
Proposed shares (000s)			7,800	3
Value per share	£0·75	£1·00	£0·846	4 = $\frac{1}{2}$
Proportion of holding (%)	54·54	45·46		

(ii) *Profits Basis*	W.	*P Ltd* (£000)	W.	*Q Ltd* (£000)
	1 × 696	696	1 × 780	780
	2 × 852	1,704	2 × 960	1,920
	3 × 828	2,484	3 × 708	2,124
	4 × 1,081	4,324	4 × 744	2,976
	5 × 1,320	6,600	5 × 900	4,500
	6 × 1,500	9,000		
	21	24,808	15	12,300
Weighted average				
Complete year's (gross)		1,181		820
Tax @ 52%		614		426
		567		394

Alternatives

The above computation can be compared with the latest three complete years. The accounting years have differing dates and ideally the periods should be brought to a common accounting date, since the difference is three months. For March compared with June we really need figures for appropriate quarters. The information is, however, given in half-years and the latest figures which exist for *both* companies are those in respect of first half-year 19x5:

	P Ltd (£000)	*Q Ltd* (£000)
Profits before tax		
1st half of 19x5	684	462
1st half of 19x4	600	432
2nd half of 19x4	720	468
19x3	1,081	744
	3,085	2,106
Less Tax (52%)	1,604	1,095
Total for $2\frac{1}{2}$ years	1,481	1,011
Equivalent to annual rate of (net)	592	404
19x5 First half-year	684	462
19x4 Second half-year	720	468
	1,404	930
Tax at 52%	730	484
	674	446

Annual rate of latest known six months:		
P Ltd 19x5 (1,500 – 684)	816	—
Q Ltd 19x5	—	462
	816	462
Tax at 52%	424	240
Profit after tax (6 months)	392	222
Profit after tax (12 months)	784	444

Any of the above might be used as a basis for capitalisation but it is suggested that for illustration purposes above the following figures are used:

	P Ltd (£000)	*Q Ltd* (£000)
Suggested profits	750	450

Bids and Counter-bids—The City Code

Interests of Shareholders

The majority of shareholders can be classified into two major groups: individual and institutional. Generally speaking, individual shareholders know little or nothing about the business in which they have shares. They buy and sell shares on advice from professional agents such as stockbrokers and may move investments frequently for taxation purposes or capital gains. Alternatively, they may leave investments untouched and so present opportunities for exploitation through mere inertia and lack of interest. The second group, the institutional investors, also tend to leave managements undisturbed so long as the companies produce results in line with what the investors see as their objectives. These may, however, be very different from the best interests of either the company or the smaller individual shareholders. The doctrine of shareholders' control is in practice open to serious doubt. Theoretically control does lie as a last resort with the shareholders but a wide distribution of the total holding may well mean that actual control and manipulative ability can be with a comparatively small power bloc.

There is no special group of legislation which particularly regulates conduct of takeovers and mergers. The acts which govern law of contract and company legislation contain safeguards whereby directors or individuals who have acted recklessly or fraudulently may be brought to task. As indicated elsewhere, the majority (over 90 per cent) of mergers are achieved quietly and with the consent of all parties. A précis of the proposals is sent to the members of the companies concerned. This would comprise:

(*a*) *Chairman's Letter*. In this is set out a summary of the proposals, including details of any additional contract entered into by the company. This contract is normally conditional upon it being ratified by the shareholders concerned and, if applicable, confirmation of permission to deal in the shares on the stock exchange. Some paragraphs are given describing the other companies involved and the advantages of the amalgamation. This would include a summary of management personnel and structure, profit and dividend prospects, change of name and amendments to share capital. The date for the extraordinary general meeting and a formal recommendation to accept the offer or endorse the scheme would also be given.

(*b*) *Appendices of supporting information.* These would comprise more detailed summaries of the relative financial positions and prospects of the parties concerned. This is verified by auditors and professional advisers who include any comment on the scheme as to its fairness. Details are also given of the bases and assumptions on which profit forecasts have been made.

(*c*) Finally, the summary would contain a list of documents available for inspection and notices of the extraordinary meeting, setting out the formal resolutions, ordinary and special, as required by the law governing such meetings.

If the proposals are endorsed at the meeting then the merger proceeds. If acceptance of the offer is confirmed by holders of 90 per cent of the shares bid for then the bidder may compulsorily acquire the remaining shares. The responsibility for ensuring that the best interests of the shareholder are being followed rests with the board of directors. They have a liability to act for the utmost benefit of the shareholders even if this conflicts with their own personal interests. Shareholders who object to a bid would have to convince the board at the meeting that their case was a better one or claim that the directors had not exercised 'duties of skill and care' to a sufficient extent.

It may be, however, that the board of directors decide to reject and fight a bid. In this event the rejection must be based on the same motive, i.e. the best interests of the shareholders. This opposition will normally be through a genuine belief that it is not in the company's interest or it may be a stalling device to obtain better terms. As above, the potential loss of employment or change of status of the directors concerned should be ignored by them if it conflicts with the best interests of the shareholders. It is the contested bid which provides the publicity, complaints and case law which exist in the specific sphere of mergers and takeovers.

However, unless a scheme is blatantly objectionable the ability of a scattered group of shareholders to be aware of the situation and take concerted action is restricted. Small shareholders are obviously at a disadvantage when prompt communication and unilateral action is necessary against the activities of a particular pressure group. In response to popular pressure, and possibly to attempt to avoid specific legislation, the City has attempted to continue the system of self-regulation by helping to set up and by supporting the City Panel on Takeovers and Mergers.

Restriction and Control of Mergers

Government Restrictions

The legislation that has been enacted in respect of mergers and takeovers is not within the objectives set out in the preceding paragraphs but in the area of the 'public interest'. Growing concern relating to the dominance of particular suppliers or manufacturers led to the formation of the Monopolies Commission and the enactment of the Monopolies and Mergers Act in 1965. Although this act has now been incorporated into the Fair Trading Act, 1973, its objectives remain unaltered. These were to ensure that mergers did not take place against the public interest. If the public interest was in doubt then the act empowered the appropriate official to refer the proposals to the Monopolies Commission. If the Commission found against the proposals then the Act could be invoked to forbid or modify the bid. The main factors on which such interference might apply would be where the merger would result in too large a market dominance, where employment would be seriously affected, or where the motive was seen as predominantly tax avoidance and/or asset stripping. It is ironic to consider that on the one hand various government agencies such as the now defunct Industrial Reorganisation Corporation were created to encourage mergers and on the other it was felt necessary to introduce counter legislation. In fairness, it should be stated that the IRC objectives were seen largely as protection of the industries concerned whereas the monopolies legislation was primarily protection of the consumer—though both of these factors could be ideally regarded as in the public interest. Criticism has often been made of the restricted use made of the power to refer and also of the comparatively small proportion of bids forbidden, but the structure still remains largely as conceived.

Panel and Takeover Code

The institutions of the City and in particular the Stock Exchange operate a vetting system primarily aimed at protecting their own reputation. In this respect the objectives are more in the spirit of ensuring equality of treatment of the shareholders and other investors concerned than considering the desirability or otherwise of the merger from the view of the public interest.

The City Panel is a body comprising members drawn from the major intstitutions which are actively engaged when mergers and takeovers are enacted. Their brief is to act as watchdogs on all aspects of the bidding activities and by virtue of their influence in the money markets they exert pressures or get sanctions imposed should advice be ignored. The most important document associated with them is the City Code on Takeovers and Mergers. While it concedes that it is impractical to devise rules in such detail as to cover all the various circumstances it directs that the spirit as well as the precise wording of the rules must be observed. The Code, which was originally produced in March 1968, has been revised several times, the latest to date being June 1974. A summary of the major provisions is given below.

(*i*) *Responsibility to shareholders.* An offer should, in the first instance, be made to the board of the offeree company or to its advisers rather than direct to the shareholders. On receipt, the directors would normally issue a notice in the press stating the offeror's name, terms and conditions and follow this with a circular stating the board's view on the acceptability or otherwise of the offer. Shareholders should have in their possession all evidence, facts and opinions upon which an adequate judgment can be reached and should have sufficient time to make a decision. In particular, the directors may not sell shares before the formal submission of the offer if by doing so the offeror would acquire 30 per cent or more of the voting rights.

(*ii*) *Minimum information required*

(*a*) The advantages claimed from the merger.

(*b*) Nature of the offer, i.e. securities or cash and if the latter endorsement that the offeror has the cash resources.

(*c*) Details of any fundamental change in the nature or structure of the business, with particular reference to the position of employees.

(*d*) Listing of the directors and associates plus statistics of shareholdings in both companies and any dealings in the preceding year.

(*e*) Profit forecasts must be verified by advisers, the nature of accounting treatment indicated and any revaluations supported by expert evidence.

(*iii*) *Offers*

(*a*) All shareholders of the same class of an offeree company shall be treated similarly by an offeror.

(*b*) An offer cannot become unconditional until the offeror has secured over 50 per cent of the voting capital.

(*c*) The minimum offer period is 21 days after posting of the offer and any revised offer must be kept open for at least 14 days.

(*d*) An acceptor is entitled to withdraw his acceptance if the offer has not become or been declared unconditional as to acceptances within 21 days of the first closing date of the initial offer.

(*e*) No offer may become or be declared unconditional as to acceptances more than 60 days after the offer is initially posted unless there is a competing offer and the panel gives its permission. An offer which has become unconditional must remain open for acceptance within a further 14 days.

(*iv*) *Price*

(*a*) A basic condition is that if the offeror or any person acting in concert with the offeror purchases shares during the offer period at above the offer price then the offer price must be increased to the highest price so paid.

(*b*) Whenever 15 per cent or more of any class of shares is purchased for cash during the offer period and the previous 12 months, the offer must be in cash or accompanied by a cash alternative.

(*e*) Any person who acquires 30 per cent or more of the voting rights obtained by himself or person acting in concert must make an offer for the remaining shares in the classes whose shares have been bought on the market and must make a comparable offer for any other class of share capital whether such capital carries voting rights or not.

These conditions may be waived at the discretion of the Panel.

Countering a Bid

If the directors of the offeree genuinely consider that the offer is not in the best interests of their company and they wish to reject the bid then they must provide evidence to shareholders to support this opinion. As in the case of the offer documents, the evidence must be produced with the same care and verified where applicable by professional experts and advisers. This is particularly important when unaudited figures are being used to justify forecasts. Shareholders will have to be notified of any fundamental differences between the position as revealed by the last published accounts and the current situation. If they can demonstrate that the bidder is, for example, interested merely in purchasing assets at a discount then they will have to show good reason why the value of the company is greater as a non-operating concern than otherwise. They will also, under these conditions, have to explain how such circumstances have arisen. If the shareholders accept the directors' assessment then they will reject the bid.

More positively, the directors may seek out an alternative buyer. If this is done there are certain criteria which have to be satisfied in respect of the City

Code, but more fundamentally the motives would have to be critically examined by the shareholders. If the offeree company has not been realising its potential it is natural that the board should resent the possible aggressive tactics of the original bidder. This in no way implies that the company approached by the offeree would be a better prospect but it puts the onus on the shareholders or their advisers to watch carefully the alternatives put to them.

Current Developments

Growth through acquisition and merger has been a major feature of the financial markets of the 1970s and 1980s. The main motives have been considered but can be repeated briefly:

(i) The target company is undervalued on the Stock Exchange in the opinion of the bidder.
(ii) The company has particular assets the bidder wants, e.g. large cash resources or prime sites.
(iii) There may be taxation advantages.
(iv) Protecting or increasing market share.
(v) Basic desire by bidder for growth.
(vi) The acquisition of a management team.

The above are mainly financial aspects in addition to the economic factors discussed on page 255. In the past most mergers have been achieved reasonably quietly but recently techniques have been more aggressive. One possible reason is that it is easier to grow by acquiring other successful businesses than to create one's own growth. There is evidence too of some relationship between takeover activity and high share prices. The purchase price can be met by issuing paper—shares—of inflated value. During 1985/6 there were mergers involving over £18 billion. The initiative lies with bidders since they can devise strategy well in advance and build up an initial holding without disclosing their hand until the proportion requiring disclosure is achieved. By contrast the largest company has only three weeks to publish its counter attack. As stated on page 279 the alternative defence was reference to the Monopolies Commission via the Office of Fair Trading. This has been weakened by recent changes in the rules which permit the bidder to change the terms of his offer should it warrant referral. In the climate of the intense activity for mergers many companies adopted more and more previously unused tactics. A favourite was large-scale advertising by both parties publishing their views and denigrating the opposition. One instance more than any other, however, which occurred in 1987 has brought into the public eye tactics which break even the flimsy rules which some parties contend are already too weak and this was the Guinness involvement.

The Guinness Affair

In 1985 there were indications that the Argyll Group (a supermarket chain) were planning to bid for Distillers (whisky refineries, etc.). James Gulliver, the Chairman of Argyll, denied this and by Takeover Panel rules was not allowed to make an offer for three months. Exactly three months later Argyll did put in a bid which was not accepted while at the same time (June 1986) Guinness made a better offer. Argyll increased their offer but once more Guinness responded with a higher bid. During this period the price of both contenders' shares were rising. There were repetitive advertisements proclaiming the merits of the offers of the two protagonists and making scathing comments on the disattraction of the opposing side. The rise in Guinness share price, however, far outstripped that of Argyll. In the critical period up to 18th April 1986 the Argyll share price rose by about 30p while the Guinness share price increased by 70p. At this point Guinness announced they had more than 50 per cent of Distillers' shares giving them control. Several merchant banks had bought shares in Guinness with the motive of increasing market price. The rules of the Takeover Panel permit this subject to disclosure and this had been done. A major element however concerned a block of shares representing roughly 3 per cent of Distillers' capital which came on the market. The brokers for Guinness found a buyer for the whole block at 705p whereas the brokers for Argyll could only find buyers for less at that level. Because of the extremely large gap Argyll reported the incident to the Takeover Panel. At this stage they found nothing to condemn but in September 1987 it changed its opinion.

A major supporter of the Guinness bid had been Ivor Boesky, an American operator. He had invested £70 million in Guinness shares which although representing over 5 per cent—a notifiable holding—had not been disclosed. There were other connections with Guinness—they had invested $100m in one of his operations. The most important thing however from the takeover point of view was that as a result of his disclosures, the panel ruled that the purchaser of the block of shares in April—Pipetec—had been acting in concert with Guinness. The implication of this would be that all Distillers shareholders would be entitled to the price paid for this slice—705p—each rather than the final price paid of 630p. On the number of shares involved this would amount to around £70m maximum. Other disclosures followed including details of a 'share support operation' whereby Guinness shares were bought in exchange for indemnity fees totalling £25 million. A substantial part of this went to Pipetec, a subsidiary of the Swiss Bank Leu. Thomas Ward, at that time a non-executive director of Guinness, was also connected with Pipetec. He subsequently resigned from the Guinness Board. The Chairman of Bank Leu, Dr Feurer, was also a non-executive director of Guinness. Subsequent investigation resulted in the dismissal of the Chairman of Guinness, Ernest Saunders. There are a number of rules in the Companies Act which cover dealings by a company in its own shares or other involvements in the form of indemnities to purchasers. The Takeover Panel concluded that their original view that there had been no irregularity was incorrect. Although Guinness appealed against this—there was a judicial review which lasted eight days ending on Wednesday 27th January—the verdict ultimately went against them.

The position at the time of writing (March 1988) is that several men are to face charges arising out of the takeover battle for Distillers in 1986. It will be a considerable time before the court battles are sorted out. Both Argyll and Distillers shareholders' representatives will be concerned with possible claims for damages of colossal amounts. The events have been summarised as briefly as possible but it is probably the single most important case of the 1980s in respect of City activities and investors' confidence. It has confirmed specialist and general opinion that the Takeover Panel may be an ineffective watchdog. The ability of the City to be a self-regulatory organisation is once again in question. It will provide an incentive to widen the scope of, and put stronger powers in, the Financial Services Act 1986 and Company Law. From the point of view of the City itself the timing of the scandal could not have been worse. After the frenetic years of the 1980s confidence slumped with the huge losses sustained in October 1987. To have such a major, well-known company at the centre of such actions was a further blow to the reputation of the City as a whole. Whatever the outcome of the court proceedings, it is certain that demand for more protection of the investor and public at large will become more persistent.

Worked Examples

Investigation into Financial State of a Potential Bidder

Part 1. ABC Ltd is an old established company of building contractors. The directors are all related to the founder of the business who died in 19x6. Most of the employees have grown up in the service of the company.

In its earlier years the company had considerable contracts for the erection of public buildings. However, in recent years it has been engaged mainly in jobbing and subcontract work.

The youngest member of the board has suggested that the company should now seek to expand its business, possibly in new areas of activity, and that this might best be achieved by acquiring an existing company. The shareholdings are widely spread with no member holding more than 7½ per cent of the total share capital.

The tables given below summarise the recent financial history of ABC Ltd.

ABC Ltd: Summary of Financial Information
(£000)

	Year ended 30th June				
	19x8	*19x9*	*19y0*	*19y1*	*19y2*
Invoiced sales	2,300	2,800	3,200	3,000	2,800
Operating profit before tax	135	128	119	116	126
Income from short-term investments	5	7	11	24	24
Profit after tax	85	80	80	85	90
Year-end balances:					
Current assets:					
Stock and work-in-progress	420	430	450	380	280
Debtors and prepayments	560	700	680	600	500
Short-term investments	100	140	225	480	780
Cash at bank	80	25	80	85	55
	1,160	1,295	1,435	1,545	1,615
Current liabilities:					
Creditors, trade	180	200	200	190	160
Taxation	50	55	55	50	55
Proposed dividend	60	60	60	60	60
	290	315	315	300	275
Net current assets	870	980	1,120	1,245	1,340

	Year ended 30th June				
	19x8	*19x9*	*19y0*	*19y1*	*19y2*
Fixed assets:					
Plant, machinery and equipment, at cost	1,400	1,450	1,470	1,470	1,460
less Depreciation	870	1,010	1,155	1,250	1,300
	530	440	315	220	160
Land and buildings, at cost 42 years ago	1,200	1,200	1,200	1,200	1,200
	1,730	1,640	1,515	1,420	1,360
Total assets employed	2,600	2,620	2,635	2,665	2,700
Financed by:					
Ordinary share capital, shares of £1 each;					
Authorised—2,500,000					
Issued and fully paid—1,700,000	1,700	1,700	1,700	1,700	1,700
Reserves	845	865	885	910	940
Deferred taxation	55	55	50	55	60
	2,600	2,620	2,635	2,665	2,700
	£	£	£	£	£
Share price during year: high	1·00	1·00	0·90	1·00	1·20

You are required to analyse the financial position of ABC Ltd and to list and comment on the financial and other characteristics desirable in the company to be taken over.

Part 2. This part cannot be answered properly unless you have answered part 1. Among the companies investigated for the purpose of takeover by ABC Ltd is XYZ Ltd, an unquoted company, which manufactures small air-conditioning units. This company was founded in 19y0 by two graduates, one with a degree in electronics and the other with a degree in business studies, with initial financial backing from a small number of friends in the City. In spite of the growth prospects of the company, it is unlikely that further finance will be available from this source.

The financial history of the company and a forecast for the years 19y3 and 19y4 are given below:

XYZ Ltd: Summary of Financial Information
(£000)

	Year ended 31st December				
	Actual			*Forecast*	
	19y0	*19y1*	*19y2*	*19y3*	*19y4*
Invoiced sales	240	540	960	1,320	2,400
Profit before tax	6	30	48	66	100
Profit after tax	6	24	30	40	60

	Year ended 31st December				
	Actual			Forecast	
Year-end balances:	*19y0*	*19y1*	*19y2*	*19y3*	*19y4*
Current assets:					
Stock and work-in-progress	30	70	114	200	280
Debtors and prepayments	48	81	66	120	160
Cash at bank	20	5	—	—	11
	98	156	180	320	451
Current liabilities:					
Creditors, trade	30	54	78	172	240
Taxation	—	—	6	18	26
Bank overdraft	28	37	26	—	—
	58	91	110	190	266
Net current assets	40	65	70	130	185
Fixed assets:					
Plant machinery and fittings, at cost	45	50	75	75	130
less Depreciation	9	19	34	49	85
	36	31	41	26	45
Land and buildings, at cost	80	120	120	120	120
	116	151	161	146	165
Research and development expenditure	—	20	57	60	60
Total assets employed	156	236	288	336	410
Financed by:					
Ordinary share capital, shares of £1 each:					
Authorised—240,000					
Issued and fully paid 150,000	150	150	150	150	150
Reserves	6	30	60	100	160
Deferred taxation	—	6	18	26	40
Loan account, at 10%	—	50	60	60	60
	156	236	288	336	410

You are required to advise:

(*a*) Whether it would be practicable for XYZ Ltd to obtain a stock exchange quotation at this stage of its development and/or what preliminary steps would be necessary to achieve a quotation.

(*b*) As to the extent to which you consider XYZ Ltd and ABC Ltd respectively could raise loan capital.

(*c*) Whether it would be to the advantage of ABC Ltd and XYZ Ltd respectively to merge.

(*d*) Within what range of prices ABC Ltd might make an offer for XYZ Ltd.

(*e*) If ABC Ltd were to acquire XYZ Ltd at the maximum price suggested, what would be the advantages and disadvantages for each company in each of the following forms of purchase consideration: (i) entirely in cash; (ii) entirely in shares of ABC Ltd; (iii) any other form of consideration you consider appropriate.

(CIMA)

Part 1

This part is concerned with assessing the potential and strength of the acquirer. Stage one is therefore to produce statistics which might be useful in indicating the strong and weak areas.

	Data identity		*19x8*	*19x9*	*19y0*	*19y1*	*19y2*
Pre-tax operating profit	1	(£000)	135	128	119	116	126
Sales	2	(£000)	2,300	2,800	3,200	3,000	2,800
Profit/Sales	$3=\frac{1}{2}$	(%)	5·9	4·6	3·7	3·9	4·5
Investment income	4	(£000)	5	7	11	24	24
Total pre-tax profits	$5=4+1$	(£000)	140	135	130	140	150
Investment income as proportion of profits	$6=\frac{4}{5}$	(%)	3·6	5·2	8·5	17·1	16·0
Short-term investments	8	(£000)	100	140	225	480	780
Return on investments	$9=\frac{4}{8}$	(%)	5·0	5·0	4·9	5·0	3·1
Post-tax profits	10	(£000)	85	80	80	85	90
Capital employed							
Total assets	11	(£000)	2,600	2,620	2,635	2,665	2,700
Operating assets	$12=11-8$	(£000)	2,500	2,480	2,410	2,185	1,920
$\frac{\text{Post-tax profit}}{\text{Total assets}}$	$13=\frac{10}{11}$	(%)	3·3	3·1	3·0	3·2	3·2
$\frac{\text{Post-tax profit}}{\text{Operating assets}}$	$14=\frac{10}{12}$	(%)	3·4	3·2	3·3	3·9	4·7
$\frac{\text{Operating profit (gross)}}{\text{Operating assets}}$	$15=\frac{1}{12}$	(%)	5·4	5·2	4·9	5·3	6·6
Share capital	16	(000s)	1,700	1,700	1,700	1,700	1,700
Earnings/share	$17=\frac{10}{16}$	(pence)	5	5	5	5	5
Share price	18	(£)	1·00	1·00	0·90	1·00	1·20
Highest p/e	$19=\frac{18}{17}$		20	20	18	20	24
Debtors	20	(days' sales)	89	91	78	73	65
Creditors	21	,,	29	26	23	23	21
Stocks	22	,,	67	56	51	46	36
Assets/share at book value	23	(£)	1·53	1·54	1·55	1·57	1·59

Financial position of ABC Ltd

On a trading basis the results require explanation. The highest turnover (19y0) corresponded to the lowest pre-tax profit to sales performance. This is particularly surprising in view of the nature of the business concerned. It can be seen that the net of tax return of post-tax profits to total assets was about 3·3 per cent for the whole of the period. The main contributory factor to this stabilisation was the increase in investment income. The return on short-term investment was constant at about 5 per cent with the exception of 19y2, but in this year the amount had risen to £78,000. The effect of this holding is to provide a strong liquidity position and the major source of this appears to be the cumulative depreciation of £430,000. The effect of investment income is emphasised in line 6, showing a rise from 3·6 per cent to a maximum (19y1) of 17·1 per cent of total profit.

The dividends and share price have been relatively constant and in view of the attraction to a potential asset stripper it is surprising that the company itself has not been subjected to a bid. The fixed assets of plant and machinery are written off, leaving land and buildings—even at cost—at 70p per share, while net current assets are worth another 80p if fully realised.

The company could consider the following courses of action:

1. It might purchase another company with a view to liquidating ABC Ltd.
2. It could consider revitalising the management, either by direct employment or by purchasing a company with evidence of managerial drive and ability.
3. The company could utilise its short-term investments to purchase a company in another line of activity as a subsidiary. On the other hand, if the depreciation has been based on a realistic life estimate, the plant and machinery will shortly be due for replacement and this cash would be needed.

The characteristics desirable in the company to be taken over are:

1. Proven managerial expertise, demonstrated by a growth record in earnings per share and returns.
2. A company possibly with liquidity problems not connected with poor management or other undesirable causes. This would enable utilisation of short-term investments in the liquidity of a proposed group.
3. How desirable is the preserving of jobs in the company? The average age of employees may be high and generous redundancy treatment financed out of sale of land may be in the long-term interest of all. This would alter the characteristics of the company sought for, as it could be a project unfettered by the existing situation.
4. A company in a related industry or activity, say manufacture of joinery for the building trade. This might result in mutual exchange and increase of business and provide a means of absorbing some of the labour skills.
5. The company sought should have surplus capacity of more up-to-date plant and machinery than ABC, which would provide a means of replacement on more economical terms than buying new on the market.
6. Alternatively, a company in a completely different field of activity could be sought to avoid a link with the vagaries of the building industry. There would then arise a crucial dependence upon the management of the company taken over and with the investment funds thus utilised ABC would become exceptionally vulnerable because of its lack of replacement of its own plant and machinery.

Part 2

(*a*) *Practicality of Quotation*

The maximum profit after tax is forecast as £60,000, whereas the latest actual performance is £30,000. Even with the forecast achieved this is only just about the minimum currently suggested flotation figure of around £50,000 p.a. post-tax profits. On a capitalisation basis of two-thirds of the p/e ratio of ABC Ltd—on the grounds that it would be a newcomer to the market—this would suggest a p/e of 12 to 16. This would provide on the highest basis a capital value of 16 × £60,000 = £960,000 and on the lowest basis 12 × £30,000 = £360,000. Neither of these figures would justify the expenses of an issue since even if permission were granted the company is too small and not sufficiently established.

(*b*) *Possibility of raising Loan Capital*

ABC Ltd. The question here is academic in the sense that one could say why do they need it with £780,000 in investments and £55,000 in cash? The tests, however, are: could they pay the interest and does the asset backing exist? The major security would be the land which, taken to be worth no more than three times its value 42 years ago, gives a current value of £3,600,000. The income aspect is more doubtful since dividends on equity have been constant over five years and trading profits declining. If the loan was required to finance an acquisition then it would be the likelihood or otherwise of this achieving the objective set out in Part 1 rather than asset support which would govern the likelihood of raising such capital.

XYZ Ltd. The cash flow statement shows a break-even position for 19y2/3 and a positive inflow of £11,000 for 19y3/4, indicating a favourable change in the cash position from the deficit of £26,000 at the end of 19y2. The working capital ratios show a poor situation on quick assets ratio, debtors and cash being about 0·6 for the whole three-year period. Debtors/Sales show a short credit period while stocks/sales ratio has also improved. The cash flow at present is unsatisfactory but if no additional plant is likely to be required for some time and the major expenditure on research has already been incurred this should improve considerably, though the company is still vulnerable to any worsening of debtors. At present the firm is overtrading but it appears to have demonstrated an ability to generate the necessary income to support its loan capital. Again, however, no dividends have been paid and it would be necessary to know what reward had been taken by the founders for their services to assess the relative situation of all parties concerned.

The asset backing is not so impressive. At present fixed assets plus current assets give a total of £161,000 + £180,000 = £341,000 (19y2). Research and development expenditure, which has been capitalised, is excluded as being of doubtful break-up value. Of the £341,000, current liabilities require £110,000 and the loan account a further £60,000, the figure remaining being £171,000. Although this could provide sufficient cover for some element of loan—say, around one-third of this amount—it is not a very appealing proposition to a lender. Viewed from the fixed asset cover, the book value of £161,000 is already supporting the loan of £60,000 and a second lender may not be willing to extend this ratio greatly, especially as the buildings in particular are newly acquired and their current value not likely to be much advanced upon the cost price.

XYZ Ltd—Relevant Statistics—Last three years

Funds flow (£000)	*Year ended 31st December* 19y2 Actual	19y3 Forecast	19y4 Forecast
Sources			
Profit before taxation	48	66	100
Depreciation	15	15	36
Debtors—reduction	15	—	—
Creditors—increase	24	94	68
Loan—increase	10	—	—
	112	175	204
Uses			
Plant and machinery	25	—	55
Research and development	37	3	—
Taxation paid	—	6	18
Stocks	44	86	80
Debtors	—	54	40
	106	149	193
Change in cash and bank	6	26	11
Ratios			
Debtors + cash (£000)	66	120	171
Current liabilities	110	190	266
Quick asset ratio	0·60	0·63	0·64
Debtors	66	120	160
Sales (£000)	960	1,320	2,400
Debtors turnover (days)	25	33	24
Stock (£000)	114	200	280
Sales (£000)	960	1,320	2,400
Stock turnover (days)	43	55	43
Profit after tax	£30,000	£40,000	£60,000
Earnings per share	20p	26·7p	40p

(c) Whether it would be to the advantage of ABC Ltd and XYZ Ltd respectively to merge

ABC Ltd. Referring to the characteristics listed as being desirable by ABC Ltd in a merger prospect:

1. XYZ Ltd shows management potential demonstrated by increased earnings per share.

2. The company has liquidity problems but predominantly short-term if forecasts are reliable.

3. The preservation of the existing company and labour force is a separate issue in this instance.

4. Possibly the company has some trade connections—i.e. air-conditioning units are used in buildings—but is sufficiently different to provide some diversification.

5. All things considered it would appear to meet the criteria quite well and would merit further investigation.

6. However, the fixed assets of XYZ Ltd are not likely to be of a nature to make good any replacement requirements of ABC Ltd.

XYZ Ltd

1. In view of the comments made in Part 2(*a*) regarding the inability of XYZ Ltd to obtain a quotation the merger with ABC Ltd would give entrance to the stock exchange indirectly and at less cost.

2. The combined companies would appear to complement each other particularly in respect of the supply of necessary short-term funds required by XYZ Ltd.

3. The increased asset strength would facilitate the ability to raise loan capital if and when required and the ability to pay interest charges, with satisfactory cover, out of annual revenue would be improved.

4. The existing loan account could be repaid with an immediate saving of £6,000 p.a. pre-tax profits, and also remove any possible deterrent to raising new loan capital.

An unqualified answer to this section at this stage cannot be given since the final assessment in either case will depend upon finalisation of stages (*d*) and (*e*).

(*d*) *Range of prices in which ABC Ltd might make an offer for XYZ Ltd*

Asset basis—XYZ Ltd	*Actual*	*Forecast*	
	19y2	*19y3*	*19y4*
	(£000)	(£000)	(£000)
Fixed assets			
Plant and machinery			
(cost less depreciation)	41	26	45
Land and buildings	120	120	120
	161	146	165
Net current assets	70	130	185
	231	276	350
Less: Required for loan account	60	60	60
	171	216	290
Price per share (150,000 shares)	£1·14	£1·44	£1·93

Research and development has been excluded and no deduction made in respect of deferred taxation. Since land, buildings and plant are less than three years old (19y2) their balance sheet valuation is fairly realistic.

Profits basis. A simple average of the 19y2 actual figure and next two years' forecast would produce profits after tax of $\frac{30+40+60}{3}=\frac{130}{3}=$ £43,000 p.a.

A weighted average, giving greater emphasis to the forecast for the same three years, would produce:

		(£000)
19x2	1 × 30 =	30
19x3	2 × 40 =	80
19x4	3 × 60 =	180
		290

$$= \frac{£290{,}000}{6} = £48{,}333$$

A simple average of the forecast period only would produce $\frac{40 + 60}{2} =$ £50,000 p.a. The latter is in round terms slightly more than the previous weighted average and, if accepted as the estimate of *average maintainable distributable future earnings*, leaves as the final element the assessment of a reasonable rate of return or p/e ratio.

ABC Ltd had a high p/e ratio which varied between 18 and 24. This was, however, probably related to its assets worth rather than genuine multiple of earnings. It would be better to examine the p/e ratio of quoted companies in similar lines of business to XYZ Ltd as this would more nearly represent the level of performance for similar risk class. Assuming this to average about 16 the capitalised value of XYZ Ltd would become 16 × £50,000 = £800,000. In the absence of more information it is not possible to give other than conditional prices. Alternative approaches would be to use the gilt-edged net income yield multiplied by a premium for risk or to use the discounted cash flow basis described in Chapter 3 once an acceptable rate of return has been established.

The range of prices on the above criteria would be between the lowest (asset) value of £171,000 and the earnings figure of £800,000. The average of these figures—i.e. that produced by a combination of assets and earnings—is known as the **Berliner method of valuation** and in this instance would produce a mean of

$$\frac{£171{,}000 + £800{,}000}{2} = £485{,}500 \simeq £500{,}000$$

This is in no way to suggest that figures between £170,000 and £800,000 would not be acceptable as a theoretical basis for discussion. In practice, as with all 'market' transactions the buyer would offer what he thought would be the minimum possible while the seller at least in the first instance would go for the maximum it was thought possible to obtain.

(*e*) *Advantages and disadvantages of alternative forms of consideration*

(Using maximum price of £800,000 suggested in Part (*d*) for illustration as requested.)

1. *Entirely in cash.* £800,000 would be required and XYZ Ltd could realise almost all this figure by selling the short-term investment holding of £780,000. Whether this would be acceptable or not to ABC Ltd would largely depend on whether the two graduates and their friends consider the reward sufficient to liquidate their entire interests. They may prefer to share in the possible

growth having borne the early risks. The owners of the loan capital should be indifferent as to whether the loan is taken over or liquidated unless the contractual rate is in excess of that likely to operate for a considerable future period. From the point of view of XYZ Ltd an all-cash offer may be self-defeating since a major objective was to import more dynamic management into the group and the graduates are hardly likely to settle for a service contract without equity interest. Moreover, it could be advantageous to ABC Ltd for the key management of XYZ Ltd to retain an interest in future performance.

2. *Entirely in shares of ABC Ltd*

ABC Ltd: Capital

Authorised shares of £1 each	2,500,000
Issued shares of £1 each	1,700,000
Available for issue	800,000

Assuming these issued at par in settlement of above then the relative holding of XYZ Ltd in the new company would be

$$\frac{800{,}000}{2{,}500{,}000} = 32\%$$

On this basis

Existing number of shares in XYZ Ltd =	150,000
New shares =	800,000

∴ Each shareholder in XYZ would be offered 16 shares in the new company for every three now held.

(At this stage it might be worth considering a less awkward fraction: 16 for 3 is the ratio between 800,000 and 150,000, but $\frac{16}{3}$ is $5\frac{1}{3}$ and we might consider a more straightforward 5:1. This would mean revising the 'maximum' answer computed in part (*d*) to £750,000 (i.e. 5 × 150,000 × £1). Under examination conditions time might preclude such reconsideration and therefore this has deliberately not been done. If the question were not stated to be the *maximum* price in part (*e*) it would be preferable to adjust the exchange ratio to 5:1 and after explanation proceed accordingly.)

Comparative statistics if merged on this basis:

	Without merger		*Merged*
	ABC Ltd	*XYZ Ltd*	
Issued ordinary shares of £1 (000s)	1,700	150	2,500
Earnings for ordinary shareholders (ABC 19y2 actual—XYZ 19y3 forecast)	£90,000	£40,000	£130,000
Earnings per ordinary share	5·3p	26·7p	5·2p
Adjusted for merger 16:3	—	5·0	—
Market value based on £1 per share (£000)	1,700	—	2,500
p/e ratio based on £1 per share	18·9	—	19·2
Tangible assets—19y2 (£000)	2,700	171	2,871
Assets per share	£1·59	£1·14	£1·15
Adjusted for merger 16:3	—	£6·08	—

The effect of this scheme would be briefly:

1. Original shareholders in XYZ would have 32 per cent of the total shares in the new company. Since none of the original shareholdings in XYZ was in excess of $7\frac{1}{2}$ per cent XYZ would have effective control of the group if the new shares had equal voting rights.
2. The earnings prospects would be reasonably distributed. Earnings per share for ABC at 5·3p are virtually unchanged at 5·2p. In the case of XYZ, although earnings per share before the merger were 26·7p, this is being exchanged at the rate of 3 for 16; therefore effective earnings per share show marginal change from 5·0 to 5·2.
3. In the case of assets backing XYZ is showing considerable gain. Their proportional adjusted holding shows a rise from 114p to 608p at the expense of ABC shareholders.

Although the scheme would probably be acceptable by XYZ Ltd, the effect of items 1 and 3 above would make the method of consideration unacceptable to shareholders in ABC Ltd as they have a lot to lose and little to gain.

3. *Any other form of consideration you consider appropriate.* The alternatives are loan stock, cash and shares or a combination of these. ABC Ltd has the capacity to raise such a security but there is little point in this since it already has short-term investments it could liquidate. Since offers entirely in cash or shares have been considered and rejected we should examine the possibilities of an offer comprising elements of each. The offer price maximum is still to be assumed as £800,000. Consider the effect of offering £500,000 in cash and £300,000 in £1 shares at par value (since existing market value of the £1 ordinaries in ABC is averaging £1).

		£
Combined earnings as above (*e*2)		130,000
Less: Interest forgone in short-term investments	£	
5% × £500,000	= 25,000	
Less tax @ 40% (at 19y2)	= 10,000	15,000
		115,000
Shares issued (1,700,000 + 300,000)		2,000,000
Earnings per share		5·75p
Asset basis		
Combined assets (£2,871,000 – £500,000)	= £	2,371,000
Assets per share	= £	1·19

The ratio of cash/shares depends on the potential preferences of the existing shareholders. Other possibilities are part cash combined with share warrants. The matter goes back to the issues raised in part *c*, i.e.

1. What are the cash requirements of XYZ Ltd?
2. Is ABC Ltd capable of supplying it?
3. Are the companies compatible?
4. What is the corporate objective?
5. What is the position of ABC Ltd without takeover?

6. What is the position of the directors?
7. Where will the control lie with any scheme?
8. Is it fair and acceptable to all parties?
9. Are there any legal impediments to proposals?

Analysis of Performance and Case for Rejection of Takeover Bid

Summaries are given below of the accounts of the PQR Ltd for the three years ended 30th June, 19x3, 19x4 and 19x5, and of those for the year ended 30th June, 19x6, which are present with the printers prior to issue. It will be noted that no dividend was paid in 19x5. In his statement accompanying the 19x5 accounts the chairman forecast the 'resumption of normal dividends' in 19x6. The interim statement for the six months to December 19x5 referred to this hope, though no interim dividend was paid.

Within the last month there has been unusual activity in the company's shares and the price has moved up to a recent high of £0·70. The board has credible information that the main buyer is the XYZ Conglomerate Group, and that an offer may shortly be made at about £0·84. This news is most unwelcome to the board, partly because it doubts the ability or the willingness of XYZ Conglomerate Group to carry through the development of the company which has been quietly planned over the past few years, and partly because the directors suspect their own future prospects would be uncertain.

Summary of Results of PQR Limited for years ended 30th June (in £000):

	19x3	*19x4*	*19x5*	*19x6*	*Comments*
Sales	2,000	2,400	2,800	3,100	
Profit before tax	400	280	20	168	Assume Corporation Tax of 50%
Dividend	65	65	—	20	
Ordinary share capital	900	1,200	1,200	1,200	Shares of £1 each
Share premium	—	126	126	126	
Other reserves	172	212	222	276	
10% Unsecured loan stock	400	400	400	400	
15% Debenture stock redeemable in 7/9 years	—	—	400	400	
Trade creditors	228	272	322	700	
Taxation	150	200	120	60	
Bank overdraft	—	—	90	194	
Total capital and liabilities	1,850	2,410	2,880	3,356	
Land and buildings	300*	400	600	750	*At cost 11 years earlier
Other fixed assets	780	800	780	806	At cost less depreciation
Stocks	400	700	900	1,150	
Trade debtors	280	450	600	650	
Cash	90	60	—	—	
Total assets	1,850	2,410	2,880	3,356	

		£	£	£	£
Share price during year:	Mean	3·50	1·80	0·60	0·63
	High	3·70	2·44	1·40	0·70
	Low	2·00	1·54	0·40	0·47

Appendix. Data relating to companies typical of high and low p/e ratio groups in the same industry:

Company	*Earnings per share* (£)	*Dividend (after ACT 35%)* (£)	*Dividend cover (times)*	*Dividend (gross)* (£)	*Share price (recent)* (£)	*p/e ratio*	*Dividend yield* (%)
A	0·08	0·02	4	0·03	0·80	10	4
B	0·15	0·05	3	0·08	2·25	15	3

The board has asked you to:

(*a*) Give your analysis of the recent performance and possible future prospects of the company, based on the figures in the summary of results.

(*b*) Advise the chairman: (i) of the grounds, if any, on which to recommend to the shareholders to reject the expected bid, having regard to the figures shown in the accounts and to the results of comparable businesses, and (ii) what defensive measures the board might take to avoid this particular bid or at least to obtain a higher offer. For this purpose your attention is directed to the statistics for companies A and B which have been extracted from the financial press this week and are reproduced in the appendix above. A and B are typical of two categories of company within the industry group to which PQR Ltd belongs. (CIMA)

This question is concerned primarily with analysis and diagnosis of past performance together with a subjective assessment of prospects, relating any statistics computed to the situation as described. Under examination conditions the volume of such statistics computed would be restricted by time, so attention must therefore be given to key ratios in each area. In practice there is no such time limit and an almost endless permutation of ratios can be computed. The tendency to produce such an endless array must, however, be resisted as the resultant confusion may hinder rather than aid interpretation. In answering Part (*a*) the relevant data have been produced in order to clarify the source of the calculations. Such repetition would not be necessary if working in a situation where time is at a premium. The use of indices related to a common base of 100 for 19x3 enables movements and trends to be compared but also at the same time enables a change between any two years to be computed as a percentage by simply subtracting the indices concerned, thus:

Sales 19x3 = £2,000,000 Index £2,000,000 = 100

19x4 = £2,400,000 $\frac{£2,400,000}{£2,000,000} \times 100 = 120$

19x5 = £2,800,000 $\frac{£2,800,000}{£2,000,000} \times 100 = 140$

This is the same as saying sales for 19x4 were 20 per cent higher than 19x3 and for 19x5 were 40 per cent higher than 19x3. The percentage change of 19x5 *relative* to 19x4 would, however, be 16·7 per cent as in this case the change is being measured relative to the immediately preceding period.

(a) *Analysis and Diagnosis of Performance*

	Data identity	(£000)				*Indices 19x3 = 100*			
		19x3	*19x4*	*19x5*	*19x6*	*19x3*	*19x4*	*19x5*	*19x6*
Sales	1	2,000	2,400	2,800	3,100	100	120	140	155
Profit (before tax)	2	400	280	20	168	100	70	5	42
Dividend	3	65	65	—	20	100	100	—	31
Ordinary share capital	4	900	1,200	1,200	1,200	100	133	133	133
Share premium	5	—	126	126	126	—			
Other reserves	6	172	212	232	276				
Equity	7 = 4 + 5 + 6	1,072	1,538	1,548	1,602	100	143	144	149
10% Unsecured loan	8	400	400	400	400	100	100	100	100
15% Debentures	9	—	—	400	400				
Total loan stock	10 = 8 + 9	400	400	800	800	100	100	200	200
Trade creditors	11	228	272	322	700	100	119	141	307
Taxation	12	150	200	120	60	100	133	80	40
Bank overdraft	13	—	—	90	194				
Total creditors	14 = 11 + 12 + 13	378	472	532	954	100	130	156	182
Capital and liabilities	15 = 7 + 10 + 14	1,850	2,410	2,880	3,356	100	130	156	181
Assets									
Land and buildings	16	300	400	600	750	100	133	200	250
Other fixed assets	17	780	800	780	806	100	103	100	103
Total fixed	18 = 16 + 17	1,080	1,200	1,380	1,556	100	111	128	144
Stocks	19	400	700	900	1,150	100	175	225	287
Trade debtors	20	280	450	600	650	100	161	214	232
Cash	21	90	60	—	—	100	66	—	—
Total current	22 = 19 + 20 + 21	770	1,210	1,500	1,800	100	157	195	234
Total assets	23 = 18 + 22	1,850	2,410	2,880	3,356	100	130	156	181
Interest payments									
10% Unsecured loan	24 = 8 × 0·10	40	40	40	40	100	100	100	100
15% Debenture	25 = 9 × 0·15	—	—	60	60				
Overdraft (assume 10%)	26 = 13 × 0·10			9	19				
Total interest	27 = 24 + 25 + 26	40	40	109	119	100	100	272	298
Profit before interest and tax	28 = 2 + 27	440	320	129	287	100	73	29	65
Profit after interest and tax	29 = 2 × 50%	200	140	10	84				
Earnings per share	$30 = \frac{29}{900}$	22p	—	—	—				
	$\frac{29}{1,200}$	—	11·7p	0·83p	7p				
		(£)	(£)	(£)	(£)				
Share price: Mean	31	3·50	1·80	0·60	0·63				
High	32	3·70	2·44	1·40	0·70				
Low	33	2·00	1·54	0·40	0·47				

Ratios	*Data identity*	*19x3*	*19x4*	*19x5*	*19x6*
Performance		(%)	(%)	(%)	(%)
$\frac{\text{Net profit (before tax)}}{\text{Capital employed}}$	$34 = \frac{2}{7 + 10}$	27	14	1	7
$\frac{\text{Net profit (after tax)}}{\text{Equity capital}}$	$35 = \frac{29}{7}$	19	9	1	5
$\frac{\text{Operating profit}}{\text{Total assets}}$	$36 = \frac{28}{23}$	24	13	4	9
$\frac{\text{Operating profit}}{\text{Fixed assets}}$	$37 = \frac{28}{18}$	41	27	9	18

Ratios	Data identity	19x3	19x4	19x5	19x6
Control					
*Working capital	38 = 22:14	2·0	2·6	2·8	1·9
*Quick assets	39 = 20 + 21:14	1·0	1·1	1·1	0·7
Stock (days)	$40 = \frac{19}{1} \times 365$	73	106	117	135
Debtors (days)	$41 = \frac{20}{1} \times 365$	51	68	78	77
Trade creditors (days)	$42 = \frac{11}{1} \times 365$	42	41	42	82
Financial					
p/e ratio Mean	$43 = \frac{31}{30}$	15·9	15·4	72·3	9·0
High	$44 = \frac{32}{30}$	16·8	20·9	168·7	10·0
Low	$45 = \frac{33}{30}$	9·09	13·2	48·2	6·7
Assets/share	$46 = \frac{23 - 10 - 14}{900}$	£1·19	—	—	—
	$\frac{23 - 10 - 14}{1,200}$	—	£1·28	£1·29	£1·34
Loans/Total capital	47 = 10:15	0·22	0·17	0·28	0·24
Total creditors/ Total capital	48 = 10 + 14:15	0·42	0·36	0·46	0·52
Loans/Net capital	49 = 10:7 + 10	0·27	0·21	0·34	0·33

* *Note.* The position of the 'taxation' item in the accounts summary—between trade creditors and bank overdraft—suggests it is all currently due, and hence its inclusion in these ratios. In practice it would comprise *provision* for future tax, which would be excluded, and current tax, which would be included, and the relative amounts would be known. With the data given one would be equally justified in omitting taxation from these ratios provided it was stated that it was assumed taxation was not currently due.

(b) Interpretation

Over the four-year period sales have increased in value by 55 per cent whereas profit has declined by 58 per cent of the 19x3 figure. No intimation is given that the results have been adjusted for inflation and sales volume change is, therefore, presumably a combination of volume and price changes. Stocks, debtors and trade creditors have increased consistently over the period at a greater rate than sales, suggesting poor management in control of working capital. The cash position too requires explanation. Share capital was increased by £300,000 in 19x4 with an attached share premium of £126,000. Additional loan capital was raised in 19x5 of £400,000, giving a total capital injection from external sources of £826,000. During the period £450,000 has been added to land and buildings, but as other fixed assets show hardly any movement the balance has gone to finance working capital, yet at the same time the cash position has moved from a favourable balance of £90,000 in 19x3 to an overdraft of £194,000 in 19x6 and the 10 per cent unsecured loan is due for redemption by 19x8.

During the period all profit ratios have fallen consistently except for 19x6. It is the change between 19x5 and 19x6 which is the critical one. If the favourable movement is the forerunner of consistent and rapid growth—which may be the reason for investment in land and buildings and working capital—then the Board may have a case for rejecting the bid. Purely on the figures for the past four years their management performance does not inspire confidence. Profits and dividends have declined consistently and seriously in absolute and relative terms. The state of the other fixed assets is critical as it is difficult to see how extra expenditure will not be due here shortly unless the nature of the business is warehousing or merchanting. This may be supported by the assumption that as stocks have increased storage accommodation has been required for them, but all the classic indications of overtrading are present.

The value of the assets per share based on book values is £1·34, which is almost double the highest market price of 19x6 and equivalent almost to the highest market price of 19x5. The land and buildings added since 19x4 will be at fairly recent prices so the questionable figures are how much is the land and buildings which cost £300,000 worth now and would any surplus offset any possible losses on enforced liquidation of current assets in the event of ceasing trading? Assuming they would near enough balance out, the p/e ratio reflects the market valuation on an earnings basis since the range for 19x6 is from 7 to 10 compared with Company A (at 10) and Company B (at 15), i.e. the share is underpriced on an assets basis and this may be a reason for the bid.

(i) The offered price is 84p against a high market price for 19x6 of 70p and an asset price of £1·34. Earnings per share for 19x6 were 7p and the p/e ratio produced by the group offer would, therefore, be 12. This compares with the external companies of 10 and 15 respectively for A and B and A also has the more similar statistics in terms of performance. The primary basis for rejection of the bid lies factually in the probable higher worth of the assets and potentially in the strength of the case of future developments beginning to come to fruition. This must be very convincing to override the poor past performance and there is not sufficient information really to assess future prospects.

(ii) Defensive measures are:

1. Confirm the real value of the assets preferably by independent valuers. This will provide a firm minimum value for defence or negotiation and will give time for preparation of an alternative case. The shareholder is unlikely to be pressurised into a quick acceptance if it can be demonstrated that he is handing over assets 'at a discount', i.e. at less than their market worth.

2. Publish the details of the 'development of the company which has been quietly planned over the last few years'. Individual shareholders can then make their own assessment of the prospects and situation.

3. Consider approaching an alternative purchaser. If there is another interested party then the offer prices will be adjusted according to the genuine desire and strength of the relevant bidding parties.

4. Consider a capital reconstruction or revision. This may be by means of extra shares to widen the equity base and provide replacement for the £400,000 due for redemption in 19x6/x8, possibly by some form of convertible security. Again it depends upon the ability of the company to show that its plans and the profits associated with it are very much better than the recent past would suggest.

Admittedly the 19x6 accounts are 'at the printers' and therefore shareholders are not yet in possession of this information. The directors will have to convince shareholders that the combination of these actual results and the poor liquidity position are more than offset by the special skills and prospects revealed by the plan. There is no realistic alternative to the Board opening up and 'laying itself on the line' publicly.

Questions

1. The company by which you are employed as a financial analyst is looking for new managers, including new senior financial management. It might be prepared to make offers to people currently employed by other companies and has identified the AB Group plc as a potential source of suitable candidates.

Your attention has been drawn to the recent annual reports of AB Group plc, extracts from which are reproduced in the Appendix to this question.

You are required to prepare detailed analyses of the strategic and financial management of AB Group plc over the years 19x4–19x6 inclusive, with summaries of your conclusions on the way in which the Group has been managed and financed.

Appendix to Question 1

AB Group plc
Consolidated Profit and Loss Account

for the Years ended 31st December	*Notes*	*19x4* £000	*19x5* £000	*19x6* £000
Turnover		10,279	9,683	9,133
Cost of sales		11,252	9,337	8,827
Gross profit/(loss)		(973)	346	306
Distribution costs		229	224	135
Administrative expenses		266	279	277
Trading loss		(1,468)	(157)	(106)
Other operating income		158	220	102
Investment income		523	500	315
		(787)	563	311
Interest payable		613	398	230
Profit/(loss) on ordinary activities before taxation	*1 & 2*	(1,400)	165	81
Tax on profit on ordinary activities		17	171	7
Profit/(loss) on ordinary activities after taxation		(1,417)	(6)	74
Minority interests		—	1	1
Profit/(loss) before extraordinary items		(1,417)	(7)	73
Extraordinary items	*3*	1,650	(29)	45
Profit/(loss) for the financial year		233	(36)	118
Dividends paid and proposed		(36)	(48)	(54)
(Loss)/retained profit for the year		197	(84)	64

AB Group plc
Consolidated Balance Sheet at 31st December

for the Years ended 31st December	*Notes*	*19x4* £000	*19x5* £000	*19x6* £000
Fixed assets				
Tangible assets	4	8,580	4,949	5,808
Investments		8	7	—
		8,588	4,956	5,808
Current assets				
Stocks	5	1,265	1,112	1,061
Debtors		2,245	1,960	2,166
Deposits		4,077	3,859	450
Other investments	6	23	33	33
Cash at bank and in hand		324	512	1,823
		7,934	7,476	5,533
Creditors: amounts falling due within one year	7	4,489	4,167	2,824
Net current assets		3,445	3,309	2,709
Total assets *less* current liabilities		12,033	8,265	8,517
Creditors: amounts falling due after more than one year	7	(4,539)	(1,663)	(1,435)
Provisions for liabilities and charges		(460)	(106)	(519)
Minority interests		(2)	(14)	(15)
		7,032	6,482	6,548
Capital and reserves				
Called-up share capital		598	598	598
Share premium account		4	4	4
Profit and loss account	8	6,430	5,880	5,946
		7,032	6,482	6,548

Consolidated Statement of Source and Application of Funds

for the Years ended 31st December	£000	*19x4* £000	£000	*19x5* £000	£000	*19x6* £000
Source of funds						
Profit/(loss) before taxation		(1,400)		165		81
Adjust items not involving the movement of funds:						
Depreciation		785		617		707
Other		138		(38)		(52)
Total funds generated from operations		(477)		744		736
Other sources:						
Proceeds from disposal of tangible fixed assets	6,193		4,001		71	
Proceeds from disposal of shares	29		—		30	

for the Years ended 31st December		*19x4*		*19x5*		*19x6*
	£000	£000	£000	£000	£000	£000
Deposits withdrawn	—		208		3,409	
Loan stock	—		600		—	
Secured bank loans	3,187		—		870	
Issue of share capital	5		—		—	
		9,414		4,809		4,380
		8,937		5,553		5,116
Application of funds						
Purchase of tangible fixed assets	5,235		572		1,705	
Acquisition of subsidiaries (*Note A*)	44		600		7	
Deposits	968		—		—	
Loan stock repaid	—		1,321		600	
Bank loans repaid	3,348		3,376		1,220	
Dividends paid	30		36		48	
Taxation paid	16		16		21	
	9,641		5,921		3,601	
Movement in working capital (*Note B*)	(800)		(525)		417	
		8,841		5,396		4,018
Increase in net liquid funds		96		157		1,098

	19x4	*19x5*	*19x6*
	£000	£000	£000
Note A *Acquisition of subsidiaries*			
Net assets acquired:			
Tangible fixed assets	—	9	—
Stock and working capital	—	2	—
Liquid funds	—	124	7
Other	7	—	—
Goodwill	37	465	—
	44	600	7
NOTE B *Movement in working capital*			
Stocks—			
Decrease/(increase)	(48)	220	51
Debtors—			
Decrease/(increase)	1,957	213	(182)
Creditors—			
Increase/(decrease)	(1,109)	92	(286)
	800	525	(417)

Notes to the Accounts

1. *Analysis of turnover and profit before tax*

	19x4		19x5		19x6	
Class of business	*Turnover*	*Profit*	*Turnover*	*Profit*	*Turnover*	*Profit*
	£000	£000	£000	£000	£000	£000
Marine engineering	3,362	124	3,815	155	4,052	200
Shipping	3,541	(1,634)	1,967	(213)	1,921	(149)
Fishing	1,546	141	2,082	106	1,892	(155)
Fish merchandising (discontinued 19x7)	1,774	(24)	1,335	(34)	505	(28)
Security services (acquired 1st May 19x5)	—	—	409	46	676	123
Marine consultancy	41	24	65	37	82	46
Travel services (discontinued 19x6)	15	(5)	10	(7)	5	(13)
Profit adjustments—discontinued insurance business	—	(62)	—	38	—	—
	10,279	(1,436)	9,683	128	9,133	24
Unattributed income		36		37		57
Profit on ordinary activities before tax		(1,400)		165		81

2. *Employees*

The average number of persons employed by the group each year was:

	19x4	*19x5*	*19x6*
	000	000	000
Engineering	88	83	82
Shipping	61	33	27
Fishing	82	103	91
Fish merchandising	34	21	8
Security services	—	5	5
Other	6	7	11
	271	252	224
Employee costs (£000) were	2,342	2,128	2,017

3. *Extraordinary items*

	19x4	*19x5*	*19x6*
	£000	£000	£000
Net surplus on disposal of ships	1,650	(29)	88
Surplus on disposal of shares in subsidiaries	—	—	41
Costs on closure of fish merchandising company	—	—	(84)
	1,650	(29)	45

4. *Tangible fixed assets* (Net book value)

	19x4	*19x5*	*19x6*
	£000	£000	£000
Ships	6,792	3,118	2,616
Ships under construction	—	—	1,402
Fishing vessels	1,005	1,062	1,051
Land and buildings	540	497	487
Machinery, equipment and motor vehicles	243	272	252
	8,580	4,949	5,808

5. *Stocks*

	19x4	*19x5*	*19x6*
	£000	£000	£000
Raw materials and consumables	146	143	221
Work-in-progress	68	58	112
Finished goods and goods for resale	1,051	911	728
	1,265	1,112	1,061

6. *Current asset investments*
These are mainly deposits, part of which are hypothecated as security for loans.

7. *Creditors*

	19x4	*19x5*	*19x6*
	£000	£000	£000
(*a*) *Due within one year*			
Trade creditors	1,114	1,190	1,036
Secured bank loans	949	418	260
Overdrafts	162	68	275
Loan stock	1,321	600	—
Corporation tax	226	1,173	693
Other	717	718	560
	4,489	4,167	2,824
(*b*) *Due after one year*			
Secured bank loans	4,539	1,571	1,343
Others	—	92	92
	4,539	1,663	1,435

All secured bank loans are secured against mortgages on specific ships and vessels.

8. *Reserves—Profit and loss account*

	19x4	*19x5*	*19x6*
	£000	£000	£000
At beginning of year		6,430	5,880
Profit/(loss) for year	197	(84)	64
Currency adjustments		(1)	2
Goodwill written off		(465)	
At end of year	6,430	5,880	5,946

(CIMA)

2. (*a*) Two companies, S plc and T plc, are engaged in the exploitation of similar mineral resources, involving highly specialised skills and considerable investment in exploration and site development costs.

Current statistics relating to the two companies are as follows:

	S plc	*T plc*
Number of shares in issue	1,064,000	800,000
Earnings	£165,000	£239,000
Earnings per share	15·5p	29·9p
Stock market price per share	£1·03	£2·40
Price/earnings ratio	6·6	8·0

Over recent years, S plc has provided its shareholders with high rates of growth in both dividends and share prices. Its plans for the next three years, however, show that the company will not have the financial strength to cope with the need for expansion within an increasingly competitive market. This is believed to be a problem only in the medium term, beyond which the prospects could be very good. T plc has not been so aggressive in exploration, but by prudent exploitation of its resources it has managed to maintain relatively stable earnings and dividends per share. Its p/e ratio is higher than that of S plc and is also in the upper quartile for the industry as a whole. The board of T plc now realises, however, that unless it undertakes major new exploration its profits are likely to peak during the next three years and then decline significantly. Unfortunately, its past policy has left the company short of certain necessary skills which are possessed in abundance by S plc.

The boards of the two companies have therefore been exploring the possibility of a merger based, so far, on the assumption that shares in T plc will be issued in exchange for the existing shares in S plc.

They are uncertain at this stage whether the number of T plc shares to be issued to the existing shareholders in S plc should be calculated by reference to the current stock market prices of shares in the two companies or whether S plc should be valued for the purpose of the merger at a p/e ratio of 8·0.

You are required to:

(i) Calculate and comment on the effects of these two alternative methods on the earnings and share values attributable to the shareholders in each company.

(ii) Indicate what factors might influence the choice of p/e ratio to be used.

(*b*) While the above merger discussions are in progress, an independent company, U plc, makes a cash offer of £1·60 per share to S plc shareholders.

You are required to explain:

(i) The main possible differences in procedures and in the form of consideration between a merger and a takeover bid.

(ii) Possible reasons why U plc can offer a price as high as £1·60 per share.

(iii) What advice you would give to shareholders in S plc.

(CIMA)

3. (*a*) The following statistics have been extracted from the five most recent years' accounts of L plc, a company engaged in transport operations.

Years ended 30th June	*19x2*	*19x3*	*19x4*	*19x5*	*19x6*
Ratios					
Profit before tax: Shareholders' funds plus long-term loans ('Total capital employed')	12·0%	12·8%	9·6%	6·9%	2·5%
Profit before tax: Sales	6·0%	5·8%	5·3%	5·7%	2·8%
Sales: Total capital employed	2·0x	2·2x	1·8x	1·2x	0·9x
Current ratio (:1)	0·9	0·8	0·9	0·7	0·5

Years ended 30th June	*19x2*	*19x3*	*19x4*	*19x5*	*19x6*
Ratios					
Total debt (current and long-term): Shareholders' funds	7·0x	6·8x	7·6x	9·1x	12·1x
Retained profit: Shareholders' funds	14·9%	17·9%	18·2%	20·3%	9·5%
Retained profit: Operating profit	20·0%	20·9%	16·7%	17·8%	8·3%
Interest cover	2·3x	2·2x	1·7x	1·7x	1·3x
Index numbers (L plc)					
Sales	100	122	179	215	262
Profit before tax	100	118	159	205	123
Fixed assets	100	125	189	362	590
Total debt	100	116	159	238	348
Long-term debt	100	107	221	431	735

Notes

1. No new issues of shares were made during the period.
2. Dividends remained constant throughout the period.
3. The ratio of Long-term debt to Shareholders' funds at 30th June, 1982 was 2·5:1.

You are required to comment briefly on the circumstances under which these figures might reflect good or bad financial management of the company.

(*b*) Various discriminant analysis models have been developed for the purpose of predicting company failure or changes in financial health.

You are required to:

(i) Give an outline description of any such model known to you.

(ii) Comment on the usefulness of such models to the independent analyst.

(iii) Discuss the extent to which such models can give any clearer indications than could be obtained from a traditional scheme of ratio analysis. (CIMA)

4. V Ltd, a close company controlled by family interests, now holds a 30 per cent stage in the equity of X plc. This interest has been built up over a number of years in the belief that an uninterrupted supply of essential non-traded commodities can be assured. V Ltd's inventories have been cut back as its influence over X plc has become apparent.

Following recent reports of predator activity, the market price of shares in X plc has increased significantly. V Ltd is considering taking advantage of this speculation by realising profits. However, its directors are concerned as to whether any intended bid is likely to make X plc divest itself of less profitable business. This could materially affect V Ltd's interests as the supply of its inputs may be in jeopardy.

A review of X plc's annual report discloses its equity to be dispersed as follows:

	Distribution by	
Number of shares held	*Number of shareholders*	*Shareholding*
1–1,000	60%	2%
1,001–10,000	30%	10%
10,001–25,000	8%	30%
over 25,000*	2%	58%

*Includes V Ltd's holding.

X plc's Articles of Association allow one vote to be cast per share held, so that V Ltd could well determine the outcome of any bid. To assist V Ltd's directors, its management accountant has provided a 'pay-off' matrix quantifying the expected effect on the current market price of X plc's shares, as follows:

	V Ltd decides to:		
	accept	*decline*	*sell out*
Others accept	−5%	−5%	0%
Others decline	−15%	−20%	0%

If the bid is successful it is recognised that the earnings per share (of the exchanged shares) will improve once X plc's facilities have been restructured. Such restructuring is likely to involve extraordinary charges against profits. If the offer is declined, X plc's management will interpret the outcome as a vindication of its low dividend policy. V Ltd's directors may try to vacillate until it is clear what the attitudes of the other shareholders are likely to be. They are anxious, however, not to be left with a minority interest.

You are required to:

(*a*) Evaluate the options open to the directors of V Ltd and identify the one you would recommend.

(*b*) Assess the strategic implications to V Ltd of the decision you have recommended.

(*c*) Explain what the advantages are to the shareholders of V Ltd of partial vertical integration with a supplier of major inputs. (CIMA)

5. What financial benefits would you expect to accrue as the result of a merger of two similar companies? Do you agree that the consequences of such a union would necessarily be beneficial? (SCCA)

6. In the role of financial director, explain to your board the steps it should pursue to resist an offer for the shares of the company that has just been received. (SCCA)

7. You are the financial manager of a medium-sized engineering firm XYZ Ltd which has just reported record profits of £250,000, after tax and interest and preference dividends, and declared an ordinary dividend of 15 per cent. Despite the record profits, which maintain the previous pattern of overall growth but with cyclical fluctuations, the company has been faced with liquidity problems which have restricted its operational flexibility.

XYZ Ltd has received a suggestion from ABC Ltd that the two companies should consider merging. ABC Ltd is a relatively new company—formed six years previously—which has had a spectacular and consistent growth in profit and whose products complement those of XYZ Ltd. The most recent profits of ABC Ltd were £375,000 after tax and interest, with an ordinary dividend of 10 per cent. The reason for suggesting the merger given by ABC Ltd is that they have also been having liquidity problems and that an enlarged size could help overcome these. ABC's initial approach did not go into any detail but simply suggests that exploratory talks should be opened and that to make these talks purposeful they should assume that both company's profits will increase by 10 per cent in the next period and that for amalgamation purposes a fair p/e ratio would be 15 for ABC and 10 for XYZ.

The executive directors have called a meeting to discuss the matter and have asked you to analyse the implications of ABC's suggestion and to list the factors which should be considered at this stage in respect of this analysis.

The summary of the most recent balance sheets of ABC Ltd and XYZ Ltd is as follows:

Summary Balance Sheets for Year Ended . . .

	ABC Ltd	*XYZ Ltd*
Net assets	£3,000,000	£2,500,000
Share capital—ordinary £1 shares	£750,000	£400,000
6% preference shares	—	100,000
Reserves	1,500,000	2,000,000
10% loan stock	750,000	—
	£3,000,000	£2,500,000

(CACA)

8. A conglomerate company, L Ltd, is considering investing cash up to £200,000 in an industry where, due to depressed market conditions, share prices are currently below a previous peak.

Two companies in that industry, M Ltd and N Ltd, which are similar in many respects, appear to be suitable candidates for acquisition. It has been decided to select the company having the management team which has demonstrated the greater improvement in financial control over the past year.

The latest balance sheet and profit and loss account of each of the two companies, together with comparative figures, are summarised below:

	M Ltd		*N Ltd*	
	Last year	*This year*	*Last year*	*This year*
Balance sheets	£	£	£	£
Fixed assets, at cost	290,000	310,000	220,000	300,000
less depreciation	150,000	175,000	101,000	141,000
	140,000	135,000	119,000	159,000
Stocks	30,000	50,000	40,000	30,000
Work-in-progress	60,000	70,000	100,000	100,000
Debtors	70,000	80,000	95,000	90,000
Cash	39,500	5,000	21,000	1,000
	£339,500	£340,000	£375,000	£380,000
Ordinary shares, £1 each	50,000	50,000	40,000	40,000
Undistributed profits	149,300	150,000	172,000	170,000
Loan stock:				
4% 19y5/z0	60,000	60,000		
9% 19x3/x4			80,000	80,000
Current taxation	2,200	500	3,000	—
Sundry creditors	78,000	79,500	80,000	90,000
	£339,500	£340,000	£375,000	£380,000
Profit and loss accounts	£	£	£	£
Sales	600,000	500,000	680,000	600,000
Increase in stocks and work-in-progress	—	30,000	—	—
	£600,000	£530,000	£680,000	£600,000
Purchases	380,000	340,000	450,000	410,000
Productive wages	100,000	90,000	80,000	70,000
Decrease in stocks and work-in-progress	26,000	—	48,500	10,000
Selling costs	37,000	40,000	42,000	42,000
Administrative costs	24,000	28,000	20,000	21,000
Depreciation	25,000	25,000	30,000	40,000
Loan stock interest	2,400	2,400	7,200	7,200
Exceptional costs	—	3,400	—	1,800
Net profit (loss)	5,600	1,200	2,300	(2,000)
	£600,000	£530,000	£680,000	£600,000

You are required:

(*a*) To analyse the figures and to recommend, with reasons, which company would provide the better investment.

(*b*) Given the following additional information, to state the approximate price per share that might be offered for the ordinary shares of M Ltd.

Five year profit record, before tax:

Year	£	
1	3,500	
2	3,500	
3	4,000	
4	5,600	as shown above
5	1,200	as shown above

There has been no change in the ordinary share capital over the five years. Current market price of shares in M Ltd is £0·60 each. Opportunity cost of capital for L Ltd is 15 per cent before taxation.

(CIMA)

9

ACCOUNTING UNDER INFLATIONARY CONDITIONS

The Nature of Inflation

At the outset it might be helpful to consider what inflation is so as to understand its general effects and more particularly its effects upon business, to which this chapter is devoted.

Basically, inflation refers to the falling value of money, and its outward characteristic is a general increase in the prices of all goods and services. It is fundamentally caused by an undue increase in the quantity of money in proportion to buying power, or the amount of money in circulation in relation to the goods or wealth created. The amount of money may be increased by lack of control, particularly of all forms of borrowing which increases potential purchasing power or increases in earnings without comparable increases in wealth produced, or by direct government action in increasing the currency in circulation.

Once a momentum is established the effects can become serious to the nation, with all sectors striving to correct their purchasing power by increased income which quickly generates further increases in prices as the producers of goods and services redress the pressures upon them.

All price increases may not, however, be due to the process of inflation itself, although the collective effects are the same. The normal effects of supply and demand still operate to aggravate or sometimes arrest the situation. World-wide failure of harvests creates international shortages of food for people and domestic animals, resulting in increased prices which permeate the consumer networks; a recent long dry summer affected agricultural output adversely with consequential shortages and higher prices, but favourable outcomes were good harvests of tomatoes and hard fruits, which at least prevented price increases for these commodities.

Supply and demand of the currency itself on the open market can have its effect upon prices. Changes in the international terms of trade can also mean inflationary increases in the prices of imports.

Inflation has been recognised as a progressive phenomenon through the ages with aggravated phases occurring in times of national calamity, particularly wars, when national output is concentrated upon war production made essentially for destruction. A graphic interpretation of price levels from 1661 to 1975 in log scale (Fig. 21), has been presented by *News of the Week*, to whom acknowledgments are extended for its reproduction.

The Impact of Inflation upon a Business

The effects of inflation upon a business can briefly be described as distorting its profit performance and valuations of its capital, which in turn affects the judgments and decisions of its management and in addition its shareholders, investors and the government through its fiscal officers.

The immediate operating effects are upon the cash flow of the business, with

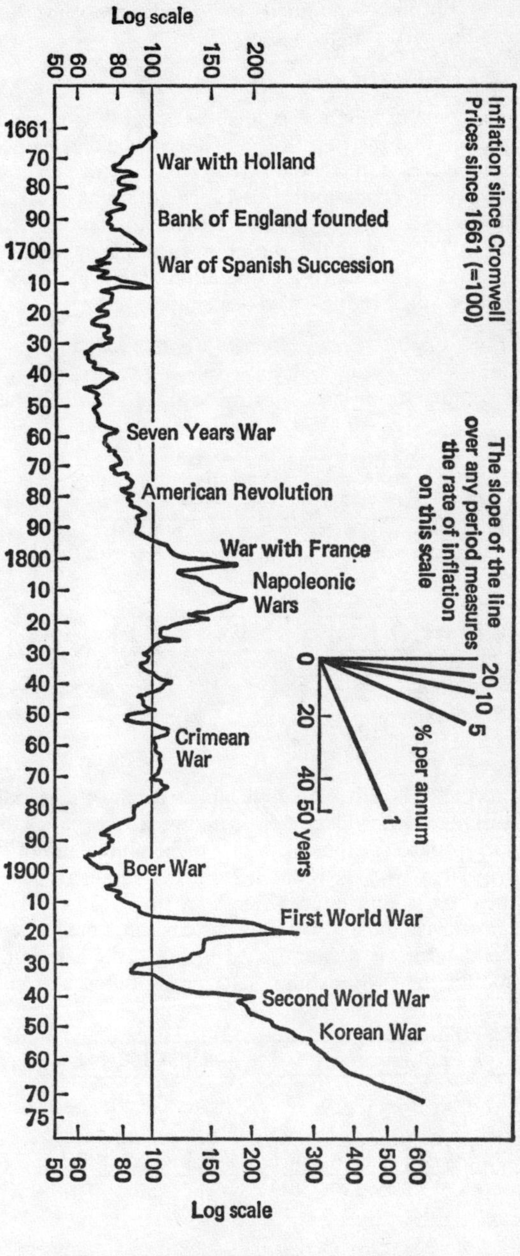

Fig. 21. Getting inflation into perspective.

emphasis upon what the inflowing cash can acquire in real terms, and it is proposed to examine these problems under three headings—working capital, fixed capital, and profits—and finally to consider problems of communication in the form of financial statements.

Working Capital

An early outcome of inflation is to divert cash flow more extensively into working capital in that increases in costs have to be met as incurred and until a compensating increase in income is received. The time-span of the cash flow cycle will subsequently contain this cost increase which invariably will be of a rising nature because of the continuing effects of inflation itself.

The longer it takes to make the compensating increases in sales prices (because of market resistance or the operation of official bodies for controlling prices), the longer will be the period of peak impact upon the working capital.

Normal Working Capital Cycle: Material Content only

In a stable business cycle, material requirements will progress consistently through the manufacturing processes up to the stage when the finished work

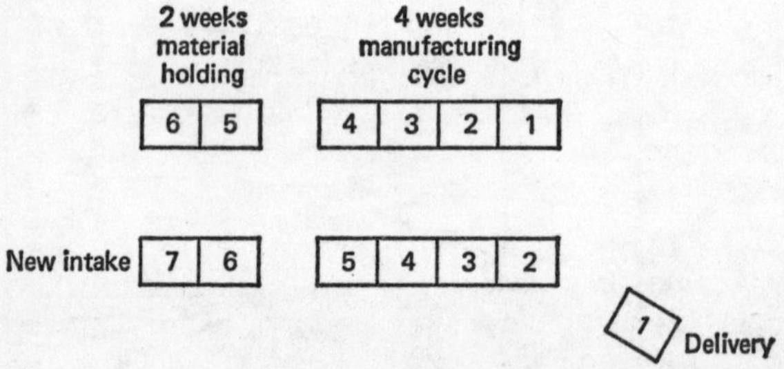

Fig. 22

is delivered to the customer. The first intake batch of materials becomes the first batch of finished products. Sequentially each week all batches of pro grammed work progress, exposing a gap at the intake end of the cycle which is immediately filled by a new batch from the suppliers. Thus the material content of the cycle is kept intact (Fig. 22).

The cash flow cycle must also cover the customer credit period, which, on four-week credit terms, is demonstrated in Fig. 23. There is thus a constant waiting period for the cash income of 10 weeks, but the effect upon the cash

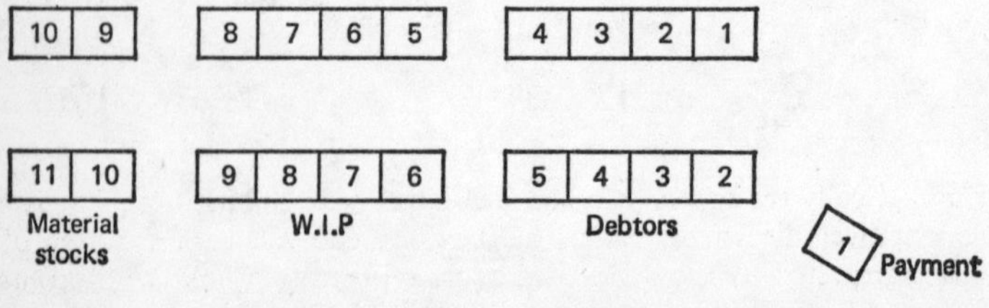

Fig. 23

flow is alleviated by any credit to suppliers for the payment in respect of materials received.

Effects of Material Price Increases

Any price increase must be absorbed into the 10-week cash flow cycle and will need to be sustained as additional working capital until such time as any selling price increase in compensation can be effected (see Fig. 24).

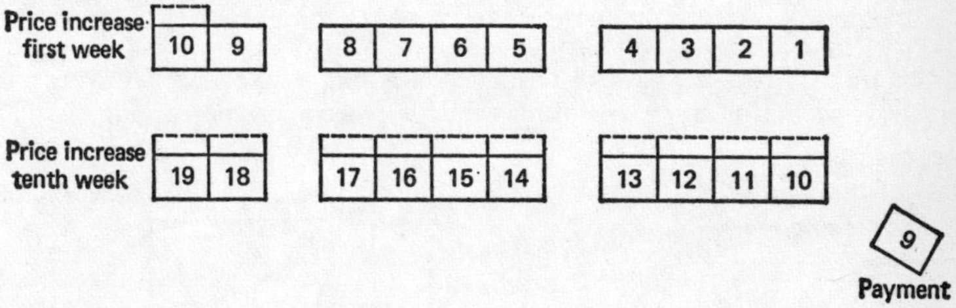

Fig. 24

The recoupment via the sales value from week 10 onwards will be at the pre-increase level (until the selling price can be increased) and therefore this cost increase will be a constant drain upon the liquid resources in the form of reduced profits after the investment build-up.

Normal Working Capital Cycle: Total Cost Content

Inflation also has effects upon wages and expenses and therefore the impact of all cost increases upon working capital can be more fully demonstrated as in Fig. 25. The triangular shape of the four-week manufacturing cycle shows

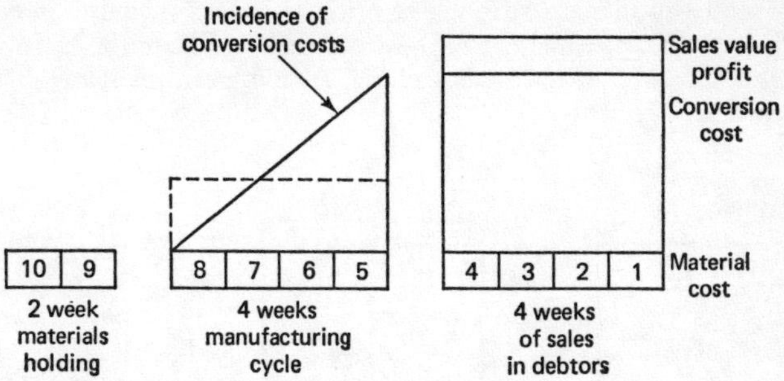

Fig. 25

diagrammatically the increase in costs as items near completion. The average investment over the whole cycle would be the equivalent of the area of the triangle interpreted by the dotted rectangle representing half the total labour cost applicable to the particular quantities in the manufacturing cycle.

Before Cost Increases

The working capital investment in stocks and debtors will therefore be—

Material stocks:	At cost
WIP stocks:	Materials at cost
	Conversion cost—at cost
Debtors:	At sales values comprising:
	Total cost and Profit

Effects of Increases in Total Cost

When an all-round phase of cost increases has worked itself through the cash flow cycle, the new investmtent position becomes that of Fig. 26. The

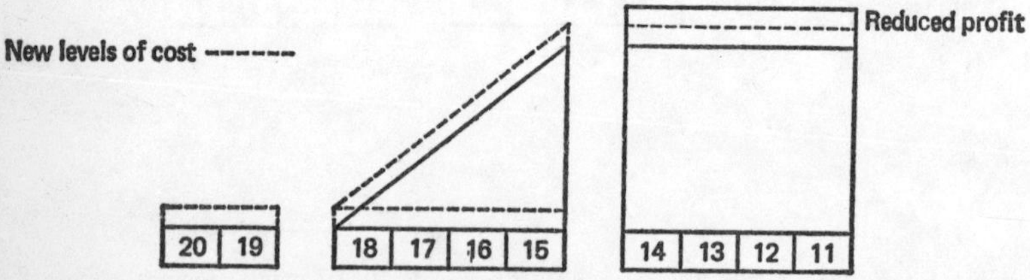

Fig. 26. Investment levels after cost increases.

investment in material stocks and work in progress is now increased by the cost increases for their respective periods of time. With no increases in selling prices the investment in debtors remains as before, but its composition differs in that the profit content is reduced, thus impairing the ability of the business to finance the new higher level of stock investment and other requirements of cash flow such as fixed capital investments.

When eventually an increase in selling prices to redress the position becomes possible there will be a time-lag of the credit period before this is translated into cash inflow and then there will be a permanent increase in debtor investment (Fig. 27).

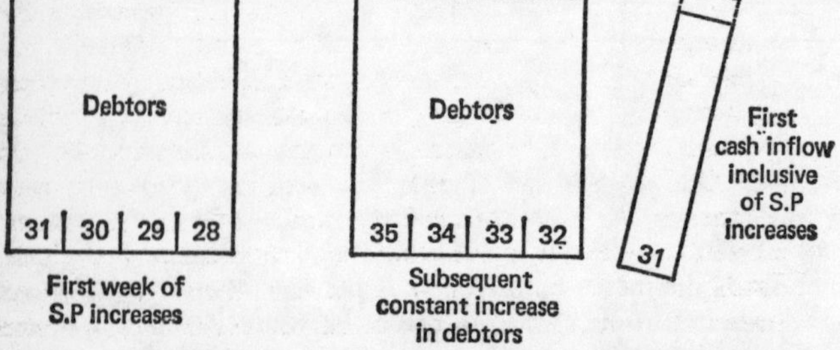

Fig. 27. Effect of selling-price increases on debtors.

Even without inflation the control of working capital can be difficult for management because it arises out of the business operations and in some respects through reasons outside the control of management. If a supplier improves upon his lead time a higher stock level can occur and should a debtor defer payments of his account beyond the normal credit terms, then a higher level of debtors will result. In other respects changes in working capital investment can result from lack of attention, inefficiency or even excess cost reduction operations, such as reducing staff, which can impair the ability to control.

The adverse effects of inflation upon working capital brings an aggravation, to the point of danger, of the normal problems experienced in exercising control, so that management must redouble its efforts with the aim of neutralising the inflationary effects by even greater effectiveness in the areas where this is possible. Some such areas are:

(*a*) Cost reductions by buying resistance causing lower prices, and changes in quality or grade of materials, alternative materials, reductions of waste and abortive effort.

(*b*) Improvements in productivity.

(*c*) Reductions in lost capacity due to machine breakdowns, shortages and lost time.

(*d*) Control of inventories by revising reorder levels, taking more risks of stock-out and ensuring that control procedures are effective.

(*e*) Re-examining credit terms on sales, establishing careful credit control procedures and effective implementation.

(*f*) Simplifying the product through design.

(*g*) Value analysis—the organised elimination of all but the functional features of the product.

(*h*) Work simplification—the re-planning of all work cycles to eliminate waste effort and ensure the most effective use of resources.

The natural desire is to increase selling prices to offset the effects of inflation on costs as soon as possible, which of course is the very inflationary spiral which makes matters worse. Certainly the business needs to be sensitive to its market and the effect increased prices could have upon the demand for its products. Any fall in volume would tend to bring more problems for the business.

Fixed Capital

The first problem the business meets with fixed assets is the effect of inflation upon their replacement. The problem is twofold in that the general increase in costs reduces the cash flow available for investment and that the replacement cost of an asset can vastly exceed its original purchase price. So to maintain its capacity the business must find increasing sums from a depleting source of funds upon which there is exerted an already growing pressure for extra working capital. Growth through new assets thus becomes a more difficult proposition.

The practical solution is adequacy of profit and depreciation, with the latter more appropriately geared to replacement value. This means taking conscious steps to evaluate future trends of replacement values and more carefully reviewing the needs of the business expressed in up-to-date values so as to express profit targets more realistically. This then promotes the challenge to management as to the means of achieving the target through product performance and design, effective marketing and efficient production methods.

Emphasis upon replacement values in turn focuses attention upon the shortcomings of interpreting values of fixed assets upon their historical costs. For very many years some companies have recognised this and for the benefits of management and their investors have periodically undertaken a revaluation of their assets, reporting this as a note to the balance sheet or actually incorporating the new information into the balance sheet. Not only does this inform about the value of the business but provides a foundation about the adequacy of profits to maintain or add to these values. Comprehensive revaluations are expensive and even companies undertaking this tend only to do so at intervals so when balance sheets are adjusted any additions during these intervals are introduced at cost. The result then becomes a conglomerate of values usually defined as 'plant and machinery at valuation or cost . . .', and so the usefulness of the operation is diminished.

When revaluations are introduced into the balance sheet certain aspects of accountancy need to be observed about the revaluation mark-up and subsequent depreciation, demonstrated as follows:

An assumed historical interpretation (relevant accounts only):

ASSET A/C

	£		
At cost	10,000		

DEPRECIATION A/C

			£
		5th Year	5,000

BALANCE SHEET

LIABILITIES	ASSETS		
		£	£
	Plant and machinery		
	at cost	10,000	
	less Depreciation	5,000	
			5,000

Upon revaluation at the end of the fifth year of a ten-year life-span, at £7,000:

ASSET A/C

	£		£
At cost	10,000	Dep'n	5,000
Mark-up to capital reserve	2,000	Bal. c/f	7,000
	12,000		12,000
Bal b/fwd.	7,000		

DEPRECIATION A/C

	£		£
Asset	5,000	5th Year	5,000

CAPITAL RESERVE A/C

			£
		Asset a/c	2,000

BALANCE SHEET

LIABILITIES		ASSETS	
	£		£
Capital reserve	2,000	Plant and machinery at valuation	7,000

Subsequently it is necessary to depreciate the new valuation of £7,000 over the remaining five years of the life-span:

DEPRECIATION A/C

		Year	£
		6 P & L a/c	1,400
		7	1,400
		8	1,400
		9	1,400
		10	1,400
			7,000

The asset has now been written down to nil and the capital reserve of £2,000 remains, but there is no asset in existence—assuming at the end of its life it is now not usable. This capital reserve has been compensated by a reduction of profit over the remaining five years of a like amount, and as there are restrictions upon the application of capital reserves, this will remain the position, even if, say, this asset was sold for £200 scrap value, thus:

REALISATION OF ASSET A/C

	£		£
Asset	7,000	Residual income	200
Profit on sale	200	Depreciation	7,000
	7,200		7,200

If, however, at Year 5 the asset was actually sold for the £7,000, and not retained and revaluated, the excess of £2,000 above written down value would accrue as a profit on realisation and could be transferred to the P & L account. It will be seen conversely that the process of revaluation seals the surplus above book value in the capital reserve.

The real benefits of revaluation are derived prior to any resale or scrapping of an asset—namely in providing more adequate information for management control during the life of the various assets. Such information will include:

Depreciation. This should now more adequately reflect the funds required for eventual replacement of assets. It does not of itself provide more cash flow but provides signals about priority claims upon the cash flow available.

Depreciation and Profit and Loss Account. The increased depreciation in turn increases total costs and indicates more clearly the real product profits which, if shown to be inadequate, will bring pressure to increase selling prices. The objective is more specifically to extract adequate income from the customer to provide an appropriate profit *and* to provide for the replacement of the assets without added cash flow strains upon the business.

The above example confined the uplift revision of depreciation to a revaluation incidence during the life of the asset, but if desired the depreciation can be assessed at the outset upon a forecast of replacement value. An important feature is to keep such a forecast up to date and reflecting contemporary trends in values. Methods being advocated for implementing this updating are discussed later in the chapter.

Asset Valuation. In addition to facilitating adequate depreciation to cover replacement values, the revaluations of assets provide helpful guidance about the current value of the business either as an interpretation of the net worth of the business for the investors, or of the capital employed in terms of current purchasing power against which to assess more adequately the profits earned.

Profits

Inflation increases costs and thus erodes profits. A business will strive to compensate by raising selling prices, but this will invariably be with a time-lag. Price may be a more sensitive marketing factor for some businesses where competition is keen and always this action will be against a background of the consumer losing purchasing power through the progressive effects of inflation upon earnings. The timing of selling price increases may be important.

In addition to market resistance, businesses are sometimes subject to Government Control in setting selling prices and require approval for price increases to be implemented. The basis of this approval is a factual demonstration of the impact of cost increases incurred, not all of which may be allowed. Such approved sales price increases will therefore always be some time after the cost increases have been incurred and after time for presentation and adjudication.

A tax concession towards the alleviation of the pressures upon cash flow was operating at the time of writing, but this has been withdrawn. It took the form of reducing the assessable profit by the amount the closing stock had increased above the opening stock. Conversely, a tax increase was incurred if and when subsequently a stock decrease arose.

Inflation by its effect on profits challenges a competent management to take every available compensating step to increase efficiency.

A pertinent consideration regarding profit is what it will buy at present prices—namely, its purchasing power—and comparisons over periods of time must take into consideration this changing interpretation of purchasing power. Various indices are available for interpreting purchasing power at different times, particularly the Retail Price Index. A prerequisite for comparable judgment is therefore to reduce the data, in this case profits, to a common basis of purchasing power, thus:

	Year 1	*Year 2*	*Year 3*
Index	100	120	135
Profit	£150,000	£160,000	£190,000
Profit (index adjusted)	£150,000	£133,333	£140,740

This demonstrates that contrary to the 'money' interpretations of profit in each year the profits in Years 2 and 3 were lower than Year 1 in terms of equivalent purchasing power, with Year 3 showing some improvement over Year 2.

When considering profitability—say, to sales or capital employed—it becomes necessary to ensure that the two sets of data related should be upon a like interpretation for purchasing power. Should they both be subject to the same index of purchasing power, their relationship will be the same whether index adjusted or not. If the index interpretation of the data to be related is different then one or, if necessary, *both* should be adjusted to a common basis of purchasing power before the relationship is demonstrated.

Capital employed provides more problems in this context because it has several different constituents, each of which may be differently affected by the impact of inflation.

Inflation therefore influences the 'money' values conveyed in financial statements, particularly about profit performance and resources, and the high inflation rate of recent years has highlighted the problems of interpretation. Much thought has been given to finding an acceptable means of solving these problems that could be commonly applied throughout business.

The effects of inflation upon a large manufacturing company were well illustrated in a speech delivered in London by the Chairman of Unilever Ltd at the Annual General Meeting in May 1975 and are still appropriate. He pointed out that profit provides for:

1. The replacement and renewal of existing resources.
2. The financing of the additional cost of stocks.
3. The payment for research which brings about technological change and the improvements which are necessary to meet the new environmental standards which society now demands, at the same time bearing in mind that scientific discovery has usually to be incorporated into new physical assets in order to produce its effects.

In viewing the world situation he demonstrated the seriousness of decreasing investments in that in many major countries real profits have shown a continuous tendency to decline over the past decade or more. In the UK this decline was as much as 40 per cent and in the USA 19 per cent. Since capital employed increased considerably, yields on capital employed in industry went down much more; comparing the early 1950s with the early 1970s the net pre-tax profits on net assets in Swedish and British manufacturing virtually halved. Although not the only reason, inflation is adjudged to be the most important reason especially when accompanied by severe price control, and certainly the decline in corporate profitability had been most marked in years when world inflation had dramatically accelerated.

In this connection the chairman revealed that in Unilever Ltd the difference between historical cost depreciation and replacement cost depreciation was almost £30 million in 1974 and £50 million in 1975. Furthermore, the extra working capital to find out of profits was even more devastating. To do approximately the same amount of business at the end of 1974 as at the end of 1973 the company needed £289 million of extra working capital, three times the retained profits in sterling for the year.

If the business cannot find the funds then it contracts and unemployment results. To some extent it is possible to bridge the gap by borrowing providing the business is sound and has good prospects of profitable growth, but borrowing is a short-term remedy only, not a permanent one. For a prudent management it has strict limits, particularly as interest rates are usually high when inflation is rampant. All of this means that when inflation is high, profits expressed in current terms have to rise. (With acknowledgements to the Information Division, Unilever Ltd.)

Inflation Accounting—The General Theory

Published financial statements reflect a company's position on the basis of historic cost, i.e. the amounts reported are based on the actual prices (pounds, dollars, lire or whatever) spent or received without regard to changes in the purchasing power of the monetary unit. While this may be acceptable for stewardship purposes—and even this is very debatable—it certainly does not provide an effective basis for management and decision making. The objective of all entrepreneurs should be to show **real**, not monetary, gains. This can only be demonstrated if changes due to performance are distinguished from monetary or fiscal changes. Academics and economists have long been aware of the varying concepts of profit, income and capital when contrasted with those generally employed by accountants. As long ago as 1949–50 the CIMA researched the problem and in 1952 produced a basic work *The Accountancy of Changing Price Levels*. The previous section attempted to demonstrate what the problems were in relation to working capital and fixed assets. The theorists devised two main approaches: one based on the idea of maintaining the purchasing power of the original investment, and the other on the objective of maintaining the operating capital of the enterprise. Both schools of thought have their adherents and both resulted in the introduction of unsuccessful standards. The main principle behind each category is now illustrated.

Current Purchasing Power (CPP)

Sometimes referred to as Constant Purchasing Power this method attempts to measure the effect that **general** inflation has on historic cost based financial data. In economic terms no profit is made unless the purchasing power of the original capital investment is maintained. In this approach the value of the original capital is adjusted to CPP before accepting that any real profit has been made thus maintaining the monetary value of the original investment.

Example 1

Consider a first year of trading in which theoretically one type of product only was sold and all stock was exhausted by the end of the period. The summarised historic accounts are:

		£000
	Sales	500
Less	Cost of sales	400
	Operating profit	100

During the year the general rate of inflation measured by the Retail Price Index is 10 per cent. Then in order to maintain the general purchasing power of the original investment—in this case the £400,000 used to provide the original goods for resale—an additional 10 per cent of £400,000 is required and this can be shown in CPP adjusted accounts as follows:

		£000	
	Sales	500	
Less	Cost of sales	400	
	Operating profit	100	
Less	Capital maintenance adjustment	40	(10% × £400,000)
	Adjusted profit	60	

The firm has made a real profit of £60,000 but had the cost of sales been, for example, £460,000 the original investment would require £46,000 from an operating profit of only £40,000 giving an adjusted loss of £6,000. This method formed the basis of the development of ED 8 and SSAP 7 (page 322).

Current Cost Accounting (CCA)

Sometimes referred to as Current Value Accounting this method attempts to measure the effect of **individual** rates of price changes on all assets and liabilities, i.e. stocks, plant, machinery, investments, loans, creditors and so on. It recognises that there may be great differences in the various rates of inflation and by using specific indices for items or groups of items attempts to match the current cost of assets used against current income generated by them. In this approach the objective is to ensure that operating capital is maintained at the appropriate level. If the trader in the example above is to continue operations the **physical** stock must be replaced for resale in period 2. If the price of this commodity has risen meanwhile by 20 per cent (compared with the general rate of 10 per cent) the position under CCA accounts will be:

		£000	
	Sales	500	
Less	Cost of sales	480	(£400,000 × 20%)
	Operating profit	20	
	Adjustment	—	
	Adjusted profit	20	

In this case the operating profit is automatically adjusted by the fact that the replacement cost of the asset has been charged in full against revenue. It can be seen that this profit is insufficient to maintain the purchasing power of the original investment by reason that the inflation rate for this particular asset is twice that based on the general collection of retail prices. To this extent it was considered that this approach would be more realistic for business purposes than CPP and formed the basis for the development of SSAP 16—Current Cost Accounting (page 324).

The Development of Accounting Standards for Inflation Accounting

Historically accounting practice has been based upon recording transactions in monetary terms. Under inflationary conditions it has come to be realised that the monetary unit no longer interprets a stable value and that this changes as the effects of inflation continue. Financial statements prepared from historical data are thus seen to embody weaknesses which can lead to misinterpretation, inadequate judgement and wrong decisions.

The high rates of inflation in the 1960s and 1970s brought a reasonable degree of unanimity to the notion that some change is required to reflect more adequately the changes in the value of money, but the methods to be employed are proving more difficult to command such general accord. In the UK the major policy of the Conservative governments of the 1980s has been to control inflation and this has been successful to a degree. The cost has been high in other areas and thus it is a matter of political preference and judgement. The resulting lower rates of inflation have, however, diverted interest away from the problem with the result that measures and schemes hurriedly introduced in the 1970s have been suspended or allowed to lapse. The problem however remains and the cumulative effect of such lower rates of inflation can be serious after a few years and most businesses are long-term operations. For example a rate of 6 per cent per annum would increase prices by 50 per cent in seven years.

It is therefore necessary to consider in detail the attempts at standardisation made by the accounting profession so far. Although the description here relates to the UK a parallel investigation was conducted in the USA by the FASB (Financial Accounting Standard Board). It issued a statement (Number 33) in September 1979 requiring disclosure of the effects of inflation on businesses. The two methods prescribed were broadly in line with those described in the previous section and those detailed on the following pages.

Over recent years a need has been demonstrated for more uniform methods of accountancy practice, chiefly in the realm of interpreting business performance in specific time periods and demonstrating changes in the value of net assets between different points in time. A code of practice in specific problem areas has been devised under the auspices of the Accounting Standards Committee, which is representative of the various professional accounting bodies of the UK. In general, following studies by a specific Working Party, the Committee makes public its recommendations in the form of an Exposure Draft, inviting consultation, debate and counter-recommendations from all interested parties. In due course there is published a formal Statement of Standard Accounting Practice on the particular subject, incorporating any revisions found to be acceptable as a result of the advance exposure.

Because of its universal importance the subject of inflation was studied, resulting in Exposure Draft ED8, published in January 1973, which in turn led to the publication of a Provisional Statement of Standard Accounting Practice (SSAP 7) in May 1974. The principal recommendations of SSAP 7 were:

General Objective

To express the accounting data in terms of a unit of constant purchasing power at different points of time. The unit of measurement is, in effect, changed each year by updating, so that the adjusted accounts become no longer expressed in units of money, but units of purchasing power. The method has become known as **Current Purchasing Power (CPP)**.

The business is thus seen as having a certain volume of purchasing power at its disposal in the form of investment with a primary objective of at least maintaining this purchasing power irrespective of movements in the general level of prices.

The Basis of Conversion

As the expressed intention was to reflect changes in the general purchasing power of the pound, it was felt that this was best reflected by retail prices of goods and services for personal use, and therefore the official Retail Price Index (RPI) was chosen, with named earlier versions for the years prior to 1962 when RPI was introduced. The RPI index is calculated monthly and thus provides a regular and consistent basis for interpreting changes in purchasing power.

The Revised Presentation

The accountancy and published accounts would continue in historical form, but a supplementary statement would be provided containing the inflation adjustments. The precise form of the supplementary statement was not specified but it was required to implement the standard of accounting practice in its information. The statement was required to be audited and also for the directors to comment upon significant features arising.

Special Features

A distinction was made between monetary and non-monetary items, thus:

Monetary items are amounts fixed by contract regardless of changes in purchasing value such as cash, debtors, creditors and loan capital. A business *gains* during inflation in equivalent purchasing value on liabilities because the pound sum is fixed so that subsequent repayment in the same pound sums is in terms of lower purchasing value (conversely for debtors and loans outwards).

Non-monetary items are fixed assets and stock contracted at a specific original cost, but whose value in terms of pounds can have improved to reflect their equivalent purchasing value. Such improvements are latent or potential.

The Conversion Process

The conversion is to demonstrate the equivalent purchasing value in revised sums of pounds as at the date of the accounts under review. The monetary items remain the same as in the historical accounts. The non-monetary items are increased in proportion to the inflation change that has occurred since acquisition or revaluation. On the first occasion this calls for a conversion of each item separately, so that irrespective of age all items are interpreted into the current purchasing value through application of the RPI for the date of the review. Even after conversion the valuations should be subject to tests of the re-stated costs versus realisable values, whichever is the lower, in the normal way.

Year-to-Year Comparisons

The supplementary statement requires the previous year's data to be uplifted to conform to the purchasing value level, at the end of the period under review. The change in the level of inflation during the accounting year is thus eliminated and both opening and closing values are on a common basis. Differences reveal changes in 'real' terms. In this conversion the monetary items are adjusted and the mark-up or reduction demonstrates the gain or loss on monetary items due to the change in the value of the pound in terms of purchasing value in the year's interval.

Profit

The movement in purchasing values of net assets will accrue to the equity holders. Such a movement will incorporate latent gains/losses and profit. The profit for the year will be converted so that its items reflect the RPI index as at the date of the accounts under review. Also adjustments will be necessary to incorporate the calculated uplifts and reductions arising from the conversion of the operating balances to the end-of-year index. This will chiefly be the changes in monetary items and the stock change, i.e. if the opening stock is increased the profit in year-end terms will be reduced. The profit thus revealed will demonstrate the performance of the business for the year in 'real' terms and will segregate the year's profit from the net asset latent gains/losses.

A great deal of controversy subsequently generated on the recommendation of SSAP 7 centred upon the use of the Retail Price Index and the treatment of monetary and non-monetary items. A report was commissioned by the government (the Sandilands Report) which was critical of CPP and supported the introduction of the main alternative system—Current Cost Accounting—which emphasised costs rather than purchasing power.

Current Cost Accounting—The Development of SSAP 16

The recommendations of the Sandilands Committee for the introduction of a system of Current Cost Accounting (CCA) were broadly accepted by the Government and the Consultative Committee of Accounting Bodies. In December 1976 the Inflation Accounting Steering group under the chairmanship of Mr (later Sir) Douglas Morpeth published an Exposure Draft (ED 18) calling for companies to produce Current Cost Accounts. The requirements were complicated and a majority of members of the English Institute of Chartered Accountants rejected them, and asked for simplfication. In June 1977 the ASC published a simplified version with notes to guidance on implementation. These were produced by a committee under the chairmanship of William (Bill) Hyde. They were termed the Hyde Guidelines and were an interim measure to assist preparation of accounts on an experimental CCA basis for periods ended on or after 3st December, 1977 and anticipated a revised standard.

Subsequently a further Exposure Draft ED 24 dated April 1979 added a CCA Balance Sheet to the requirements. This was followed finally in March 1980 by the introduction of a further standard, SSAP 16 which accepted the need for experiment; it was required from large companies only and expected to remain unaltered for a period of three years, effective for accounting periods beginning on or after 1st January, 1980.

SSAP 16 Current Cost Accounting—Objectives

The standards' objective was to provide more useful information in the accounts as to:

(*a*) The financial viability of the business.
(*b*) Return on investment.
(*c*) Pricing policy, cost control and distribution decisions.
(*d*) Gearing.

The objective is achieved in two stages:

(*i*) *Current cost operating profit:* calculated by making three adjustments to the historic profit before interest on net borrowing and taxation. These adjustments are made in respect of:

(*a*) Depreciation (i/c profits and losses on sale of fixed assets).
(*b*) Cost of sales.
(*c*) Monetary working capital.

The purpose of these adjustments is to charge against revenue the value to the business of assets consumed in earning that revenue.

(*ii*) *Current cost profit attributable to shareholders:* If a company is financed by loan capital or other forms of debt finance (excluding short-term debt) a further adjustment is required to determine 'profit attributable to shareholders'. This includes adjustment in respect of interest paid or received and is known as the gearing adjustment.

Current Cost Balance Sheet

To achieve the objective listed the opening and closing Balance Sheets must similarly be stated in current cost terms. This is achieved by revaluing assets at their value to the business defined as:

(*a*) net current replacement cost—or if a permanent diminution to below net current replacement cost has been recognised then;
(*b*) recoverable amount (disposal value).

Current Cost

An asset's current cost is its value to the business. In the majority of cases it is synonymous with replacement cost. Where this is not available it must be assessed from indices or directors' valuation.

Current Cost Adjustment/Depreciation Adjustment

This is the difference between the charge based on an asset's current cost and that based on its historic cost as charged in arriving at historic profit.

The process of adjustment consists first in obtaining the current value to the business of all the company's fixed assets and second in establishing the proportion of the fixed assets consumed in a period based on such current values. When the first accounting period is adjusted there will be a substantial adjustment in respect of past years which is not relevant to the current year's profit. This is in respect of previous years and is usually referred to as 'prior year backlog'. Even in subsequent years if it is known or assumed that changes in fixed assets have taken place at an even rate during the year then annual adjustment will be divisible into several components. The objective is to charge to the Current Cost Profit and Loss Account the difference between the computed charge for the current value of assets consumed *in the period* and the depreciation calculated on the historical cost basis. Any other adjustments are passed directly through the *Current Cost Reserve* (CCR).

Example. Included in the Current Cost Balance Sheet of X Ltd, at 31st December, 19x0 were fixed assets valued at £550,000 which originally cost £500,000 and which were being written off on a 5 year straight line basis. The price indices relative to the fixed assets were:

January 19x1	110
December 19x1	130

Compute the depreciation adjustment on an average basis.

Solution

Average index for year $= \dfrac{110–130}{2} = 120$

All assets at gross current cost at 1st Jan 19x1	$= £550,000$
Adjusted to average current cost during year	$= £550,000 \times \dfrac{120}{110}$
	$= £600,000$
Depreciation $- \frac{1}{5} \times £600,000$	$= £120,000$
Less depreciation charged in Historic account	$= £100,000$
Depreciation Adjustment	$= £20,000$

This is an over simplification as in most instances there will be adjustments in respect of previous years (prior year backlog)—if an averaging method is used—adjustments in respect of the current year between the amount attributable to the Profit and Loss Account (depreciation adjustment) and the full requirement to update the balance sheets (current year backlog). The figures above are given primarily to show the presentation of the final results (below). More typical treatment is to distinguish between current year and prior year backlog and also to assume assets are used up at an average rate during the year.

Cost of Sales Adjustment (COSA)

This is the difference between the current cost of the stock consumed and the cost charged in the historic Profit and Loss Account. The COSA is the difference between the stock charge over the year at *average cost* for the year and at historic cost: unless the actual items can be identified and valued or some other more acceptable basis is used.

Example

Stock at 1st January 19x0	£100,000	Index 200
" " 31st December 19x0	£140,000	Index 240

Assuming that stocks have risen steadily during the year COSA is calculated as follows:

Average index for year $= \dfrac{240 + 200}{2} = 220$

	Historic Cost		*Average Cost*
Opening Stock	£100,000	$\times \dfrac{220}{200} =$	£110,000
Closing Stock	£140,000	$\times \dfrac{220}{240} =$	£128,333
COSA	= £40,000	less	18,333
		= £21,667	

The figure of £21,667 represents the increase in stock value due to changing prices as distinct from changing quantities with 220 used as the average index through the year as computed above.

Monetary Working Capital Adjustment (MWCA)

In addition to stocks most businesses have working capital items of a monetary nature. These include assets such as trade debtors and prepayments and liabilities such as creditors and accruals. Bank and cash balances are excluded unless they fluctuate with stock and net monetary assets, i.e. the difference between monetary assets and liabilities.

Example. AB Ltd has the following balances recorded in the accounts:

	Debtors	*Creditors*	*Net*
	£	£	£
1st January, 19x0	600,000	400,000	200,000
31st December, 19x0	800,000	500,000	300,000

Index No. January 19x0 250
" " December 19x0 300

$$\text{Average index} = \frac{250 + 300}{2} = 275$$

	Historic		*Average*
	£		£
Net Monetary Assets 1 June, 19x0	200,000	$\times \frac{275}{250} =$	220,000
Less " " 31 December, 19x0	300,000	$\times \frac{275}{300} =$	275,000
MWCA =	100,000	less	55,000
=		£45,000	

In this example debtors exceed creditors and the adjustment is a charge against profits. Where creditors exceed debtors and prices are rising the adjustment will be a credit to profit but this should not exceed the Cost of Sales Adjustment.

Current Cost Adjustments

The three adjustments typified above are totalled and applied to the historic profit to determine (before interest) the current cost profit:

i.e. £20,000 + £21,667 + £45,000 = £86,667

The Gearing Adjustment

This is the part of Current Cost Adjustments attributable if a proportion of the net operating assets is financed by net borrowing. It is required to determine the Current Cost Profit attributable to the shareholders and is calculated by:

(*a*) expressing net borrowing as a proportion of the net operating assets using average figures for the year from current cost balance sheets; and

(*b*) multiplying the total of the charges or credits made to allow for impact on the net operating assets of the business by the proportion determined at (*a*).

This adjustment will be a credit if prices are rising.

Example. The *abbreviated* Balance Sheets of AB Ltd in current cost values at the beginning and end of 19x1 are as follows:

	1st January, 19x1	*31st December, 19x1*
	£	£
Fixed assets	550,000	600,000
Stock	200,000	230,000
Net Monetary Assets	200,000	220,000
Total	950,000	1,050,000
Share Capital	400,000	400,000
Reserves	250,000	350,000
Sub-total	650,000	750,000
Loan Capital	300,000	300,000
Total	950,000	1,050,000

If the Current Cost Profit is £93,333, *after* the three adjustments similar to those for X Ltd above but *before* interest of £28,000, tax of £25,000 and dividends of £40,000, the gearing adjustment would be:

$$\text{Average capital employed for year} = \frac{£950,000 + £1,050,000}{2}$$

$$= £1,000,000$$

Loans = £300,000

Current Cost adjustments = £86,667

$$\text{Gearing Adjustment} = \frac{\text{Loans}}{\text{Total Capital}} \times \text{CCA}$$

$$= \frac{£300,000}{£1,000,000} \times £86,667 = £26,000$$

Current Cost Profit	= 93,333	
Add Depreciation Adjustment	20,000	
COSA	21,667	86,667
MWCA	45,000	
Historic Profit before interest and tax	180,000	

Current Cost Profit and Loss Account
for year ended 31st December, 19x1

Profit as per Historic Profit and Loss Account before		£
interest and taxation		180,000
Less Current Cost Adjustment		86,667
Current Cost Operating Profit		93,333
Gearing Adjustment	(26,000)	
Interest	28,000	2,000
		91,333
Taxation		25,000
		66,333
Dividends		40,000
Profit retained		26,333

The profit retained of £26,333 does not equate with the change in reserves of £100,000 derived from the Balance Sheet. The difference incorporates the Current Cost Reserve (see below) and provisions for tax and dividends.

Current Cost Reserve

The effect of revaluation of assets is to require some adjustment to the liabilities side of the balance sheet. An equivalent amount to the revaluation is credited (net of current cost depreciation in the case of fixed assets) to the Current Cost Reserve.

The treatment of assets in respect of revaluation will be as follows:

(*i*) *Stocks*. Adjusted to replacement cost where known or revalued by indices as described in COSA.

(*ii*) *Investments in Associated Companies*. The appropriate proportion of Associated Companies' net assets at current cost, or directors' best estimate.

(*iii*) *Investments* (Non Current Assets). At directors valuation or 'listing'.

(*iv*) *Intangible Assets* (excluding goodwill). At the best estimate of value to the business.

(*v*) *Goodwill arising on Consolidation*. At the value prescribed by SSAP 14—that is the difference between purchase consideration and the value of net tangible, and identifiable intangible assets to the purchaser.

(*vi*) *Current Assets* (Other than those subject to a cost of sales adjustment). At historical cost.

(*vii*) *Liabilities*. All liabilities are shown on an historical cost basis.

Chief Advantages Claimed for CCA

1. Will permit returns on capital employed to be more usefully assessed.
2. Separation of classifications of gains more adequately distinguishes productive efforts from fortuitous results.
3. Separation of classifications gives better guidance to managements.
4. The revaluation of assets in balance sheets and some forms of valuing

stocks have anticipated this formal CCA; therefore the content of the report is seen as being evolutionary not revolutionary.

Implementation

The report suggested the appointment of a steering group to supervise the implementation of the changes envisaged, and also that these be introduced in company annual reports after 24th December, 1977, for:

(*a*) Listed companies.
(*b*) Others with a turnover exceeding £10 million per year.
(*c*) Others with assets exceeding £10 million.
(*d*) Nationalised industries.

Present Position Regarding Published Accounts

The SSAP 16 was never universally received or endorsed and some company chairmen chose to ignore some or all of its requirements even where this meant qualification of the accounts by auditors. The slowing down of the rate of inflation in the UK in the 1980s removed some of the impetus to distorting results. The position at the end of August 1987 was that compliance with SSAP 16 was no longer mandatory for companies within the criteria referred to above. A new exposure draft ED35 was being issued while a new approach was formulated. The Accounting Standards Committee has also issued a *Handbook on Accounting* for the effect of changing prices. Not much greater progress has yet been made internationally. In the USA the Financial Accounting Standard Boards Statement 33—Financial Reporting and Changing Prices has been amended to remove the requirement to disclose historical cost/constant dollar information. The problem of dealing with accounts in unstable monetary units still remains and until—if at all—a generally accepted method of dealing with this phenomena is achieved, the controversy will continue.

Summary of Main UK Developments

1974 ASC publish provisional standard on Current Purchasing Power (CPP) method of accounting for inflation.
1975 Government rejects CPP and sponsors Sandilands Committee with brief to examine adjustment on basis of replacement costs termed Current Cost Accounting (CCA).
1976 ASC accept CCA principle and Morpeth Committee publish Exposure Draft 18 calling for all companies to produce Current Cost Accounts. Withdrawn after criticism of complications.
1977 ED18 modified gearing adjustment added. Hyde guidelines developed as encouragement to use and ED24 refines existing ideas. Hyde guidelines add requirement for CCA Balance Sheet.
1980 SSAP 16 published—mandatory for large companies.
1987 Mandatory requirement withdrawn and position under review.

The results of a MORI survey of preparers and users of accounts towards accounting for inflation (commissioned by the Chartered Association of Certified Accountants) tended to confirm the above as follows:

(*a*) At current levels of inflation nine out of ten of both preparers and users of accounts believe that historic cost accounts present a reliable picture.

(*b*) Over three-quarters of those surveyed believe that at current levels of inflation it does not matter which system is used.

(*c*) Ten per cent is considered to be the rate needed before there would be great concern.

(*d*) A small majority of users and preparers agreed a new practice statement was needed from the Accounting Standards Committee.

Inflation and Management Control Information

The basic purpose of management control information is to demonstrate management performance against planned objectives and to isolate the differences into causes and under responsibilities so that management can make decisions and implement action to alter the adverse causes, counter them and improve upon the beneficial trends.

In comparing actual performance with plan in financial terms the impact of inflation can adversely affect results and distort interpretation, so that it becomes highly desirable to ensure that the data under comparison be similarly constituted as to money values. This then confines differences to aspects of performance. To make this possible the plan can be adjusted for inflation so that plan and actual performance each contain their elements of inflation, or alternatively the plan avoids any inflation content and the actual performance information is reduced net of price and wage rate increases by the normal process of variance accounting.

If inflation is anticipated in the budget, practitioners find that the only aspect about which there is certainty is that the degree and timing of the inflation content will be wrong and for this reason it is not encouraged for fixed budgets. Improved accuracy is forthcoming from adjustments to short-term budgets such as the rolling next quarter (updating the next three months progressively), when the rates and timing of inflation would be more informed. However, experts are confounded when forecasting inflation even in the short term, so that a more reliable method is to rely only upon published data of actual changes in the value of money. This invites a process of introducing the known degree of inflation into a flexible budget as a separate operation from that of adjusting for output volume.

Critics can advance the point that any published index of prices such as the Retail Price Index does not necessarily reflect the effect of inflation upon a particular business, and the Sandilands Report and ED18 endorsed this view. This criticism directs attention to the advantages of isolating the price variances from the performance data as they occur, as this would then demonstrate the actual impact of inflation upon the business. These price variances can be analysed under suitable categories and the degree of change related to nationally monitored changes within similar categories by government or trade associations. In such a manner the ability to shield the business from the full impact of price increases relative to it can be demonstrated. An efficient buying function deserves its contribution to be recognised if it is able to keep the impact of prices down to, say, half the national rate.

The actual expenditure, now devoid of price variance, provides a more adequate means of reflecting performance and the segregation of price variances of costs can be monitored against price variances of sales. Businesses subject to control of selling price changes may have to demonstrate the extent of cost increases incurred and a properly analysed price variance control can be of immense assistance in substantiating claims for compensating sales increases.

As a budget year progresses a price variance account can assume very generous proportions and in the later stages appear somewhat incongruous. However, the purpose of the procedure should be recognised as that of isolating the impact of inflation so as to reveal the actual performance data so vital for effective management.

The establishment of price standards for standard costing and budgeting will require careful consideration especially as to the degree of price change which should, or should not, be anticipated. Replacement values at the opening date of the budget would be the more advisable basis. It should perhaps be realised that standard costing is a means of facilitating control accounting and not of demonstrating product costs from time to time. The procedure for maintaining current product costs in a standard costing system is a separate operation from the accounting processes. It will be important to monitor and demonstrate the effects of progressive price changes upon current costs within the standard cost model as for all other changes such as methods, design, material substitutes, so that changes of product contribution are under regular management review in so far as they may affect pricing, product mix and marketing policies.

Inflation and Investment Appraisal

Investment appraisal involves the forecasting and assessment of the future incomes to be derived from an investment and it could well be judged helpful to translate estimates of future cash inflows with some reflection of inflation, so as to indicate the flow in the money terms of the future dates.

It is important, however, to present and judge forecast data in terms of common purchasing power so that any interpretation of inflation-adjusted flow of money must first be converted into purchasing power equivalent, which simply means converting back any index which has already been used to convert into inflated currency. This process is demonstrated as follows:

A Forecast—Inflation Included

	Current year	*Year +1*	*Year +2*	*Year +3*
Index	155	167	177	184
	£	£	£	£
Sales	200,000	215,500	274,100	368,000
Costs	160,000	172,400	219,250	299,000
Profit	40,000	43,100	54,850	69,000

To interpret the above in terms of purchasing power equivalent to the current year, the forecast years are arithmetically adjusted using the indices of the respective years, thus:

	Current year	*Year +1*	*Year +2*	*Year +3*
Index adjustment	*at* 155	$\times 155$ / 167	$\times 155$ / 177	$\times 155$ / 184

	£	£	£	£
Sales	200,000	200,000	240,000	310,000
Costs	160,000	160,000	192,000	252,000
Profit	40,000	40,000	48,000	58,000

Making allowance for inflation in forecast information is thus frequently considered as being superfluous, as evaluation, to be meaningful, must be in terms of common purchasing power. Forecasts can therefore be made in terms of the purchasing power at the time of forecasting on the general assumption that inflation changes will affect the future currency interpretations of sales and costs and thus profits by a common factor.

However, it is usual for sales price increases to lag behind cost increases and the latter may apply to different costs with varying degrees of price impact. Thus where it is felt that a common element of inflation will not apply it is advisable to interpret the variable levels item by item into an inflation-adjusted forecast as a first step. In the above example (Inflation Included) it was assumed that Year +1 was commonly influenced by an index of 167; had this year been subject to variable inflation factors the 'Inflation Included' forecast compared with the current year could be:

	Current year		*Year +1*			
			Index	*Inflation-reduced*	*Inflation-adjusted*	
	£	£		£	£	£
Sales		200,000	167	200,000		215,000
Materials	80,000		175	80,000	90,300	
Labour	25,000		167	25,000	26,900	
Overheads variable	30,000		167	30,000	32,300	
Overheads fixed	20,000		170	20,000	22,000	
Interest	5,000	160,000	—	5,000	5,000	176,500
Profit		40,000		40,000		38,500

The inflation-adjusted profit of approximately £39,000 results from the conglomerate of the inflation adjustments but it is not reflecting the same purchasing power as the current year. To make it so it must be deflated by the general index applicable to its year:

$$\pounds 39{,}000 \times \frac{155}{167} = \pounds 36{,}200$$

which now compares with the current year profit of £40,000.

In turning to use of forecasts of future cash flows in investment appraisal procedures it is seen as advisable for the investment and the incomes to be reflected in terms of common purchasing power as at the investment date. Such an appraisal presentation in terms of net present value could be:

Year		*Cash flow* £	*Discount factor* @ 10%	*Present value* £
0	Investment—Out	–100,000		–100,000
1	Cash income—In	40,000	0·91	36,400
2		48,000	0·83	39,840
3		58,000	0·75	43,500
	Net present value			£19,740

The cash income and thus the net present value is expressed on a basis of purchasing power common with the investment. The investment can be replaced out of income with a surplus in hand of £19,740 (net present value equivalent) providing that the replacement value of the asset at the close of the project has kept in step with the inflation factor applicable to the income—it assumes a commonly applied inflation factor throughout.

However, it may be assumed that the inflation factor applicable to the replacement of the asset in due course may be greater than the general inflation level at that time. Such difference must be evaluated and converted into the equivalent purchasing power at the time of the investment. It may be that this is undertaken at the outset—namely, £100,000 initial cost will become £105,000 replacement cost in equivalent purchasing power.

On the other hand, the assessment may be that plant replacement prices will be 5 per cent higher than the general price index of 184 at the end of the third year—say, 9 points higher at 193. The replacement cost in +3 years' terms of value would be £124,645, which must be found out of the income value of the time—namely the 184 index. In terms of the equivalent purchasing power of the original investment this becomes

$$\pounds 124{,}645 \times \frac{155}{184} = \pounds 105{,}000$$

Under the circumstances of the above net present value demonstration, the replacement value of £105,000 is substituted for the original cost of £100,000 and the net present value is seen capable of withstanding this and still provide a positive surplus. Of course, such a surplus will be conditional upon the discount rate and should the cost of capital be higher then it would be demonstrated that the income would be incapable of supporting the replacement value of the asset.

The extra £5,000—the difference between £105,000 and £100,000—is the additional sum to be found out of the monetary income over the period of the project. If it was thought that the rate of inflation was going to increase at a constant annual rate over the period then this could be adjusted in the discount rate. Thus if the required rate of return was 10 per cent p.a. and the inflation rate was a constant 8 per cent p.a., the total rate used for discounting would be 18 per cent. It is most important, however, that the purpose of the two elements of the rate be clearly appreciated. The 10 per cent is the cost of capital, which is the reward expected by the lenders of the capital or the reward to the owners of the business for investment for the appropriate period and risk class. The extra 8 per cent is to compensate for the decline in purchasing power of the interest or dividend being paid. It should be noted that if the capital is borrowed by some form of contractual rate of investment, e.g. debentures, the monetary loss will fall on the lender. If the capital is in equity then—ignoring other factors—inflationary gains or losses will be borne by the shareholders. The manner of raising the capital will therefore affect the necessity or desirability of such adjustments to the rate which is used for the investment appraisal.

The examples used tend to oversimplify the inflation problem in respect of investment appraisal since they have concentrated upon a short-term scale. Most investments projects are being assessed over much longer periods. A difficulty then arises in forecasting the degree of inflation into the future and, more particularly, in assessing any differential between the general index of inflation and that applicable to particular assets—and the longer the period the more likelihood of error. This can be demonstrated in an example where it is assumed that the general price index is 100 and that an annual price rise of 10 per cent p.a. is anticipated over the next 10 years. Furthermore, it is anticipated that prices of machine tools will rise by 15 per cent p.a. over the same period. The purchasing power equivalents in each case can be compared at compound interest at 10 per cent and 15 per cent respectively:

Years			*Rates*	
			@ 10%	@ 15%
			£	£
Cost at year	0	(per £)	1·0	1·0
	1		1·10	1·15
	2		1·21	1·32
	3		1·33	1·52
	4		1·46	1·75
	5		1·61	2·01
	6		1·77	2·31
	7		1·94	2·66
	8		2·14	3·06
	9		2·35	3·52
	10		2·59	4·04

Thus at the end of 10 years items within the general price index which cost £1,000 at Year 0 would cost £2,590 and machine tools £4,040. Note that this is equivalent to saying that the present value of £1,000 received at the end of 10 years at 10 per cent general inflation p.a. is equivalent to £1,000 $\times \frac{1}{2{\cdot}59} =$ £386·10, whereas £1,000 at 15 per cent inflation p.a. as for machine tools becomes £1,000 $\times \frac{1}{4{\cdot}04} =$ £247·50.

Several writers such as Professor A. McCosh have suggested that when making this kind of forecast the use of a geometric progression for long periods would be unrealistic. They maintain that large price differentials would encourage managers either to find a substitute or change the methods of production and thus reduce the demand for the asset in question. This would have the effect of reducing the price levels and thus the inflation rate for that particular type of asset. The effect of this has been termed the 'decay' factor.

The proponents of this reasoning suggest that before long-term predictions are made at constant annual rates, some experimenting is undertaken to assess the effects of various response levels and decay factors upon rates of price increase in order to remove the bias error which they claim could occur using a persistent differential.

The objective of exercises of this nature should be distinguished from that of alternative standard formats such as Consumer Purchasing Power (CPP) and Current Cost Accounting (CCA). These are primarily designed for published accounts and therefore stewardship reporting. In internal management decision-making, methods of treatment to reflect the impact of inflation are the choice of the management accountant and the management concerned.

Worked Examples

Example 1

Following the Sandilands report the controversy over the preparation and presentation of annual accounts has been given a new urgency and the debate between historic cost (HC), Current Purchasing Power (CPP), and replacement cost (RC) continues.

The CPP technique is based on the same conventions as the HC technique; the only difference between them is the adjustment for general inflation.

Replacement cost has several varieties. The one you are asked to consider in part (*a*) of this question is that which requires adjustment to an RC basis of fixed asset values in the balance sheet, and of annual depreciation in the profit and loss account plus an adjustment to an RC basis of stock values in the balance sheet and of the cost of stocks used in the profit and loss account. In addition 'holding gains' (excess of RC over HC cost) are credited to replacement reserve and are not transferred to profit and loss account as the asset is realised (i.e. stock sold or asset depreciated).

Consider the following data (all transactions are cash transactions; no credit is given or received):

1 Jan.	Company formed with issued share capital of £1,500
	Raises loan of £500
	Buys goods £1,000
	Buys an accounting machine £1,000
	General price index = 100
30 Jun.	Sells goods for £1,200
	Replaces goods for £1,100
	General price index = 108
31 Dec.	Sells goods for £1,320
	Replaces goods for £1,200
	Pays loan interest £50
	General price index = 116
	To replace the accounting machine would cost £1,300
	Depreciation 10% p.a. straight line

The summarised cash account is provided to show (*a*) the balance at 31st December, and (*b*) the adjustments made under the customary working schedule to reflect the change in purchasing power between the date of transaction and 31st December.

Summarised Cash Account

	£H		×	÷	£	December
Cash Receipts						
1st Jan.	1,500		116	100	1,740	
1st Jan.	500		116	100	580	
30th Jun.	1,200		116	108	1,289	
31st Dec.	1,320		116	116	1,320	
		4,520				4,929
Cash Payments						
1st Jan.	1,000		116	100	1,160	
1st Jan.	1,000		116	100	1,160	
30th Jun.	1,100		116	108	1,181	
31st Dec.	1,200		116	116	1,200	
	50		116	116	50	
		4,350				4,751
Net balance		170				178

You are required to:

(*a*) Prepare the profit and loss account for the year ended 31st December and balance sheet at this date using the three different techniques.

(*b*) Comment upon the differences.

(Ignore taxation)

(ICAEW)

Suggested Answer—Part A

PROFIT AND LOSS ACCOUNTS

	Historic cost basis		*Current purchasing power basis*		*Replacement cost basis*	
	£	£	£	£	£	£
Sales	1,200		1,289		1,200	
	1,320	2,520	1,320	2,609	1,320	2,520
Material cost of sales	1,000		1,160		1,100	
	1,100	2,100	1,181	2,341	1,200	2,300
Gross profit		420		268		220
Depreciation	100		116		130	
Interest	50	150	50	166	50	180
Operating profit		270		102		40
Net gain/loss on monetary items:						
Gain on loan: £500 × $\frac{116}{100}$			80			
(Loss) on cash receipts		(409)				
Gain on cash payments		401	(8)	72		
Adjusted profit		270		174		40

BALANCE SHEETS

	£	£	£	£	£	£
	HC basis		*CPP basis*		*RC basis*	
Fixed assets	1,000		1,160		1,300	
Less Depreciation	100	900	116	1,044	130	1,170
Stocks		1,200		1,200		1,200
Cash		170		170		170
		2,270		2,414		2,540
Financed by:						
Share capital		1,500	bal.	1,740		1,500
Operating profit		270		174		40
Holding gain		—		—		500
Total equity interest		1,770		1,914		2,040
Loan capital		500		500		500
		2,270		2,414		2,540

Suggested Answer—Part (b)

Historical Cost Basis. It is now generally agreed that this traditional presentation has weaknesses in inflationary conditions such as demonstrated in the question. The answer above emphasises the following such weaknesses:

(*a*) The monetary income and costs absorbed produce a profit value which does not reflect the purchasing power of the resulting sterling figure.

(*b*) The asset values do not reflect current values and there is inadequate provision against profit for their eventual replacement.

(*c*) The profitability is misleading on two counts: (i) the profit appears higher than its current value; (ii) assets appear lower than their current value.

Current Purchasing Power Basis. This presentation sets out to correct the above weaknesses by interpreting the transactions at the purchasing power valuations at the end of the year—namely, general index 116 against opening general index 100 (i.e. money has lost value).

The assets are valued at the end of the year on this basis. Thus £1,160 suggests that it is this money expression at December 31st which will be required to provide an accounting machine compared with £1,000 a year ago. The general index may not specifically be correct for the accounting machine and the replacement cost basis seeks to correct this. This basis suggests that the £270 operating profit on the historic basis will only acquire the equivalent of £102 of value on the market at December 31st.

The net gain/loss on monetary items is a contentious aspect not supported by the Sandilands Report. The adjustments claim that the loan of £500, being a legal commitment at that figure, represents a surrender of $£500 \times \frac{100}{116}$ of purchasing power, i.e. £420 in January 1st values, and therefore represents a gain of £80 worth of purchasing power.

The equity interest is the balance between the revalued assets and the non-equity items, i.e. £2,414 − £500 = £1,914, of which £174 can be identified as the adjusted profit.

A general criticism of CPP has been that the presentation is difficult to comprehend as the unit of purchasing power is deemed somewhat artificial and the net gain/loss on monetary items seems particularly so. The general price index is not necessarily pertinent to specific assets, which is the case here in respect of the accounting machine.

Replacement Cost Basis. This method uses the normal units of currency to reflect the cost of replacing assets at the time. Such valuations are appropriate to each asset in the context of the particular business. Uplifted depreciation relative to the replacement value is provided to help in providing for the replacement of the asset in due course. Thus depreciation on the accounting machine becomes £130 against £100 under historic cost and £116 under current purchasing value.

Sandilands contends that operating profit should be after providing for the replacement cost of goods and services absorbed in generating the output of the period, resulting in only £40 profit for the year.

The holding gains are shown in the balance sheet as an increase in the equity interest, demonstrating the fortuitous gain arising from just owning the assets. The total of £500 comprises:

		£	£
December 31st:	Replacement value of stock	1,200	
January 1st:	Original cost of stock	1,000	200
December 31st:	Replacement value of accounting machine—*as new*	1,300	
January 1st:	Original cost of accounting machine	1,000	
			300
			£500

There is here an alternative interpretation as to the replacement value of the accounting machine. The profit and loss account and balance sheet above assume the phrase to mean 'replacement value—*as new*', in which case the value £1,300 becomes subject to 10 per cent reduction at the end of its first year of life. However, the phrase could be interpreted as meaning 'replacement value—*as now, one year old*', in which case the calculation would become:

	£
Replacement value—as new	1,444
One year's depreciation @ 10%	144
Replacement value—one year old	1,300

In this event the operating profit of £40 would become £26.

Example 2

The following is a summary of the accounts of a company over a period of 23 years:

Balance Sheets at year end

	1944	*1951*	*1958*	*1966*	*1967*
	£000	£000	£000	£000	£000
Fixed assets at cost	200	200	317	504	519
less depreciation	25	132	148	235	243
	175	68	169	269	276
Trading assets, net	200	300	460	560	580
Quick resources	35	66	(5)	3	1
Equity capital and retained profits	410	434	624	832	857

Profit and Loss Accounts for the year

Trading profit	80	120	184	224	232
Depreciation	25	10	24	39	40
Profit before taxation	55	110	160	185	192
Taxation	15	56	80	95	97
Dividend, gross	24	30	50	70	70
Retained	16	24	30	20	25
	55	110	160	185	192

Index numbers

Wholesale prices	100	150	230	280	290

A financial commentator suggests that, because of the changing value of money, the company has in effect been paying dividends out of capital. You are asked to comment on this statement, saying whether:

(*a*) You agree with the commentator's calculations and with his interpretation of the facts.

(*b*) In your view the company has fulfilled its obligations to its shareholders.

(CIMA)

Suggested Answer—Part (a)

P. & L. Accounts Adjusted for Inflation at 1967 Value Equivalents

	1944	*1951*	*1958*	*1966*	*1967*
Indices	100	150	230	280	290
	£000	£000	£000	£000	£000
Trading Profit	232	232	232	232	232
Depreciation	72·5	19	30	40	40
Profit before tax	159·5	213	202	192	192
Taxation	43·5	108	101	98	97
Earnings	116	105	101	94	95
Dividends	70	58	63	73	70

In each of these selected years the earnings exceed the dividends in real terms and therefore the dividends were *not* paid out of capital.

Equity Capital Adjusted for Inflation at 1967 Value Equivalents

	£000	£000	£000	£000	£000
Historical values	410	434	624	832	857
Adjusted to 1967 values	1,189	839	767	862	857
Variations between dates		−350	−62	+95	−5
Variations 1944–1967					−332

This information suggests that the equity capital has not been kept intact in real value terms. This supports the contention of the financial commentator that because of the changing value of money, the company has in effect been paying dividends out of capital. However, because in the five sample years dividends are shown not to have been paid out of capital, the statement should be amended to read that dividends were paid out of capital in *some* years.

Suggested Answer—Part (b)

The company can be said to have prime obligations to improve the equity value of the business or at least to maintain the value. If dividends are paid, as has been so in this case, then to maintain the value would be acceptable.

Comparison of principal assets:

	1944 @ 1967 values	*1967*
	£000	£000
Fixed assets at cost	580	519
Less Depreciation	72·5	243
At present condition	507·5	276
Trading assets = Stock	580	580

The year 1944 appears to be the first year of operation as the depreciation charged to P. & L. account in that year is equivalent to the cumulative depreciation shown in the balance sheet.

By 1967 the cumulative depreciation is 47 per cent of cost; with the resulting life-span of the fixed assets in existence in 1967 therefore being about half expired there must be some aged assets not yet replaced. Although the cumulative depreciation is £243,000 in 1967 there are no liquid funds to undertake replacements—the 'Quick' resources have only £1,000 of net favourable balances.

On the basis of current purchasing power interpreted by the given indices it can be said that the company has not fulfilled its obligation of maintaining the equity value of the business.

Questions

1. 'Because the rate of inflation is now well below five per cent the historical cost convention is once again the most appropriate basis upon which to measure accounting profit.'

Discuss. (ICAEW)

2. Current cost accounting seeks to make four adjustments to the profit and loss account as drafted for publication to shareholders.

You are required to discuss the situations in which each of these adjustments might be applied to the purposes of management accounting. (CIMA)

3. On 1st January, 1969, Pontus Ltd purchased a plot of land for £80,000. The directors are now considering a development of the land. Plans have been prepared, at a cost of £45,000, for building a block of 40 flats. Building could start on 1st January, 1976. It is estimated that construction would cost £500,000, £200,000 payable on 1st January, 1976, and £300,000 payable on 1st January, 1977. The flats would be ready for occupation on 1st January, 1978.

The flats would be let on annual tenancies. Rents would be increased by 10 per cent p.a., in step with the increase expected in the index of consumer prices.

The plot of land is expected to have a market value of £200,000 on 1st January, 1976. The building would have an expected life of 20 years, i.e. it would be let for the last time during the year ended 31st December, 1997. It would have to be demolished at that time at an estimated cost of £1·5 million. The estimated market value of the land on 31st December, 1997, is £5 million.

Pontus requires a rate of return on investment of $15\frac{1}{2}$ per cent p.a., in money terms. Assume that receipts for rent arise on the last day of the calendar year to which they relate.

You are required to:

(*a*) Calculate the minimum rental per flat for 1978 at which it would be worthwhile for Pontus to undertake the development instead of holding the land in its present condition: include a note in justification of your treatment of the cost of preparing plans.

(*b*) Comment shortly on the opinion expressed by one of the directors that, in view of the great uncertainty about the future rate of inflation, it would be advisable to be conservative and express all estimates in terms of current prices.

Ignore taxation.

(ICAEW)

4. A newspaper recently reported that a manager had stated that, under conditions of inflation, businessmen were unwilling to undertake plans for expansion because rapid increases in sales and profits could cause cash flow problems.

Do you consider this to be a fair statement of fact?

(CIMA)

5. The financial manager in his day-to-day decisions must take into consideration the impact of inflation. However, for long-term decisions such as the appraisal of capital projects he can ignore this because in the long-run an average inflation rate applied to all the variables will produce the same answer as if inflation had been ignored.

Comment.

(CACA)

6. 'The figures shown in the balance sheet for long-term assets and for stocks of goods are in most cases based on historical costs, which may represent the purchasing power of many months or years ago. The capital figures shown in the balance sheet are also inadequate because no allowance is made for the decline in purchasing power that has taken place since the capital was obtained.'

Discuss the problems of adjusting for the effects of inflation in reporting results to shareholders and other external parties. Give your own views on the desirability of making such adjustments.

(SCCA)

7. Everest Ltd is considering the replacement of a group of machines used exclusively for the manufacture of one of its products, the Yeti. The existing machines have a book value of £65,000 after deducting straight-line depreciation from historical cost; however, they could be sold only for £45,000. The new machines would cost £100,000. Everest expects to sell Yetis for four more years. The existing machines could be kept in operation for that period of time if it were economically desirable to do so. After four years, the scrap value of both the existing machines and the new machines would be zero.

The current costs per unit of manufacturing Yetis on the existing machines and the new machines are as follows:

	Existing machines		*New machines*
	£		£
Materials	22·00		20·00
Labour (32 hours @ £1·25)	40·00	(16 hours @ £1·25)	20·00
Overheads (32 hours @ £0·60)	19·20	(16 hours @ £1·80)	28·80
Total cost	81·20		68·80

Overheads are allocated to products on the labour hour rate method. The hourly rates of 60p and £1·80 comprise 25p and 62·5p for variable overheads and 35p and £1·175 for fixed overheads, including depreciation.

Current sales of Yetis are 1,000 units per annum at £90 each; if the new machines were purchased, output would be increased to 1,200 units and selling price would be reduced to £80.

Everest requires a minimum rate of return on investment of 20 per cent p.a. in money terms. Materials costs, overheads and selling prices are expected to increase at the rate of 15 per cent p.a., in step with the index of retail prices. Labour costs are expected to increase at the rate of 20 per cent p.a. Assume that annual receipts and payments would arise annually on the anniversary of the installation of the new machinery.

You are required to:

(*a*) Give calculations to show whether purchase of the new machines would be worthwhile.

(*b*) Explain shortly your treatment of inflation.

Ignore taxation.

(ICAEW)

8. Zambesi Ltd has just completed, over a period of one year, the development of a new product, the Umfuli. It now wishes to decide whether to proceed with manufacture of the product. The following information is available:

(i) Development required three man-years of the time of employees in the research department; these employees earned £3,500 each p.a., on average. Various materials and components had to be purchased specially for the development work at a cost of £4,270.

(ii) The selling price of the product would be set at £82 per unit in current terms and would be increased in step with the index of retail prices. It is expected that sales would be 5,000 units p.a. for eight years.

(iii) Production of the Umfuli would require at current prices: materials costing £26 per unit; 15 labour hours per unit at a wage rate of £2 per hour; and would increase variable overhead costs by £16 per unit. All these costs would be expected to increase in step with the index of retail prices.

(iv) A machine would have to be purchased specially for manufacture of Umfulis at a cost of £350,000; it would have a residual value of £30,000 at the end of eight years.

(v) The index of retail prices is expected to increase at the rate of 15 per cent p.a. and the cost of capital in money terms is expected to be 15 per cent p.a.

Sales may be assumed to take place and production costs to be incurred on the last day of each year.

You are required to:

(*a*) Calculate the worthwhileness of producing Umfulis on the basis of the estimates given.

(*b*) Calculate the effect on the worthwhileness of production of a fall in expected inflation to 5 per cent p.a. and in the money cost of capital to 10 per cent p.a.

(*c*) Calculate the minimum annual sales volume at which the production of Umfulis would be just worthwhile, assuming that the original estimates (other than sales) hold good.

(*d*) Explain how the calculations presented in your answers to sections (*a*), (*b*) and (*c*), together with the calculations which you think may be necessary, would be used in reaching a final decision.

Ignore taxation.

(ICAEW)

10

INVESTMENT MANAGEMENT

Introduction and Taxation Background

It may be asked why it should be necessary to consider individual investors in a text on financial management since, so far, we have been concerned with companies and institutions. The answer is that if the financial manager is required to devise, suggest or approve possibly only one of the varying methods by which capital might be raised he must be as aware as practicable of the likely success or otherwise of such an issue. This means in turn that he must assess or anticipate the effect of factors which influence the actions of particular individuals or institutions which supply such capital.

Investors

These may be individual or institutional. In either event the ultimate source of all finance is savings. In the case of the individual the savings represent postponed consumption and he may invest funds directly in a trading or manufacturing company, as when he subscribes to a particular issue of securities, or indirectly as when he puts his savings into a financial institution or intermediary. In making a choice, the individual will consciously or unconsciously make one that embraces the same principles as will the institution to which he in turn lends—that is, he will assess the relevance of rate of return, anticipated risk and the time-span, or 'horizon', to his own particular needs. This process is termed **securities analysis**. Many small investors do not take this process of analysis very far since the most common choices of savings are bank deposit accounts and building societies.

It will be necessary to have a brief look at the taxation environment before considering the relative merits to an individual of particular forms of savings as this factor has a very significant influence on the relative advantages and disadvantages. The general movement is, however, against direct equity investment by the small investor. Stockbrokers are less willing to act on their behalf when dealing with small sums and in any event if they are prepared so to act the charges become such that substantial gains are required to offset them. By virtue of these developments individual savings tend to be channelled, as far as industrial and commercial investment is concerned, through institutions such as investment trusts, unit trusts, insurance societies and pension funds.

The desire and ability to save is at any time a function of liquidity preferences. Individuals, institutions and companies having an income also have necessary and unavoidable outgoings. Any surplus can be saved but one individual may desire short-term facilities combined with ease of withdrawal while another may be prepared to tie up his capital for a longer period for a higher contracted rate of return. The objectives of holding investments may therefore be summarised as follows.

Income

If this is the dominant objective then income or dividend yields will be more important than security of the capital sum. In fairly stable monetary conditions bank deposits and local and central government stocks would meet this requirement. In a more inflationary condition the 'decline in purchasing power' of the constant monetary sum received may require a closer look to be taken at alternatives of equity investment. Theoretically the average value of shares and income from them in monetary terms should rise and be a hedge against the inflationary loss experienced with fixed-income securities, but if inflation is severe a different phenomenon occurs. Investors are made so apprehensive in terms of risk that the market is depressed and, paradoxically, the yield on so-called risk (equity) style investments becomes higher than that on risk-free fixed-interest government securities. This is particularly the case when high interest rates are combined with high inflation and lack of confidence.

Capital Protection

Investors with this preference have desires for a specific sum at some known future date either for a specified objective—e.g. repayment of a loan, lease or mortgage—or against a certain situation—e.g. retirement from active employment. Again, inflation makes it harder for such investors to choose if the specific sum is one to be determined by themselves, i.e. how much should they require for retirement? It is different if the specific time of repayment and amount is fixed in monetary terms. In the latter event, if one is sure inflation will continue, the gain in real terms will be with the borrower.

Speculators

The number of individual investors who fall into this category is unknown and their significance open to debate. They are likely to be successful if in possession of advance information, as are those engaged in so-called insider dealings. Their activities are usually summarised in three categories:

Bull. This represents a situation where stock is being bought in anticipation of price rises. The stock may be held or resold (if the prediction is correct) before the end of the stock exchange settlement period and the profit taken without cash outlay.

Bear. In this situation the speculator 'sells' securities he has not bought in anticipation of a fall in price. He can then purchase them at the lower price before making delivery.

Stag. This term describes investors who apply for substantial allotments of a new issue it is anticipated will be successful in order to resell the shares at a profit when dealings commence.

The terms 'bull' and 'bear' may also be used in the general sense to describe a situation where share prices are expected to rise or fall respectively.

Taxation

Since the preferences of individuals in particular are likely to be conditioned by the after-tax position rather than before, it may be salutary to consider in outline the more common alternative systems so that their effect may be more clearly discussed subsequently.

Company Taxation

In 1965 the classical Corporation Tax system of taxation was introduced. Under the previous system the company paid income tax, choosing whether to distribute the balance as dividends or retain it. In addition to income tax the company would have been liable at some periods to additional taxation at various rates (profits tax) depending on whether fiscal policies were designed at the particular time to encourage or restrict distribution.

Corporation Tax was a simpler system in principle. The companies paid Corporation Tax at one rate and the individuals were liable to income tax on the distributed profits. Companies paid their own Corporation Tax bill and also acted on behalf of the revenue authorities by withholding income tax at the declared standard rate from the distribution made. The cost of a dividend to the company was the gross amount—irrespective of whether paid to the shareholder—and revenue and dividend cover calculations were simple and consistent. The cover was the relationship

$$\text{Times Covered} = \frac{\text{Distributable Earnings (after Corporation Tax)}}{\text{Gross Dividend (before Income Tax)}}$$

Imputation System

With effect from 1973 legislation was introduced which made the deriving of comparable statistics a somewhat more complex procedure. This was the introduction of the so-called imputation system. A major change was that a company did not, as previously, deduct income tax from the payment. Rather the distribution, termed a qualifying distribution, required that an amount of Advance Corporation Tax (ACT), equal to tax at the basic rate, on the notional gross dividend be paid to the Inland Revenue within a maximum of 15 weeks of the dividend payment date. The 'mainstream' Corporation Tax, i.e. the major tax assessed relative to the period is due, normally, from 9 to 21 months after the relevant accounting period—hence the use of the word 'advance'. The basic rate applied is that effective at the date of the dividend payment, not that at the time the dividend is proposed.

The company passes on to the shareholder the benefit of the ACT payment in the form of an 'imputed tax credit'. The individual shareholder's income for tax purposes is the dividend received plus the tax credit, but the tax credit satisfies the basic rate tax on the income, so only if the shareholder's tax rate is higher than the basic rate will any further tax be payable. If the personal circumstances of the receivers of the dividend render them not liable for tax at the basic rate then this credit can be reclaimed. Subject to certain conditions the ACT paid by the company is recoverable against Corporation Tax, but not for a considerable period of time. The result was, therefore, in the first instance to bring forward part payment of the taxation charge. This created a once-for-all shift as far as the liquid resources of the companies were concerned but it also affected the means by which dividend rates were stated and fundamental ratios expressed. In planning broad financial policies and requirements, internal standardisation of 'approach' within the firm is permissible and this is why in other sections of the book taxation treatment has been simplified. In comparing performances from external sources, however, a common approach is to be preferred. Unfortunately the main authorities have not agreed on which methods should be used exclusively and the major alternatives are briefly explained.

Comparison of the position immediately before and after introduction of the Imputation System—assuming all profits distributed

Pre-Imputation System		*Post-Imputation System*		*Company tax*
	£		£	
Profits	1,000		1,000	
Corporation Tax 40%	400	50%	500	500
Earnings	600		500	
Dividends: Gross	600	Cash to shareholder	500	
Income tax at 40%	240	ACT ($\frac{3}{7}$ × 500)	213	−213
Cash to shareholder	360	Gross equivalent	713	287 main-stream
Full Distribution				
Shareholder receives	£360		£500	
Out of profits of	£1,000		£1,000	
∴ Total taxation	£640		£500	
Equivalent to	64%		50%	
Nil Distribution				
Profits after taxation	£600		£500	
∴ Total taxation	£400		£500	
Equivalent to	40%		50%	

thus making it more beneficial to distribute profits than previously.

Summary of position Post-Imputation System

	£	£	
Gross income		1,000	
Company taxation (mainstream)	287		Total Corporation Tax
Shareholders' taxation	213		
Cash to shareholders	500		
		1,000	

Notes

(*a*) The fraction $\frac{3}{7}$ is dependent upon and derived from the basic rate of personal taxation existing in a particular period. In this example the basic rate was 30 per cent and any figure which had originally been subjected to this deduction would result in a net figure of 70 per cent. If the net figure is known or proposed then the equivalent gross figure can be found by adding back $\frac{30}{70}$ per cent, or $\frac{3}{7}$. Thus if net dividends of £700 are payable the ACT of $\frac{3}{7}$ would be equivalent to £300 and gross figures equal to £1,000. The check is that 30 per cent of £1,000 is equal to the personal taxation due of £300. If the basic rate of personal taxation is 35 per cent then the ACT would be $\frac{35}{100-35}=\frac{7}{13}$ of the net figure. An ordinary share dividend is now declared as a net rate payable: the equivalent gross figure can be determined by adding back the tax credit in the manner used for computing ACT. It was confirmed that a company paying a preference dividend after 5th April, 1973, must pay such net dividend as, when added to the rate of ACT in force at 6th April, 1973 ($\frac{3}{7}$), equals the gross dividend previously payable under the pre-April 1973 system. Thus a company paying a gross dividend of 10 per cent prior to 6th April, 1973, must pay a net dividend of 7 per cent under the new system *indefinitely*, to which ACT is then applied at *the rate in force at date of payment*.

(*b*) There is a limitation of ACT set-off, being the basic rate income tax percentage of the company's income of the period. If the Corporation Tax rate is 52 per cent and the basic rate of income tax 35 per cent, the mainstream Corporation Tax bill cannot be less than 17 per cent.

(*c*) The surplus ACT may be carried forward or (subject to limitations) backward, provided the minimum mainstream requirement is satisfied in the periods to which it is carried forward or back.

(*d*) The ACT can only be set off against the Corporation Tax on income, not on chargeable gains.

(*e*) As stated above, the ACT is set off against the Corporation Tax bill for the period in which the dividend (and hence the ACT) is paid, not necessarily that to which it relates.

(*f*) Standard practice is to show outgoing dividends in the accounts at the amounts actually paid or payable; therefore the charge for taxation in the profit and loss account consists of the full amount of Corporation Tax, i.e. the mainstream Corporation Tax and ACT are aggregated and the total then deducted from the amount of income before taxation..

(*g*) Credit for foreign tax paid is only given against the mainstream Corporation Tax, i.e. after deducting the ACT paid.

(*h*) ACT can only be counted as an advance payment of UK tax. It cannot be used to offset foreign taxes.

Under the Imputation System the amount available (earnings) for paying ordinary dividends can be dependent upon the actual dividend declared. It is desirable that earnings statistics are computed independent of dividend policy. Three alternative methods are in use and it must be stated (or ascertained) which base is being used by a particular source.

'Full' distribution basis. Earnings are computed on a maximum possible basis. The dividend cover in this instance will represent the ratio of the maximum dividend which can be paid to the actual dividend paid.

'Nil' distribution basis. Earnings are taken as the profit after taxation and all other prior charges but including unrelieved ACT.

'Net' or 'Actual'. This method uses as earnings the retained profits plus the net dividend allowing for any tax shortfall. Thus the difference between this and the previous method would be the amount of unrelieved ACT.

In practice use of the Nil or Net basis will produce identical results in the majority of cases. The difference becomes significant only where a company derives a large part of its earnings from overseas.

Example 1

The capital structure of the XYZ Co. Ltd, a quoted company, is as follows:

	£000
Share capital	
Authorised and issued:	
5 million ordinary shares of £1 each	5,000
1 million 9% (npw 6·3% plus tax credit) preference shares at £1 each	1,000
	6,000
Long-term liabilities	
10% mortgage debentures	750
11% unsecured loan stock	750
	7,500

The profit for Corporation Tax purposes for the year ended 19... is £1,600,000 and the proposed dividend (net) is 8·4 per cent. The current price of the ordinary shares on the stock exchange is 310p.

You are required to calculate the company's price/earnings ratio on the net (or actual) distribution basis and on a nil distribution basis, and the dividend cover on a full distribution basis. The relevant taxation rates are to be assumed as Corporation Tax 50 per cent and rate of tax on dividends 30 per cent.

(CACA)

Tax Calculation

		£000	£000	
Profits			1,600	
Corporation Tax (50%)		800		50% of £1,600,000
ACT preference	27			$\frac{3}{7}$ of £63,000
ordinaries	180	207	593	$\frac{3}{7}$ of £420,000
			1,007	
Dividends				
Preference	63			
30% ACT	27		90	
			917	
Ordinary (net)	420			
30% ACT	180		600	
Retained profits			317	

(*i*) *Full Distribution*

Profits before tax	1,600
Corporation Tax 50%	800
	800
Net preference dividend	63
Net earnings available	737

$$\therefore \text{ Dividend cover} = \frac{£737 + (\frac{3}{7} \times £737)}{£600} = \frac{£737 + £316}{£600} = \frac{£1{,}053}{£600} \simeq 1{\cdot}8$$

i.e. it represents the relationship between the maximum possible dividend and that paid (gross).

Check: Assuming £737,000 net had been paid out in ordinary dividends:

	£000	£000	£000	
Profit before taxation			1,600	
Corporation Tax at 50%		800		
ACT preference shares	27			($\frac{3}{7}$ × £63,000)
ACT ordinary shares	316			($\frac{3}{7}$ × £737,000)
		343		
			457	
			1,143	
Preference dividends (net)		63		
ACT thereon		27		
(Gross)			90	
			1,053	
Ordinary dividend (net)		737		
ACT thereon		316		
			1,053	
			—	

(*ii*) *Nil Distribution*

	£000
Profits before taxation	1,600
Corporation Tax at 50%	800
	800
Preference dividends (net)	63
Earnings	737

$$\text{p/e ratio} = \frac{5\text{m} \times £3{\cdot}10}{£737{,}000} = 21{\cdot}03$$

(*iii*) *Net or Actual Basis*

	£000
Retained profits	317
Ordinary dividend (net)	420
Earnings	737

$$\text{p/e ratio} = \frac{5\text{m} \times £3{\cdot}10}{£737{,}000} = 21{\cdot}03$$

Choice of Investment

The main opportunities for investment and their major features are as follows:

Investment	*Features*
Bank deposit accounts	Minimum interest rates. Flexibility. Special terms for large sums and longer deposit periods.
Building societies	Favoured by the general investor. Taxed at special rate but subject to surcharge if deposit holder liable. Variable schemes available. Rates subject to change.
Local authority bonds	Fixed term. Interest paid regularly, usually at half-year intervals.
Central government bonds	Includes so-called 'gilt-edged'—usually dated. Actual yield depends on fixed interest rates at launch date, market prices of bond and redemption period.
Industrial and commercial debentures and loan stocks	Fixed interest—usually redeemable. Secured against fixed or floating charges. 'Blue chip' signifies those with greatest security (notwithstanding that some firms in this group have failed).
Convertible loan stock	Combines features of fixed interest and equity investment. Allows investor to keep options open.
Equity Investment	
Direct	Investment by shares in company of choice either through successful application for a new issue, or purchase on the stock exchange, banks, share shops and other outlets.
Indirect: investment trust	Investment by shares in an investment trust of one's own choice, in effect buying a share in a large portfolio. Trusts are general or specific to countries, types of commodities, or special objectives such as capital growth. Shares in investment trust companies are, assuming a quoted company, traded in the normal way on the stock exchange.
Indirect: unit trust	Differs from the investment trust in being more closely controlled by legislation. Created mainly in response to small savers' desire to partake in equities in past boom periods. Shares are in units and can be traded in small volumes directly with the managers of the trust. Again tend to be specialised by commodity groups or objectives such as high income, capital growth, etc.
PEP (Personal Equity Plan)	A scheme to encourage investment in UK shares and unit trusts by individuals. Up to

£3,000 per year may be invested with no tax on dividends or capital gains subject to some restrictions.

Insurance — Offers all forms of policies from death benefit through a whole range such as guaranteed income mortgage protection, school fees, endowment with or without profits. The latter is among the most popular with small savers. It is from these sources that insurance companies obtain the funds to invest as institutional shareholders. Income and capital gains from these investments provide the source of their own profits for distribution.

Pension funds — The 'investor' subscribing to a pension fund probably has no choice. It is a common condition of employment that employees pay a minimum sum towards their own superannuation. The employer then supplements this or in some instances provides the entire amount. These monies may be funded by the firms themselves, i.e. separately constituted, or may be passed on to group schemes run by specialists from insurance companies or other sources. It is the pension fund which is the investor in the market sense but the savings come from the individuals and the firms concerned. The portfolio management will thus be directed to providing maximum income now and in the future together with the highest possible security. In either event the employer must have greater awareness of the factors governing alternatives and the financial manager is the man likely to be held responsible.

Useful Terms and Indicators

Nominal (or Par Value)

This is the 'face' of the share and is the amount in which the nominal share capital is expressed, and to which the dividend rate is related. The confusion between nominal rates and dividend amounts can be avoided by expressing dividends per share. This method has been preferred since the introduction of the Imputation System. Shares of no par value are shares issued without a nominal value—at present they are not permitted in the UK. Their introduction has been consistently advocated by committees on company law reform at various times from 1954 but to date the necessary legislation has not been enacted. A no par value share simply entitles the holder to an appropriate fraction of the assets of the company and thus all income would automatically be expressed per share.

Coupon

The coupon rate is the interest rate payable on fixed-interest securities such as debentures or the fixed dividend rate payable on preference-type shares. Again it is less important from the investor's point of view than the yield but its relationship to the nominal value above determines the absolute amount of liability of the company as far as payment is concerned.

Yields

The use of the term 'yield' normally indicates a relationship between the income and the market value of the investment from which it derives as opposed to its nominal value. Such yields may be expressed as **gross** (before taxation) or **net** (after taxation). A **flat** yield is one confined to income statistics.

Gross Yield

Sometimes termed the gross flat yield, this is interpreted by the ratio

$$\frac{\text{Interest or Dividend}}{\text{Market Price}} \times 100$$

If the interest or dividend is expressed as a percentage of the nominal rate it must be converted to an amount per share—for example:

Nominal value of share	25p
Dividend paid (gross)	40%
Market price per share	£1·20

The dividend per share is 40% of 25p = 10p

$$\text{Gross (flat) yield} = \frac{10\text{p}}{£1{\cdot}20} \times 100 = 8{\cdot}3\%$$

Net Yield

Similar to the gross yield but after taxation. This will vary in most instances according to the personal circumstances of the individual. A general indication would be the yield after taxation at the basic rate. A typical rate is 25 per cent and in this case the net yield of the above share would be

$$\frac{10\text{p} - (25\% \times 10\text{p})}{£1{\cdot}20} \times 100$$

$$= \frac{7{\cdot}5\text{p}}{£1{\cdot}20} \times 100 = 6{\cdot}25\%$$

Redemption Yield

The above ratios are the only ones which apply to irredeemable securities such as ordinary shares. Preference shares and particularly debentures and government stocks are normally redeemable at predetermined dates. Thus the amount due at redemption is a factor which influences the effective rate in the manner described on page 98, i.e. it comprises the flat yield in respect of income plus an element in respect of the capital gain. In order to assess the annual equivalent to the capital gain some interest rate must be attributable to run for the period concerned. Published statistics relating stocks of this type are always quoted as a price per £100 nominal without reference to this fact. Thus if stock with a coupon rate of 12 per cent gross is quoted at 91 this means that £100 nominal value can be purchased for this figure. The (gross) flat yield is therefore

$$\frac{12}{91} \times 100 = 13{\cdot}2\%$$

If the stock was dated, however (i.e. it had a redemption date), then a redemption yield could be calculated, and this would depend on the time and conditions of repayment. Assuming the stock above was repayable at par in four years' time, then in addition to the income stream we shall receive a £9 capital profit. This is not worth £9 at present, however, due to the time-value of money. The gross yield to redemption is therefore a rate which will equate all future cash flows to the present cost, i.e. the DCF rate which will make £12 p.a. for the next four years and £100 receivable at the end of four years equate with £91 now. At 15 per cent the relative figures would be—

£12 × 2·855 =	34·26	(present value of an annuity of £12 p.a. for 4 years)
£100 × 0·5717 =	57·17	(present value of £100 received in 4 years' time)
	91·43	

The 15 per cent was 'discovered' by trial and error for the above example but in practice the redemption yields can be obtained from a standardised list prepared by computers for published indices and special users such as actuaries and insurance companies.

Net Redemption Yield

This is the gross redemption yield adjusted for taxation. Not only is it affected by the income tax but by capital gains in most instances. Because of the complexity of these computations any example would be very artificial and any reader with a particular interest is referred to a standard text, but it must be for the relevant legislation and period.

Price/Earnings Ratio

Originally this was

$$\frac{\text{Market price per share}}{\text{Earnings (after Corporation Tax) per share}}$$

This ratio always required agreement as to what constituted earnings. With the Imputation System, 'earnings' became open to more debate and the way in which this ratio is expressed should be specified.

Dividend Cover

This was originally defined as

$$\frac{\text{Earnings available for distribution}}{\text{Dividends per share}}$$

This now requires qualification in accordance with the bases used—as explained on pages 347–51.

Ex Dividend

If a share is quoted 'ex dividend' it means that shares bought at this price are not entitled to the dividend most recently announced.

Financial Indicators

There is an abundance of data, indices, comment and articles on shares, monetary movements, bonds and all financial matters appertaining thereto in specialist papers such as *The Financial Times*, bank reviews and circulars from advisers. In the UK even the more popular daily papers carry main share movements and financial commentary. The most popular UK indicators are, however, the Financial Times (FT) Indices and they are the most regularly quoted. The more common of these are:

FT Industrial Ordinary Share Index

This is often referred to as the FT30 index as it is based on a selection of thirty major companies assumed to reflect the overall stock market performance. It was started in 1935 but the list of firms included is revised from time to time. Some names disappear as a result of reconstruction or mergers but some original big names—ICI, Marks and Spencer, Glaxo—are still there as representative of their sector of activity. The base in 1935 was 100. It has gone down over the years to a low of 49·4 (June 1940). By the late 1960s it had risen to over 500 but fell again in June 1975 to a low of 146. Between 1978 and 1985 it moved from over 500 to over 1,000. This was the so-called 'go go period' and the bull market continued until 1987. At the beginning of 1987 it was 1,320 moving to a high of 1,926 and a low of 1,232 at the time of the crash.

FT All Shares Index

The 'all shares' of the title is really a misnomer as it does not include all the shares listed on the Stock Exchange. It does, however, include about 750 shares which in total value account for over 90 per cent of the total value of the market listing. It is a better indicator than the FT30 since it includes representation from most sectors.

FT SE 100 Index

This gives a rating in between that of the previous two figures since it comprises the 100 largest companies in terms of capitalisation. It was started in 1984 from a base of 1,000. On 2nd March 1988 it stood at 1,808·7 compared with 2,002·7 a year previously. This 10 per cent fall reflected at this date how far the market had to go to achieve the position even of one year previously.

There are also over forty specialised **Financial Times Actuaries Indices** classified according to sectors of the economy, e.g. Capital Goods, Consumer, Others, Industrial and Financial. These main sectors are divided into subgroups as, for instance, the Financial Group contains Banks, Insurance Investment Trusts, Property. An extract from these indices for 7th April 1988 is reproduced as Figure 28 together with those for British Government Stocks. These indices are accurate histories of what has happened. The extent to which they can be used for prediction or decision using any of the techniques mentioned in the following section, with the salutary experience of October 1987 still very much in evidence is a matter for individual judgement and choice.

FT–ACTUARIES INDICES

These Indices are the joint compilation of the Financial Times, the Institute of Actuaries and the Faculty of Actuaries

	EQUITY GROUPS & SUB-SECTIONS Figures in parentheses show number of stocks per section	Thursday April 7 1988 Index No.	Day's Change %	Est. Earnings Yield% (Max.)	Gross Div. Yield% Act at (25%)	Est. P/E Ratio (Net)	xd adj. 1988 to date	Wed Apr 6 Index No	Tue Apr 5 Index No.	Thu Mar 31 Index No.	Year ago (approx) Index No.
1	CAPITAL GOODS (207)	740.14	+0.9	10.20	4.03	12.28	4.47	733.49	730.39	733.91	837.55
2	Building Materials (29)	1004.57	+0.7	10.01	3.76	12.42	1.21	997.67	991.69	997.24	1020.41
3	Contracting, Construction (34)	1550.68	+0.7	9.40	3.37	14.07	3.84	1539.90	1533.77	1536.88	1396.18
4	Electricals (12)	1947.47	....	10.40	5.00	12.23	1.20	1946.87	1958.02	1956.85	2090.69
5	Electronics (32)	1463.74	+0.7	11.30	3.64	11.54	11.75	1453.75	1452.83	1460.81	1876.81
6	Mechanical Engineering (56)	386.86	+1.1	10.05	4.37	12.54	1.79	382.52	380.93	383.42	474.85
8	Metals and Metal Forming (7)	439.65	+1.5	9.75	3.99	12.37	0.00	433.06	430.93	436.48	458.51
9	Motors (13)	264.55	+1.1	12.27	4.60	9.43	3.85	261.59	259.79	2[illegible]2.27	329.95
10	Other Industrial Materials (24)	1238.42	+1.4	9.14	4.45	13.08	15.91	1221.74	1211.70	1213.51	1418.51
21	CONSUMER GROUP (188)	1033.52	+1.1	8.86	3.58	14.37	3.86	1022.29	1020.04	1024.21	1145.21
22	Brewers and Distillers (21)	1055.33	+1.1	10.47	3.61	12.15	4.24	1043.38	1044.46	1047.55	1045.99
25	Food Manufacturing (23)	809.14	+0.7	9.91	4.11	12.92	7.61	803.48	803.89	808.38	878.98
26	Food Retailing (16)	2070.23	+2.0	7.76	3.01	17.35	7.65	2029.35	2025.36	2029.14	2117.94
27	Health and Household (12)	1794.68	+1.5	6.77	2.66	17.52	0.45	1767.38	1762.64	1765.77	2206.80
29	Leisure (31)	1256.45	+0.9	7.93	3.72	16.18	9.64	1244.87	1238.01	1239.95	1243.85
31	Packaging & Paper (16)	479.80	+1.4	9.21	3.95	14.04	2.18	473.11	474.74	485.38	600.48
32	Publishing & Printing (16)	3343.11	+0.8	8.18	4.42	15.23	4.21	3317.50	3315.19	3329.02	3488.12
34	Stores (35)	804.82	+0.6	9.45	3.81	14.19	1.44	799.79	796.79	800.17	960.46
35	Textiles (18)	563.73	+0.5	12.26	4.34	9.37	0.34	561.17	552.75	559.35	685.86
40	OTHER GROUPS (93)	867.98	+1.2	10.87	4.31	11.51	4.08	857.83	849.10	851.17	968.50
41	Agencies (19)	1151.47	+2.9	6.99	2.25	18.45	8.04	1118.48	1112.40	1105.28	1415.28
42	Chemicals (20)	989.89	+1.3	12.00	4.88	10.22	18.33	977.08	971.71	979.57	1225.06
43	Conglomerates (14)	1156.58	+1.4	10.07	4.50	11.58	3.27	1140.54	1125.86	1125.99	1249.84
45	Shipping and Transport (12)	1908.61	+0.1	9.66	4.45	13.71	2.66	1906.21	1881.97	1881.03	1956.88
47	Telephone Networks (2)	953.92	+0.8	11.29	4.32	11.80	0.00	946.62	933.47	932.82	981.02
48	Miscellaneous (26)	1124.26	+1.2	12.67	4.47	9.47	0.69	1110.45	1103.13	1115.25	1316.36
49	INDUSTRIAL GROUP (488)	922.96	+1.1	9.76	3.89	12.92	4.24	913.17	908.67	912.15	1029.96
51	Oil & Gas (12)	1786.66	+1.9	9.82	5.69	12.67	37.52	1753.26	1754.81	1768.78	1815.66
59	500 SHARE INDEX (500)	995.90	+1.2	9.77	4.15	12.88	7.01	984.17	980.14	984.48	1096.44
61	FINANCIAL GROUP (122)	653.43	–0.8	–	4.96	–	7.67	658.75	657.05	657.73	684.41
62	Banks (8)	610.26	–4.8	24.42	6.50	5.50	15.42	640.80	642.24	641.79	718.78
65	Insurance (Life) (8)	968.61	+0.9	–	5.16	–	5.76	959.70	960.37	958.03	945.37
66	Insurance (Composite) (7)	527.72	+1.5	–	5.61	–	5.78	519.75	515.64	513.38	539.47
67	Insurance (Brokers) (7)	833.10	+1.2	14.47	7.62	8.81	16.98	823.41	827.35	836.84	1158.27
68	Merchant Banks (11)	337.65	+0.6	–	4.16	–	1.82	335.74	334.73	337.68	373.88
69	Property (51)	1117.32	+0.5	4.92	2.73	26.01	1.90	1111.71	1104.06	1107.58	948.49
70	Other Financial (30)	386.25	+0.7	10.01	4.30	12.56	2.66	383.48	381.66	384.67	457.20
71	Investment Trusts (82)	853.74	+1.1	–	2.98	–	5.24	844.72	841.09	847.73	961.85
81	Mining Finance (2)	440.93	+1.8	10.31	3.80	10.93	2.01	432.96	432.56	432.96	445.99
91	Overseas Traders (8)	996.33	+1.8	10.22	5.27	11.60	14.93	978.82	968.52	978.44	908.66
99	ALL-SHARE INDEX (714)	904.61	+0.9	–	4.24	–	7.02	896.64	893.16	896.75	986.51
		Index No.	Day's Change	Day's High	Day's Low	Apr 6	Apr 5	Mar 31	Mar 30	Mar 29	Year ago
	FT-SE 100 SHARE INDEX ‡	1761.0	+16.0	1767.4	1758.4	1745.0	1737.6	1742.5	1756.9	1765.1	1962.8

FIXED INTEREST

	PRICE INDICES	Thu Apr 7	Day's change %	Wed Apr 6	xd adj. today	xd adj. 1988 to date
	British Government					
1	5 years	123.31	–0.02	123.34	–	3.64
2	5-15 years	142.78	–0.08	142.90	–	2.95
3	Over 15 years	151.58	–0.18	151.85	–	4.16
4	Irredeemables	170.38	+0.08	170.25	–	1.54
5	All stocks	138.81	–0.08	138.92	–	3.35
	Index-Linked					
6	5 years	126.04	–0.11	126.18	–	0.51
7	Over 5 years	119.02	–0.07	119.11	–	0.88
8	All stocks	119.43	–0.07	119.52	–	0.85
9	Debentures & Loans	120.37	–0.25	120.67	–	2.27
10	Preference	88.79	+0.01	88.79	–	1.47

	AVERAGE GROSS REDEMPTION YIELDS		Thu Apr 7	Wed Apr 6	Year ago (approx.)
	British Government				
1	Low	5 years	8.54	8.59	8.08
2	Coupons	15 years	9.01	8.97	9.01
3		25 years	8.88	8.87	9.04
4	Medium	5 years	9.04	9.02	9.05
5	Coupons	15 years	9.20	9.18	9.22
6		25 years	9.06	9.05	9.23
7	High	5 years	9.13	9.12	9.19
8	Coupons	15 years	9.33	9.31	9.35
9		25 years	9.10	9.08	9.17
10	Irredeemables	†	8.86	8.86	9.01
	Index-Linked				
11	Inflation rate 5%	5yrs.	2.30	2.25	2.69
12	Inflation rate 5%	Over 5 yrs.	3.77	3.77	3.34
13	Inflation rate 10%	5 yrs.	1.41	1.36	2.09
14	Inflation rate 10%	Over 5 yrs.	3.62	3.61	3.21
15	Debs &	5 years	10.77	10.75	9.86
16	Loans	15 years	10.59	10.55	10.05
17		25 years	10.59	10.55	10.08
18	Preference	†	10.16	10.16	10.82

‡Opening index 1764.2; 10 am 1765.3; 11 am 1766.7; Noon 1767.0; 1 pm 1766.9; 2 pm 1767.0; 3 pm 1765.9; 3.30 pm 1759.7; 4 pm 1758.5

† Flat yield. Highs and lows record, base dates, values and constituent changes are published in Saturday Issues. A new list of constituents is available from the Publishers, The Financial Times, Bracken House, Cannon Street, London EC4P 4BY, price 15p, by post 32p.

Fig. 28. Typical FT–Actuaries Share Indices compiled jointly by the *Financial Times*, the Institute of Actuaries and the Faculty of Actuaries.

Portfolio Management

This is the term used to describe the process of selection and changes of individual securities or groups of securities, forming a total holding, in order to attain the objective set out for the investments. Such an operation may be by or on behalf of an individual using his own initiative or through the services of a professional adviser such as an accountant, banker or stockbroker, or it may constitute the function of an entire organisation as with investment trusts and unit trusts. The basic theory and principles are independent of this, however, and relate primarily to the variables involved—large or small.

Methods

The background to Portfolio Analysis has already been introduced in discussion on the Capital Asset Pricing Model on page 110. Indeed the works mentioned there were developed in the first instance for portfolio selection rather than investment appraisal. The mathematical techniques expounded by Markowitz represented advanced theoretical treatment, but the contention that all investors are 'risk averse' implying that they are reluctant to invest and must be tempted to part with their money by payment of a risk premium is sound. Individual investors will have their own opinion as to what are the most desirable investments to include in a portfolio. Anyone proffering advice, e.g. a bank manager, an accountant or a financial adviser would ask what the major objectives were. These would include maximisation of income or maximisation of capital growth, the acceptable degree of risk, the amount of liquidity required and the time horizon for each section of the portfolio. This would govern the diversity and flexibility of the combination deemed most acceptable. The expected return is, as previously stated, the weighted average of the expected return of each investment in the portfolio. The weighting is in respect of risk but historical data represents attitudes now passed. It is the evaluation of future risk levels which is the difficulty and no one has yet solved how this can be precisely predetermined. The catastrophic results of October 1987 demonstrated this and this must be borne in mind when considering the following section on Prediction.

Prediction and Selection

The methods, or rather aids, described here are more basic than the complex theory above and in any event are applicable to selection of individual shares, and the timing of the selling or buying of them, rather than portfolio management, i.e. they are concerned with securities analysis. The extent to which they are used by an individual or investment manager will depend upon his own ideas and preferences.

Technical Analysis and Chartists

'Chartists' is the collective term used for investors or advisers who practice technical analysis. Chartists analyse and graph movements of share prices. The variables involved are the range of prices at which dealings have been made, the relative times and volume of such dealings. From these data they build up graphs and look for relationships such as regression correlation, trends and cycles, as described in Chapter 1. Its reliability is very much in doubt for the basic reasons that the past is always subject to restriction when used as an indicator for the future. Its critics maintain that ignoring fundamentals such as quality of company management and earnings and dividends performances of individual shares makes for incorrect forecasting. Its advocates argue that shares are simply another commodity whose value is determined by supply and demand and this is likely to be revealed by considering market movements primarily—the other factors having been weighted in this. The chartists have a terminology of their own which is very descriptive using such terms as 'rounded bottoms', 'rounded tops', 'multiple bottoms', and 'head and shoulders'. In spite of the sophistication of the systems, different conclusions are frequently drawn from the same shapes by advocates of the method. It is more likely to be used to confirm opinions arrived at on other bases than in isolation.

There are other forms of technical analysis. Although given a variety of names, they are variations of statistical analysis used for measuring averages of the first or second order. A 'rate of change' index, for example, is concerned primarily with trend movement of a share or group of shares. The techniques used here would be those used for forecasting first-order averages and computed on such bases as moving average, logarithmic scales and so on. Other techniques used are those concerned with dispersion and variances in order to test the 'significance' statistically of the range of movements about the change line predicted.

Fundamental Analysis

As the name implies this is the basic method, its advocates claiming that they concentrate on fundamentals. In this instance the fundamentals are those related to price determination of a particular share. The analysis is therefore related to a particular firm. At the extreme it is claimed the share has an intrinsic value related to its future earnings, but we saw in Chapter 4 how difficult it was to assess this figure. The present value of the future profit streams required computation of future cash flows and/or growth rates together with a cost of capital. The value computed would therefore only be as good as the figures used in the model. It is not the model which is deficient but the reliability of data used in it. Obviously if such mathematical models could make completely accurate predictions everyone would use them and the market would be nearer perfection.

In practice the fundamental analysis will be attempting to forecast the expected return which would appear in the theoretical computation of the intrinsic value. The major factors would be those affecting earnings. These would be divided into two groups: first those affecting the particular type of share in its relation to the general state of the economy, and secondly industry in general. For example, if the economic and political situation is unstable demand for capital goods—say buildings—would decline. A detailed study would then be made of firms in the building industry, the objective being to assess the effect of the situation on all firms in the industry.

Finally an analysis would be made of individual firms within the group. Here the study would be in relation to management performance as reflected in share price, earnings per share, dividends, financial control and growth record. We are endeavouring to determine within a given industry (or risk category) which are the better performers. But this by its very nature must be a subjective assessment, i.e. it depends upon the individual making it and therefore must depart from the 'intrinsic' value.

In summary, then, fundamental analysis is a technique whereby individual shares or industrial groups are assessed by studying the general and specific external conditions in which the form is operating and the performance of a particular firm within it. It relies to a great extent on sources of published information such as the annual accounts of quoted companies, but these are of necessity dated, and as was seen earlier in this chapter, are not necessarily reliable as a guide to performance or value. With the exception of chairmen's statements, interim reports, genuine or assumed genuine inside information the analysis has only the past to work on. Empirical research generally supports the hypothesis that the past is a poor indicator of the future. Two theories developed from this type of analysis are mentioned below since they are commonly referred to without definition in commentaries on the subject of share prices.

Random Walk Hypothesis

This states that changes in share prices are random and no formal system of analysis can be used to predict share price movements, particularly in the short run. It therefore negates the arguments for supporting either of the two basic systems of fundamental and technical analysis. Because most information is available to all investors simultaneously any advantage accruing to a particular investor is deemed due to fortuitous choice or 'inside' information, i.e. the result of being in a privileged position as far as knowledge of a company's position and prospects are concerned.

Higgledy-Piggledy Growth

This technique examines past growth in a company's earnings to see if this could be used as a predictor for future earnings and thus anticipate which shares would represent the better investment. Again, as the name suggests, there is little empirical evidence to suggest that the past is a reliable indicator of the future. Managements may change or falter in performance, changes in taxation policies, particularly VAT and similar taxes on sales, may be suddenly introduced and alter market conditions; the list of possibilities is endless.

The stages in construction of a portfolio are therefore easy to state but difficult to implement. Whether the portfolio is for a huge pension fund or individual investor they are the same—namely:

(*a*) *Define objective:* e.g. short-term or long-term, income priority or capital priority.

(*b*) *Specify time span:* alternatively termed the 'horizon'—compute the length of period over which the objective is to be achieved.

(*c*) *Assess risk:* decide acceptable degree of risk in relation to objective. This ranks from pure speculation (gamble) to minimum practical (fixed-term government or 'blue chip' stocks).

(*d*) *Tax planning:* particularly in the case of individuals, age, circumstances and tax liability on income and capital gains can be the predominant factor.

Protecting the Investor

In the early days of company flotation and management, cases abounded of abuse by promoters and officials in their capacity as trustees of others' wealth and investment. These activities resulted first in a gradual and then an ever-increasing volume of legislation designed to protect the shareholder, primarily against his own inability to get information to act sufficiently quickly to protect his own interests but sometimes against his own greed or indifference. There are still individuals who make use of the 'separate person' status of the limited liability company to ensure that in the event of their business failure they are still themselves financially secure—and this by legal means. There must be some balance between the ultimate risk taken by entrepreneurs and shareholders and the enticing of funds from more gullible investors in order to ensure that finance flows freely for genuine business transactions.

There are three major sources of instruments by which the Government and other interested parties attempt to hold the ring or otherwise maintain a balance of interests between all parties concerned. These are direct legislation, 'self-policing' by the Stock Exchange and other City institutions, and standardisation of practices by reporting authorities such as accountants, investment analysts and the financial press.

Legislation and quasi-legislation exist to try to ensure that shareholders and investors are protected against their own ignorance, apathy and lack of expertise. Tacit acceptance of the expert's opinion and standing is, however, being challenged by the users of all processed accounting information. A mood of self-criticism has been engendered by a variety of legal actions and other matters which have reflected on the profession generally. The Cross Committee of the ICA debating professional standards; the proposals for greater dissemination of information to employees; worker participation; the inflation controversy and 'peer reviews' introduced by larger accounting firms; these are but a few symptoms of the more complex climate in which the investor and his advisers, auditors and agents now operate.

During 1977 the Government instituted an official inquiry into the banking system. There were two major aspects to this inquiry—headed by Sir Harold Wilson. First it was to review the recurrent criticism that the banking institutions had failed to function as suppliers of finance for investment. This was a repeat of the brief of two previous committees, the Macmillan Committee on Finance and Industry in 1931, and the Radcliffe Report on the Working of the Monetary System of 1959. The former identified a need for Financial sources for small and medium companies (the so-called Macmillan Gap) and the latter debated the extent to which the gap had been filled. The gap was to some extent filled by organisations already discussed (e.g. ICFC, now part of FFI) and by the growth of secondary banking institutions not members of the clearing system, such as factors, lessors and the merchant banks. Some of these institutions, together with their customers and investors ran into grave difficulties in the depressed period of the early 1970s and in extreme instances went insolvent or had to be rescued by operations mounted by the major clearing banks.

Secondly, the Wilson inquiry reviewed the activities of the City and its associated institutions including aspects of mergers, takeovers, the operation of the City Code, the restriction and prevention of insider dealing, existing and proposed company legislation. The committee reported on the 'Functioning of Financial Institutions' in June 1980. It stated that it had examined the various aspects of the availability of finance to small and medium companies and made a detailed examination of the entire UK finance system. It concluded that 'it was not generally convinced that real investment in the UK had been unnecessarily constrained by shortages in the supply of external finance—in general it was the price of finance relative to expected profitability which was the major constraint on real investment at the time'.

Reference has already been made to the growth of investment activity in terms of corporate and individual activities over the last ten years, particularly in the 1980s (see Chapter 4). Expansion in terms of £ volume and transactions has been tremendous. The explosion of activity envisaged by the 'Big Bang' was subject to analytical techniques as described. None of these techniques were helpful in predicting the immediate and complete collapse which occurred worldwide on 19th October, 1987 (Black Monday). In the USA the Dow Jones Industrial Average fell 800 points in less than five trading days. One of the longest runs of rising prices had ended. Panic selling exaggerated the situation. Unit trust holders are entitled to cash repayment on selling and millions of holders encashed their investment. This caused a liquidity demand near crisis proportions. A major reason attributed to the New York collapse was a system of Portfolio Investment which used computer models for predicting buying and selling practices. In Tokyo the market fell steeply accompanied by large falls in Hong Kong, Sydney and other world centres. The values on the London market fell by 10 per cent on that particular Monday morning. There was considerable pressure to close some Stock Exchanges and the Hong Kong market did close briefly. By Tuesday 19th October in the USA the government had intervened. One conclusion was that it was a market panic similar to 1929. The movement was out of Stocks and Shares and into Short Dated Treasury Bills—a substitute for cash. Such movements were exaggerated by speculation and the international integration of major international centres like New York, London and Tokyo. On the Monday concerned the New York Dow Jones index fell a record 22·6 per cent in one day. London showed a similar proportional drop and in Tokyo the Nikkei average went down almost 15 per cent. At the end of the day the Dow Jones Index was 36 per cent below the 1987 previous highest and the FT index 32 per cent below the comparable figure. The Japanese average fared better as most overseas selling on the Tokyo Stock Exchange was taken up by local Japanese institutional and individual investors.

At the time of writing (March 1988) the FT SE Index had achieved the 1800 for the first time since the October 1987 crash. The Dow Jones Index had fallen from 2600 to 1700 in October 1987 but had recovered to about 2000 in March 1988

Financial Services Act 1986

Although given the opportunity to create an effective self-regulating system the UK government was not satisfied that all was being done to protect the investor. A spate of scandals, offences and failures coincided with the growth in volume of the numbers of investors concerned. Ultimately the Financial Services Act was introduced with the stated objectives of creating a comprehensive system of investor protection. It proposed the creation of a Securities Investment Board (SIB) and this will control most investment business carried on in the UK. This replaces the non-statutory rules of the Stock Exchange itself. At the time of writing the detailed instruments are not finalised but the SIB will operate through two main forms of control on investment businesses and advisers. The personnel concerned with investment business will have to be members of a Self Regulating Organisation (SRO) or a Recognised

Professional Body (RPB). The first of these will be organisations such as the Financial Intermediaries, Managers and Brokers Regulatory Association (FIMBRA) whose function lies entirely in the investment sector. The second group recognises members of certain professional bodies as being eligible to give financial advice and direct investment business. In this case—a firm of accountants for instance—the firm's **main** business must be the practice of the profession of investment adviser. Investment business comprises five categories of activity: dealing in investments; arranging deals in investments; managing investments; giving investment advice; and finally establishing, operating or winding up collective investment schemes. The proportion of business so conducted will be assessed on fee income.

A great deal of criticism has been levelled at the haste with which the Act has been introduced and the complex nature of the legislation. Since investors will be given a statutory right to claim damages for contravention of the rules it is not surprising that practitioners are seeking clarification. It is a matter of waiting to see how the rules develop and the act operates in practice. What is clear is that the days of self-regulation are permanently over and satisfying the requirements of the Act could be very demanding in both time and money. This aspect alone may help in narrowing the numbers and types of personnel previously operating in this area.

Example 2

Advice on Investment Situations

'This circular is important—if you are in any doubt as to what action to take you should consult your stockbroker, bank manager, solicitor, accountant or other professional adviser immediately.' The following are extracts from examples which have been circulated:

Charterhouse Group Limited (20th February, 19x6):

Conversion of $8\frac{1}{2}$ per cent Convertible Unsecured Loan Stock 1990/95

By notice given between 25th February, 19x6, and 25th March, 19x6, you are entitled to convert the whole or a part (being £1 or a multiple of £1) of your Stock holding into Ordinary Shares of 25p each of the Company and to require the Company to allot as at 25th March, 19x6, fully paid Ordinary Shares in exchange for and in satisfaction of such amount of Stock held by you as you may specify. The basis of Conversion is £34·39 nominal amount of share capital for each £100 nominal amount of Stock and so in proportion for other nominal amounts of Stock. Shares representing fractional entitlements will be sold and the net proceeds in excess of £1 distributed to the persons entitled thereto.

If you do not wish to exercise your conversion rights now there will be a further and final period in 19x7 during which such rights may be exercised in accordance with the conditions printed on Stock certificates.

On 19th February, 19x6 (the last practicable date before the despatch of this circular), the middle market quotation on The Stock Exchange, London, of the Ordinary Shares of the Company was 58p per Ordinary Share and of the Stock was £83 per £100 nominal of the Stock.

Consolidated Gold Fields Limited (16th January, 19x6):

Proposed Repayment of Preference Shares

. . . an announcement was made on the 18th December, 19x5, of the proposal to repay the entire issued Preference share capital at a price of 75p per share together with dividends accrued to the date of repayment. This represents an increase of more than 50 per cent over the mid-market prices of the Preference shares on the 17th December, 19x5.

BICC Limited (24th March, 19x6):

Proposed rights issue of ordinary shares

It was announced on 23rd March, 19x6, that the Board proposed to offer 23,852,173 new ordinary shares by way of rights at 87p per ordinary share on the basis of one new ordinary share for every five ordinary shares held at the close of business on 3rd March, 19x6. The issue, which has been underwritten by Morgan Grenfell & Co. Limited, will raise approximately £19·95 million (net of expenses).

Dividend

As will be seen from the summary of Group results, it is proposed to pay a final dividend of 4·36p per share in respect of the year ended 31st December, 19x5, on the existing ordinary shares, making a total of 6·61p per share for the year.

The Directors expect, in the absence of unforeseen circumstances, to recommend a maintained rate of total dividend for the year to 31st December, 19x6, amounting to 6·61p (net) per ordinary share, on the share capital of the Company as increased by the rights issue. The total dividend, with related tax credits at the current rate, would be equivalent to a gross dividend of 10·16923p per share for the year (19x5; same), which would represent a gross yield of 11·69 per cent on the issue price.

From the *Financial Times* dated 24th March, 19x6, you see that the ordinary shares of BICC were quoted at 109, down 10 from the previous day.

You are required to:

(*a*) Prepare notes on the advice you would have given to the security holder who consulted you the day after receiving the appropriate circular. State clearly any assumptions you make regarding the circumstances of your client.

(*b*) Explain the probable reason(s) for the companies' proposals.

(ICAEW)

Charterhouse Group Limited

(*a*) *Value of the offer:* £34·39 nominal value of share capital is equivalent to (4 × £34·39) = 137·56 in shares of 25p each nominal. The market price of each 25p share is 58p. Therefore

Market value of shareholding = 58p × 137·56 = £79·78

	£
Value of £100 nominal stock	83·00
Value of shareholding	79·78
Loss on conversion	3·22

$$\text{Gross yield (loan stock)} \quad \frac{£8{\cdot}50}{£83} \times 100 = 10{\cdot}24\%$$

Advice to Security Holder: The difference between the market value of £83 and conversion of £79·78 is approximately 4 per cent of the market price and would roughly represent the dealer's turn and expenses if traded in by you personally. The capital exchange is reasonable therefore. There will be only one further opportunity to convert in 19x7 and it is a question of whether a more favourable situation will exist then. More stock may be traded in on this final occasion and if this is so, there being more on the market, the price could fall.

The gross yield on the loan stock is 10·24 per cent, whereas the yield on the ordinary shares is unknown (this would normally be known so that some realistic comment could be made). The attraction or otherwise of the offer depends on your own tax position and liquidity preferences. If income is predominant then the loan stock should be retained, otherwise reference to the accounts and forecasts from the last chairman's report should give an indication of the likely rate of growth over the next few years.

(*b*) *Reason for proposals.* It is probably intended by the company that the exchange should be done in instalments. The degree of interest shown by investors at this stage may indicate a likely result of the final offer. Attention can thus be given in advance to changes likely to be brought about in capital structure and tax planning, since they would be substituting dividend for interest, and the effect on ownership since the loan stock may be in considerable amounts by particular investors.

Consolidated Gold Fields

(*a*) *Value of the offer.* 75p per share together with dividends accrued means that the mid-market price is about 50p if the offer is 50 per cent above this figure.

Advice to security holders. On a straight comparison the offer would appear to be satisfactory. It is a proposal and any action to reject it would have to be taken at the meeting or by established procedure. Without further information such action would not appear justified.

(*b*) *Reasons for offer.* Since the introduction of Corporation Tax and the Imputation System a lot of companies have sought to 'tidy up' their capital structure. They have been able to offer inducement to the preference shareholder and also ease their own earnings requirements at the expense of the lower tax bill. The company must either have liquid funds to finance the repayments or be thinking about a substitute form of financing which should in the long term be more beneficial.

BICC Limited

(*a*) *Value of the offer:*

		£
23,852,173 shares at 87p share	=	20,751,390
Expected net realisation	=	19,950,000
Anticipated expenses		801,390

Value of rights		p
Lower market price		109
Price of new share		87
Value of rights (total)		22
Value of rights per old share		$\frac{22}{5} = 4{\cdot}4\text{p}$
Dividend		
Net dividend paid	6·61	
ACT$\left(\frac{3{\cdot}5}{65} \times 6{\cdot}61\right)$	3·55923 (standard rate)	
	10·16923	

$$\text{Gross yield on present holding} = \frac{10{\cdot}16923\text{p}}{109\text{p}} = 9{\cdot}33\%$$

$$\text{Gross yield on new share} = \frac{10{\cdot}16923\text{p}}{87\text{p}} = 11{\cdot}69\%$$

$$\text{Gross yield on total holding} = \frac{6 \times 10{\cdot}16923\text{p}}{(5 \times 109) + (1 \times 87)} = 9{\cdot}65\%$$

Advice to security holders. The expenses seem reasonable at around 3·8 per cent of the gross value of the issue. If you possess cash resources the offer is attractive as the opportunity can be taken to increase the holding with the benefits computed above. There is a gain of 4·4p per share held and there is a gross yield increase on the entire holding from 9·33 per cent to 9·65 per cent. This is created by the favourable yield on the rights price of 87p.

Should you desire to sell your rights the gain will be free of capital gains tax as the value of the rights at approximately 4 per cent of the market price qualifies for exemption.

(*b*) *Reasons for offer*. These could include a need for liquid funds, either to supplement working capital or to finance some major capital project. It could be a combined operation aimed to provide a restructuring of capital or the repayment of a long-term debt.

Relationships between Dividends and Share Prices

The board of a public company considers that one of its financial objectives should be to maximise the wealth accruing to its ordinary shareholders. You are required to advise on:

(*a*) How wealth should be defined in this context.

(*b*) The relationship between this objective and the goal of share-price maximisation.

(*c*) The way in which dividend policy might theoretically be used to assist the achievement of the objective.

(*d*) The practical problems you would envisage in realising this aim.

The following data relate to the recent history of the company, and may be used to illustrate your answer:

	Year ended 31st March				
	19x1	*19x2*	*19x3*	*19x4*	*19x5*
Earnings per share (after tax), in pence	28·4	29·2	27·0	30·2	35·4
Dividend per share—net (in pence)	7·1	7·1	7·1	8·0	8·4
Share price (£)					
Before dividend declaration	2·30	2·38	2·10	1·80	1·75
After dividend declared	2·30	2·36	2·09	1·79	1·77
Ex-dividend	2·24	2·31	2·03	1·72	1·85

Press comment at the time indicated that the dividends declared in 19x2 and 19x4 were both slightly less than had been expected by the market, while the extent of the increase in 19x5 had not been fully anticipated.

(CIMA)

(*a*) Wealth in this context could be defined as maximisation of the market value of the company plus the income distributed. This in turn will be determined by the market value of the shares, which is influenced by the potential buyer's impression of a company's assets worth, earnings potential and dividend policies. The change in shareholders' wealth can be determined by taking the change in value of the shares between two specific dates and adding to this the dividends received in the same period. The change in the ex-dividend value per share in the example between 19x1 and 19x5 was a reduction of £0·39 (£2·24 – £1·85). During this period the shareholder had received 30·06p in dividends. The net effect of this was a reduction of 39 – 30·06 = 8·4p per share. Such changes can be expressed in purely monetary terms or adjusted to eliminate the effect of various price movements, i.e. inflation.

(*b*) The relationship between this and the objective of share price maximisation is a direct one, since in the definition above wealth depended on market valuation of the shares. This is achieved by the maximisation of earnings, maximisation of dividend or both. Discussion of these objectives was made in the text. A company may be forced to operate within artificial constraints in this respect. In the 1960s and early 1970s for example EPS dominated as the main indicator of company prosperity and shareholder wealth. Two major facts contributed to this. First, most equities were growing in value at a relatively higher rate than the inflation rate so equities were bought as a hedge against inflation, and companies with high earnings achieved highest share price. Secondly, in the UK the continuous policy of enforced dividend restraint prevented boards of directors from experimenting with large dividend changes in order to achieve wealth maximisation.

(*c*) Theoretically the dividend should be paid at such a rate that the sum of the dividend plus the resultant change in market prices would be maximised. In 19x2 the price *before* declaration of the dividend was £2·38. After the dividend was declared the price fell to £2·36 so that the implication is that a dividend in excess of 7·1p was expected—up to 2p more. After the share had gone ex-dividend the price of £2·31 reflects an optimistic view of the forthcoming period since the sum of the dividend received (7·1p) and the share price (£2·31) equals £2·381, which is slightly higher than the price of £2·38 which applied before the dividend declaration. A summary of the change in wealth—i.e. income received plus value of the share at the end of cash year compared with the opening share price—is given herewith:

Year	Share price before div declared £	Share price after div declared £	Dividend £	Ex-div price £	Total value £	Change £
19x1	2·30	2·30	0·071	2·24	2·311	+0·011
19x2	2·38	2·36	0·071	2·31	2·381	+0·001
19x3	2·10	2·09	0·071	2·03	2·101	+0·001
19x4	1·80	1·79	0·08	1·72	1·80	—
19x5	1·75	1·77	0·084	1·85	1·934	+0·184
	a	*b*	*c*	*d*	*e* (= *d* + *c*)	*f* (= *e* − *a*)

The total value (column *e*) represents the wealth realised if the share is sold in that year after the dividend has been received. The change (*f*) represents the change in wealth for a shareholder purchasing at the beginning of the year. Although there was a brief depression in the share price immediately after the dividend declaration in 19x2 and 19x4, change at the end of the year was negligible. On the other hand, the extent of failure to anticipate the increased dividend was relatively much greater as the significant gain of +£0·184 at the end of 19x5 indicates. Over the period earnings have increased by 25 per cent and dividends by less than 20 per cent.

(*d*) Practical problems which would occur in realising the aim would be:

(i) Legal interference such as dividend restraint preventing a firm from following a desired dividend policy.

(ii) The distribution and financing policies of this company relative to others of a similar size, status and group in the stock exchange.

(iii) Effect of economic and political influences such as changed taxation rates or systems and the sensitivity of the market to these influences in the case of particular industries and/or firms. Resisting temptation to adjust dividend rates in response to factors which have other underlying courses, e.g. movements of interest rates as a result of fiscal policies, may affect the share price to which the dividend yield will then be related but we must distinguish cause from effect.

Foreign Currency Dealings and Transactions

Most companies are involved in exporting overseas and multinational firms have operating subsidiaries and divisions also abroad. Some companies have large imports of basic raw materials and commodities, e.g. cocoa buying for chocolate manufacture, which are negotiated well in advance and possibly in local currencies. Markets exist dealing in currencies for present and future use and advance dealing in commodities. If activities of this kind are considerable the gain or loss on exchange or commodity futures may contribute substantially to increasing profits made from the major activities of the business or creating losses if judgement is defective. Optimising the effect of these transactions to the firm's advantage is a major part of the treasury function. This embraces banking, broking and other activities. The effects of these transactions on the accounts have to be presented to distinguish as clearly as possible between the manufacturing or trading gains/losses and those created by exchange and commodity price differences. Guidance on the accounting treatment is given in Statement of Standard Accounting Practice 20—Foreign Currency Translation.

Requirements of SSAP 20

A company may engage in foreign currency operations in two ways:

(*a*) Entering directly into business transactions which are denominated in foreign currencies, e.g. pricing exports in francs, USA dollars, yen etc. These will have to be translated into the currency in which the company reports, i.e. £ sterling in the case of a UK company.

(*b*) Conducting operations through a foreign enterprise which maintains its accounting records in a currency other than that of the investing company. In this case the problems of translation arise on consolidation of the accounting results of the foreign enterprise into the currency used for reporting purposes by the investing company.

The objective of the standard was to devise rules which would ensure, as far as possible, reporting a true and fair view of managerial action. The problem is separated basically therefore into two parts: (i) the results of dealing in foreign currency over a period; and (ii) expressing on consolidation the value of overseas interest at an appropriate figure.

Foreign Currency Dealings—Accounting Methods

Where trading accounts have been settled in the reporting period the gain or loss on exchange will be ascertainable precisely. If Brown UK sells goods to a USA buyer on 1st June for $9,000 when the exchange rate is $1·8 to £1 then this will be recorded in Brown's books as a sale of £5,000. If the customer pays three months later when the rate is $1·7 then Brown will receive £5,294. A gain of £294 will have been made on this particular transaction. The net effect of all such movements can be analysed and ascertained for the period. The problem arises when the debt has not been paid by end of the period. A valuation is required, both for balance sheet purposes and profit evaluation so the value must be translated at an acceptable rate. If there is a contracted rate this can be used, and similarly if 'forward' rates have been agreed. If rates do not vary a great deal some form of averaging can be used but specific rates are better.

(*a*) *The Temporal Method*. Where transactions are mainly of the nature of those above the standard recommends the use of the temporal method, i.e. translation is made where possible at the rate prevailing at the time of the transaction. It is the method used when a company is involved with overseas trading but to less considerable extent than that requiring consolidated accounts as below. Once non-monetary assets, e.g. plant and machinery, have been translated their value is carried in local currency. Long-term monetary items are evaluated on the best information available at balancing time. Average rates may be used if variation is small.

(*b*) *The Net Investment Method*. The standard recognises that investment of a company with substantial overseas holdings is in the net worth of the foreign activity rather than a direct investment in the individual assets and liabilities.

The overseas company is a subsidiary of the holding company and consolidation rules apply. When preparing consolidated financial statements the exchange risk of the holding company is limited to its 'net investment'. This is translated each year with the objective of separating the gain or loss on investment from the operating results of the group. Under this method the amounts in the balance sheet of the foreign enterprise are translated into the reporting currency of the investing company using the rate of exchange ruling at the balance sheet date. Exchange differences arise if this rate differs from the previous balance sheet. Amounts in the profit and loss account are translated at the closing rate or an average rate for the accounting period. Gains or losses are transferred to reserves, possibly a Currency Translation Reserve, so that gains or losses may be offset.

The Foreign Exchange Market

In multinational and international organisations the financial director may frequently be referred to as the treasurer as his duties are much concerned with money management—home and abroad. There are risks attached to international and overseas activities in addition to the normal ones associated with home enterprise. There may be restrictions on the volume of currency taken into or remitted from the country concerned. Exchange control, fluctuation and manipulation may be rife. The political and cultural differences may be associated with economic instability. In addition to assessing the banking aspects of exchange transactions in the case of new investment the treasurer must provide appraisal, assessing the risk associated with the factors of instability described above. The board will look to him for advice on the most appropriate source of finance be it national, international or Euromarkets. Some forms of activity, particularly large retailing organisations have large liquid resources available from overnight to much longer periods. Again he will be expected to advise on short to medium-term investment. This implies extensive knowledge of short and long-term foreign financing. There is space here only for an introduction to the problem and treatment is in two parts. First the activities of the foreign exchange market in currency translation are considered, followed by a brief resumé of the nature of international finance.

The terminology of more common foreign exchange transactions is familiar from the daily information given in the financial press and other media. Rates are quoted against the most popular currencies, in particular the US dollar, the West German mark and the Japanese yen. The most familiar is the 'spot' rate, that is the rate quoted by the market for transaction on the day in question, with settlement of the exchange in forty-eight hours. The broker quotes two rates, the lower at which he is prepared to buy and the higher at which he is prepared to sell. Thus, in the example below the dealer or bank is prepared to buy £ at a rate of 1·4375 dollars to the pound or sell £ at 1·4755 dollars to the pound.

Most tourist, business or government currency requirements are for commitment or settlement at a future date. They may not need the currency concerned for some time, but may prefer to have a definite amount known rather than wait for the 'spot' rate on the day concerned. The action taken by the institution, individual, exporter or government will depend upon what they expect to happen in the next month, three months or whatever is the time period concerned. They may prefer to 'hedge' the transaction—that is attempt to secure themselves against loss or reduce risk by partaking in compensating transactions. They can take out a contract to be fulfilled at a definite time in the future at a rate quoted now by a dealer—the so-called forward rate. If currency rates move against them they will lose but perhaps not as much as if they had waited for the period concerned and bought at the spot rate ruling then.

Because money has a time value the company may combine the exchange operation with use of the money market. By means of a 'back to back' loan a sum of money lent to the bank in the 'home' country is converted into foreign currency at the spot rate. An agreement is made both for the interest rate to be paid by the bank and the forward conversion rate. The transactions are reversed when the contract is completed. Swaps are similar but may not necessarily involve the money market, i.e. loans and interest.

Example 3

The finance director of Plottit Incorporated, a large New York based company has been studying exchange rates and interest rates relevant to the United Kingdom and the USA. Plottit Inc. has purchased goods from the United Kingdom at a cost of £2,350,000 payable in pounds in 3 months' time. In order to maintain profit margins the finance director wishes to adopt, if possible, a risk free strategy that will ensure that the cost of the goods to Plottit is no more than $3,555,000.

Exchange rates (New York)

	£/$
Spot	1·4735—1·4755
1 month forward	1·4896—1·4933
3 months forward	1·5163—1·5181

Interest rates (available to Plottit Inc.)

	New York		*London*	
	Deposit Rate (%)	*Borrowing Rate (%)*	*Deposit Rate (%)*	*Borrowing Rate (%)*
1 month	13·25	16·5	6·5	10·5
3 months	13·25	17·0	6·75	10·75

Required:

(i) Calculate whether it is possible for Plottit Inc. to achieve a cost directly associated with this transaction of no more than $3,555,000 by means of a forward market hedge, money market hedge or a lead payment. Transactions costs may be ignored.

(Two-thirds of the marks for question 6(c) are allocated to c(i).)

(ii) If, after one month, the British supplier was to suffer a fire which destroyed all stock and meant that the contract could not be fulfilled, and Plottit had bought pounds three months forward to pay for the goods, what action would you suggest that Plottit should take on the foreign exchange markets? Assume that there is no insurance protection for Plottit Inc.

(iii) What is an option forward contract? Would such a contract be of value to Plottit Inc. in this situation? (CACA)

Note that the question implies looking at the situation from the point of view of a US-based importer.

Forward market hedge. The cost of £1 purchased three months forward is \$1·5181, therefore the cost of £2,350,000 purchased three months forward is \$3,567,535. This is higher than \$3,555,000 and therefore not acceptable to Plottit.

Money market hedge. £2,350,000 is required in London (UK) in three months' time. The interest rate (deposit) in London is 6·75 per cent per annum which for three months will be $\frac{6{\cdot}75}{4} = 1{\cdot}6875$ per cent.

The value of £1 invested for three months will be 1·016875, therefore the present value of £1 will be $\frac{1}{1{\cdot}016875} = 0{\cdot}9834$. Therefore the present value of £2,350,000 will be 2,350,000 × 0·9834 = £2,310,990, with which payment can be made and the pound can be purchased spot for £2,310,990 × 1·4755 = \$3,409,865 which is acceptable as it is less than \$3,555,000.

If Plottit has to *borrow* the funds in New York the rate is 17 per cent per annum which is 4·25 per cent for three months. The total cost of borrowing \$3,409,865 would be 3,409,865 + (4·25% × 3,409,865) = \$3,554,784. It is therefore possible to avoid risk by taking the latter course, since the total cost does not exceed \$3,555,000.

A lead payment involves buying pounds now and the cost would be £2,350,000 × 1·4755 = \$3,467,425. The opportunity cost of \$3,467,425 is the borrowing rate of $\frac{17}{4}$ per cent = 4·25 per cent per quarter.

The total cost of the lead payment would therefore be 3,467,425 × 1·0425 = \$3,614,791 which is higher than \$3,555,000.

(ii) The pounds are no longer required but the contract will remain. Plottit could sell the pounds at two months forward since this is the period remaining. We would need to know the two months rate applicable at the time. Dependent upon how the rates had moved the result might be favourable or otherwise purely on the transaction.

(iii) With an option forward contract the company could buy or sell currency on the market at any time between specified dates. The rate applicable is that least favourable for the period of the option. The option relates to the time when the contract is settled, not the choice of rate in the period and is of no value to Plottit for this transaction.

International Money Markets

Multinational, or even smaller companies may utilise overseas financial institutions as long-term sources of finance. Such funds may be for local, overseas or home operations. Countries with large trading surpluses such as Japan are always looking for opportunities to invest. There are opportunities to operate in Foreign Bonds if the company itself has a surplus. In addition to the more obvious centres such as New York, Tokyo, London etc., as the sources of dealing there is a specialised market which has grown considerably since the 1950s and which with the finalisation of the Common Market in 1992, is likely to grow even more. This is the Eurocurrency market. After the Second World War the European nations involved were generously assisted toward recovery by means of the Marshal Aid funded by the USA. The dollars provided assisted reorientation to peacetime production. By the 1950s progress had been favourable enough for Europeans to accumulate surplus dollars from their exports. This could be used to purchase American goods or recycled around the monetary system. Because of the strength and general demand for American currency the owner of dollars in England could use them to pay off a debt in German marks rather than spend them in the US. As these transactions grew the Eurocurrency market was created. In the early days the market was short term and almost exclusively US dollars but as the trading importance of West Germany and Japan emerged it became larger, more international and long term. The format is in departments within international banks in all the European capitals rather than a single institution such as the London Stock Exchange. The treasurer may look to this source rather than the national market. For short or medium-term finance he may raise a Eurocurrency loan—credit in the appropriate currency supplied by the bank. Another form of investment is Eurobonds which are longer term instruments.

These markets, together with the more international activities, are highly specialised and in the case of certain borrowing countries, extremely risky and volatile. The recent accounts of major UK banks particularly Barclays and Midland show profits eroded by millions of pounds, due to extensive write off of overseas debts to Third World companies.

The above is a resumé only of the situation to emphasise how wide the present day rule of financial management is. If actively engaged, selection of a good advising firm is the first priority.

Transfer Pricing

Another problem which accountants and corporate treasurers face in large companies is that of Transfer Pricing. Most groups indulge in interdivision and intercompany trading both between home-based units and others possibly located overseas. Difficulties arise when choosing a method of valuation to apply to these transfers. Systems must be devised to achieve both the fairest system of reporting, motivation for control and maximum efficiency in the individual operating units. The objectives of the transfer pricing system are:

(*a*) To enable performance of operating divisions to be effectively assessed.
(*b*) To ensure comprehension by line, product and divisional management.
(*c*) Such that any decisions made will be best for the group or company as a whole rather than the individual operating unit.
(*d*) To enable some means of comparison with outside performance.

A popular method is to create 'profit centres' whereby performance is assessed by measuring profitability in relation to the capital employed by the centre. This enables make or buy decisions—when the alternative of purchase from an outside supplier exists—to be made on the basis of comparison with market prices, even though other bases may be used for intercompany trading and accounting. The use of profit centres also enables comparison to be made to motivate efficient performance by the managers. This system utilises **Market Prices** and is the most effective basis if such comparable data is available. Obviously it can only be used where outside suppliers of similar products or components exist. It is not practical in many situations because output of the operating division or profit centre may not be in a marketable form. A compromise may be cost-determined prices on the basis of one of the methods listed below, plus a profit or contribution mark-up. Alternatively, individual managers may be permitted to negotiate the transfer price with arbitration as necessary from more senior levels.

Cost Based Methods

These can be based on actual or standard costing systems. There are problems with either technique. Capacity decisions affect overhead absorption rates and therefore unit total costs. The variances calculated in a standard cost system may be written off against the profit of the producing unit or reallocated to charge the receiving division with full unit cost. Standard cost bases are preferable since the chosen treatment of the variances does not affect the group profit but the amounts do provide guidance on efficiency of operating and management. There is, under either technique, a choice to be made from the following cost methods:

Total Cost

This is the full cost comprising direct elements and absorbed overhead. Even this may not include all costs. It may be deemed more convenient to include Production Overheads only, treating items such as Administration, Selling and Research as group costs.

Marginal Cost

The transfer price is based only on the variable costs of the producing centre. All fixed costs are treated as policy costs. It avoids problems of overhead apportionment and absorption, but only provides management with an incentive to control direct costs and variable overhead.

Cost Plus Profit

In this system a margin for national profit or contribution is added to full cost or marginal cost respectively. The intention is to create profit related to the cost centres, as an incentive to better performance and control. It also provides a basis of comparison with market prices in situations such as those described previously where they exist.

In the case of international companies or multinational groups the problem is more complex. Prices are affected by changes in foreign exchange rates, custom and tariff rates, import/export quotas and anti-dumping regulations. The implication for group profits are more important here than satisfying the best theoretical cost treatment. To satisfy custom duty requirements a market value or full cost basis may have to be used. The resolution of the optimum solution is again an accounting or treasury activity, requiring much extended study from one engaged in such activities and reference should be made, if concerned, to one or more of the works listed in the bibliography.

Questions

1. Mr Solimon, the Financial Director of Zaide plc, has prepared a forecast of the company's cash requirements for the twelve months ending 31st July, 19x8. This forecast indicates that £1·6 million of the company's present cash surplus will not be required to finance its operations for the coming year. Mr Solimon has proposed that the surplus of £1·6 million should be placed on twelve month deposit at 11·5 per cent per annum on the London Money Market.

Ms Osmin, a non-executive director and major shareholder, has criticised the above proposal, arguing that the surplus cash should be returned to the shareholders in the form of an increased dividend. She has been advised by her stockbroker that the current equity cost of capital of Zaide plc is 20 per cent per annum.

Discuss the validity of Ms Osmin's argument and its implications for corporate treasurers.

Note: Ignore taxation.

(ICAEW)

2. (*a*) A company operating in a country having the dollar as its unit of currency has today invoiced sales to the United Kingdom in sterling, payment being due three months from the date of invoice. The invoice amount is £3,000,000 which, at today's spot rate of 1·5985 is equivalent to $4,795,000.

It is expected that the exchange rate will decline by about 5 per cent over the three-month period and in order to protect the dollar proceeds from the sale, the company proposes taking appropriate action through either the foreign exchange market or the money market.

The $/£ three-months forward exchange rate is quoted as 1·5858—1·5873. The three-months borrowing rate for Eurosterling is 15·0 per cent and the deposit rate quoted by the company's own bankers is currently 9·5 per cent.

You are required to explain the alternative courses of action to the company, with relevant calculations to four decimal places, and to advise which course of action should be adopted.

(*b*) You are required to discuss whether a multinational company should hedge translation exposure by incurring transaction exposure.

(CIMA)

3. Dolphins plc is a large UK company which manufactures and sells a range of household goods. It currently has no manufacturing or selling operations. The marketing director has recently returned from an overseas tour and is enthusiastic about the potential market for the products of Dolphins plc in a number of Third World countries. The marketing director's enthusiasm is shared by the other directors.

The company's project analyst has been instructed to prepare a report for consideration by the board of directors on the possibility of meeting this potential demand by setting up a subsidiary company in a Third World country to manufacture and distribute Dolphins plc's range of products.

Discuss the factors to be considered by the project analyst when making recommendations for dealing with the financing of the initial investment in setting up the overseas subsidiary company.

Note: Ignore taxation.

(ICAEW)

4. P & Q plc is a UK-based manufacturing company having subsidiary companies in the USA and various European countries and also a number of overseas agencies.

The company has been growing rapidly and the finance director has recently put in hand a major reorganisation of the finance department, including the setting up of a separate treasury function.

You are required to draft a report from the finance director to the board:

(*a*) Describing the proposed responsibilities of the treasury functions.
(*b*) Stating the advantages to the company of having such a specialist function.

(CIMA)

5. When a UK company wishes to invest in operations in other countries, it can transfer funds out of the United Kingdom or raise the funds in the country where it is to invest or raise the funds in one of the international financial markets.

You are required to:

(*a*) Explain in general terms how exchange rate risks may be incurred by companies operating in more than one country.

(*b*) Review the extent to which these possibilities of risk might occur under the three alternative methods of financing mentioned above.

(*c*) Explain the terms 'back-to-back loan' and 'currency swap' in relation to foreign currency borrowing.

(*d*) Explain the possible advantages to a business of obtaining an equity quotation in the country where the investment is to take place.

(*e*) List *five* factors, other than fluctuations in exchange rate, that might influence the extent to which profits of a foreign subsidiary might be remitted to the parent company or to other members of the group.

(CIMA)

6. Foreign exchange rate forecasts can be used for strategic policy decisions, budgeting and exposure management.

You are required to:

(*a*) Outline the following theories of exchange rate determination:
- (i) purchasing power parity;
- (ii) the monetary theory.

(*b*) Explain how forecasts would be made using each of the above theories and identify possible problems and weaknesses in each case.

(*c*) Outline the technical analysis approach to exchange rate forecasting and state possible strengths and weaknesses of that approach.

7. A group includes two divisions that trade with each other and with companies outside the group. Division 1 sells three products, X, Y and Z. Its major customer for all products is Division 2, but up to 20,000 kgs of product X can also be sold outside the group at a price of £32 per kg though special packaging costs of £1 per kg are incurred in supplying such orders.

The capacity of Division 1 is 150,000 hours per annum. All products are made on the same equipment. The processing times and variable costs for each product are:

Product	*Processing time* hours per kg	*Variable cost** £ per kg
X	2·5	12
Y	3·0	25
Z	2·0	34·5

* Includes the cost of processing time.

The marketing policy of the Division is to sell a minimum of 12,000 kgs per annum of each product. Its fixed overhead is £300,000 per annum.

Division 2 sells four products, L, M, N and P, to customers outside the group. Their selling prices, the usage of X, Y and Z in their production, and the other variable costs incurred in Division 2 are:

	Products (per tonne)			
	L	M	N	P
Selling price	£31,000	£37,000	£24,000	£35,000
Usage of product				
X (kgs)	220	400	—	—
Y (kgs)	400	—	250	150
Z (kgs)	—	300	200	450
Other variable cost	£4,680	£5,570	£3,305	£5,635

* 1 tonne = 1,000 kgs.

Division 2 can buy product X from outside the group at £26 per kg but it is of inferior quality and the Division has to reduce its selling price by 5 per cent if it uses the outside material.

It can also buy up to 10 tonnes per annum of product Z at a cost of £38 per kg delivered.

Division 2's capacity is 100 tonnes of output. Its policy is to sell a minimum of 15 tonnes per annum per product. Its fixed overhead is £600,000 per annum.

The group's rules for fixing transfer prices between Divisions are:

1. Where a product is sold outside the group, the average external price (less any special packaging costs) is to be used.
2. If the product is not sold outside the group, the transfer price per kg comprises the sum of: the variable cost; the fixed cost that would apply if equal quantities (in kgs) of each product were sold; 5% margin on the total of variable cost plus fixed cost.

You are required to state, with supporting evidence:

(*a*) Whether the transfer pricing rules make for goal congruence between the Divisions.

(*b*) What arrangement of production, purchasing and selling of products achieves the most profitable outcome for:

(i) The group as a whole.
(ii) Division 2.

(CIMA)

8. A shareholder in a quoted company is concerned because she receives such small dividends. She has looked at the last annual report and seen that there is a large bank balance. In addition, the balance sheet shows the following items which she believes could be used to increase the dividend.

1. A large 'share premium account'.
2. Substantial 'unappropriated profits'.
3. A large 'reserve for general contingencies'.
4. A large 'provision for depreciation'.
5. A substantial 'provision for deferred taxation'.

You are required to prepare a brief explanation of the nature of these items suitable for this shareholder, indicating which of the items, if any, are relevant to her problem.

(ICAEW)

9. Write brief notes on four of the following:

1. Contango.
2. Efficient portfolio.
3. Resistance level.
4. Sensitivity analysis.
5. Issue by Prospectus, Issue by Tender.
6. Diluted earnings per share.
7. Added value.

(CACA)

10. As investment manager for your company's private pension fund you are asked the following questions:

(*a*) What should be the object of your investment policy?

(*b*) Assuming equity investment to be permitted, it may be desirable for the fund manager to be able to take advantage of short-term changes in market prices. What are the practical difficulties in doing this?

(*c*) How would you calculate at any time the yield to redemption on a long-dated government stock?

(*d*) When the market rate of interest changes, what effect would you expect this to have on the prices of various gilt-edged stocks having different coupon rates and varying lives to maturity?

(*e*) What do you understand by 'technical analysis' and 'fundamental analysis' of share prices? Discuss their merits in deciding your equity investment strategy.

(CIMA)

APPENDICES

TABLES OF DISCOUNTED VALUES OF £1

The DCF Calculations in the text have normally been made with the use of four-figure tables, and tables of at least four figures are advisable for practical problems by virtue of the large sums involved. The two-figure present-value indices (Table A) minimise arithmetical calculations and enable a greater range of rates to be included. They are suitable for practice exercises and examination problems. Present value for annuity purposes can be obtained by adding the figures at the appropriate rate of interest for the years concerned.

Table B is included as indicative of the more normal format to four decimal places and for interest rates up to 16 per cent.

Table C is present value of £1 received per period for a given number of periods (n) when the interest rate is for the same period of time. If the time is in years and the interest rates per annum then the table becomes equivalent to annuity tables.

More detailed tables together with useful reference notes will be found in *Tables for Dscounted Cash Flow, Annuity, Sinking Fund and Annual Capital Charge Calculations*, by G. H. Lawson and D. W. Windle, published by Oliver and Boyd.

Table A. Present value of £1

The table shows the value today of £1 to be received or paid after a given number of years

After	At 1%	2%	3%	4%	5%	6%	7%	8%	9%	10%
1 year	0.99	0.98	0.97	0.96	0.95	0.94	0.93	0.93	0.91	0.91
2 years	0.98	0.96	0.94	0.92	0.90	0.89	0.87	0.86	0.83	0.83
3	0.97	0.94	0.92	0.89	0.85	0.84	0.80	0.79	0.76	0.75
4	0.96	0.92	0.89	0.85	0.81	0.79	0.75	0.74	0.70	0.68
5	0.95	0.91	0.86	0.82	0.77	0.75	0.70	0.68	0.64	0.62
6	0.94	0.89	0.84	0.79	0.73	0.70	0.65	0.63	0.58	0.56
7	0.93	0.87	0.81	0.76	0.69	0.67	0.60	0.58	0.53	0.51
8	0.92	0.85	0.79	0.73	0.65	0.63	0.56	0.54	0.48	0.47
9	0.91	0.84	0.77	0.70	0.62	0.59	0.52	0.50	0.44	0.42
10	0.91	0.82	0.74	0.68	0.59	0.56	0.49	0.46	0.40	0.39

After	At 11%	12%	13%	14%	15%	16%	17%	18%	19%	20%
1 year	0.90	0.89	0.88	0.88	0.87	0.86	0.85	0.85	0.84	0.83
2 years	0.80	0.80	0.78	0.77	0.76	0.74	0.73	0.72	0.71	0.69
3	0.72	0.71	0.69	0.67	0.66	0.64	0.62	0.61	0.59	0.58
4	0.65	0.64	0.61	0.59	0.57	0.55	0.53	0.52	0.50	0.48
5	0.58	0.57	0.54	0.52	0.50	0.48	0.46	0.44	0.42	0.40
6	0.52	0.51	0.48	0.46	0.43	0.41	0.39	0.37	0.35	0.33
7	0.47	0.45	0.43	0.40	0.38	0.35	0.33	0.31	0.30	0.28
8	0.42	0.40	0.38	0.35	0.33	0.31	0.28	0.27	0.25	0.23
9	0.38	0.36	0.33	0.31	0.28	0.26	0.24	0.23	0.21	0.19
10	0.34	0.32	0.29	0.27	0.25	0.23	0.21	0.19	0.18	0.16

Table B. Present value of £1
$(1+r)^{-n}$

n	1%	2%	3%	4%	5%	6%	7%	8%
1	0.9901	0.9804	0.9709	0.9615	0.9524	0.9434	0.9346	0.9259
2	0.9803	0.9612	0.9420	0.9246	0.9070	0.8900	0.8734	0.8573
3	0.9706	0.9423	0.9151	0.8890	0.8638	0.8396	0.8163	0.7938
4	0.9610	0.9238	0.8885	0.8548	0.8227	0.7921	0.7629	0.7350
5	0.9515	0.9057	0.8626	0.8219	0.7835	0.7473	0.7130	0.6806
6	0.9420	0.8880	0.8375	0.7903	0.7462	0.7050	0.6663	0.6302
7	0.9327	0.8706	0.8131	0.7599	0.7107	0.6651	0.6227	0.5835
8	0.9235	0.8535	0.7894	0.7307	0.6768	0.6274	0.5820	0.5403
9	0.9143	0.8368	0.7664	0.7026	0.6446	0.5919	0.5439	0.5002
10	0.9053	0.8203	0.7441	0.6756	0.6139	0.5584	0.5083	0.4632
11	0.8963	0.8043	0.7224	0.6496	0.5847	0.5268	0.4751	0.4289
12	0.8874	0.7885	0.7014	0.6246	0.5568	0.4970	0.4440	0.3971
13	0.8787	0.7730	0.6810	0.6008	0.5303	0.4688	0.4150	0.3677
14	0.8700	0.7579	0.6611	0.5775	0.5051	0.4423	0.3878	0.3405
15	0.8613	0.7430	0.6419	0.5553	0.4810	0.4173	0.3624	0.3152
16	0.8528	0.7284	0.6232	0.5339	0.4581	0.3936	0.3387	0.2919
17	0.8444	0.7142	0.6050	0.5134	0.4363	0.3714	0.3166	0.2703
18	0.8360	0.7002	0.5874	0.4936	0.4155	0.3503	0.2959	0.2502
19	0.8277	0.6864	0.5703	0.4746	0.3957	0.3305	0.2765	0.2317
20	0.8195	0.6730	0.5537	0.4564	0.3769	0.3118	0.2584	0.2145
21	0.8114	0.6598	0.5375	0.4388	0.3589	0.2942	0.2415	0.1987
22	0.8034	0.6468	0.5219	0.4220	0.3418	0.2775	0.2257	0.1839
23	0.7954	0.6342	0.5067	0.4057	0.3256	0.2618	0.2109	0.1703
24	0.7876	0.6217	0.4919	0.3901	0.3101	0.2470	0.1971	0.1577
25	0.7798	0.6095	0.4776	0.3751	0.2953	0.2330	0.1842	0.1460
26	0.7720	0.5976	0.4637	0.3607	0.2812	0.2198	0.1722	0.1352
27	0.7644	0.5859	0.4502	0.3468	0.2678	0.2074	0.1609	0.1252
28	0.7568	0.5744	0.4371	0.3335	0.2551	0.1956	0.1504	0.1159
29	0.7493	0.5631	0.4243	0.3207	0.2429	0.1846	0.1406	0.1072
30	0.7419	0.5521	0.4120	0.3083	0.2314	0.1741	0.1314	0.0994
35	0.7059	0.5000	0.3554	0.2534	0.1813	0.1301	0.0937	0.0676
40	0.6717	0.4529	0.3066	0.2083	0.1420	0.0972	0.0668	0.0460
45	0.6391	0.4102	0.2644	0.1712	0.1113	0.0727	0.0476	0.0313
50	0.6080	0.3715	0.2281	0.1407	0.0872	0.0543	0.0339	0.0213

9%	10%	11%	12%	13%	14%	15%	16%	*n*
0.9174	0.9091	0.9009	0.8929	0.8850	0.8772	0.8696	0.8621	**1**
0.8417	0.8264	0.8116	0.7972	0.7831	0.7695	0.7561	0.7432	**2**
0.7722	0.7513	0.7312	0.7118	0.6931	0.6750	0.6575	0.6407	**3**
0.7084	0.6830	0.6587	0.6355	0.6133	0.5921	0.5718	0.5523	**4**
0.6499	0.6209	0.5935	0.5674	0.5428	0.5194	0.4972	0.4761	**5**
0.5963	0.5645	0.5346	0.5066	0.4803	0.4556	0.4323	0.4104	**6**
0.5470	0.5132	0.4817	0.4523	0.4251	0.3996	0.3759	0.3538	**7**
0.5019	0.4665	0.4339	0.4039	0.3762	0.3506	0.3269	0.3050	**8**
0.4604	0.4241	0.3909	0.3606	0.3329	0.3075	0.2843	0.2630	**9**
0.4224	0.3855	0.3522	0.3220	0.2946	0.2697	0.2472	0.2267	**10**
0.3875	0.3505	0.3173	0.2875	0.2607	0.2366	0.2149	0.1954	**11**
0.3555	0.3186	0.2858	0.2567	0.2307	0.2076	0.1869	0.1685	**12**
0.3262	0.2897	0.2575	0.2292	0.2042	0.1821	0.1625	0.1452	**13**
0.2992	0.2633	0.2320	0.2046	0.1807	0.1597	0.1413	0.1252	**14**
0.2745	0.2394	0.2090	0.1827	0.1599	0.1401	0.1229	0.1079	**15**
0.2519	0.2176	0.1883	0.1631	0.1415	0.1229	0.1069	0.0930	**16**
0.2311	0.1978	0.1696	0.1456	0.1252	0.1078	0.0929	0.0802	**17**
0.2120	0.1799	0.1528	0.1300	0.1108	0.0946	0.0808	0.0691	**18**
0.1945	0.1635	0.1377	0.1161	0.0981	0.0828	0.0703	0.0596	**19**
0.1784	0.1486	0.1240	0.1037	0.0868	0.0728	0.0611	0.0514	**20**
0.1637	0.1351	0.1117	0.0926	0.0768	0.0638	0.0531	0.0443	**21**
0.1502	0.1228	0.1007	0.0826	0.0680	0.0560	0.0462	0.0382	**22**
0.1378	0.1117	0.0907	0.0738	0.0601	0.0491	0.0402	0.0329	**23**
0.1264	0.1015	0.0817	0.0659	0.0532	0.0431	0.0349	0.0284	**24**
0.1160	0.0923	0.0736	0.0588	0.0471	0.0378	0.0304	0.0245	**25**
0.1064	0.0839	0.0663	0.0525	0.0417	0.0331	0.0264	0.0211	**26**
0.0976	0.0763	0.0597	0.0469	0.0369	0.0291	0.0230	0.0182	**27**
0.0895	0.0693	0.0538	0.0419	0.0326	0.0255	0.0200	0.0157	**28**
0.0822	0.0630	0.0485	0.0374	0.0289	0.0224	0.0174	0.0135	**29**
0.0754	0.0573	0.0437	0.0334	0.0256	0.0196	0.0151	0.0116	**30**
0.0490	0.0356	0.0259	0.0189	0.0139	0.0102	0.0075	0.0055	**35**
0.0318	0.0221	0.0154	0.0107	0.0075	0.0053	0.0037	0.0026	**20**
0.0207	0.0137	0.0091	0.0061	0.0041	0.0027	0.0019	0.0013	**45**
0.0134	0.0085	0.0054	0.0035	0.0022	0.0014	0.0009	0.0006	**50**

Table C. Present value of £1 received per period

$$\frac{1-(1+r)^{-n}}{r}$$

n	1%	2%	3%	4%	5%	6%	7%	8%
1	0.9901	0.9804	0.9709	0.9615	0.9524	0.9434	0.9346	0.9259
2	1.9704	1.9416	1.9135	1.8861	1.8594	1.8334	1.8080	1.7833
3	2.9410	2.8839	2.8286	2.7751	2.7232	2.6730	2.6243	2.5771
4	3.9020	3.8077	3.7171	3.6299	3.5460	3.4651	3.3872	3.3121
5	4.8534	4.7135	4.5797	4.4518	4.3295	4.2124	4.1002	3.9927
6	5.7955	5.6014	5.4172	5.2421	5.0757	4.9173	4.7665	4.6229
7	6.7282	6.4720	6.2303	6.0021	5.7864	5.5824	5.3893	5.2064
8	7.6517	7.3255	7.0197	6.7327	6.4632	6.2098	5.9713	5.7466
9	8.5660	8.1622	7.7861	7.4353	7.1078	6.8017	6.5152	6.2469
10	9.4713	8.9826	8.5302	8.1109	7.7217	7.3601	7.0236	6.7101
11	10.3676	9.7868	9.2526	8.7605	8.3064	7.8869	7.4987	7.1390
12	11.2551	10.5753	9.9540	9.3851	8.8633	8.3838	7.9427	7.5361
13	12.1337	11.3484	10.6350	9.9856	9.3936	8.8527	8.3577	7.9038
14	13.0037	12.1062	11.2961	10.5631	9.8896	9.2950	8.7455	8.2442
15	13.8651	12.8493	11.9379	11.1184	10.3797	9.7122	9.1079	8.5595
16	14.7179	13.5777	12.5611	11.6523	10.8378	10.1059	9.4466	8.8514
17	15.5623	14.2919	13.1661	12.1657	11.2741	10.4773	9.7632	9.1216
18	16.3983	14.9920	13.7535	12.6593	11.6896	10.8276	10.0591	9.3719
19	17.2260	15.6785	14.3238	13.1339	12.0853	11.1581	10.3356	9.6036
20	18.0456	16.3514	14.8775	13.5903	12.4622	11.4699	10.5940	9.8181
21	18.8570	17.0112	15.4150	14.0292	12.8212	11.7641	10.8355	10.0168
22	19.6604	17.6580	15.9369	14.4511	13.1630	12.0416	11.0612	10.2007
23	12.4558	18.2922	16.4436	14.8568	13.4886	13.3034	11.2722	10.3711
24	21.2434	18.9139	16.9355	15.2470	13.7986	12.5504	11.4693	10.5288
25	22.0232	19.5235	17.4131	15.6221	14.0939	12.7834	11.6536	10.6748
26	22.7952	20.1210	17.8768	15.9828	14.3752	13.0032	11.8258	10.8100
27	23.5596	20.7069	18.3270	16.3296	14.6430	13.2105	11.9867	10.9352
28	24.3164	21.2813	18.7641	16.6631	14.8981	13.4062	12.1371	11.0511
29	25.0658	21.8444	19.1855	16.9837	15.1411	13.5907	12.2777	11.1584
30	25.8077	22.3965	19.6004	17.2920	15.3725	13.7648	12.4090	11.2578
35	29.4086	24.9986	21.4872	18.6646	16.3742	14.4982	12.9477	11.6546
40	32.8347	27.3555	23.1148	19.7928	17.1591	15.0463	13.3317	11.9246
45	36.0945	29.4902	24.5187	20.7200	17.7741	15.4558	13.6055	12.1084
50	39.1961	31.4236	25.7298	21.4822	18.2559	15.7619	13.8007	12.2335

9%	10%	11%	12%	13%	14%	15%	16%	*n*
0.9174	0.9091	0.9009	0.8929	0.8850	0.8772	0.8696	0.8621	1
1.7591	1.7355	1.7125	1.6901	1.6681	1.6467	1.6257	1.6052	2
2.5313	2.4869	2.4437	2.4018	2.3612	2.3216	2.2832	2.2459	3
3.2397	3.1699	3.1024	3.0373	2.9745	2.9137	2.8550	2.7982	4
3.8897	3.7908	3.6959	3.6048	3.5172	3.4331	3.3522	3.2743	5
4.4859	4.3553	4.2305	4.1114	3.9975	3.8887	3.7845	3.6847	6
5.0330	4.8684	4.7122	4.5638	4.4226	4.2883	4.1604	4.0386	7
5.5348	5.3349	5.1461	4.9676	4.7988	4.6389	4.4873	4.3436	8
5.9952	5.7590	5.5370	5.3282	5.1317	4.9464	4.7716	4.6055	9
6.4177	6.1446	5.8892	5.6502	5.4262	5.2161	5.0188	4.8332	10
6.8051	6.4951	6.2065	5.9377	5.6869	5.4527	5.2337	5.0286	11
7.1607	6.8137	6.4924	6.1944	5.9176	5.6603	5.4206	5.1971	12
7.4869	7.1034	6.7499	6.4235	6.1218	5.8424	5.5831	5.3423	13
7.7862	7.3667	6.9819	6.6282	6.3025	6.0021	5.7245	5.4675	14
8.0607	7.6061	7.1909	6.8109	6.4624	6.1422	5.8474	5.5755	15
8.3126	7.8237	7.3792	6.9740	6.6039	6.2651	5.9542	5.6685	16
8.5436	8.0216	7.5488	7.1196	6.7291	6.3729	6.0472	5.7487	17
8.7556	8.2014	7.7016	7.2497	6.8399	6.4674	6.1280	5.8178	18
8.9501	8.3649	7.8393	7.3658	6.9380	6.5504	6.1982	5.8775	19
9.1285	8.5136	7.9633	7.4694	7.0248	6.6231	6.2593	5.9288	20
9.2922	8.6487	8.0751	7.5620	7.1015	6.6870	6.3125	5.9731	21
9.4424	8.7715	8.1757	7.6446	7.1695	6.7429	6.3587	6.0113	22
9.5802	8.8832	8.2664	7.7184	7.2297	6.7921	6.3988	6.0442	23
9,7066	8.9847	8.3481	7.7843	7.2829	6.8351	6.4338	6.0726	24
9.8226	9.0770	8.4217	7.8431	7,3300	6.8729	6.4641	6.0971	25
9.9290	9.1609	8.4881	7.8957	7.3717	6.9061	6.5906	6.1182	26
10,0266	9.2372	8.5478	7.9426	7.4086	6.9352	6.5135	6.1364	27
10.1161	9.3066	8.6016	7.9844	7.4412	6.9607	6.5335	6.1520	28
10.1983	9.3696	8.6501	8.0218	7.4701	6.9830	6.5509	6.1656	29
10.2737	9.4269	8.6938	8.0552	7.4957	7.0027	6.5660	6.1772	30
10.5668	9.6442	8.8552	8.1755	7.5856	7.0700	6.6166	6.2153	35
10.7574	9.7791	8.9511	8.2438	7.6344	7.1050	6.6418	6.2335	40
10.8812	9.8628	9.0079	8.2825	7.6609	7.1232	6.6543	6.2421	45
10.9617	9.9148	9.0417	8.3045	7.6752	7.1327	6.6605	6.2463	50

BIBLIOGRAPHY

General

Management of Company Finance, J. M. Samuels and F. M. Wilkes, Van Nostrand Reinhold.

Managerial Finance, J. F. Weston and E. F. Brigham, Holt Reinhart & Winston.

Financial Management and Policy, J. C. Van Horne, Prentice Hall International.

Chapters 1–4

Investment Appraisal, S. Lumby, Van Nostrand Reinhold.

Capital Allocation Theory, G. A. Fleischer, Appleton Century Crofts.

Teach Yourself Operational Research, M. S. Makower and E. Williamson, Hodder and Stoughton.

Chapters 5–6

Capital Budgeting Decision, H. Bierman and S. Smidt, Collier Macmillan.

Cost and Management Accounting Made Simple, Joseph Baggot, Heinemann.

How to Use Management Ratios, C. A. Westwick, Gower Press.

Chapter 10

Introduction to Investment Management, C. R. Sprecher, Houghton Miflin.

British Financial Markets and Institutions, K. V. Peasnell and C. W. R. Ward, Prentice Hall International.

Useful Paperbacks

Economics of Business Decisions, B. Carsberg, Penguin.

Economics of Capital Budgeting, M. Bromwich, Penguin.

Insight into Management Accounting, J. Sizer, Penguin.

Index